Conflict Management in Law Enforcement

SECOND EDITION

James Pardy

2005
EMOND MONTGOMERY PUBLICATIONS LIMITED
TORONTO, CANADA

Emond Montgomery Publications Limited
60 Shaftesbury Avenue
Toronto ON M4T 1A3
http://www.emp.ca/college

Printed in Canada.

We acknowledge the financial support of the
Government of Canada through the
Book Publishing Industry Development Program
(BPIDP) for our publishing activities.

The events and characters depicted in this book are
fictitious. Any similarity to actual persons, living or
dead, is purely coincidental.

Acquistions editor
James Black

Copy editor
David Handelsman, WordsWorth Communications

Production editor and typesetter
Nancy Ennis, WordsWorth Communications

Proofreader and indexer
Paula Pike, WordsWorth Communications

Cover designer
John Vegter

Library and Archives Canada Cataloguing in Publication

Pardy, James, 1958–
    Conflict management in law enforcement / James
Pardy. — 2nd ed.

Includes index.
ISBN 978-1-55239-106-8

    1. Police—Canada—Textbooks.   2. Conflict management—
Textbooks.   3. Family violence—Canada—Textbooks.   4. Offenses
against the person—Canada—Textbooks.   I. Title.

HV7936.P75P37 2005   363.2'3   C2005-903725-3

Contents

CHAPTER 5
Elder Abuse

CHAPTER 6
Mental Illness and Psychological Disorders

CHAPTER 7
Suicide

CHAPTER 8
Crime Victims

GLOSSARY

Preface

Policing has the unenviable reality of being, in many situations, the last intervention option available. When other crisis intervention professionals are unable to effectively deal with an escalating situation, they have the option of withdrawing and calling for assistance from police. Police do not have the alternative of dialing 911 when situations intensify.

Police are required to respond in circumstances where no other professional will attend. Police officers are expected to have the ability to effectively communicate, counsel, mediate, advise, empathize, protect, and console. Officers are expected to be intelligent and possess a thorough understanding of federal and provincial legislation and its application. They must also have the physical capacity and willingness to forcibly intervene, and to do so without malice. Police are expected to calmly and compassionately render assistance to the public and at the same time deal firmly with the criminal element of society. This may seem an impossible endeavour; but to make the task even more daunting, police officers are asked to perform these feats several times each day without complaint, and many times without thanks.

This book recognizes that policing is a profession that does not have an established daily routine—each day will bring different occurrences, challenges, and problems. It is therefore impossible for a text to address every situation that a police officer may encounter. Rather than make such a vain attempt, this text will examine several of the most difficult occurrences faced by police officers. Two problem-solving models, CAPRA and PARE, are used in much of this text. Although there are other problem-solving models that may also be effective, both of these models have proven to be particularly effective in policing situations. By understanding how the CAPRA and PARE models are used in the situations described in the text, officers can later apply that knowledge to situations they encounter in their professional future.

This text is written for those who wish to enter the profession of policing, and who have a thorough knowledge of federal and provincial statutes and their applications. No attempt has been made to identify the "facts in issue" of any particular offence, although there are some procedural explanations. Students are expected to have an understanding of evidence and investigative procedures, as well as an understanding of what is required to effectively communicate with the persons involved in a conflict.

The goal of this text is to expose students to relevant situations that they will encounter in their future policing career and to provide examples of safe procedures to follow to enhance the likelihood of successful interventions.

The first chapter of the text deals with factors that precipitate a conflict or crisis situation, followed by a discussion of problem-solving and intervention techniques. The next three chapters deal with child, spousal, and elder abuse, followed by a chapter addressing psychological and emotional disorders.

Next is a chapter on suicide intervention—often one of the most emotionally difficult situations faced by police officers. Intervention techniques and recognition of risk are discussed in this chapter along with elements of officer safety. The final chapter deals with victims of crime and also examines some potentially emotional situations that happen on a too-frequent basis, such as missing persons and break and enters.

The text includes self-study exercises that will assist students in applying their understanding of the course material. Many of the scenarios used in the self-study exercises are taken from actual occurrences and represent common situations that police officers will encounter.

CHAPTER 1

Stress in Conflict and Crisis Situations

Chapter Objectives

After completing this chapter, you should be able to:

- Describe the physical and mental changes produced by stress.
- Describe the signs and symptoms of a person in crisis.
- Describe how stress can impair the performance of a police officer.
- Explain how post-traumatic stress disorder arises and describe its potential effects.

CONFLICT AND CRISIS

This book looks at issues of conflict and crisis. Stress is a major contributor to many crisis situations. The stress caused by conflict situations may escalate to a point where the conflict becomes a crisis. **Conflict** means a disagreement that may not require police intervention—for example, a dispute between siblings that does not become violent. This does not mean that police intervention will never be required in a conflict situation. Intervention may be required to prevent escalation or to keep the public peace. A conflict may result in a crisis situation.

A person pushed beyond his or her ability to cope with stress from any source is a **person in crisis**. The person's equilibrium has been upset and his or her coping skills have become ineffective. Such persons may, under normal circumstances, be non-violent and non-confrontational, but under severe stress become unpredictable and display inappropriate behaviour toward others or themselves. Immediate assistance is needed, although not always from the police. Community and social service agencies may be the best source of help.

conflict
a disagreement that may not require police intervention

person in crisis
a person pushed beyond his or her ability to cope with stress from any source

THE NATURE OF STRESS

Stress affects everybody at one time or another. It is an ordinary part of our daily lives. When handled properly, stress can be a positive force that enhances our

stressor
something that causes a stress reaction or response

stress
a response to a perceived threat or challenge or change; a physical or psychological response to a demand

physical and mental capabilities. It may, however, lead to problems when **stressors**—sources of stress—overpower a person's ability to cope.

Stress can be defined as "a response to a perceived threat or challenge or change … a physical or psychological response to a demand" (Mitchell & Brady, 1990). Assume that you are a police officer on lunch break. A call for assistance from a fellow officer is received. Your response is to immediately drop your lunch and assist the officer in need. Your muscles tense, your pupils dilate to enhance your vision, your heart rate increases because you will need extra blood flow to your muscles to cope with the threat, your digestion shuts down so that blood can be directed to more important bodily tasks in response to the threat, and your mind begins to process information more quickly. This is a survival stress reaction, and these changes are only a few of the many complex responses exhibited by the body as it adapts to stressors. As long as this reaction is not triggered too often and does not become permanent, it will help you survive stressful situations. But, if it becomes permanent, it can cause physical, emotional, and mental health problems.

The stress reaction can be controlled with proper stress reduction and management techniques. Learning to handle the stress reaction is beyond the scope of this text. A course in lifestyle management will give you the information you need to manage stress.

The stress reaction developed as a survival mechanism in humans. During times of severe stress a "fight or flight" response occurs. In primitive times, the threat might have been a tiger or other wild animal; today, work pressures can trigger the same response. Tigers or work, the body recognizes only a stressor, and responds identically. The reaction is both physical and psychological. Chemical compounds are released into the body in reaction to the stressor. These chemicals cause many physical and mental changes, including increased muscle tension, faster respiration, increased heart rate, heightened mental alertness, and faster thought processing (Mitchell & Brady, 1990). This hyperalert condition gives the body the ability to fight or escape from a threat.

In modern society our high-pressure, fast-paced daily environment produces a continual triggering of the stress reaction. Adverse emotional, physical, and cognitive changes can occur when improper means are used to handle this stress. Angry outbursts, abuse of sick time, and alcohol abuse are all common results of improper stress management. One may begin to lose one's mental efficiency, have difficulty remembering details, become more easily distracted, lose the ability to focus on a particular task, and begin to distrust others. One may appear to be detached and unapproachable. A simple question or action can result in an exaggerated emotional response.

TYPES OF STRESS

Cumulative Stress

cumulative stress
stress that is caused by long-term, frequent, low-level stress

Cumulative stress, or chronic stress, is caused by long-term, frequent, low-level stress. The cumulative effect of these low-level stressors may cause problematic reactions. Cumulative stress reactions result from the buildup of work-related and non-work-related stressors. These stressors may accumulate over a period of months or years before becoming problematic.

Police officers perform their duties under often extremely stressful conditions and suffer greatly from accumulated stress. Compounding the problem are the improper coping techniques common in policing. Angry outbursts, abuse of sick leave, and alcohol abuse are all common police reactions to stress and examples of improper coping. Physical and cognitive reactions to constant stress result in poor concentration, loss of objectivity, and, if allowed to continue, apathy.

Cumulative stress is preventable if the signs and symptoms are recognized early and corrective action is taken. However, recognizing cumulative stress is difficult. The condition usually develops slowly over several years and the subtle signs and symptoms are not easily recognizable as reactions to stress.

Cumulative stress reactions are generally experienced in four distinct phases.

1. WARNING PHASE

During the warning phase, the reactions are usually emotional in nature. The person may experience feelings of vague anxiety, depression apathy or emotional fatigue. Unfortunately, the sufferer may not be able to readily identify stress as the cause of these symptoms. If recognized at this stage, the reactions may be reversed by actions as simple as taking a vacation, changing exercise habits, or discussing feelings.

2. WORSENING SYMPTOMS

Failure to recognize and address the warning signs may lead to more serious but still treatable stress reactions. In this phase, the initial emotional symptoms may now be accompanied by physical symptoms. The person may experience sleep disturbances, frequent headaches, muscle aches, fatigue, irritability, and increased depression to the point where social contact is difficult.

At this stage, the reaction may be treated through a lifestyle change that reduces stressors. Also, short-term professional counselling may enhance the person's ability to recover.

3. ENTRENCHED STRESS

This phase occurs when the initial stages of the stress reaction are ignored or not adequately addressed. Once entrenched, stress is very difficult to recover from without assistance from mental and other medical health professionals. Some of the symptoms that may be experienced include:

- physical and emotional fatigue,
- intense depression,
- increased use of alcohol or other drugs,
- cardiac problems,
- elevated blood pressure,
- migraine headaches,
- loss of sexual drive,
- intense anxiety,

- withdrawal, and
- sleeplessness.

4. DEBILITATING STRESS

Ignoring or failing to identify the symptoms of stress for a long period of time may lead to debilitating stress. Some of the signs and symptoms of this severe stress reaction include:

- heart attack,
- severe depression,
- low self-esteem,
- low self-confidence,
- inability to manage daily activities,
- uncontrolled emotions,
- suicidal thoughts,
- agitation,
- poor concentration and attention span,
- carelessness,
- paranoia, and
- thought disorders.

It is extremely unlikely that a person suffering from debilitating stress will be able to participate in the workforce. At this stage, the sufferer is physically and emotionally incapable of interacting with society. The sufferer's increased potential for self-destructive behaviour and inability to interact socially negate the possibility of his or her being an effective participant in the community. Symptomatic control through the use of psychotherapy and pharmaceutical means is a probable method of intervention at this stage. Full recovery is unlikely.

Acute Stress

acute stress
a reaction to one or more specific critical incidents that are beyond the individual's ability to cope

Acute stress, also called critical incident stress, is more easily identified than chronic stress. Acute stress is a reaction to one or more specific critical incidents that are beyond the individual's ability to cope. Law enforcement officers respond to many incidents that can cause acute stress reactions:

- the death of a fellow worker,
- the suicide of a friend or family member,
- a natural or other disaster,
- a severe accident,
- a violent assault, or
- the death or serious injury of a child.

The signs and symptoms of acute stress are shown in table 1.1 below.

Acute stress reactions may begin at the time of the incident or shortly afterward. Although it is not unusual for the reaction to occur days, weeks, or even years after the incident. A delayed reaction can make it difficult to identify the nature of the symptoms experienced. In many cases, professional help is required to ascertain and address the problem.

Some acute stress reactions evoke the fight or flight response. The response is divided into three phases: alarm, resistance, and exhaustion. During the alarm stage, the threat, real or perceived, is identified. The body initiates the fight or flight response. During the resistance phase, the person resists the threat through disengagement (flight) or through a physical or verbal encounter (fight). Resistance continues until the threat is eliminated or the person is not capable of further

TABLE 1.1   Signs and Symptoms of Acute Stress

Signs and symptoms that require immediate corrective action

Physical	*Cognitive*
Chest pain	Decreased alertness or hyperalertness
Difficulty breathing	Difficulty making decisions
Excessive blood pressure	Mental confusion
Collapse from exhaustion	Disorientation to surroundings
Excessive dehydration	Slowed thinking
Dizziness	Problem recognizing familiar people
Vomiting	

Emotional	*Behavioural*
Panic reactions	Change in speech patterns
Shocklike state	Excessive angry outbursts
Phobic reaction	Crying spells
General loss of control	Antisocial acts
Inappropriate emotions	Extreme hyperactivity

Signs and symptoms that require timely, but not immediate, action

Physical	*Cognitive*
Upset stomach	Confusion
Profuse sweating	Lowered attention span
Chills	Memory problems
Sleep disturbance	Distressing dreams
Muscle aches	Disruption in logical thinking
Fatigue	Reliving an event over and over

Emotional	*Behavioural*
Denial	Withdrawal
Grief	Becoming suspicious of everything
Feeling hopeless	Increased or decreased food intake
Feeling overwhelmed	Excessive humour
Feeling lost	Excessive silence
Feeling worried	Increased alcohol intake and smoking
Wanting to hide	Change in interaction with others

resistance. The person then enters the exhaustion phase, when the body attempts to recover from the encounter.

Physical reactions of the response include the following:

- The body releases epinephrine (adrenalin). This alerts the brain that a stressor has been or will be encountered.

- The brain prepares the body for the encounter through stimulation of the pituitary gland. The pituitary releases a chemical called adrenocorticotropic hormone. This hormone prepares the body for fight or flight.

- The muscles tighten.

- The pupils dilate.

- Breathing rate increases.

- Heart rate increases.

- Blood pressure increases.

- Fat cells are released into the bloodstream to be used by the liver to increase the amount and rate of glucose production.

- Protein and antibody levels in the blood increase.

In modern society, most people seldom experience the fight or flight response. This is not true in the law enforcement profession. The response may be evoked several times during one shift. The officer may not have the opportunity to enter the recovery stage. The response, while advantageous in some situations, is a definite health hazard if evoked too frequently. Severe physical, psychological, and emotional problems may develop within persons functioning for extended periods in the alarm and resistance stages.

RECOGNIZING A PERSON IN CRISIS

Stress is generally the underlying issue that precipitates a crisis situation. A person functioning normally within his or her individual stress threshold may experience an occurrence of unusual stress caused by a single incident or by multiple incidents. The person attempts to deal with the stressor(s) by using his or her usual coping mechanisms. If the coping mechanisms prove ineffective and the person cannot effectively deal with the stressors, a crisis occurs. The person will begin a downward spiral of maladaptive behaviours.

A crisis develops in three stages.

Stage 1. An incident occurs. This may be a critical incident, such as the death of a fellow worker, or a seemingly trivial incident that evokes a disproportionate response. This disproportionate response could be the result of cumulative stress.

Stage 2. The person's ability to deal with the incident is compromised. He or she is unable to effectively deal with the acute or cumulative stress evoked by the incident.

Stage 3. The person requires additional resources to deal with their stress response. This is the stage where police are usually involved. Police involvement may be through direct intervention or through referral.

Recognizing the characteristics of a person in crisis is a critical skill that officers must possess. A person in crisis may exhibit certain characteristics (Mitchell & Brady, 1990):

- A distorted view of reality: the person imagines that certain events are taking place.

- Personality changes, such as a normally talkative person becoming quiet, or vice versa.

- In serious cases, unresponsiveness.

- Feelings of anger or fear.

- Chest pains or other sorts of physical discomfort, shortness of breath, and excessive perspiration.

- Agitation, extreme restlessness, and hyperactivity.

Here are some indicators of a crisis state that may be readily identifiable during a brief conversation with the person (Mitchell & Brady, 1990):

- *Apathy.* "Nothing can help me now."

- *Helplessness.* "I can't take care of myself."

- *Urgency.* "I need help now."

Officer safety is a major concern when dealing with persons in crisis. The officer wants to help, but must not forget the need for safety. A person in crisis can be extremely dangerous, and may be experiencing a temporary loss of control over his or her thoughts and actions. Recognizing such potentially dangerous persons depends on the officer's ability to interpret verbal and non-verbal messages. The appropriate response depends on the situation and rests with the officer's judgment.

In many cases it will be immediately obvious that a person is in crisis. At other times, there are several questions that officers can ask themselves when dealing with a possible person in crisis and attempting to assess the situation:

1. Are any physical or cognitive crisis indicators present?

2. What events have recently taken place in the person's life?

3. What is the person expressing through his or her verbal and non-verbal communications?

4. Can the police assist this person or is the problem beyond the abilities of the officers on the scene?

5. Is it safe to leave this person alone? If not, an appropriate, legally sanctioned response must be determined.

INTERVENTION

intervention
for the purposes of this
chapter, any verbal or
physical extraneous
interference by police to
change an event's
negative outcome

When interacting with a person in crisis, an officer must attempt to identify the problem(s) that caused the crisis. In situations where the problem is not readily identifiable, it is unlikely that police **intervention** will be of much assistance in alleviating the stress. Intervention may be defined, for the purpose of this text, as extraneous interference by police for the purpose of managing the course of events in an effort to change or modify any negative outcome of the "event" through verbal and physical methods.

It is imperative that the officer listen actively and effectively to ascertain whether the problem can be addressed through police intervention. Responding to the person may be a delicate process. Care must be taken not to judge. Judging the person's words or actions usually serves only to sever communications. People in crisis may cease to reveal their feelings or express their problems if they believe that the officer has prejudged them. Advice should not be given until the basis of the problem is understood and the person in crisis asks for assistance in dealing with the problem.

Crisis Intervention Models

There are three fundamental crisis intervention models: the cognitive model, the psychosocial transition model, and the equilibrium model.

1. THE COGNITIVE MODEL

The cognitive model is based on the premise that crises originate from unsound thinking about the environment in which the person interacts. First, the person has negative thought patterns that distort his or her view of reality. Then, his or her thoughts become self-fulfilling prophecies. Finally, the person begins a continuously downward spiral.

The cognitive model seeks to remedy the person's behaviours through therapies designed to change thought patterns. The person learns to view his or her environment more realistically and positively.

Unfortunately, the time commitment and expertise required to use this model make it impractical for police.

2. THE PSYCHOSOCIAL TRANSITION MODEL

The psychosocial transition model presumes that people are a product of their learning experiences in the social environment. When people lack adequate coping mechanisms, they are unable to adapt to everchanging social environments. The psychosocial transition model considers all elements of the person's life in seeking to address the state of crisis. Effective treatment may require changes to the person's internal coping mechanisms, thought patterns, and social supports. Like the cognitive model, this model is best applied after the person in crisis has reached a state of balance. Due to time constraints and required expertise, this model, too, is unsuitable for police intervention.

3. THE EQUILIBRIUM MODEL

The equilibrium model is the model most suited to police intervention. This model is based on the premise that a person in crisis is operating in a state of disequilibrium. His or her usual coping mechanisms and problem-solving methods have failed. The person may feel, and may act, out of control and disoriented.

The goal of the equilibrium model is to return the person to a state of stability through contextual discussions of the problem. The officer may, through effective communication, try to assist the person in identifying the cause of his or her crisis. Once the source of the problem is identified, the officer may be able to suggest a short-term solution to the problem. This allows the person to deal with his or her crisis until a more permanent solution can be found. Finally, a followup referral to a community agency is generally required to complete the intervention.

STRESS AND POLICING

The duties of police may be dangerous and require bravery and heroism; or they may be tedious and require inordinate patience. The obvious stressors such as physical confrontations or gunplay are more easily recognized as being harmful. But the unseen social and psychological stressors can be equally debilitating. These unseen stressors are many-faceted. They include intrapersonal and interpersonal stressors; organizational and administrative stressors; and operational stressors that are inherent to the very nature of police duties.

Intrapersonal stress can occur when a person believes that his or her abilities do not coincide with his or her position in life. For example, an officer may believe that she should be working at a higher rank but, for some reason, has not achieved that rank. The greater the discrepancy between the person's perceived deserved status and his or her actual status, the greater will be the intrapersonal stress.

intrapersonal stress
stress that can occur when a person believes that his or her abilities do not coincide with his or her position in life

To address the problem of intrapersonal stress, realistic personal evaluation and objective, informed, outside opinions are used to identify unrealistic goals or performance levels beyond a person's ability. Strategies that may assist in alleviating intrapersonal stress include lowering of unrealistic expectations or raising the level of performance to be closer to the individual's perceived potential.

Interpersonal stress often emanates from the police service itself, including policies and procedures that govern and direct the officer's actions. These procedures often require copious and onerous amounts of paperwork. In many police services, street-level officers do not have much input into policies or procedures, even though these regulations directly affect them. Other organizational stressors include insufficient in-service training, compounded with a lack of promotional opportunities or rewards. Officers may perceive that they do not receive adequate organizational support and that the only time they are noticed is when they make a mistake and are reprimanded.

interpersonal stress
stress that emanates from the police service itself, including policies and procedures that govern and direct the officer's actions

The introduction of an expedited, simplified public complaints process may reinforce this perception of lack of organizational support. This process could be viewed by some officers as a betrayal of the traditionally internalized complaints process, where problems are resolved out of the public eye. Further, the public complaints process may be seen as an effort by administrative bodies to encourage the public to complain about trivial matters.

A 1999 study of municipal and provincial police officers in Ontario (Kohan & Mazmanian, 2003) focused on organizational and operational stressors of police officers. The average age of the participants was 36.5 years with an average of 13 years' policing experience in a wide range of functions. There was no discernible difference in the replies of municipal or provincial police officers.

The study revealed that, as a group, officers were more stressed by operational stressors (dealing with the public) than by organizational stressors (dealing with the department). This overall finding was different when the officers' replies were divided into subgroups of patrol and supervisory officers. Patrol officers reported more operational stressors while supervisory officers reported more organizational stressors.

Part of the study identified some of the negative aspects of operational and organizational stressors. The most obvious was "burnout," which the study defined as "an extreme state of depleted resources that can result from chronic exposure to work stress." Burnout was examined from the perspective of emotional exhaustion (depleted mental energy and fatigue), depersonalization (cynicism toward the organization), and diminished personal accomplishment.

Officers that reported having more organizational hassles felt more emotionally exhausted and cynical toward the organization. Those employees may be more inclined to leave policing or take more time off. When on the job, their contributions and efforts may be minimal.

Conversely, officers that reported positive organizational experiences tended to be more loyal employees who were willing to participate in organizational betterment.

This study, while not definitive, may indicate that organizational stress is a controllable variable in the cumulative stress experienced in policing. Fewer organizational stressors may reduce stress-related organizational problems such as absenteeism and poor work effort.

Although operational stress cannot be eliminated, there are stress reduction techniques that may assist officers.

One of the best strategies to reduce acute stress is to thoroughly prepare officers for situational encounters, such as armed suspect encounters or multiple victim occurrences. Training is one aspect where organizational behaviour can have a positive influence on the reduction of operational stress. An officer receiving adequate technical and interpersonal training may be less likely to suffer from critical incident stress and will likely be more confident and less indecisive in operational situations. Although it is not possible to prepare police officers for all potential encounters, preparation through classroom and scenario-based training can greatly assist with stress reduction and enhance officer safety. When faced with highly stressful situations, officers will most often revert to behaviours ingrained through training.

Health and Stress

Although training may assist with short-term stress reduction, it will not reduce the effects of long-term stress. Long-term coping strategies are the responsibility of individual officers. Proper eating habits and regular exercise are two of the most controllable and effective strategies available. Officers in good physical condition are usually more confident in their physical ability to effectively control a situation.

Good health also allows the officer to recover more quickly from the unavoidable stressful encounters experienced in policing.

Good health benefits officers in another way. As discussed earlier, when an officer encounters a stressful situation, the stress response is triggered. The stress response prepares the body for intense physical activity through chemical and hormonal stimulation. However, stressful encounters in policing rarely result in all-out physical exertion, and the chemical compounds that the body produced are not significantly reduced after the encounter. These compounds, described earlier, may be caustic and cause damage at a cellular level. Physical exercise will help reduce this overabundance of unused compounds and help return the body to a more balanced level. Aerobic exercise appears to be best for this purpose.

The following are some suggestions that may assist with keeping stress within tolerable levels (Greenstone & Leviton, 2002):

- Ensure proper nutrition.

- Get adequate sleep and don't rely on caffeine to get through the shift.

- Exercise regularly.

- Reduce intrapersonal stress through realistic assessments of your abilities and expectations.

- Schedule regular recreational and vacation times. Quality time spent on recreation can greatly reduce stress.

- Try to maintain an optimistic outlook.

- Set realistic goals for yourself.

- Recognize that you are responsible for your well-being.

Post-Traumatic Stress Disorder

The American Psychiatric Association identifies a diagnosis of **post-traumatic stress disorder (PTSD)** as meeting the following conditions and symptoms.

1. The person must have been confronted with an event involving actual or threatened death or serious injury.

2. The traumatic event is re-experienced in at least one of the following ways:

    - recurrent, distressing recollections of the event;

    - recurrent nightmares of the event;

    - flashback episodes involving sensory perceptions of the incident; and

    - intense psychological distress upon exposure to cues resembling some aspect of the event.

3. The person persistently attempts to avoid re-experiencing the incident and exhibits at least three of the following signs and symptoms:

    - attempts to avoid thoughts, dialogues, or feelings associated with the event;

post-traumatic stress disorder (PTSD) disorder in which a person is unable to recover from physical, emotional, and psychological stress caused by exposure to an extremely traumatic event

- inability to recall important aspects of the traumatic event;

- significantly diminished interest in previously enjoyed activities;

- emotional and social detachment;

- inability to react to situations within normal emotional ranges; and

- pessimistic outlook on all aspects of life.

4. The person displays increased nervous system arousal indicated by

- difficulty falling or staying asleep, and

- irritability or angry outbursts.

5. The person is unable to maintain employment and social relationships, or engages in substance abuse brought about by psychological disturbances as a result of the disorder.

Mitchell and Brady (1990) have identified some additional signs that may indicate PTSD: loss of concentration; excessive suspiciousness and cautiousness toward others and hypervigilance; and an inability to relax.

Post-traumatic stress disorder can be experienced by anyone who has gone through or witnessed an extremely traumatic event. PTSD occurs when a person is unable to physically, emotionally, and psychologically recover from an extremely stressful incident. Traumatic incidents that may lead to PTSD occur frequently in policing. They include losing a partner in the line of duty, having to take a life in the line of duty, being violently assaulted, attending occurrences where children have been killed, intervening in or witnessing a suicide, and attending motor vehicle collisions where severe injury or death resulted. This list is far from exhaustive.

Police regularly respond to occurrences that have the potential to cause PTSD if the officer is unable to deal with the stress of the incident and does not seek help. These traumatic events may be referred to as "critical incidents." One or more of these critical incidents may precipitate the initial stages of PTSD. Without treatment, the condition is often permanent. The condition is extremely serious and may lead to personality changes, illness, and, if ignored, suicide. Proper treatment must be provided by a knowledgeable and skilled mental health professional.

1. TREATMENTS FOR POST-TRAUMATIC STRESS DISORDER

Treatment for PTSD can involve psychological intervention as well as medications. Psychological intervention is particularly helpful in treating "re-experiencing" symptoms and social or vocational problems caused by PTSD.

cognitive behavioural therapy
psychological treatment to change maladaptive thoughts, feelings, beliefs, and habits

The main treatment for PTSD is **cognitive behavioural therapy**. This involves examining the thought processes associated with the trauma, the way memories return, and how people react to them. The goal of therapy is to accelerate the natural healing or forgetting process. Discussing memories of the trauma in a safe environment may help the sufferer become less frightened or depressed by those memories. This is called desensitization, which is often combined with cognitive behavioural therapy.

Most people with PTSD will benefit from taking antidepressant medications, whether or not clinical depression accompanies their PTSD. These medications are particularly helpful in treating the avoidance and arousal symptoms, such as social withdrawal and angry outbursts, as well as any anxiety and depression.

2. FACTORS THAT CONTRIBUTE TO POST-TRAUMATIC STRESS DISORDER

For PTSD to occur, the stress caused by the critical incident must be severe and exceed the officer's coping abilities. The severity required to induce PTSD varies from person to person. A situation that one officer may find overwhelming, intolerable, disgusting, or terrifying may not have such a severe effect on another. Note that PTSD does not always manifest itself immediately. The symptoms may not become noticeable until several months after the traumatic event.

The factors that may contribute to PTSD include the following (Mitchell & Brady, 1990):

- *The proximity of the person to the event.* The more involved the person is in the event, the more likely it is that the person will be affected by the disorder.

- *The person's mental, emotional, and physical state.* If the person enters the traumatic situation in a weakened state, he or she is more likely to suffer serious negative effects from the resulting stress.

- *The significance of the event to the person.* Some events may have special significance to the officer. For example, the event may awaken a childhood memory of a traumatic event or arouse latent responses in the officer that stem from unresolved losses or traumas of a similar type.

- The person's general character. A person who can effectively handle large amounts of stress has probably developed his or her coping mechanisms to the point that susceptibility to PTSD is diminished.

- The amount of help that the person receives after experiencing the traumatic event. Support from fellow workers, superiors, and, if required, mental health professionals can help alleviate the symptoms before they become problematic.

3. REDUCING THE EFFECTS OF POST-TRAUMATIC STRESS DISORDER

To help reduce the effects of critical incident stress and PTSD, police services have developed critical incident stress debriefings. These debriefings are primarily confidential discussions about the critical incident that emphasize emotional venting and expression of reactions to the incident. Advice on how to handle the stress may be given, or the officer may simply elect to express his or her feelings about the incident. The major goals of these debriefings are to reduce the impact of the incident, expedite the officer's recovery, and reduce the possibility of PTSD.

Over the past decade psychologists have evaluated treatments for PTSD. The popular one-session procedure, referred to as a critical incident debriefing, appears to be of little benefit in reducing psychological distress. However, brief cognitive behavioural therapy (five to six sessions) provided to very distressed people shortly after a traumatic event appears helpful in reducing PTSD symptoms. Also, short-term (8 to 30 hours) behavioural and cognitive therapies have been shown to alleviate PTSD symptoms in chronic sufferers.

Common therapeutic components of successful treatments include giving people the opportunity to repeatedly describe the traumatic event and their emotional responses to it. Assistance with stress-coping skills helps patients examine concerns about personal safety ("I can never be safe again") and allows them to gradually re-establish more realistic beliefs about personal safety through changes in thinking patterns ("It is safe to go into tall buildings again").

PTSD does not disappear by itself. If you recognize the symptoms in yourself or a fellow officer, get help. Ignoring PTSD may lead to the loss of your job, relationship problems, personality changes, alcohol and drug abuse, and even suicide.

KEY TERMS

acute stress

cognitive behavioural therapy

conflict

cumulative stress

interpersonal stress

intervention

intrapersonal stress

person in crisis

post-traumatic stress disorder (PTSD)

stress

stressor

REFERENCES

American Psychiatric Association. (2000). *Diagnostic and statistical manual of mental disorders* (4th ed.). Washington, DC: Author.

Canadian Psychological Association. Koch, W.J. (1994). *Did you know that ... Psychology works for posttraumatic stress disorder (PTSD)*. Retrieved from Canadian Psychological Association website: http://www.cpa.ca/factsheets/PTSD.htm.

Greenstone, J.L., & Leviton, S.C. (2002). *Elements of crisis intervention: Crises and how to respond to them.* Toronto: Thomson Learning.

Kohan, A., & Mazmanian, D. (2003). Police work, burnout, and pro-organizational behavior: A consideration of daily work experiences. *Criminal Justice and Behavior, 30,* 559–583.

Mitchell, J., & Brady, G. (1990). *Emergency services stress.* Scarborough, ON: Prentice Hall.

EXERCISES

True or False

_____   1. Stress reactions are always obvious.

_____   2. Stress cannot cause serious health problems.

_____   3. Stress affects only the body, not the mind.

_____   4. Work-related stress cannot affect one's home life.

_____   5. The effects of stress can be eliminated from one's life.

_____   6. The effects of stress may not be felt for several months.

_____   7. Persons in crisis situations will exhibit predictable behaviours.

_____   8. Only mentally unstable police officers suffer from the effects of stress.

Multiple Choice

1. Stress is

    a. a response to a real danger

    b. a response to a perceived danger

    c. a response to a real or imagined danger

    d. a response to poor physical conditioning

2. The stress reaction is

    a. an emotional reaction

    b. a physical reaction

    c. a psychological reaction

    d. a physical and psychological reaction

3. The best way to handle stress is to

    a. use alcohol and illegal drugs

    b. learn proper stress reduction techniques

    c. ignore it

    d. use prescription drugs such as tranquilizers

4. Stress reactions allow the body to

    a. perform at a higher level mentally and physically

    b. combat a threat

    c. escape from a threat

    d. all of the above

5. The intervention model most suited to police interventions is

   a. the cognitive model

   b. the psychosocial transition model

   c. the equilibrium model

   d. the anti-psychotic model

6 Which of the following physical symptoms of acute stress requires immediate corrective action?

   a. chest pain

   b. difficulty breathing

   c. excessively high blood pressure

   d. collapse from exhaustion

   e. all of the above

7. Which of the following cognitive signs of acute stress requires immediate corrective action?

   a. decreased alertness

   b. difficulty making decisions

   c. hyperalertness

   d. mental confusion

   e. all of the above

8. Which of the following emotional signs of acute stress requires immediate corrective action?

   a. panic reactions

   b. shock-like state

   c. phobic reaction

   d. general loss of control

   e. all of the above

9. Which of the following behavioural changes resulting from acute stress requires immediate corrective action?

   a. change in speech patterns

   b. excessive angry outbursts

   c. crying spells

   d. antisocial acts

   e. all of the above

Short Answer

1. Is police intervention always the best way to help a person in crisis?

2. List five behaviours that may indicate a person in crisis.

3. Why is officer safety a major concern when dealing with a person in crisis?

4. Briefly describe post-traumatic stress disorder (PTSD).

5. List four factors that may contribute to PTSD.

6. How do critical incident stress debriefings help officers cope with the after-effects of highly stressful situations?

7. Explain intrapersonal stress.

8. Identify two strategies that may be used to reduce levels of intrapersonal stress.

CHAPTER 2

Problem Solving

Chapter Objectives

After completing this chapter, you should be able to:

- Identify and explain each component of the SARA, CAPRA, and PARE problem-solving models.

- Describe communication techniques for de-escalating conflict and crisis situations.

- Describe the common personality traits of a violent person.

- Identify the outward signs of a possibly violent person and explain how the potential for violence in a police encounter with such a person can be reduced.

- Discuss how the mediation process can facilitate problem solving.

INTRODUCTION

Problem solving is an integral part of policing. Problem solving and improvisational skills are paramount in allowing officers to successfully and safely complete their duties. An officer's problem-solving skills will determine how successful he or she will be as a police officer.

In many instances, however, the police cannot solve a problem, although they may be able to prevent a problem from escalating. Conflicts, of course, usually arise without police involvement. When the officers have had no involvement in the conflict, and therefore have no knowledge of the situation that led to it, they may not be able to resolve the conflict themselves. But they may, by using the proper techniques and relying on referrals to third parties, be able to assist the parties in resolving their dispute. There are also some situations where successful intervention by the police is impossible. There are situations, as well, where conflict management may require removal, through voluntary departure or arrest, of one or more of the parties. Although removal may appear to bring an end to the dispute, in many instances it only postpones it. Nevertheless, removal may be necessary to protect the parties or the public.

Problem-solving skills can be learned by almost anyone with a positive attitude. The key ingredients are a willingness to learn and a desire to help people with their problems.

ATTITUDE

In any conflict situation, a police officer must remain professional and objective. The persons involved in the conflict look to the officer to provide unbiased responses. The officer should remain as polite as possible under the circumstances, but always remember the possible need for forceful verbal or physical intervention.

The officer should be patient and allow the parties time to adequately explain their problem. The officer's questions should be directed toward the problem only, and he or she should attempt to respect the parties' privacy by not searching for unnecessary personal details.

The attitude displayed by the officer will have a substantial effect on the attitude of the parties. A positive attitude should be displayed even if the officer is unsure of the outcome of his or her intervention. The parties may be more likely to engage in meaningful conversation if the officer displays the attitude that the situation is solvable.

Motivating the parties to address the situation in a positive manner can alleviate tension. If a solution is not immediately reached, the officer should remain patient and continue to seek a resolution. The officer must remain calm even if the conversation among the parties becomes heated. Emotional outbursts on the officer's part may reinforce the parties' perception that the situation is out of control and that the officer cannot help.

An officer should intervene with empathy but not with sympathy. "Empathy" means trying to see a situation from another's perspective. It can be displayed by accepting emotions and by displaying respect for the worth of another. "Sympathy" means feeling sorry for someone. An officer who shows sympathy may lead one party in a dispute to believe that the officer is on his or her side.

Officers should offer cautious guidance, but not solutions, to individuals involved in a dispute. The officer can be helpful, but cannot solve someone else's problems. Officers must also remain aware that the need for non-verbal intervention can arise at any time. Police officers should always be prepared for a possible escalation to violence.

PROBLEM-SOLVING PROCESS

Along with the proper attitude, officers must have a method of sequentially addressing a problem—that is, they must break down the process into steps.

SARA
a problem-solving process with four components: scan, analysis, response, and assessment

One such problem-solving process, known by the acronym **SARA** (scanning, analysis, response, and assessment), is used by many police services throughout Canada. The SARA problem-solving model was first used in Virginia in the early 1980s. The SARA process is not as detailed as the processes discussed later in this chapter, but it is easy to use and allows quick and effective intervention. Many of the later problem-solving models are based on the SARA model.

The SARA model contains four steps:

1. *Scan.* The purpose of scanning is to determine whether the problem may benefit from police intervention. If more than one problem is identified, the problems must be prioritized.

2. *Analysis.* The analysis considers all perspectives of the problem. The victim, the offender, the location of the occurrence, etc.

3. *Response.* The response is a strategy based on the analysis of the problem and implementation of the strategy.

4. *Assessment.* The assessment evaluates the response strategy. Was the response effective? Why? Why not? What could be done to make it more the effective and easier to implement?

The SARA model can be quickly adapted to most situations but, as with all police interventions in conflict situations, the process may be interrupted by the arrest of an offender.

There are other popular problem-solving models that may require more time than the SARA model but generate more in-depth information and response options. That being said, these problem-solving models are substantially based on the concepts of the SARA model.

The two most popular of these models are the CAPRA problem-solving model, used by the Royal Canadian Mounted Police as its operational model, and the PARE model, used by the Ontario Provincial Police as its community policing operational model.

THE CAPRA CONFLICT MANAGEMENT SYSTEM

This book uses an adaptation of the **CAPRA** system of problem solving, which is similar to the RCMP operational policing model developed in the early 1990s. The system can be successfully applied to any conflict or crisis situation once its components are fully understood. The following is a description of the system's components. Each letter in the acronym CAPRA relates to a different aspect of the system.

CAPRA
a problem-solving system with five components: clients (and communication skills), acquiring and analyzing information, partnerships, response, and assessment

Components of the CAPRA System

C CLIENTS

The C in CAPRA stands for client. Officers must be able to identify the client—the person in need, or the person that should be addressed. The person may have a problem or may be creating a problem. A **client** may be anyone directly or indirectly involved in an occurrence, or in any way affected by it. "Direct clients" are the persons with whom an officer comes into contact in everyday occurrences. They include suspects, victims, witnesses, and concerned citizens. Indirect clients are persons with whom an officer may not have direct contact but who are affected by the officer's actions. Indirect clients include business communities, special interest and cultural groups, and the general public. Getting to know a client's needs and

client
anyone directly or indirectly involved in an occurrence, or in any way affected by it

expectations greatly promotes efficiency when problems arise and may assist in appropriately allocating resources for the client.

The C in CAPRA also refers to the communication skills that an officer must possess in order to successfully intervene.

Importance of Knowing Your Clients

The better the officer understands a client, the more quickly and effectively he or she can

- meet the client's service delivery needs, demands, and expectations;

- dissipate potentially violent situations;

- resolve community safety problems;

- generate workable and sustainable preventive action; and

- mobilize the community to assist in achieving a safe environment.

Expectations of Clients of Police

The following are some examples of clients' expectations in particular policing situations:

- *Call for assistance.* Be polite, caring, and respectful. Provide referral and follow-up where appropriate.

- *Call to an incident in progress.* Attend to victims. Apprehend the suspect. Have the goods returned. Reduce the likelihood of recurrence.

- *Call to an incident after the fact.* Increase likelihood of successful prosecution based on appropriate evidence collected according to law and policy.

- *Interaction with a suspect/prisoner.* Control suspect/prisoner to ensure public and police safety. Treat him or her with respect and dignity.

- *Testimony in court.* Provide concise, objective, honest, and accurate testimony to ensure the fair outcome of the trial.

- *Community group call for assistance.* Ensure sensitive and full participation in preventive problem solving to arrive at a mutually agreed upon strategy.

A   ACQUIRING AND ANALYZING INFORMATION

The officer must be able to acquire and analyze relevant information not only to help resolve an incident but also to investigate possible offences. Acquiring and analyzing information may also help an officer determine who the primary client should be. Gathering and analyzing information requires knowledge of procedure, legislation, and investigative techniques, as well as an open mind unclouded by prejudice or bias. Information can be obtained from many sources. The officer's task is to determine where information can be found, which information is relevant, and which sources are the most credible. Sources of information include victims, witnesses, the Canadian Police Information Centre (CPIC) database, libraries, community groups, experts, and fellow officers with appropriate experience. Officers must not overlook pertinent information obtainable through unpleasant activities such as interviewing belligerent witnesses or searching garbage containers.

To acquire and analyze information effectively, officers must use their crime analysis, leadership, communication, and time management skills. A combination of these skills will permit quicker identification of problems, allowing a more immediate response.

P PARTNERSHIPS

Officers must remember that problem solving requires partnerships. They need to know and understand that they can draw community-based resources as well as available police resources to solve problems. For example, an officer may determine that a person's problem is beyond the officer's ability to solve. The officer must be able to direct that person to another person or to a community-based organization that may be able to help. Knowing what the relevant community-based organizations can offer is essential to making a proper referral. Partnership with these organizations is an instrumental component of providing police services. Specialized services may also be found within the police service itself. Some examples of available partners include:

- *Experts within and outside the police service.* Doctors, psychiatrists, social workers, psychologists, scientists, lab technicians, dog specialists, firefighters, clergy, and colleagues with experience or expertise in a particular area.

- *Community groups.* Cultural groups, halfway houses, and organizations supporting battered women and other victims.

- *Individual citizens.* Volunteers or individuals who may be privy to information that can help solve the problem.

"Partnership" also refers to the relationship that the officer may build with the parties to a conflict or with witnesses. To establish a working partnership, the officer needs effective interpersonal communication skills and should display qualities such as integrity and respect for others. Such partnerships may help immensely in acquiring information. By working together, the partners may be able to remove the source of the problem.

Although the officer may choose to establish a working relationship with one or more parties, he or she must remain in control of the situation. Indeed, the officer is present because the parties are unable to resolve the conflict. The partnership extends only so far as to allow a fuller disclosure of the problem and the possibility of a solution. The officer must set clear boundaries that establish the limits of allowable participation by the partners.

Importance of Establishing and Maintaining Partnerships

Establishing and maintaining partnerships on an ongoing basis will

1. develop trust to ensure that partners are available when they are required;

2. ensure that the officers are aware of all the potential partners that do exist so that the best available information or assistance is available to clients as soon as possible;

3. ensure that there are contingency plans in place for cases where a preferred partner is unavailable, so that when assistance is required, it is still immediately available; and

4. ensure that clients receive assistance and followup through volunteers when the police have other priorities to attend to.

R   RESPONSE

"Response" encompasses incident and risk management, officer and public safety, decision making, and handling of suspects and prisoners. It can include arrest, use of force, mediation, referral, non-involvement, and a number of other incident-specific responses. The type of response depends on the officer's skills in areas such as communication, negotiation, and the use of force, and on the officer's physical condition. Responses will vary but must remain within the confines of legislation and the policies of individual police services.

Four categories of response are available:

1. *Service.* Referral of the client to partner agencies.

2. *Protection.* Protection of the public interest and safety through appropriate action.

3. *Enforcement.* Enforcement of the law by arrest or other means. (Enforcement is not always the ideal response but it is sometimes necessary.)

4. *Prevention.* Prevention of conflicts. This is the ultimate goal of policing. If workable community strategies are in place and officers possess the knowledge and ability to implement these strategies, all of society benefits.

A   ASSESSMENT

An officer must continually assess his or her actions. Self-evaluation can improve an officer's ability to intervene in conflict situations. Mistakes may have serious consequences, but should be viewed as opportunities to learn. A single mistake is a learning experience—a repeated mistake displays incompetence. Assessment gives the officer the opportunity to continually enhance his or her skills and knowledge.

"Assessment" also encompasses an officer's ability to assess the outcome of a decision before any action is carried out. The ability to predict the likely outcome of an action enhances the officer's ability to make better choices in a given situation.

To assess his or her actions, an officer should first establish some criteria for self-evaluation, such as whether the chosen response met the needs of the client(s) and whether the response fell within the guidelines of the police service. Then, the officer should compare his or her performance with recognized standards of performance. Whenever possible, clients should be consulted. Clients can identify areas for improvement and point out opportunities for not repeating mistakes.

Application of the CAPRA System

Effective application of the CAPRA system requires that the officer know what information must be obtained, how to obtain the information, and how to determine and assess his or her response. The following are some questions that may help the officer work through the process:

- *Clients.* Who are the clients (direct and indirect)?

- *Acquiring and analyzing information.* What is the apparent problem? What are the underlying issues in the dispute? What are the clients' expectations, needs, and demands? What sources of information are available?

- *Partnerships.* Who are the potential partners that may help define the problem or resolve the issue?

- *Response.* Which type of response does this situation require: service, protection, enforcement, or prevention?

- *Assessment.* What are the possible consequences of the chosen response? Are the identified consequences acceptable in this situation? Was the chosen response correct for this situation? What can be learned from the occurrence?

THE PARE PROBLEM-SOLVING MODEL

The **PARE** model is a sequential problem-solving model that was developed in 1997 by the Ontario Provincial Police. Its fundamental components are similar to those of the CAPRA model.

The PARE model was developed with the goals and philosophies of community policing in mind. It may be more applicable to community-type problems than the CAPRA model, which has been adapted for use in occurrences involving specific individuals and more "personalized" problems.

PARE
a problem-solving system with four components: problem identification, analysis, response, and evaluation

Components of the PARE Model

P   PROBLEM IDENTIFICATION

The most crucial step in problem solving is accurately identifying the problem. When trying to ascertain the true nature of a problem, officers should do the following:

- Consider all perceptions of the problem. Does everyone see the same problem?

- Determine whether the problem is longstanding. Is the identified problem overshadowing an underlying issue? Longstanding problems usually cannot be solved through police intervention. A referral may be of assistance.

- Examine the problem using the "five Ws": Who? What? When? Where? and Why?

- View the problem in context with the available information. Who is involved? Who has contributed to the problem?

A ANALYSIS

In analyzing the problem, officers should

- try to determine the underlying causes of the problem.

- gather all available information on the victim, offender(s), and the situation—the information may be obtained on scene, through previous contact with the parties, from occurrence reports, from other officers, or from other sources; and

- numerically rate (prioritize) the problem.

The Ontario Provincial Police has developed a scale to numerically rate problems based on the impact, seriousness, complexity, and solvability of the problem. This numeric ranking system may be helpful in determining how to allocate resources in situations of multiple, simultaneous occurrences. Problems ranking numerically higher may be more easily resolved, or should receive immediate attention depending on the overall context of the problem. However, situations involving injury or the threat of violence should receive first priority regardless of their numerical ranking. The ranking system is set out below.

1. Impact   1 least – 5 most

2. Seriousness   1 least – 5 most

3. Complexity   1 most – 5 least

4. Solvability   1 difficult – 5 easy

To determine the numerical ranking for each of these criteria, officers must ask themselves the following questions:

- *Impact of the problem.* Is it a big problem? Who is affected by the problem?

- *Seriousness of the problem.* Would it be dangerous to not address the problem? Is the public concerned?

- *Complexity of the problem.* Are resources available to address the problem? Is it a "police problem"?

- *Solvability of the problem.* Can the problem be solved by police with the resources available?

OPP Ranking System: An Example

The following example shows how police might use the OPP ranking system to deal with two simultaneous calls for assistance.

Call one: Several youths are loitering in front of a convenience store. They are not impeding customers, but the store owner wants them removed from the area. He doesn't think they are good for business.

Call two: A store owner reports that approximately 10 minutes ago two persons broke his store window, took several MP3 players that were on display, and fled on foot.

Both calls originate in the same commercial area. After applying the numerical ranking system to these simultaneous calls, the officers decide that call one should be addressed first. Why not call two? Because call two will consume considerably more police time and will be difficult to solve. Further, there is no immediate danger and there is little chance that the suspects can be immediately apprehended. Call one, on the other hand, is in the general area of call two and will likely consume very little police time. More importantly, addressing call one first may prevent a violent escalation of the situation. Police might rank these occurrences as follows:

Call one		*Call two*		
Impact	1	Impact	2	no injury
Seriousness	2	Seriousness	1	
Complexity	5	Complexity	1	
Solvability	5	Solvability	1	

R   RESPONSE

In responding to a problem, officers must consider the objectives of their response and their response options.

Objectives of Response

- *Eliminate the problem.* Usually, police can eliminate only simple problems. It is difficult for police to eliminate more complex problems.

- *Reduce the harm.* Police can usually manage problems in a manner that reduces the harm.

- *Improve the response through improved community services to victims.* Police can establish programs such as the Victim Crisis Assistance and Referral Service (VCARS). (See chapter 8.)

- *Redefine responsibility for the problem.* Determine whether other community agencies may be better equipped to address the problem.

Response Options

Note that many of the responses below may not be traditional policing responses, but may still be effective pre-emptive solutions to problems.

- *Investigation and enforcement.* Arrest and charging may manage and, in some situations, eliminate the problem. Enforcement is usually only a short-term solution, but in some situations it is necessary.

- *Focused strategies.* Usually a small number of criminals are responsible for a large number of offences. Removing these offenders may greatly reduce crime.

- *Interagency strategies.* Collaboration with other agencies is an effective way to manage long-term problems. Community agencies often have more problem-specific expertise and time than police.

- *Use of non-criminal legislation.* Examples include the *Tenant Protection Act, 1997* and municipal bylaws.

- *More discriminating use of law enforcement.* Police using this response focus on prevention rather than enforcement.

- *Community education.* Fraud prevention programs are a good example.

- *Community mobilization and crime prevention programs.* The Neighbourhood Watch and Block Parent programs are two examples.

- *Environmental design.* Community design features, such as well-lit areas, can assist in crime reduction. Although not directly under the control of a police service, consultation on environmental design with the aim of crime prevention can be an effective strategy.

At this point, the problem has been identified and analyzed, and a response option has been chosen. An intervention plan is now developed and implemented based on the information obtained through the process. The response must now be evaluated.

E   EVALUATION

To evaluate the effectiveness of their response, officers should ask the following questions:

- Was the response easy to implement?

- What problems were encountered?

- What can be done to make this response more effective in future similar situations?

Application of the PARE Problem-Solving Model

To effectively apply the PARE problem-solving model, officers should ask themselves the following self-directed questions. These questions are adapted to the format of the model to allow self-assessment.

PROBLEM IDENTIFICATION

- Can the problem be solved or managed through police intervention, or is it a long-term problem that cannot be effectively addressed by police?

- Do all involved parties agree with the accuracy of the identified problem?

ANALYSIS

- Does anyone require medical assistance?

- Is there any threat of violence?

- Has all information available about the victim, the offender, and the situation been considered?

- Does the description of the problem by the victim and the offender match the available evidence?

- Are the statements of the victim and the offender credible?

- Has information obtained through previous occurrences been considered?

- If more than one problem has been identified, have the problems been prioritized?

- How complex is the problem?

- Can the problem be solved or managed through the necessarily brief police intervention?

RESPONSE

- Would there be any repercussions if police do not intervene?

- Is the problem a police problem or are the parties responsible for the solution?

- Is enforcement through charging an appropriate response?

- Is mediation an appropriate response?

- Would referral to a community agency be an effective response?

- Is arrest necessary?

EVALUATION

- Was the response appropriate based on the circumstances and information available at the time?

- What difficulties were encountered when implementing the response?

- In hindsight, was there a better option available?

- What resources could have been used that were not used or available initially?

- How could these resources be accessed in the future?

- Was the outcome of this intervention positive or negative?

- Was the intervention a learning experience?

- Will knowledge gained enhance the effectiveness of interventions in future similar incidents?

COMMUNICATION IN A CONFLICT SITUATION

Police officers rely on their communication skills to define and defuse problems in conflict situations. The officer's most important tool in such instances is his or her ability to observe what is happening and relay accurate information to the parties involved. The officer relies on his or her verbal and non-verbal communication skills to control the incident and mediate disagreements.

The following are some basic criteria for more effective communication in a conflict or crisis situation:

- *Calmness.* A police presence can sometimes escalate a conflict. Because the parties feel safe and protected with the police around, they may resort to violence. The officers must ensure that nothing is said or done that may inadvertently arouse antagonism or provoke further conflict. If a party is shouting, the officer may decide to allow him or her to continue as long as, in the officer's opinion, the shouting will not inflame the situation. Such venting may allow some of the party's hostility to be harmlessly alleviated.

- *Honesty.* The officer should tell the parties why the police are present. The officer should explain that he or she is there to help if possible and will use all reasonable means to resolve the situation, but if necessary will make an arrest. The officer should not threaten arrest, but should tell the parties that arrest is a possibility.

- *Positive atmosphere.* Whenever possible, the officer should try to create a positive atmosphere. People are more likely to discuss their disagreements if they believe that a solution to the problem exists. The officer should maintain a professional bearing and treat everyone present with equal respect and in as dignified a manner as possible.

- *Verbal and non-verbal communication.* The officer's body language should communicate as much "openness" as safety allows. Such openness may encourage dialogue. The officer, however, must ensure that non-verbal messages are consistent with verbal communication. And for his or her own safety, the officer must always be aware of his or her physical proximity to the parties.

  Controlling the volume and pitch of one's voice demonstrates that one is in control of a situation. Voice can be used to convey empathy, a positive attitude, or an impression of authority.

  Questions posed by the officer should be clear and directed to the person who possesses the information that the officer requires.

- *Control.* The officer should ensure that he or she does not argue with the parties. Arguing may suggest a loss of objectivity. Arguments directed toward the officer should be dealt with by a calm reply such as "My beliefs are irrelevant in this situation." The officer must remain in command of the situation and should maintain control of the conversation. This may be accomplished through verbal direction or, possibly more effectively, through non-verbal communication such as eye contact.

- *Information gathering.* If an officer is to provide help, he or she must clearly understand the subject's responses. The officer should paraphrase a subject's responses to determine whether he or she has understood the responses correctly, but at the same time avoid interpreting or explaining the feelings of the other person.

- *Unbiased perspective.* The officer must be careful not to judge the parties. As long as their actions and ideas are legal, the officer should not criticize them or interject personal opinions. Also, the officer must control his or her non-verbal forms of expression. Non-verbal messages can relay information to a person more quickly than verbal messages and can send mixed messages that disclose the officer's beliefs, biases, or prejudices.

DEFUSING CONFLICT SITUATIONS

Calm, persuasive communication by the police may reduce the risk of violence in a confrontation. An officer should try to influence an individual's behaviour rather than coerce that person. The following are some actions that may help to de-escalate a situation and reduce the potential for violence:

- *Respond in a calm, reassuring manner.* This will help defuse the situation by allowing the disputants to see that the police are ready to help in an unemotional and unbiased manner, and that the police are in control of the situation. Emotional outbursts by the officer may exacerbate the situation.

- *Separate the parties to alleviate tensions.* The officer should try to separate the parties so that their eye contact is broken. At the same time, the officer should maintain eye contact with fellow officers.

- *Where separating the parties does not de-escalate the situation, take verbal, or, if necessary, a greater degree of physical, command of the situation.* However, the officer should not give ultimatums or make assurances that cannot be kept; statements such as "Do what I say or else" may aggravate the situation. The officer's voice, demeanour, and actions should communicate the fact that an opportunity to solve the problem or to withdraw from the conflict with dignity is available, but that escalation of the conflict will not be tolerated.

- *Maintain an authoritative demeanour.* The most important factor in defusing a conflict or crisis situation and preventing an escalation of violence is the officer's outward behaviour and attitude. Knowledge of legislation and use of force tactics have their place, but with the appropriate non-violent intervention techniques most situations can be defused without resorting to force.

- *Address the concerns of the parties as soon as possible.* The officer should ascertain the nature of the problem and determine whether police intervention is appropriate. If it is not, the appropriate referrals should be made. If the matter requires police intervention, the officer should listen to the parties with a view to helping defuse the situation, while still investigating whether an offence has been committed.

- *Where a situation escalates and there is a potential for violence, remove the parties.* The police have a duty to protect the person and property of all citizens. Knowledge of the appropriate provincial and federal arrest powers is essential at this point to enable the officer to legally apprehend the person or persons responsible for the escalation.

  If arrest is deemed necessary and is legal, it should be carried out. Although an arrest may not solve a problem, it may be necessary to prevent violence. Arrestees should be clearly told that they are being arrested for their actions, not for failure to obey an officer's directions. If force must be used to stop or prevent violence, the action taken should commence without warning and be as non-invasive as possible. This denies the arrestee time to plan a response to the police intervention and thus reduces the need for greater force on the part of the police.

- *Do not use the threat of force to compel a member of the public to obey a command.* It is hypocritical to use the threat of force to prevent another person from using force. Arrest should not be threatened if there are no legal grounds to make an arrest (an officer can appear inept if the threat is made but cannot be legally executed).

VIOLENCE

violence
for the purposes of this chapter, any unwanted act of aggression resulting in physical contact

For the purpose of this section, **violence** may be defined as any unwanted act of aggression resulting in physical contact. Violent behaviour can be a consequence of stress that has overwhelmed a person's ability to cope. This part of the chapter is directed toward fostering a better understanding of violent behaviour and how to handle it.

Violence is not hereditary. It can, however, be a product of one's environment, which may explain why it seems to run in families. In such families it may be a learned behaviour that is considered an acceptable alternative to peaceful conflict resolution.

Common Characteristics of Violent Persons

There appear to be some common personality traits possessed by violent persons:

- *Below-average intelligence.* Persons of below-average intelligence may resort to violence more frequently than the general population. This does not mean that lower intelligence is a cause of violence. Instead, these individuals may lack the ability to adequately problem solve and may see violence as their only viable option.

- *Impulsivity and a lack of self-control.* People who are impulsive and lack self-control show a greater potential for violence.

- *An inflated sense of self-worth.* Individuals with this characteristic may consider the views of others as being beneath their consideration. Such persons may react aggressively and violently in situations where they believe their superiority is being challenged.

- *An intense craving for social power and esteem.* Persons with this trait demonstrate rigid, egocentric thought patterns, prejudicial beliefs, and an intense focus on obtaining power. They may treat those of perceived lower social standing with disdain, and may react aggressively and violently during confrontations with these persons.

Potential Causes of Violence

Here are some potential causes of violence (Hafen & Frandsen, 1985):

- *Stress.* Chronic stress may lead to violence. The stressor need not be the object or target of the violent behaviour, and may be related to work, family, or finances.

- *Personality disorders.* Violence related to personality disorders is usually explosive. The person may have a long record of violence, as a victim or a perpetrator.

- *Alcohol and drugs.* Alcohol and drugs can impair one's ability to control impulsive responses to stress.

- *Threats.* Physical, emotional, or financial circumstances, as well as many other kinds of circumstances, can be perceived as a threat.

- *Panic.* Persons may feel that they are losing control over their lives. Violent reactions can give them the sense of restoring power over some portion of their lives.

- *Societal influences.* A sense of power may be gained through violence and intimidation. Society sometimes grants respect, money, and prestige to boxers and others who gain power this way. A person who commits a violent act may thus be searching for respect.

Predicting Violent Behaviour

Certain kinds of violent behaviour are specific to policing, such as the violence displayed by a person resisting arrest or by a person who postures before the police in an attempt to gain respect from peers or onlookers. It is impossible to predict with complete accuracy whether a person will respond violently to an encounter with the police. Situations, personalities, and personal experiences vary too widely. Officers should therefore respond to all incidents involving members of the public as if the potential for violence exists.

Although anyone has the potential for violent behaviour, males are generally more likely than females to handle a situation violently. Statistics over the past several decades indicate that males are charged with violent offences approximately 6.5 times more frequently than females. According to Statistics Canada, in 2003 there were 304,515 violent crimes reported to police across Canada. Adult males were charged with approximately 87 percent of these crimes.

Certain common indicators can help an officer determine whether the subject is violence prone:

- Has the person ever been charged with committing violent acts (not only assaults, but acts such as robbery, disturbing the peace, and harassment)?

- Have complaints of violence that did not result in a conviction been lodged against the person? Complaints of violence may be unfounded or lack sufficient evidence to prosecute or obtain a conviction. However, such complaints may indicate a history of violent behaviour. The relevant information may not be available on the Canadian Police Information Centre (CPIC) system but may be obtained by checking local records and the Ontario Municipal and Provincial Police Automated Computer Cooperative (OMPPAC) system.

- Has the person ever threatened violence? The threat of violence is sometimes the result of an emotional outburst, but should not be taken lightly. Did the person carry out the threat? If so, the person poses a substantial risk of further violence. The threat was a preconceived idea showing that the person did not act on impulse.

- Does the person abuse alcohol or drugs? Alcohol and drugs affect one's ability to reason, making one commit acts that are out of character.

- Does the person's history include being a victim of child abuse, a history of cruelty to animals, or symbolic acts of aggression such as the violent destruction of photographs or clothing? These and certain other experiences greatly increase the possibility of violence, although they may be difficult for the officer to uncover.

Officers also need to learn the outward signs of a possibly violent person. Recognition can allow officers to handle a situation more safely, by giving them more time to remove or lessen the impact of whatever is agitating the person. The signs include the following (Hafen & Frandsen, 1985):

- Loud, aggressive speech.

- Lack of emotion or, conversely, extreme emotion and volatility.

- Tense and alert posture (for example, sitting on the edge of a chair and appearing ready to move).

- Irritability. Everything is "bugging" the person in question.

- Short attention span. The person's mind is wandering and unable to focus, which can cause frustration and make the person lash out.

- Threatening gestures (for example, clenching or shaking fists, hitting the table with fists, or slamming doors) or destroying the person's own property.

- Refusal to discuss the situation. The person who remains silent and expressionless may be contemplating his or her next move or have already decided what to do next.

Some other indicators of potential violence include:

- Pacing.

- Finger drumming, wringing of hands, or other restless, repetitive movements.

- Change in voice or subject matter.

- Staring or avoiding eye contact.

- Change in facial colour and expression.

- Trembling.

- Shallow, rapid breathing.

The most important indicators of possible violence are non-verbal. The officer must use his or her judgment to interpret non-verbal communication. If the person's body language does not match what he or she is saying, the officer should rely on the body language. Body language usually reflects a person's true emotions and can account for about 70 percent of the information transmitted in an interaction (Stewart, 1995).

Dealing with Violent Persons

In general, police officers try to avoid violent responses to conflict or crisis situations. However, an officer may experience an adrenalin rush when a potentially violent situation is encountered—for example, when a suspect taunts or otherwise verbally abuses the officer. This may affect the officer's judgment. Therefore, officers must not react to rudeness, aggression, sarcasm, or any other provocation. It will only escalate the situation.

The officer must act within the bounds of the law and use good judgment at all times. It may be difficult for the officer to control his or her emotions, but control is an ability that the officer must possess.

The officer should not hurry into the situation or try to solve the problem in a few minutes. He or she should move and speak slowly when engaging the subject. Physical contact should be avoided except when there is an immediate danger of harm to the officer, the subject, or anyone else.

The officer should try to determine the problem by engaging the person in conversation, always speaking in a calm, rational manner. It is normal to feel fear when confronted with a potentially violent situation, but the officer should try not to allow the fear to show in his or her voice or body language.

The person may be irrational and may not respond to spoken words. Instead, he or she may react to the non-verbal messages that the officer is sending. Therefore, the officer should avoid using body language that can be perceived as threatening, such as placing hands on hips, crossing the arms, pointing, and rolling the eyes.

The officer should try to reduce the level of potential violence by attempting to persuade the person to put away any weapons and move away from any areas where there is ready access to weapons. Eye contact with the person should never be broken. When the person has moved to a "neutral" area, he or she can be offered a non-alcoholic drink, food, or a cigarette. This may temporarily distract the person's attention from the problem. When the person has become calm, the officer will need to decide on a further course of action.

Of course, preventing criminal acts and protecting the officer and the public from violence supersede allowing a person to vent his or her emotions. Accordingly, immediate arrest may be necessary in lieu of the process described above.

EFFECTIVE LISTENING AND PROBLEM IDENTIFICATION

Effective Listening

For the proper information to be obtained, the officer must employ active listening techniques. **Active listening** means devoting complete attention to a message to ensure full and accurate understanding. The techniques for active listening are as follows:

active listening
devoting complete
attention to a message to
ensure full and accurate
understanding

- *Concentrate on the message.* It may be necessary to make a conscious effort to concentrate on verbal messages. Because we think faster than we speak, we tend to try to predict what a person will say, instead of focusing solely on the information being relayed.

- *Show empathy and acceptance.* Empathy allows the officer to view the problem from the other's viewpoint. Empathy must not be confused with sympathy. Feeling sorry for someone involved in a conflict may taint an officer's opinion, resulting in a loss of objectivity.

- *Accept the message.* The officer must not jump to conclusions and form an opinion before the person has finished expressing himself or herself. It is acceptable for the officer to try to predict the outcome of a person's actions but it is nearly impossible to accurately predict the thoughts of another.

- *Take responsibility for accurately understanding the completed message.* The officer should verify that his or her understanding of the message is accurate by summarizing it for the speaker and asking for feedback.

Effective active listening allows the officer to obtain the information necessary to proceed to the next phase of the intervention process, problem identification.

Problem Identification

A solution to a problem cannot be reached until the problem is accurately identified. The problem may be obvious to the parties involved but not to an outsider. Perception is reality: if the person believes there is a problem, then there is one.

The officer should be careful when attempting to determine the cause of a problem. The immediate occurrence may merely be evidence of a deeper problem. For example, consider a call to a domestic disturbance involving a spouse who habitually comes home from work drunk and starts arguments with the other spouse. Addressing the current problem is necessary, but may do little to resolve the fundamental cause of the conflict. Careful observation and active listening may help identify the fundamental cause of the conflict and increase the officer's chances of resolving it.

To accurately diagnose the fundamental causes of a problem, an officer must be methodical and collect all pertinent information relating to the conflict. The officer must use his or her judgment to determine what information is important and what is not. Proper analysis of the conflict will allow the officer to more precisely identify the problem. Proper analysis requires good judgment, an understanding of verbal and non-verbal modes of communication, and the ability to remain objective.

If the person describes his or her problem vaguely, makes ambiguous statements, or presents non-verbal behaviour that does not agree with his or her verbal message, the officer should seek clarification. The person is likely to elaborate and clarify when asked non-intrusive, non-threatening questions. However, the officer must use this technique carefully and sparingly. Continually asking the person to clarify his or her statements could make him or her feel uneasy and distrust the officer's ability to assist.

Another effective method of identifying the problem is to ask the person to restate or rephrase the problem. The person will often respond positively to the officer if the problem has been identified or will explain the problem more clearly if he or she believes that the officer is sincerely trying to understand.

If an officer is unsure whether he or she has accurately identified the problem, he or she should admit to being confused and ask the person for clarification. As with restating and rephrasing, this method shows the person that the officer is interested in what is being said.

The officer may also need to ask questions, in addition to requesting clarification. Officers should pose questions in a non-accusatory manner, for the purpose of clarification and not interrogation. The questions may be closed or open. A closed question elicits a brief response (for example, "yes" or "no"), whereas an open question encourages further discussion in order to narrow the focus of the problem.

While seeking clarification, the officer should direct his or her attention to the person's non-verbal behaviours. As stated earlier, if the non-verbal behaviours are incongruous with the spoken message, the non-verbal message will generally be more reliable. Even so, the non-verbal message must always be contextually considered. It is possible that the action is a habit or nervous behaviour with no significant meaning.

To identify a problem and determine whether intervention is appropriate, officers must be alert to the specific attitude that the person presents. The following are examples of common attitudes that people present and the behaviours that indicate each attitude.

- Openness
  - open hands
  - hands spread apart
  - palms up
  - body leaning forward during conversation
- Defensiveness
  - arms crossed
  - legs crossed
  - hands closed into fists
- Cooperation
  - head tilted
  - significant eye contact (may differ culturally)
  - hand-to-face gestures
  - body leaning forward

- Evaluating
  - ❑ head tilted
  - ❑ pacing
  - ❑ chin stroking
  - ❑ pinching the bridge of the nose
- Readiness
  - ❑ hands on hips
  - ❑ body leaning forward
  - ❑ moving into another person's personal space
- Suspicion
  - ❑ avoiding eye contact (may differ culturally)
  - ❑ rubbing the eyes
  - ❑ rubbing the ears
  - ❑ sideways glance
- Confidence
  - ❑ elevated position on chair or platform
  - ❑ hands clasped behind the back
  - ❑ body leaning back with hands behind the neck
  - ❑ fingers steepled

By using effective communication skills, clarifying issues, and observing non-verbal behaviours, the officer should be able to decide whether the problem should be addressed through police intervention.

When the problem has been identified, the officer should ask the parties whether his or her assessment is accurate. Parties involved in a heated exchange may not immediately recognize whether the officer is correct. The officer should try to build a consensus with the parties and try to make reaching an agreement the priority.

The officer needs to determine what police response is appropriate at this stage. Mediation (discussed in the next section) may be applicable.

In some situations it will not be possible for an officer to accurately identify the underlying problem. For example, in the case of domestic strife that has lasted 25 years, there may be issues that cannot be identified in the time the officer has available, or that are beyond the officer's expertise. Likewise, in situations involving the abuse of alcohol or drugs, the officer may not have the ability to help. In such instances the officer must at least be able to identify the immediate problem and refer the parties to the appropriate community or social service agencies.

The officer must always remain aware that physical intervention may be necessary to prevent an offence or halt the continuance of one. Such intervention may have to be at the expense of determining the underlying cause of the problem.

MEDIATION

Mediation may be defined as assisted negotiation. The goal of mediation is to have the disputants resolve their disagreement themselves. The officer can assist, but in most cases cannot solve a problem that was created by others.

mediation
assisted negotiation in which a third party helps the disputants resolve their disagreement themselves

Effective mediation by police relies on several assumptions:

- the parties voluntarily agree to mediation;

- the parties agree to discuss their issues in a non-adversarial manner;

- the police will act as a neutral third party;

- the parties agree to hear the submissions of each party involved in the conflict; and

- the parties agree to allow the police to help them reach a consensus (if possible).

Conflicts more likely to be resolved through mediation are those isolated incidents where the parties are unlikely to have future contact with each other, or situations where police are involved at the first instance of the conflict. For example, in a situation involving two strangers arguing over a parking space, timely mediation by police is likely to be effective in resolving the dispute.

If the problem is a recent one, the officer may be able to offer assistance or advice. But, solving a long-term problem is beyond the scope of the police function and, in all probability, the capabilities of intervening officers.

The officer must determine whether the problem is a one-time acute problem or an ongoing, chronic problem. To determine whether the problem is acute or chronic, the officer analyzes the information acquired through investigation. A chronic problem may require long-term intervention and/or counselling by professionals who are better equipped to deal with the nature of the problem. Referral to the appropriate community or social agency may be the officer's best response to chronic problems after ensuring that the officer's immediate presence is of little value in helping solve the problem. However, referral should not be the first option for chronic problems where the officer believes that the conflict could escalate to the point where public or personal safety is threatened. The officer's first priority, after officer safety, is to protect all involved parties. This may require enforcement responses, including arrest that may do nothing to alleviate the problem.

Some situations, such as child custody disputes, family property disputes, or similar disputes, are better dealt with through means other than police mediation. In such situations, it is not possible for police to reach a legal agreement between the parties. Police may give advice on how to proceed to civil or family court or may refer the disputants to the services of a lawyer. The role of police in such matters is that of a peacekeeper.

After determining the nature of the problem, the officer will either try to mediate the problem or conclude that the problem is beyond immediate help.

If the decision is to mediate, the officer should formulate a plan for the medication. The following suggestions may help the officer achieve a successful outcome:

- *Reiterate the nature of the problem.* All parties should clearly understand and agree on the nature of the problem.

- *State the intended outcome of the mediation.* All parties should understand and agree on the goals and purpose of the mediation.

- *Physically separate the parties, but ensure that they are within speaking distance.* Keeping the parties separate reduces the probability of physical confrontations.

- *Ensure that one officer is in charge of the mediation.* Conflicting comments by different officers can confuse the parties and hinder the mediation process.

- *Establish the ground rules for the interaction.* The parties will each be allowed to speak and explain their views on the dispute. The parties will be asked to hear the concerns of each other without interruption. Everyone concerned will be asked to agree to the ground rules. If agreement is not reached, the mediation may be a wasted effort, because the parties may not be sincere in their commitment to resolve the problem.

- *Separate personalities from the problem to avoid bias and help speed up the process.* The parties should be directed to address the problem, not personalities. Personal bias, if allowed to enter into the process, may negate any advantage of mediation. For example, if a particular individual is perceived to be the problem and is treated as such, the other parties may not be willing to listen to his or her suggestions about resolving the issues, because they already "know" who the problem is. Their bias may predetermine the outcome of the mediation and doom it to failure.

- *Summarize the parties' understandings of the problem once they have had the opportunity to speak.* The officer's summary should be presented to the parties, and each party should be asked whether the problem has been clearly stated. There should be a consensus among the parties about the accuracy of the officer's problem identification.

- *Ask the parties for solutions once the problem has been identified.* They created the problem, and only they can resolve it.

- *Take care not to ridicule any proposed solutions.* An officer must remember that the dispute is not the officer's problem, and therefore that it is not the officer's place to belittle proposed solutions.

- *When a solution is proposed, ask the other parties whether the proposal is viable.* Care must be taken not to interject personal opinion. If asked for an opinion, the officer should politely decline.

- *When an adequate compromise is reached, ask each person whether he or she is willing to abide by the agreement.* Once a consensus is reached, the officer should leave, after confirming that all parties are satisfied and a police presence is no longer required.

It may not always be possible for the parties to reach a consensus within a reasonable time. What is a reasonable time? There is no single answer. It depends on the complexity of the problem, the time available to the officer, and the willing-ness of the disputants to work toward a consensus. The officer must use his or her judgment to determine what is reasonable. The officer may have to concede that the police are unable to effectively mediate the situation and are unable to help the parties reach an agreement within a reasonable time. Referral to community and social service agencies may be appropriate in such situations.

PERSONAL ANGER MANAGEMENT

Mediation may be a frustrating process for officers who think that they are the problem solvers. This frustration may lead to feelings of anger, either about the initial circumstances of the problem or about the inability of the involved parties to reach a consensus or to follow the mediation rules as outlined above. Any display of anger by the officer is unacceptable. Anger displays show that the officer is not in control and may even aggravate the situation. The following are some questions that officers should ask themselves to help recognize and overcome anger or at least prevent those feelings of anger from becoming apparent.

1. Have I avoided linear thinking? Did I resort to all-or-nothing solutions, anticipate the thoughts and responses of the parties involved, or magnify the problem or perceived personality "problems" of the parties involved?

2. How have I reacted to confrontation by the parties? Did I take the confrontational situation personally? Did I remain calm and in control?

3. How well did I recognize and control my anger? Did I recognize my own body signals (tense muscles, increased heart rate, agitation, etc.)? Did I use breathing and internal relaxation techniques to control my feelings?

4. Did I deal with my feelings after the occurrence? Did I talk to someone about stress management? Have I made a plan to alleviate my anger in future situations—for example, control my overall stress through healthy physical and relaxation activities?

KEY TERMS

active listening	PARE
CAPRA	SARA
client	violence
mediation	

REFERENCES

Hafen, B., & Frandsen, K. (1985). *Psychological emergencies and crisis intervention*. Scarborough, ON: Prentice Hall.

Stewart, J. (1995). *Bridges not walls*. Toronto: McGraw-Hill.

EXERCISES

True or False

_____ 1. The CAPRA system is applicable only to law enforcement.

_____ 2. When intervening in a conflict situation, a police officer will never partner with one of the parties.

_____ 3. Properly applying the CAPRA system will allow a police officer to solve any problem.

_____ 4. Arrest is an option provided for by the CAPRA system.

_____ 5. With some guidance, most parties can solve their own problems.

_____ 6. The attitude of the attending officer has no bearing on the outcome of an intervention.

_____ 7. A non-violent situation can become violent as a result of the arrival of the police.

_____ 8. Non-violent disputants should be physically separated and their eye contact with each other broken.

_____ 9. Delivering an ultimatum is a good way for police officers to defuse a situation.

_____ 10. In mediation, a solution to a dispute should come from the disputants themselves.

Multiple Choice

1. Mediation is an effective problem-solving technique

   a. in most of the situations that police face

   b. in only a few situations that police face

   c. in none of the situations that police face

   d. only in domestic situations

2. Police intervention may be required

   a. in domestic disputes

   b. in landlord and tenant disputes

   c. in property ownership disputes

   d. all of the above

3. The appropriate options for officers in a conflict or crisis situation include

   a. arrest

   b. inaction

   c. mediation

   d. all of the above

4. The most important ability officers must possess in a conflict or crisis situation is

   a. the ability to defend oneself

   b. the ability to communicate

   c. the ability to use common sense and good judgment

   d. none of the above

5. If an officer cannot assist a person with a problem, the officer should

   a. tell the person that he or she cannot help, and then leave the scene

   b. call a relative of the person

   c. refer the person to an appropriate community or social service agency

   d. remain on the scene as long as the person wishes

Short Answer

1. Briefly describe the four components of the SARA problem-solving model.

2. Briefly describe the four components of the PARE problem-solving model.

3. Briefly describe the five components of the CAPRA system.

4. Explain why it is important for an officer to remain calm when intervening in an emotionally charged dispute.

5. Explain why the potential for violence between the disputants arises when officers enter a previously non-violent situation.

6. What is the fundamental obligation of police officers when intervening in a conflict situation?

7. Briefly describe five potential causes of violent behaviour.

8. List five outward signs of a possibly violent person.

9. Briefly explain the procedure for dealing with a potentially violent person.

10. Explain active listening and why it is an important skill for police officers.

11. Explain the phrase "perception is reality" in the context of problem identification.

Case Analysis

Case 2.1

You are a police officer dispatched to a call for assistance at an apartment building. You are met at the entrance by Mr. Smith. He tells you that the building owner refuses to rent him an apartment because he is collecting social assistance. The owner, Mr. Collins, comes to the entrance to speak with you. He tells you he doesn't want to rent the apartment to someone on social assistance because the last time he did, the tenants wrecked the apartment.

Using the CAPRA system, answer the following questions:

1. Who are the clients in this scenario?

2. What information do you need? From which sources can you obtain this information?

3. What partners are available to assist you in this situation?

4. What is an appropriate response?

5. Assess your response. What are some possible outcomes?

Case 2.2

You are a police officer responding to a complaint at the residence of the local community college. You are met in the lobby by a young female student. She complains that one of her professors, Professor Doe, has been harassing her. She explains that Professor Doe has continually been making comments rife with sexual innuendoes. Professor Doe has never called her at home but takes every opportunity to comment on her looks and actions.

Using the CAPRA system, answer the following questions:

1. Who are the clients in this scenario?

2. What information do you need? From which sources can you obtain this information?

3. Which partners are available to assist you in this situation?

4. What is an appropriate response?

5. Assess your response. What are some possible outcomes?

Case 2.3

You are the owner of a small fitness club. Several patrons have approached you to complain that they have to wait too long to use the exercise equipment during the busy noon-hour period. You tell them that you will look into the matter. Your staff tell you that there is indeed a problem. Some patrons are waiting as long as 20 minutes to use some of the equipment. In the opinion of the staff, six new pieces of equipment are required to alleviate the problem. The cost of the new equipment is about $60,000, which is beyond your financial capabilities.

Using the CAPRA system, propose some solutions to this problem. Assess the possible outcomes of each solution.

Case 2.4

You are an employee at a fast-food restaurant. Three other employees work the late shift with you. For the past four Fridays, two employees, John and Jane, have been highly intoxicated when they come to work. Because of this, they have been unable to work, so you and the remaining employee, Abe, have had to do their share of the work.

You arrive at the restaurant for your Friday shift and meet Abe in the parking lot. The two of you discuss the situation. Abe is tired of having to work harder because of John and Jane, and says, "We should do something about it." You agree.

John and Jane arrive about 30 minutes late. They are again highly intoxicated. They stagger to the employee change room, telling you they will be right out. The restaurant is quite busy. After 30 minutes they have still not come out of the room. You check the room and find them both passed out on the floor. Attempts to revive them are unsuccessful. You go back to serving customers while Abe is busy in the kitchen.

About four hours later John walks out of the change room and asks, "What's going on?" He is still intoxicated. Luckily the restaurant is closed. You tell him, "It's time to clean up around here." He tells you he is too sick and is going home. He also tells you he has been having problems at home and that he is in financial trouble and may lose his car. He then walks out the door. Jane is still sleeping in the change room. You and Abe have to work an extra three hours to finish cleaning.

Using the CAPRA system, propose some solutions to this problem. Assess the possible outcomes of each solution.

Case 2.5

You are teaching a law class of 45 students. Not for the first time, two students in particular are having difficulty grasping an advanced concept. You therefore take a few minutes in class to re-explain the concept. After class you are approached by three students who complain that the class is going too slowly. They are becoming bored and want the class to progress faster. They are tired of your always having to stop and re-explain concepts to the same two students. They are paying a lot of money to take this course and want an immediate change. You explain that the two students in question are working full-time and raising families, and that they can't stay after class for extra help. The response is, "We don't care. If they can't afford to be in college, they shouldn't be here."

Using the CAPRA system, propose some solutions to this problem. Assess the possible outcomes of each solution.

Case 2.6

You are a police officer responding to a complaint at the public library. You obtain the following information.

There are three picnic tables at the rear of the building that are used as a place of relaxation by library staff and families with their children. The last six mornings in a row, there were human feces in the middle of each table. The area is open to the public. There is no fence. The feces were deposited sometime between closing at 2200 and 0600, when staff arrive. Cleaning staff cleaned and disinfected the tables each morning after the incidents occurred, but neither the library staff nor the public has been made aware of the situation.

Video cameras had been set up but captured only a grainy image of a person committing the act. The person could not be identified from the video. His face was covered. The library manager is irate and wants something done immediately.

What will you do? Apply the PARE problem-solving model to this problem.

Case 2.7

You are a police officer in charge of community policing. You are participating in a public meeting regarding community problems.

Several residents of Birch Street complain about the noise on the street after closing time at a nearby college bar. There is shouting, swearing, fighting, and cars "squealing" their tires. One complainant tells you that his two children, ages two and three, are awakened by the noise on Thursday, Friday, and Saturday nights. They are afraid to go to sleep because of the loud noises that awaken them.

Others complain of drunken students walking through their yards. One person, living directly behind the college, tells you that some of them are urinating in her garden. They want something done about the problem.

Apply the PARE problem-solving model to this problem.

Case 2.8

During the same meeting, the Residential Safety Committee brings forth a complaint that children are not wearing helmets while riding their bicycles. The chair of the committee, Dr. Bain, states that this complaint was brought to the Police Services Board on three consecutive meetings. The board advised police to enforce the helmet bylaw. The committee has checked the number of bylaw charges regarding bicycle helmets. In the past three months, no charges have been laid. They demand that something be done to rectify the situation. They warn that if nothing is done, they will make a complaint to the Ontario Civilian Commission on Policing Services regarding the inability of the police service to provide adequate services.

Apply the PARE problem-solving model to this problem.

Case 2.9

The final complaint brought to your attention at the meeting regards pedestrians standing in the turning lane on the highway. The Residential Safety Committee cites several incidents where pedestrians have been observed standing in the turning lane during periods of heavy traffic.

The area in question has two lanes on either side of the turning lane. Pedestrians have been running from the sidewalk to the turning lane, where they wait for a break in the traffic before running across the other two lanes of traffic. Dr. Bain tells you that on three occasions (times and dates were noted), a police cruiser drove past the pedestrians as they stood in the turning lane. She asks you: "Will you address the problem of the pedestrians and the officers neglecting their duty or will you also neglect to do your duty?"

Apply the PARE problem-solving model to this problem.

CHAPTER 3

Child Abuse

Chapter Objectives

After completing this chapter, you should be able to:

- Identify different types of child abuse.

- Differentiate between punishment and abuse.

- Recognize and understand general investigation techniques regarding child abuse.

- Explain the application of the *Child and Family Services Act* of Ontario.

- Identify possible criminal offences and applicable criminal law relating to child abuse.

- Develop effective responses to scenarios involving child abuse.

INTRODUCTION

Children of all ages, from babies to teenagers, and from all kinds of homes and from all types of ethnic, religious, social, and economic backgrounds, suffer from abuse. There are many kinds of abuse and these are not specific to certain age groups. Infants may be sexually abused and teenagers may be emotionally abused by humiliation and rejection.

The *Child and Family Services Act* (CFSA) of Ontario affirms the fervent desire of society to protect the well-being of its most vulnerable members. Section 79(1) of the Act defines **abuse** as "a state or condition of being physically harmed, sexually molested or sexually exploited." Section 37(2) defines the conditions under which a child may be in need of protection. It expands on the definition of abuse by including neglect and emotional and psychological abuse. It also states that a child is in need of protection when there exists the risk of abuse.

The term "risk" allows child protection workers and police to use their best judgment in determining whether the child is at risk of harm. If they are in doubt and if there is any reasonable possibility of risk, child protection workers are encouraged to first consider the best interests of the child. It is preferable to remove the child through the use of authorized apprehension authorities, and inconvenience or upset the person in care of the child, than to have the child injured in any way.

child
generally, a person under the age of 18; under some legislation, a person under the age of 16 or 14

abuse
in the *Child and Family Services Act*, a state or condition of being physically harmed, sexually molested, or sexually exploited

Although any child that interacts with adults has the potential to be abused, some children are at greater risk, including:

- children with behavioural problems or other special needs that consume a great deal of the parent's time;

- children of teenage mothers (stressors on such mothers, including lifestyle changes such as full-time childcare obligations and financial problems due to limited employment opportunities, may be contributing factors);

- children who continually demand attention or, conversely, children who do not communicate; and

- children that fall short of the parent's expectations, for example, in athletics or academic achievement.

CHILD ABUSE STATISTICS

Although many cases of abuse are not reported either to police or to child welfare authorities, data from police reports and child welfare authorities are still the most important sources of information about child abuse. A recent study conducted through Health Canada, the Canadian Incidence Study of Reported Child Abuse and Neglect (CIS), estimated the extent of child abuse in Canada based on data from child welfare authorities (Trocmé et al., 2001).

The Canadian Incidence Study of Reported Child Abuse and Neglect (CIS)

The CIS provides a snapshot of children who were reported to, and investigated by, child welfare services during a three-month period, from October to December 1998. The highlights presented below on physical abuse, sexual abuse, neglect, and emotional maltreatment are based on 7,672 investigations from 51 sites in all provinces and territories.

The CIS estimates that there were 135,573 child maltreatment investigations in Canada in 1998—a rate of almost 22 investigations for every 1,000 children in Canada. Child welfare workers were able to confirm that the abuse had occurred in almost half of all cases. (Note: Due to rounding of percentages, and more than one type of abuse occurring in each incident, the totals below may not equal 100 percent.)

In 1998, there were an estimated 21.52 investigations of child maltreatment per 1,000 children in Canada. Of these, 45 percent were substantiated, 22 percent remained suspected, and 33 percent were found to be unsubstantiated. Child maltreatment investigations were divided into four primary categories:

1. physical abuse,

2. sexual abuse,

3. neglect, and

4. emotional maltreatment.

FIGURE 3.1   Substantiated Child Maltreatment

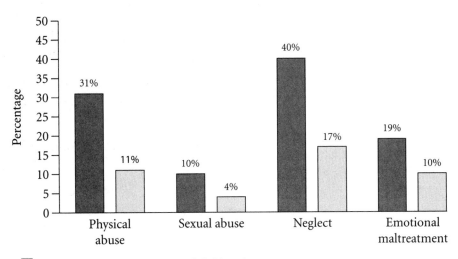

■ Percentage of investigations of child maltreatment
☐ Percentage of substantiated child maltreatment investigations

Figure 3.1 shows the percentage of each type of maltreatment that was investigated and what percentage of those investigations were substantiated.

PHYSICAL ABUSE

The study divided physical abuse into three forms: inappropriate punishment; other forms of abuse; and shaken infant syndrome. The majority of the substantiated reports of physical abuse involved inappropriate punishment while other forms of physical abuse accounted for almost one-third of the cases. Shaken infant syndrome accounted for the smallest percentage of substantiated cases. The table below shows each form of physical abuse and its percentage of substantiated cases.

Form of physical abuse	Percentage of substantiated cases
Inappropriate punishment	69
Other	31
Shaken infant syndrome	1

SEXUAL ABUSE

The CIS tracked seven forms of sexual abuse. Touching and fondling genitals was the most common form of substantiated child sexual abuse. Attempted and completed sexual activity accounted for over one-third of all substantiated reports. Adults exposing their genitals to children was reported in about one-eighth of cases. Sexual exploitation and sexual harassment were less common forms of child sexual abuse. There were an insufficient number of cases of voyeurism to permit estimates of this form of abuse. The table below shows the most common forms of sexual abuse and the percentage of substantiated cases for each.

Most common forms of sexual abuse	Percentage of substantiated cases
Touching and fondling of the genitals	68
Attempted and completed sexual activity	35
Adults exposing their genitals	12

NEGLECT

The CIS tracked eight forms of neglect. Failure to supervise leading to physical harm represented roughly half of the substantiated cases, while physical neglect, permitting criminal behaviour, abandonment, educational neglect, medical neglect, failure to provide necessary treatment, and failure to supervise leading to sexual harm represented the rest of the substantiated cases. The table below shows the most common forms of substantiated neglect and the percentage of substantiated cases for each.

Most common forms of neglect	*Percentage of substantiated cases*
Failure to supervise leading to physical harm	48
Physical neglect	19
Permitting criminal behaviour	14
Abandonment and educational neglect	12

EMOTIONAL MALTREATMENT

The CIS tracked four forms of emotional maltreatment. The most common form was exposure to family violence. This was followed by emotional abuse and emotional neglect. Failure to develop emotionally occurred too infrequently to be estimated in the study. The table below shows each form of emotional maltreatment and its percentage of substantiated cases.

Form of emotional maltreatment	*Percentage of substantiated cases*
Exposure to family violence	58
Emotional abuse	34
Emotional neglect	16

Police officers rarely intercede in cases of emotional abuse unless another type of abuse is present. Professional childcare or social workers, such as those employed by a Children's Aid Society, have the knowledge and time necessary to handle cases of emotional abuse, and are generally better equipped to address the emotional needs of children. The role of the police is usually confined to interceding in cases of sexual abuse, physical abuse, and neglect.

IDENTIFYING CHILD ABUSE

Section 37(2) of the CFSA identifies situations where a child is in need of protection. In many of these situations, police can offer only initial intervention, such as child apprehension or referral to an appropriate community agency, because they lack the required expertise and resources.

CHILD IN NEED OF PROTECTION: CHILD AND FAMILY SERVICES ACT, SECTION 37(2)

A child is in need of protection where,

(a) the child has suffered physical harm, inflicted by the person having charge of the child or caused by or resulting from that person's,

(i) failure to adequately care for, provide for, supervise or protect the child, or

(ii) pattern of neglect in caring for, providing for, supervising or protecting the child;

(b) there is a risk that the child is likely to suffer physical harm inflicted by the person having charge of the child or caused by or resulting from that person's,

(i) failure to adequately care for, provide for, supervise or protect the child, or

(ii) pattern of neglect in caring for, providing for, supervising or protecting the child;

(c) the child has been sexually molested or sexually exploited, by the person having charge of the child or by another person where the person having charge of the child knows or should know of the possibility of sexual molestation or sexual exploitation and fails to protect the child;

(d) there is a risk that the child is likely to be sexually molested or sexually exploited as described in clause (c);

(e) the child requires medical treatment to cure, prevent or alleviate physical harm or suffering and the child's parent or the person having charge of the child does not provide, or refuses or is unavailable or unable to consent to, the treatment;

(f) the child has suffered emotional harm, demonstrated by serious,

(i) anxiety,

(ii) depression,

(iii) withdrawal,

(iv) self-destructive or aggressive behaviour, or

(v) delayed development,

and there are reasonable grounds to believe that the emotional harm suffered by the child results from the actions, failure to act or pattern of neglect on the part of the child's parent or the person having charge of the child;

(f.1) the child has suffered emotional harm of the kind described in subclause (f) (i), (ii), (iii), (iv) or (v) and the child's parent or the person having charge of the child does not provide, or refuses or is unavailable or unable to consent to, services or treatment to remedy or alleviate the harm;

(g) there is a risk that the child is likely to suffer emotional harm of the kind described in subclause (f) (i), (ii), (iii), (iv) or (v) resulting from the actions, failure to act or pattern of neglect on the part of the child's parent or the person having charge of the child;

(g.1) there is a risk that the child is likely to suffer emotional harm of the kind described in subclause (f) (i), (ii), (iii), (iv) or (v) and that the child's parent or the person having charge of the child does not provide, or refuses or is unavailable or unable to consent to, services or treatment to prevent the harm;

(h) the child suffers from a mental, emotional or developmental condition that, if not remedied, could seriously impair the child's development and the child's parent or the person having charge of the child does not provide, or refuses or is unavailable or unable to consent to, treatment to remedy or alleviate the condition;

(i) the child has been abandoned, the child's parent has died or is unavailable to exercise his or her custodial rights over the child and has not made adequate provision for the child's care and custody, or the child is in a residential placement and the parent refuses or is unable or unwilling to resume the child's care and custody;

(j) the child is less than twelve years old and has killed or seriously injured another person or caused serious damage to another person's property, services or treatment are necessary to prevent a recurrence and the child's parent or the person having charge of the child does not provide, or refuses or is unavailable or unable to consent to, those services or treatment;

(k) the child is less than twelve years old and has on more than one occasion injured another person or caused loss or damage to another person's property, with the encouragement of the person having charge of the child or because of that person's failure or inability to supervise the child adequately; or

(l) the child's parent is unable to care for the child and the child is brought before the court with the parent's consent and, where the child is twelve years of age or older, with the child's consent, to be dealt with under this Part.

In some of these situations, it is obvious that police, beyond initial intervention, cannot adequately address the needs of the child. Intervention by child protection authorities is the better recourse in such situations. The Act requires that, in situations of suspected abuse, child protection authorities be apprised of the possibility that a child may be in need of protection.

DUTY TO REPORT CHILD IN NEED OF PROTECTION: CHILD AND FAMILY SERVICES ACT, SECTION 72(1)

Despite the provisions of any other Act, if a person, including a person who performs professional or official duties with respect to children, has reasonable grounds to suspect one of the following, the person shall forthwith report the suspicion and the information on which it is based to a society: [The Act then lists the situations where a child is in need of protection. See s. 37(2), above.]

Although police officers may not have the expertise or resources to address the verbal, emotional, or psychological aspects of child abuse, they do have the expertise and legislative authority to address the criminal aspects. Physical abuse, sexual abuse, and neglect may be effectively dealt with through police intervention in conjunction with child protection authorities.

IDENTIFYING PHYSICAL ABUSE

Child physical abuse can take the form of punches, kicks, or any other method of striking a child. Where small children are concerned, it may involve shaking or throwing. The abuse may produce extreme injuries such as burns, scalds, broken bones, concussions, bites, and severe bruising. Such abuse can cause the child's death.

Signs of Physical Abuse in Children

There are many behavioural and physical clues to possible abuse (Children's Aid Society of Algoma, 1998). Behavioural signs include the following:

- The child is unable to recall how injuries suggestive of abuse occurred.
- The child is very aggressive or extremely withdrawn.
- The child has a vacant stare, as if unaware of his or her surroundings.
- The child indiscriminately seeks affection.
- The child is compliant and eager to please.
- The child caters to his or her parent's needs (role reversal).
- The child models negative behaviour when playing, such as using violence to deal with disagreements or shouting at playmates.
- The child dresses inappropriately in an attempt to hide injuries.
- The child runs away from home or expresses a fear of going home.
- The child describes incidents of abuse.
- The child behaves in a way that provokes punishment.
- The child flinches or pulls away if touched unexpectedly.

Physical signs of abuse include unexplained bruises, welts, or lacerations. Most physical signs involve injuries to parts of the body that, among children, typically tend not to be injured. Children frequently injure themselves while playing or when involved in sports. These common injuries usually take the form of bruises, lacerations, or abrasions at the joints or on the hands. By contrast, abusive injuries often appear at suspicious locations, such as the lips, mouth, and other parts of the face. They are also common on the backs of the legs, the buttocks, and soft tissue areas such as the abdomen, which usually are not visibly injured as a result of a child's daily activities. Abusive injuries may have a regular pattern, as in the case of tooth marks, handprints, or the imprints of objects such as belts, cords, and rulers. As time passes, the injuries suffered by the child may become more severe or obvious.

BRUISES

Common areas where children bruise include shins, elbows, knees, and to a lesser extent the forehead. When investigating potential abuse, look for bruising in areas uncommonly injured in daily activities. Children rarely bruise themselves in areas such as the small of the back, buttocks, or abdomen.

Pattern bruises may also indicate abuse. The bruising may be in the pattern of a hand with bruising from the abuser's thumb and fingers. Bruising from bite marks may be present. Human bite marks may be easily distinguished from those of common house pets such as dogs or cats. The animals' teeth are designed to tear flesh, whereas the human bite mark will compress the flesh, leaving a distinct bruise pattern.

Finally, bruises on non-ambulatory or very young children may indicate abuse. Children who cannot walk or who are confined to bed have less opportunity to bruise themselves. Observations by medical personnel at the Hospital for Sick Children in Toronto found that less than 0.5 percent of children under 6 months of age had any type of bruising, whereas 11.5 percent of children between 9 and 12 months of age had bruising. (Note: This was not a study of possible abuse, merely observations of the presence of bruising.)

Bruises can sometimes be dated according to their colour. This method is not exact but may be used to estimate the time when bruising occurred. Most bruising is gone within two to four weeks, depending on the severity of the injury.

- Red and swollen—Usually less than 2 days old.

- Red, blue, or dark purple—Usually 1–3 days old.

- Green—Usually 4–7 days old.

- Yellow—Usually 7–14 days old.

- Brown—Usually more than 14 days old.

BURNS

Burn injuries should arouse suspicion if the parent's or caregiver's explanation does not fit with the extent and category of the burn. There are three main categories of burns: scalding burns, contact burns, and flame burns.

- Scalding burns are caused by spilling, splashing, or immersion in a hot liquid. Spill burns will exhibit an inverted arrow pattern with the narrow area of the pattern at the "bottom" of the spill. Immersion burns are caused by immersing part of the child in hot water. The burn is evidenced by the distinct burn line dividing the immersed from the non-immersed parts of the body. A child that "accidently pulled a boiling pot from the stove" will not have the distinct burn pattern consistent an intentional immersion burn.

- Contact burns are caused by contact with hot or acidic objects. These burns often mirror the shape of the object used. For example, small circular burns on the hands or soles of the feet may indicate a cigarette burn. The investigating officer should consider the age of the child when weighing the probability of the explanation provided. For example, it is extremely unlikely that an infant who is not yet able to crawl will accidently incur a contact burn.

  Not all contact burns are the result of abuse. There are pattern burns that may occur in diapered babies where the shape of the burn will resemble the edge of the diaper. This could be an acidic burn caused by urine or stool where the baby's diet is high in fruit products. Such burns should be categorized only by qualified medical personnel.

- Flame burns are caused by contact with direct flame. Such burns have random patterns, depending on the source of the flame.

The injury resulting from a burn depends on:

- the cause of the burn,

- the temperature of the mechanism of the burn, and

- the duration of exposure.

Burns are classified as first, second, and third degree burns.

- First degree burns involve the epidermis, or outer layer of skin. A first degree burn exhibits as redness of the epidermis.

- Second degree burns extend into the dermis, the layer of skin below the epidermis.

  Partial thickness burns extend into the outer layers of the dermis. Such burns are painful and generally blister, but they heal well, often without scarring.

  Deeper second degree burns extend deeper into the dermis and cause a great deal of pain. Such burns heal more slowly and often leave a scar.

- Third degree burns involve burning of the entire dermis, and possibly the underlying tissues. These burns are not painful because all the pain sensors have been destroyed. However, the damage caused by third degree burns is serious and possibly life-threatening if the burned area is large.

The table below provides estimates of the amount of time required at a given temperature to produce a third degree burn of a child's bare skin. Officers can use this information to evaluate the credibility of information they receive from a parent or caregiver regarding the cause of the burn injury.

Temperature	Time
49 degrees Celsius	300 seconds
54.5 degrees Celsius	30 seconds
60 degrees Celsius	5 seconds
65 degrees Celsius	1.5 seconds

HEAD AND NECK INJURIES DETECTED DURING DENTAL EXAMINATIONS

Section 72 of the Ontario *Child and Family Services Act* requires that all health care professionals report suspected cases of child abuse.

Physical abuse, sexual abuse, and neglect may be revealed through dental examination. Through a program called PANDA (Prevent Abuse and Neglect through Dental Awareness), dentists throughout Ontario have been provided with information to assist them in identifying child abuse ("Reporting Suspicions of Child Abuse," 1999).

Studies have indicated that approximately 65 percent of child physical abuse injuries occur in the head and neck area; these are areas easily viewed and examined by dental health care professionals (Stechey, 2001).

Injuries readily identified by dental health care professionals include:

- gag marks caused by the abuser tying something around the child's mouth to muffle sounds;

- injuries caused by direct trauma to the facial area;

- bruising of the hard and soft palate from forced oral sex;

- injuries on the soft tissues inside the mouth caused by forcefully holding the child's mouth shut, usually to quiet the child;

- venereal warts, which may indicate sexual abuse;

- multiple abscesses and caries due to neglect;

- tongue lacerations, which may indicate physical abuse; and

- marks on the neck, which may indicate strangulation by hands, rope, or similar means.

BITE MARKS

In inflicting abuse, a perpetrator may bite his or her victim. The resulting bite pattern can serve as a unique identifier of the aggressor. As discussed above, human bite marks are distinct from the bite marks of other animals. This distinctiveness may assist in the apprehension and prosecution of the abuser.

Officers should keep in mind that a child can suffer bite marks through interactions with other children. However, if there is any doubt as to the origin of the bite mark, officers should err on the side of safety and take steps to protect the child.

A dental health care professional experienced in the field of forensic odontology can assess bite mark patterns to implicate or exonerate suspects. The odontologist can compare the bite marks with the suspect's dental records or impressions of the suspect's teeth.

Bite mark analysis can also be used to determine whether the suspect was at the crime scene and whether the suspect inflicted the injury. Investigators should ask the victim whether he or she was bitten by the assailant as well as whether the victim bit the assailant. Bite marks on the victim could contain the DNA of the suspect. Bite marks on the suspect that match those of the victim could put the suspect at the scene.

Section 487.092(1) of the *Criminal Code* allows police to obtain a warrant requiring a suspect to provide an impression of his or her teeth to be used for comparison purposes:

A justice may issue a warrant in writing authorizing a peace officer to do any thing, or cause any thing to be done under the direction of the peace officer, described in the warrant in order to obtain any handprint, fingerprint, footprint, foot impression, teeth impression or other print or impression of the body or any part of the body in respect of a person if the justice is satisfied

(a) by information on oath in writing that there are reasonable grounds to believe that an offence against this or any other Act of Parliament has been committed and that information concerning the offence will be obtained by the print or impression; and

(b) that it is in the best interests of the administration of justice to issue the warrant.

TELLTALE INJURIES

There are other injuries that are more definite indicators of physical abuse. These include:

- *Injuries to the face.* Common examples are broken teeth or a black eye. These injuries may have been caused by schoolyard fights or sporting activities, but warrant an investigation into the origin of the injury.

- *Fractures.* Infants rarely fracture bones. Look for signs of deformities of limbs, swelling, or inability to move the limb. In older children, there may be a viable explanation for the injury. Police should investigate the explanation. Fractures that do not receive immediate medical attention should be treated as suspicious.

- *Fractures of the chest area.* These may be more difficult for police to detect. Look for signs of breathing distress and deformities in the area of the rib cage.

- *Abdominal injuries.* These are also difficult to detect. Look for distention, bruising or swelling of the abdominal area. Abdominal injuries can result in death due to internal bleeding.

When questioning the parent or other involved parties about the injuries, look for discrepancies in their explanations. Compare the explanations with the injuries observed to identify possible inconsistencies.

If there is any risk that the child is being abused, consider the child to be "in need of protection."

Shaken Infant Syndrome

The term "shaken infant syndrome" describes a classic injury pattern seen in shaken infants and very young children. The victim is held around the chest by an adult and violently shaken back and forth. This causes the extremities and the head to whiplash back and forth. Violent shaking creates shearing forces on the extremities, which may cause fractures of the growth plate (skull). These fractures are highly specific to this type of abuse.

The violent shaking causes similar shearing forces in and on the brain. This may cause large amounts of brain matter to tear and may also cause bleeding to occur on the surface of the brain if the brain strikes the skull during shaking. With violent shaking, serious brain damage may occur. In fact, infants have died after being violently shaken.

The tight grasp around the chest that accompanies this shaking may also cause rib fractures (these are also highly specific for abuse). These rib fractures may be incidentally found on chest X-rays performed for other reasons, such as diagnose pneumonia.

FACTS ABOUT SHAKEN INFANT SYNDROME

Officers should know the following facts about shaken infant syndrome to aid them in their investigations:

- It is a non-accidental trauma caused by violently shaking the infant.

- It usually occurs in children less than three years old, although the majority of victims are less than one year old.

- The most common perpetrators are (in order) the father, boyfriend of the mother, female babysitter, and mother of the child.

- Injuries occur as the result of severe back and forth motion of the infant's head.

- It usually causes brain injuries.

- It may also cause retinal hemorrhages.

- Approximately 50 percent of severely injured victims die from the abuse.

- Most victims are left with a severe disability.

- Victims that appear to fully recover are often left with developmental difficulties.

Some common explanations put forth by the perpetrators of this crime include:

- the baby suffered an accidental fall;

- the injuries were inflicted by chest compressions from CPR;

- another child in the home caused the injuries;

- the injuries are the cumulative result of several accidents; or

- the injuries are due to an illness, such as meningitis, a bleeding disorder, or a genetic disease.

Thorough investigation by medical practitioners and police generally reveals the fallacy of these "defences."

CRIMINAL OFFENCES RELATED TO THE PHYSICAL ABUSE OF CHILDREN

The definition of assault is found in s. 265 of the *Criminal Code*.

ASSAULT: CRIMINAL CODE, SECTION 265(1)

A person commits an assault when

> (a) without the consent of another person, he applies force intentionally to that other person, directly or indirectly;

> (b) he attempts or threatens, by an act or a gesture, to apply force to another person, if he has, or causes that other person to believe on reasonable grounds that he has, present ability to effect his purpose; or

(c) while openly wearing or carrying a weapon or an imitation thereof, he accosts or impedes another person or begs.

The degree of injury caused by the assault will determine the section of the *Criminal Code* that has been violated and the severity of the punishment for the assault. Several different kinds of assault and physical abuse are described in the sections of the *Criminal Code* listed below.

ASSAULT: CRIMINAL CODE, SECTION 266

Every one who commits an assault is guilty of

(a) an indictable offence and is liable to imprisonment for a term not exceeding five years; or

(b) an offence punishable on summary conviction.

This section can be used where the assault was not severe and there is evidence that the child was assaulted. A child's statement that he or she was assaulted can be enough to support a charge under this section.

ASSAULT WITH A WEAPON OR CAUSING BODILY HARM: CRIMINAL CODE, SECTION 267

Every one who, in committing an assault,

(a) carries, uses or threatens to use a weapon or an imitation thereof, or

(b) causes bodily harm to the complainant,

is guilty of an indictable offence and liable to imprisonment for a term not exceeding ten years or an offence punishable on summary conviction and liable to imprisonment for a term not exceeding eighteen months.

Section 267 may be used in situations where the child was struck with an object or suffered bodily harm. Bodily harm has been defined as injuries that are not transient in nature.

AGGRAVATED ASSAULT: CRIMINAL CODE, SECTION 268(1)

Every one commits an aggravated assault who wounds, maims, disfigures or endangers the life of the complainant.

If the child's injuries are severe (as in the case of broken bones) or life-threatening, aggravated assault may be an appropriate charge.

Section 268(3) of the *Criminal Code* recognizes the practice of female "circumcision" as a criminal offence if the procedure is carried out upon a female under the age of 18 years. The procedure may be legally performed as an approved surgical procedure for medical reasons or upon consent when the person is 18 years of age.

EXCISION: CRIMINAL CODE SECTION 268(3)

For greater certainty, in this section, "wounds" or "maims" includes to excise, infibulate or mutilate, in whole or in part, the labia majora, labia minora or clitoris of a person, except where

(a) a surgical procedure is performed, by a person duly qualified by provincial law to practise medicine, for the benefit of the physical health of the person or for the purpose of that person having normal reproductive functions or normal sexual appearance or function; or

(b) the person is at least eighteen years of age and there is no resulting bodily harm.

CORRECTION OF CHILD BY FORCE: CRIMINAL CODE, SECTION 43

There may be instances where the parent claims that force was applied to a child as a corrective punishment. The *Criminal Code* of Canada, since its inception in 1892, has included a provision granting permission to parents, and persons standing in place of parents, to use force to correct a child's behaviour. The provision in the 1892 legislation is reproduced below.

CRIMINAL CODE OF CANADA 1892: SECTION 55

It is lawful for every parent, or person in the place of a parent, schoolmaster or master, to use force by way of correction towards any child, pupil or apprentice under his care, provided that such force is reasonable under the circumstances.

The authority has evolved over the past century but remains substantially the same. The provision for corrective punishment in the current *Criminal Code* is reproduced below.

CORRECTION OF CHILD BY FORCE: CRIMINAL CODE, SECTION 43

Every schoolteacher, parent or person standing in the place of a parent is justified in using force by way of correction toward a pupil or child, as the case may be, who is under his care, if the force does not exceed what is reasonable under the circumstances.

Challenges to the Validity of Section 43

The CIS found that 69 percent of all substantiated abuse investigations involved inappropriate physical punishment. Such statistics have led many to question the use of force as a method of correcting a child's behaviour. The validity of s. 43 of the *Criminal Code* has been challenged by the Canadian Foundation for Children, Youth and the Law. The issue was brought before the Supreme Court of Canada in the case of *Canadian Foundation for Children, Youth and the Law v. Canada (Attorney General)*. The court was asked to invalidate s. 43 of the *Criminal Code* on a number of constitutional violations.

The judgment of the court was delivered by Chief Justice Beverley McLachlin on January 30, 2004. Below are sections of the judgment applicable to law enforcement. A summary of the judgment follows the excerpt.

[1] THE CHIEF JUSTICE: The issue in this case is the constitutionality of Parliament's decision to carve out a sphere within which children's parents and teachers may use minor corrective force in some circumstances without facing criminal sanction. The assault provision of the *Criminal Code*, RSC 1985, c. C-46, s. 265 prohibits intentional, non-consensual application of force to another. Section 43 of the *Criminal Code* excludes from this crime reasonable physical correction of children by their parents and teachers.

. . .

[19] The purpose of s. 43 is to delineate a sphere of non-criminal conduct within the larger realm of common assault. It must, as we have seen, do this in a way that permits people to know when they are entering a zone of risk of criminal sanction and that avoids ad hoc discretionary decision making by law enforcement officials. People must be able to assess when conduct approaches the boundaries of the sphere that s. 43 provides.

. . .

[21] Section 43 delineates *who may access* its sphere with considerable precision. The terms "schoolteacher" and "parent" are clear. The phrase "person standing in the place of a parent" has been held by the courts to indicate an individual who has assumed "*all* the obligations of parenthood": *Ogg-Moss*, [[1984] 2 SCR 173], at p. 190 (emphasis in original). These terms present no difficulty.

[22] Section 43 identifies less precisely *what conduct* falls within its sphere. It defines this conduct in two ways. The first is by the requirement that the force be "by way of correction." The second is by the requirement that the force be "reasonable under the circumstances." The question is whether, taken together and construed in accordance with governing principles, these phrases provide sufficient precision to delineate the zone of risk and avoid discretionary law enforcement.

[23] I turn first to the requirement that the force be "by way of correction." These words, considered in conjunction with the cases, yield two limitations on the content of the protected sphere of conduct.

[24] First, the person applying the force must have intended it to be for educative or corrective purposes: *Ogg-Moss*, *supra*, at p. 193. Accordingly, s. 43 cannot exculpate outbursts of violence against a child motivated by anger or animated by frustration. It admits into its sphere of immunity only sober, reasoned uses of force that address the actual behaviour of the child and are designed to restrain, control or express some symbolic disapproval of his or her behaviour. The purpose of the force must always be the education or discipline of the child: *Ogg-Moss*, *supra*, at p. 193.

[25] Second, the child must be capable of benefiting from the correction. This requires the capacity to learn and the possibility of successful correction. Force against children under two cannot be corrective, since on the evidence they are incapable of understanding why they are hit (trial decision (2000), 49 OR (3d) 662, at para. 17). A child may also be incapable of learning from the application of force because of disability or some other contextual factor. In these cases, force will not be "corrective" and will not fall within the sphere of immunity provided by s. 43.

[26] The second requirement of s. 43 is that the force be "reasonable under the circumstances." The Foundation argues that this term fails to sufficiently delineate the area of risk and constitutes an invitation to discretionary *ad hoc* law enforcement. It argues that police officers, prosecutors and judges too often

assess the reasonableness of corrective force by reference to their personal experiences and beliefs, rendering enforcement of s. 43 arbitrary and subjective. In support, it points to the decision of the Manitoba Court of Appeal in *R v. K.(M.)* (1992), 74 CCC (3d) 108, in which, at p. 109, O'Sullivan JA stated that "[t]he discipline administered to the boy in question in these proceedings [a kick to the rear] was mild indeed compared to the discipline I received in my home."

[27] Against this argument, the law has long used reasonableness to delineate areas of risk, without incurring the dangers of vagueness. But reasonableness as a guide to conduct is not confined to the law of negligence. The criminal law of negligence, which has blossomed in recent decades to govern private actions in nearly all spheres of human activity, is founded upon the presumption that individuals are capable of governing their conduct in accordance with the standard of what is "reasonable." But reasonableness as a guide to conduct is not confined to the law of negligence. The criminal law also relies on it. The *Criminal Code* expects that police officers will know what constitutes "reasonable grounds" for believing that an offence has been committed, such that an arrest can be made (s. 495); that an individual will know what constitutes "reasonable steps" to obtain consent to sexual contact (s. 273.2(b)); and that surgeons, in order to be exempted from criminal liability, will judge whether performing an operation is "reasonable" in "all the circumstances of the case" (s. 45). These are merely a few examples; the criminal law is thick with the notion of "reasonableness."

[28] The reality is that the term "reasonable" gives varying degrees of guidance, depending upon the statutory and factual context. It does not insulate a law against a charge of vagueness. Nor, however, does it automatically mean that a law is void for vagueness. In each case, the question is whether the term, considered in light of principles of statutory interpretation and decided cases, delineates an area of risk and avoids the danger of arbitrary *ad hoc* law enforcement.

. . .

[30] The first limitation arises from the behaviour for which s. 43 provides an exemption, simple non-consensual application of force. Section 43 does not exempt from criminal sanction conduct that causes harm or raises a reasonable prospect of harm. It can be invoked only in cases of non-consensual application of force that results neither in harm nor in the prospect of bodily harm. This limits its operation to the mildest forms of assault. People must know that if their conduct raises an apprehension of bodily harm they cannot rely on s. 43. Similarly, police officers and judges must know that the defence cannot be raised in such circumstances.

[31] Within this limited area of application, further precision on what is reasonable under the circumstances may be derived from international treaty obligations. Statutes should be construed to comply with Canada's international obligations: *Ordon Estate v. Grail*, [1998] 3 SCR 437, at para. 137. Canada's international commitments confirm that physical correction that either harms or degrades a child is unreasonable.

. . .

[36] Determining what is "reasonable under the circumstances" in the case of child discipline is also assisted by social consensus and expert evidence on what constitutes reasonable corrective discipline. The criminal law often uses the concept of reasonableness to accommodate evolving mores and avoid successive "fine-tuning" amendments. It is implicit in this technique that current social consensus on what is reasonable may be considered. It is wrong for caregivers or

judges to apply their own subjective notions of what is reasonable; s. 43 demands an objective appraisal based on current learning and consensus. Substantial consensus, particularly when supported by expert evidence, can provide guidance and reduce the danger of arbitrary, subjective decision making.

[37] Based on the evidence currently before the Court, there are significant areas of agreement among the experts on both sides of the issue (trial decision, at para. 17). Corporal punishment of children under two years is harmful to them, and has no corrective value given the cognitive limitations of children under two years of age. Corporal punishment of teenagers is harmful, because it can induce aggressive or antisocial behaviour. Corporal punishment using objects, such as rulers or belts, is physically and emotionally harmful. Corporal punishment which involves slaps or blows to the head is harmful. These types of punishment, we may conclude, will not be reasonable.

[38] Contemporary social consensus is that, while teachers may sometimes use corrective force to remove children from classrooms or secure compliance with instructions, the use of corporal punishment by teachers is not acceptable. Many school boards forbid the use of corporal punishment, and some provinces and territories have legislatively prohibited its use by teachers: see, e.g., *Schools Act, 1997*, SNL 1997, c. S-12.2, s. 42; *School Act*, RSBC 1996, c. 412, s. 76(3); *Education Act*, SNB 1997, c. E-1.12, s. 23; *School Act*, RSPEI 1988, c. S-2.1, s. 73; *Education Act*, SNWT 1995, c. 28, s. 34(3); *Education Act*, SY 1989-90, c. 25, s. 36. This consensus is consistent with Canada's international obligations, given the findings of the Human Rights Committee of the United Nations noted above. Section 43 will protect a teacher who uses reasonable, corrective force to restrain or remove a child in appropriate circumstances. Substantial societal consensus, supported by expert evidence and Canada's treaty obligations, indicates that corporal punishment by teachers is unreasonable.

. . .

[40] When these considerations are taken together, a solid core of meaning emerges for "reasonable under the circumstances," sufficient to establish a zone in which discipline risks criminal sanction. Generally, s. 43 exempts from criminal sanction only minor corrective force of a transitory and trifling nature. On the basis of current expert consensus, it does not apply to corporal punishment of children under two or teenagers. Degrading, inhuman or harmful conduct is not protected. Discipline by the use of objects or blows or slaps to the head is unreasonable. Teachers may reasonably apply force to remove a child from a classroom or secure compliance with instructions, but not merely as corporal punishment. Coupled with the requirement that the conduct be corrective, which rules out conduct stemming from the caregiver's frustration, loss of temper or abusive personality, a consistent picture emerges of the area covered by s. 43. It is wrong for law enforcement officers or judges to apply their own subjective views of what is "reasonable under the circumstances"; the test is objective. The question must be considered in context and in light of all the circumstances of the case. The gravity of the precipitating event is not relevant.

Summary of the Judgment

Below are summaries of the sections of the judgment reproduced above.

USE OF FORCE FOR CORRECTIVE PURPOSES: PARAGRAPHS 24, 25

The court clearly stated that the use of force must be for corrective purposes. Striking a child out of anger or frustration does not meet the requirement of s. 43 of the *Criminal Code* that the force be "by way of correction." Paragraph 25 states another condition: The child must be capable of learning from the corrective force. If the child is too young or lacks the ability to understand why he or she is being punished, the use of force is not permissible.

FORCE THAT IS "REASONABLE UNDER THE CIRCUMSTANCES": PARAGRAPHS 26, 27, 28, 40

In interpreting "reasonable under the circumstances," the court clearly stated that police officers must not base their opinions only on subjective views. Instead, they must determine whether criminal behaviour has occurred by using an objective test (discussed below). The court was satisfied that police officers could determine what is "reasonable for the circumstances" by applying the objective test, and could reach an accurate conclusion of what actions constitute criminal behaviour.

Paragraph 27 of the decision refers to the ability of police to determine a standard of reasonableness such as the determination of "reasonable grounds" as found in s. 495 of the *Criminal Code*.

Paragraph 40 refers to the need for police to objectively consider their opinion of "reasonable under the circumstances."

The objective test is described in the decision of *R v. Storrey*. Although the subject of the decision is the validity of an arrest, the objective test that it proposes for determining reasonable grounds also applies to the issue of the reasonable use of force.

> [A]n arresting officer must subjectively have reasonable and probable grounds on which to base the arrest. Those grounds must, in addition, be justifiable from an objective point of view. That is to say, a reasonable person placed in the position of the officer must be able to conclude that there were indeed reasonable and probable grounds for the arrest.

FORCE CANNOT CAUSE BODILY HARM: PARAGRAPH 30

The application of corrective force cannot cause bodily harm. The court went further by adding the words "or raises a reasonable prospect of harm." If the force used causes bodily harm or raises the reasonable prospect of bodily harm, s. 43 cannot be relied upon for a defence by the person who administered the punishment.

RESTRICTIONS ON THE USE OF CORPORAL PUNISHMENT: PARAGRAPH 37

Paragraph 37 sets out several restrictions:

- The use of force to correct a child under the age of two has no demonstrated corrective value and has been shown to be harmful. Therefore, corrective force will not be authorized in such circumstances.

- Corporal punishment of teenage children can cause aggressive and/or antisocial behaviour and therefore will not be permitted.

- Corporal punishment using objects will not be permitted.

- Blows to the head, including slaps, are not reasonable and therefore are not permitted.

USE OF FORCE BY TEACHERS: PARAGRAPHS 38, 40

A teacher may only use force to restrain a child, to ensure compliance with instructions, or to remove a child from the classroom in appropriate circumstances. The use of corporal punishment by teachers is not acceptable.

PUNISHMENT VERSUS ABUSE

This section addresses situations where a person legally authorized to use force to correct a child has used force, and the child has been harmed or a complaint has been made. It may be used as a guide for determining whether a child is in "need of protection" within the meaning of s. 37 of the CFSA.

These guidelines, along with the above discussion of *Canadian Foundation for Children, Youth and the Law v. Canada*, should assist officers in determining whether the force used against a child is an appropriate punishment or a criminal offence.

Abusive (inappropriate) physical punishment includes the following:

- The use of generally accepted types of physical punishment, such as slapping hands or buttocks, that is unduly prolonged or that is applied with an excessive amount of force.

- The use of generally unaccepted or inappropriate types of physical punishment, such as continual or lengthy beating, striking with fists, kicking, burning, scalding, or suffocating.

The decision in *Canadian Foundation for Children, Youth and the Law v. Canada* provides the following guidelines on the use of force:

- The force used must be for corrective purposes.

- The child must be capable of understanding why he or she is being punished.

- The child must be over the age of 2 and under the age of 13.

- The force used must be reasonable. Unreasonable force includes:

  ❑ causing bodily harm,

  ❑ administering strikes to the head, and

  ❑ using objects to strike a child.

Description of Physical Punishment

The purpose of the descriptions that follow is to give guidelines to child protection workers regarding the use of force to correct a child. Protection of the child rather than consideration of proof of a criminal offence was the overriding concern in their drafting. However, police officers must also know when physical punishment constitutes a criminal offence so that they can act accordingly. Child protection should be foremost when determining whether to apply criminal or provincial legislation in child abuse cases.

The punishment identified in the following descriptions is in order of most to least amount of force used.

1. EXCESSIVE OR INAPPROPRIATE PHYSICAL FORCE USED, RESULTING IN SEVERE INJURY

Examples of severe injuries requiring immediate medical attention include bone fractures, internal injuries such as those caused by shaking, intentional burns, brain or spinal cord injury, and wounds or punctures. This level of injury meets the definition of a child in need of protection. A criminal offence has likely been committed.

2. EXCESSIVE OR INAPPROPRIATE FORCE USED, RESULTING IN MODERATE INJURY

Moderate injuries are those that are not life-threatening even in the absence of medical treatment. Examples include sprains, mild concussions, broken teeth, bruising, and small fractures. This level of injury also meets the definition of a child in need of protection. A criminal offence has likely been committed.

3. EXCESSIVE OR INAPPROPRIATE FORCE USED, RESULTING IN SUPERFICIAL INJURY

Superficial injuries involve no more than broken skin. These injuries include localized bruises, welts, and abrasions. This level of injury may meet the definition of a child in need of protection. A criminal offence may have been committed, depending on the circumstances in which the force was applied. A welt from a single slap on the buttocks may not constitute a criminal offence, but a strike to the head or face has been found by the Supreme Court of Canada to be unreasonable. The entirety of the situation must be considered.

Case Law: Supreme Court of Canada 1995

"In *R v. Halcrow* (1993), 80 CCC (3d) 320, 40 WAC 197 (BCCA), aff'd. [1995] 1 SCR 440, 95 CCC (3d) 94, 90 WAC 72, 179 NR 63, Southin JA in her opinion (dissenting in part) considered that the word 'reasonable' in this section means 'moderate' or 'not excessive' and what is or is not excessive should depend solely upon the age and physical condition of the child. Factors such as the gravity of the offence, the character of the child, and the likely effect on the character of the child are relevant only to the issue of the accused's purpose, whether the force was applied by way of correction." (*Martin's Annual Criminal Code, 1999*)

Case Law: Supreme Court of Canada 2004

In *Canadian Foundation for Children, Youth and the Law v. Canada*, [2004] 1 SCR 76, 2004 SCC 4, Chief Justice Beverley McLachlin, in delivering the court's ruling, stated: "Corporal punishment which involves slaps or blows to the head is harmful. These types of punishment, we may conclude, will not be reasonable."

4. EXCESSIVE OR INAPPROPRIATE FORCE USED, RESULTING IN INJURY

The child is not physically injured but may experience considerable temporary pain. The potential for injury is present. An example is several slaps on the buttocks. This level of injury may meet the definition of a child in need of protection. A criminal offence may have been committed, depending on the circumstances in which the force was applied.

5. PHYSICAL PUNISHMENT USED, BUT NOT EXCESSIVE OR INAPPROPRIATE

The person in care of the child uses a generally accepted method of physical punishment—for example, a slap on the buttocks. The force used does not ordinarily leave any marks on the child. It is unlikely that the child is in need of protection, nor is it likely that a criminal offence has been committed. The punishment is allowed under s. 43 of the *Criminal Code* in cases where the person has used the punishment to correct the child's behaviour.

6. NO PHYSICAL PUNISHMENT USED ON THE CHILD

Non-physical, non-assaultive methods of correction are used on the child. Examples are taking away privileges and verbal disapproval. The child is not in need of protection. A criminal offence has not been committed unless the person in care of the child fails to provide the necessities of life, which is an offence under s. 215 of the *Criminal Code*. This offence would be established in only the most extreme cases such as locking a child in a room and not providing food or water for several days. In rare circumstances such as this, the child would also be in need of protection.

Police officers must use their expertise and judgment in establishing whether the punishment rendered was permissible and reasonable and whether an offence was committed. By following the preceding guidelines and by using the objective test, the officer should be able to reach a defensible conclusion as to whether a child has been abused. If the officer is unsure whether a criminal offence has taken place, but still suspects abuse, he or she must adhere to the provisions of s. 72 of the CFSA and report the suspected abuse to the Children's Aid Society.

SEXUAL ABUSE

Child sexual abuse includes any activity or behaviour that is sexual in nature and directed toward a child. Generally speaking, the *Criminal Code* defines a child as a person under the age of 18.

child sexual abuse
any activity or behaviour that is sexual in nature and directed toward a child

Pedophiles

Pedophiles are people who are sexually attracted to children. A pedophile is most often male and may be attracted to both male and female children. Pedophiles sometimes know that their actions are wrong but may be unable to control their urges. They are aroused sexually by young, usually prepubescent children. They may be further stimulated by engaging in or observing violent sexual acts with children.

There are sexual predators who are opportunistic and will randomly abduct a child for sexual purposes. These predatory offences are investigated in the same

pedophile
a person who is sexually attracted to children

way as any other random act of sexual violence. It is unlikely that the predatory pedophile will attack the same child again. The majority of pedophiles, however, are known to the child and are usually family members or family friends.

A CONVERSATION WITH A PEDOPHILE

The following information was obtained voluntarily from a pedophile during a conversation with an undercover police officer. The officer was posing as a person who could provide access to children for sexual purposes. The officer surreptitiously recorded the conversation on audio tape. The content of the summary that follows addresses the modus operandi used by the pedophile to gain access to children for sexual purposes. The perpetrator in this case was "successful" in gaining access to approximately 20 children (established through investigation; the number could be greater). The information is specific to the case but has many commonalities that may assist police in understanding the modus operandi of a pedophile.

Below is a summary of the conversation, with quotations from the pedophile:

- Spoke of the desire to create sexual videos involving self and children.

- Often masturbated while watching child pornography.

- Sat in parks, not far from his home, waited for kids to approach him. Stated that having a puppy dog was a good idea, "brings the kids to you." Stated that it was not a good idea to approach kids because "everyone is telling them to stay away from strangers."

- "You have to groom them gradually. Not too fast."

- Brought children to his home. Candy and soft drinks provided. Possibly alcohol for the older kids. Older meaning under 14.

- Discussed his age limits. Too difficult with kids over 13. As part of the conversation, he identified a situation where he tried to have sexual contact with a 14-year-old male. The male reported to police. Created a "bad situation."

- As part of the grooming process, he allowed the children to use his computer to play games.

- Gradually exposed the children to sexual images on his computer.

- Progressed to child pornography on his computer and through the use of pornographic books that he "left around" his home.

- The exposure to child pornography escalated using books and video to the point of becoming constant.

- He used child pornography to "show them what to do."

- "Don't force them. I had bad luck with that. The kid fought back and told his parents."

In the remainder of this section, note the following commonalities of pedophiliac behaviour identified in this summarized conversation:

- secrecy

- exposure to pornography

- personal use of pornography

- grooming.

The Phases of Abuse

Child sexual abuse may be categorized into five phases: engagement, sexual inter-action, secrecy, disclosure, and suppression (Murphy, 1985). Each phase is dis-cussed below.

ENGAGEMENT

In the engagement phase, the abuser communicates with the child with the objec-tive of engaging the child in sexual activity. The abuser may entice the child into sexual activity through the use of trickery or rewards. Entrapment may be used to manipulate the child into feeling that he or she has no choice but to participate. The abuser may use his adult authority to impose feelings of guilt and convince the child that he or she is responsible for the abuse. Threats of harm may be used to force the child into participating in sexual activity. The threat may be to the child or a family member. The abuser, most often a family member, may convince the child that he will commit suicide if the child does not participate. The abuser may use alcohol or other drugs to subdue the child or may simply use his superior size and strength to overpower the child.

The majority of abusers rely on enticement or entrapment to engage the child in sexual activity. The engagement strategy, if successful, is likely to be repeated and not escalate into violent strategies. Pedophiles tend to repeat their modus oper-andi, often for many years, until they are discovered or the child grows up and the pedophile loses interest.

Pedophiles often prey on children who have recently begun using the Internet and who complain of not having many real friends. These children are easy prey. They are more susceptible to someone trying to befriend them and they are less likely to talk about their online conversations with anyone. They're lonely, and the pedophile poses as a much-needed friend. Pedophiles look for kids who are having problems at home. The pedophile tries to win the child over and further separate the child from his or her family by complaining about parents generally. A common modus operandi for the online pedophile is to first gain the trust of the child and then make arrangements to meet him or her some place where they can talk privately. The child has no way of knowing whether he or she is meeting with a 14-year-old peer to discuss teenage problems or with a 44-year-old pedophile.

In 2002, provisions were added to the *Criminal Code* to prohibit the contacting of a child through means of a computer for the purpose of sexual activity. The provisions are set out below.

LURING A CHILD: CRIMINAL CODE SECTION 172.1(1)

Every person commits an offence who, by means of a computer system within the meaning of subsection 342.1(2), communicates with

(a) a person who is, or who the accused believes is, under the age of eighteen years, for the purpose of facilitating the commission of an offence under subsection 153(1), section 155 or 163.1, subsection 212(1) or (4) or section 271, 272 or 273 with respect to that person;

> (b) a person who is, or who the accused believes is, under the age of sixteen years, for the purpose of facilitating the commission of an offence under section 280 with respect to that person; or

> (c) a person who is, or who the accused believes is, under the age of fourteen years, for the purpose of facilitating the commission of an offence under section 151 or 152, subsection 160(3) or 173(2) or section 281 with respect to that person.

SEXUAL INTERACTION

Sexual interaction is the second phase of child sexual abuse. Types of abuse may include masturbation, fondling, digital penetration, oral or anal penetration, intercourse, and pornography.

SECRECY

In the secrecy phase, the objective of the abuser is to continue with the activity. This necessitates his avoiding detection and maintaining access to the child. The abuser may use threats or guilt to coerce the child into keeping the abuse a secret.

DISCLOSURE

In the disclosure phase, the abuse may be discovered accidentally, or the child may intentionally disclose the abuse. When a child discloses abuse, it is usually to a family member. This can cause tremendous emotional turmoil within the family if the family member refuses to believe that the abuse occurred.

SUPPRESSION

In the suppression phase, the family attempts to keep the secret of the abuse within the family and chooses not to disclose it to police and child welfare authorities. This phase may begin as soon as disclosure takes place and may continue through investigation by police and child welfare authorities. There are many reasons for suppression: desire to protect the family's reputation, to protect the child, or to protect the abuser; fear of legal repercussions; fear of involvement with the legal system, particularly of being a witness; avoidance of responsibility; or feeling of inadequacy due to failure to protect the child. Subsequent police investigation may reveal that failing to act immediately upon disclosure may have allowed the abuse to continue.

Signs of Sexual Abuse in Children

A sexually abused child may not have any readily visible physical signs of abuse. However, the abused child may exhibit changes in behaviour. There are some common behaviours that a young child who has experienced or is experiencing sexual abuse may exhibit (Children's Aid Society of Algoma, 1998). These behaviours are age-related, although there is no definite age at which they are exhibited:

- The child engages in age-inappropriate sexual play with toys, in which the toys are used to mimic sex acts.

- The child touches himself or herself sexually at inappropriate times.

- The child produces age-inappropriate sexually explicit drawings or descriptions.

- The child shows evidence of sophisticated sexual knowledge, beyond that of children of the same age.

- The child refuses, for no apparent reason, to go home or to the home of a relative or family friend.

- The child fears being in a particular area of the home.

- The child fears being left alone with a person of a particular sex.

- The child hints that he or she is engaged in sexual activity or has been abused.

Older children, including but not limited to teens, may exhibit behavioural changes in addition to those noted above:

- depression;

- self-destructive behaviour such as alcohol or drug abuse;

- aggressive or sexually suggestive behaviour;

- unusual or out-of-context sexual statements;

- promiscuity or prostitution;

- recurring physical complaints without a physiological basis;

- recurring references to sexual abuse in school projects or essays; or

- sudden interest in sex, sexually transmitted diseases, or pregnancy.

When an officer responds to a complaint of sexual abuse, the complainant, often a teacher or family member, may initially be the best source of information. The responding officer, having no prior knowledge of the child's behaviour, will have no basis for comparing the child's past and present behaviour. Consultation with others familiar with the child may reveal behavioural changes that indicate sexual abuse.

There may be some physical indicators, too, although most cannot be readily identified by the responding officer (Children's Aid Society of Algoma, 1998):

- the presence of a sexually transmitted disease;

- unusual or excessive itching or pain in the genital or anal area;

- blood in the stool or urine;

- bruises, lacerations, redness, swelling, or bleeding in the genital or anal area;

- torn, stained, or bloody underclothing; or

- pregnancy.

Physical force is rarely necessary to prompt a child to engage in sexual activity. The abuser is often in a position of trust toward the child. The child can be tricked, bribed, threatened, or pressured into sexual activity, or may willingly engage in such activity because he or she trusts and depends on the abuser and wants to gain his or her approval. The goal of the abusive act, as in most sex crimes, is not sexual gratification but power and control. The abuser takes advantage of his or her position of trust for personal gratification.

In most instances where the child is under 14, his or her consent is irrelevant and cannot be used by the abuser as a defence.

Consent by a Child

CONSENT NO DEFENCE: CRIMINAL CODE, SECTION 150.1(1)

> Where an accused is charged with an offence under section 151 or 152 or subsection 153(1), 160(3) or 173(2) or is charged with an offence under section 271, 272 or 273 in respect of a complainant under the age of fourteen years, it is not a defence that the complainant consented to the activity that forms the subject-matter of the charge.

"Subsection (1) provides that the consent of the complainant, who is less than 14 years old, is no defence to the sexual assault offences (ss. 271 to 273) and no defence at all, no matter what the age of the complainant, to the other enumerated offences, such as sexual exploitation (s. 153)." (*Martin's Annual Criminal Code, 2005*)

EXCEPTION: CRIMINAL CODE, SECTION 150.1(2)

> Notwithstanding subsection (1), where an accused is charged with an offence under section 151 or 152, subsection 173(2) or section 271 in respect of a complainant who is twelve years of age or more but under the age of fourteen years, it is not a defence that the complainant consented to the activity that forms the subject-matter of the charge unless the accused
>
> > (a) is twelve years of age or more but under the age of sixteen years;
> >
> > (b) is less than two years older than the complainant; and
> >
> > (c) is neither in a position of trust or authority towards the complainant nor is a person with whom the complainant is in a relationship of dependency.

"Subsection (2) provides an *exception* to subsec. (1) and permits the defence of consent to be raised to the offences of sexual interference (s. 151), invitation to sexual touching (s. 152), indecent exposure to a person under 14 (s. 173(2)), or sexual assault (s. 271) if the complainant is at least 12 but less than 14 years old and the additional requirements of the subsection are met. The further conditions which must be met for the exception to apply are as follows: (a) the accused is at least 12 but less than 16; (b) the accused is less than two years older than the complainant; (c) the accused is neither in a position of trust nor is the complainant in a relationship of dependency with the accused." (*Martin's Annual Criminal Code, 2005*)

Within the realm of consent, an accused may rely on the defence of mistake of age to explain sexual interactions with a person under 14 years of age.

MISTAKE OF AGE: CRIMINAL CODE SECTION 150.1(4)

It is not a defence to a charge under section 151 or 152, subsection 160(3) or 173(2), or section 271, 272 or 273 that the accused believed that the complainant was fourteen years of age or more at the time the offence is alleged to have been committed unless the accused took all reasonable steps to ascertain the age of the complainant.

The accused must have taken all reasonable steps to determine the age of the person before engaging in sexual activity with him or her. Otherwise, the accused cannot rely on mistake of age as a defence.

MISTAKE OF AGE: R v. OSBORNE

"The accused, in order to rely on the defence of mistake, need only raise a reasonable doubt. The accused must, however, have made an earnest inquiry or there should be some compelling factor that obviates the need for such an inquiry. Thus, the accused must show what steps he took and those steps were all that could be reasonably required of him in the circumstances: *R v. Osborne* (1992), 17 CR (4th) 350, 102 Nfld. & PEIR 194 (Nfld. CA)." (*Martin's Annual Criminal Code, 2005*)

MISTAKE OF AGE: R v. P.(L.T.)

In *R v. P.(L.T.)*, the court identified some criteria for determining whether the mistake of age was reasonable in the circumstances.

"Where the accused raises the defence of honest but mistaken belief in the complainant's age, the Crown must prove beyond a reasonable doubt that the accused did not take all reasonable steps to ascertain the complainant's age or did not have an honest belief as to the complainant's age. The issue to be determined is what steps would have been reasonable for the accused to take in the circumstances. While in certain circumstances a visual observation may suffice, where it does not, further reasonable steps should be considered having regard to the complainant's physical appearance, her behaviour, the ages and appearance of those in whose company the complainant was found, the activities engaged in, the times, places and other circumstances in which the accused observes the complainant and her conduct. The accused's subjective belief is relevant but not conclusive of this determination: *R v. P.(L.T.)* (1997), 113 CCC (3d) 42, 142 WAC 20 (BCCA)." (*Martin's Annual Criminal Code, 2005*)

The issue of consent in cases of sexual assault was addressed by the Supreme Court of Canada in the 1999 decision of *R v. Ewanchuk*. This case did not involve a child but may be referred to when investigating situations where the victim is 14 years of age or older. The decision refers to a situation where the accused alleges that the victim consented to the sex act through the victim's non-response or non-refusal to participate.

NO CONSENT WHERE FEAR OF PHYSICAL HARM: R v. EWANCHUK

"There is no defence of implied consent to sexual assault. The absence of consent is subjective and must be determined by reference to the complainant's subjective internal state of mind towards the touching at the time it occurred. The complainant's statement that she did not consent is a matter of credibility to be weighed in light of all of the evidence including any ambiguous conduct. If the trier of fact accepts the complainant's testimony that she did not consent, no matter how strongly conduct may contradict her claim, the absence of consent is established. The trier of fact need only consider s. 265(3) if the complainant has chosen to participate in sexual activity or her ambiguous conduct or submission has given rise to doubt regarding the absence of consent. There is no consent where the complainant consents because she honestly believes that she will otherwise suffer physical violence. While the plausibility of the alleged fear and any overt expressions of it are relevant in assessing the complainant's credibility that she consented out of fear, the approach is subjective: *R v. Ewanchuk*, [1999] 1 SCR 330, 131 CCC (3d) 481, 22 CR (5th) 1." (*Martin's Annual Criminal Code, 2005*)

This decision removes a measure of ambiguity from the concept of consent. If the victim acquiesces through an honest belief that he or she may suffer physical harm if he or she resists, consent is not given. In the information presented to the court in the *Ewanchuk* case, the victim did not adamantly refuse the advances of the accused. The court ruled that the victim could have honestly believed that such refusal could result in physical harm. This may often be the case in situations of child sexual assault. The perpetrator of the crime is most likely to be physically larger than the victim, leading the victim to fear for his or her safety.

Sexual Offences Involving Children

There are specific sections in the *Criminal Code* that address the sexual abuse of children. A child, for the purpose of ss. 151 and 152, is a person under the age of 14.

SEXUAL INTERFERENCE: CRIMINAL CODE, SECTION 151

> Every person who, for a sexual purpose, touches, directly or indirectly, with a part of the body or with an object, any part of the body of a person under the age of fourteen years is guilty of an indictable offence and liable to imprisonment for a term not exceeding ten years or is guilty of an offence punishable on summary conviction.

This offence is made out when a person touches a child, directly or indirectly, for a sexual purpose.

The following provincial court ruling confirms the inability of a child to consent to sexual activities.

NO CONSENT WHERE CHILD SUGGESTS SEXUAL INTERACTION: R v. SEARS

"An accused who intends sexual interaction of any kind with a child and with that intent makes contact with the body of a child, 'touches' the child within the meaning of this section, even where the sexual interaction is suggested by the child: *R v. Sears* (1990), 58 CCC (3d) 62 (Man. CA)." (*Martin's Annual Criminal Code, 2005*)

INVITATION TO SEXUAL TOUCHING: CRIMINAL CODE, SECTION 152

> Every person who, for a sexual purpose, invites, counsels or incites a person under the age of fourteen years to touch, directly or indirectly, with a part of the body or

with an object, the body of any person, including the body of the person who so invites, counsels or incites and the body of the person under the age of fourteen years, is guilty of an indictable offence and liable to imprisonment for a term not exceeding ten years or is guilty of an offence punishable on summary conviction.

"The section applies regardless of whether the accused invites the touching of his or herself or another person or incites the person under 14 to touch their own body." (*Martin's Annual Criminal Code, 2005*)

NO PROOF OF PHYSICAL CONTACT REQUIRED: R v. FONG

"This offence does not require proof of actual physical contact between body parts or an invitation to engage in that level of contact. This section covers not only actual touching but 'indirect' touching and thus includes an invitation by the accused to the complainant to hold a tissue onto which the accused ejaculated: *R v. Fong* (1994), 92 CCC (3d) 171 (Alta. CA), leave to appeal to SCC refused 94 CCC (3d) vii." (*Martin's Annual Criminal Code, 2005*)

SEXUAL EXPLOITATION: CRIMINAL CODE, SECTION 153(1)

Every person who is in a position of trust or authority towards a young person or is a person with whom the young person is in a relationship of dependency and who

(a) for a sexual purpose, touches, directly or indirectly, with a part of the body or with an object, any part of the body of the young person, or

(b) for a sexual purpose, invites, counsels or incites a young person to touch, directly or indirectly, with a part of the body or with an object, the body of any person, including the body of the person who so invites, counsels or incites and the body of the young person,

is guilty of an indictable offence and liable to imprisonment for a term not exceeding five years or is guilty of an offence punishable on summary conviction.

DEFINITION OF "YOUNG PERSON": CRIMINAL CODE, SECTION 153(2)

In this section, "young person" means a person fourteen years of age or more but under the age of eighteen years.

"This section creates the hybrid offence of *sexual exploitation of a young person.* Section 153(2) provides a definition of 'young person,' namely a person between 14 and 17 years old inclusive. The offence is predicated upon either the accused being in a position of trust toward the young complainant or the young person being in a relationship of dependency with the accused. If either relationship exists and the accused commits acts amounting to either sexual interference (s. 151) or invitation to sexual touching (s. 152) then the offence is committed. (Note that it must be shown that the accused had a *sexual purpose.*)" (*Martin's Annual Criminal Code, 2005*)

DEFINITION OF "DEPENDENCY": R v. GALBRAITH

"The term 'dependency' is to be read *ejusdem generis* [of the same class] with two other categories of trust or authority and contemplates a relationship in which there is a *de facto* [in reality, actual] reliance by a young person on a figure who has assumed a position of power, such as trust or authority over the young person along non-traditional lines. The disentitling condition of dependency must exist independently of a sexual relationship: *R v. Galbraith* (1994), 90 CCC (3d) 76, 30 CR (4th) 230 sub nom. *R v. G.(C.)*, 18 OR (3d) 247, 71 OAC 45 (CA), leave to appeal to SCC refused 92 CCC (3d) vi." (*Martin's Annual Criminal Code, 2005*)

INCEST: CRIMINAL CODE, SECTION 155(1)

Every one commits incest who, knowing that another person is by blood relationship his or her parent, child, brother, sister, grandparent or grandchild, as the case may be, has sexual intercourse with that person.

Note that this offence requires that the act of sexual intercourse be committed.

PUNISHMENT: CRIMINAL CODE, SECTION 155(2)

Every one who commits incest is guilty of an indictable offence and liable to imprisonment for a term not exceeding fourteen years.

DEFENCE: CRIMINAL CODE, SECTION 155(3)

No accused shall be determined by a court to be guilty of an offence under this section if the accused was under restraint, duress or fear of the person with whom the accused had the sexual intercourse at the time the sexual intercourse occurred.

DEFINITION OF "BROTHER" AND "SISTER": CRIMINAL CODE, SECTION 155(4)

In this section, "brother" and "sister," respectively, include half-brother and half-sister.

There is a rarely used section of the *Criminal Code* that addresses the corruption of children. Note that police may commence proceedings only with the permission of the attorney general. However, the charge may be brought forth by the Children's Aid Society without the permission of the attorney general.

CORRUPTING CHILDREN: CRIMINAL CODE, SECTION 172

(1) Every one who, in the home of a child, participates in adultery or sexual immorality or indulges in habitual drunkenness or any other form of vice, and thereby endangers the morals of the child or renders the home an unfit place for the child to be in, is guilty of an indictable offence and liable to imprisonment for a term not exceeding two years. ...

(3) For the purposes of this section, "child" means a person who is or appears to be under the age of eighteen years.

(4) No proceedings shall be commenced under subsection (1) without the consent of the Attorney General, unless they are instituted by or at the instance of a recognized society for the protection of children or by an officer of a juvenile court.

"This section makes it an indictable offence to indulge in behaviour, in a *child's home*, which corrupts children. Children are defined in s. 172(3) as being *under or apparently under* the age of *18*. The prohibited activities listed in the section are expansively defined by adultery, sexual immorality, habitual drunkenness, or *any other form of vice*. However, it must be shown that the result of this behaviour is to *endanger the morals* of a child or to make the house unfit for a child to live in." (*Martin's Annual Criminal Code, 2005*)

SEXUAL IMMORALITY AND THE CORRUPTION OF CHILDREN: R v. E.(B.)

"The offence of engaging in sexual immorality in the home of a child requires proof that the accused intentionally engaged in the prohibited conduct including knowledge or at least wilful blindness that the children were aware of the sexually immoral conduct. 'Sexual immorality' requires an objective consideration of conduct by reference to community standards of tolerance that are tied directly to the harm caused or threatened by the conduct. 'Participation' requires proof of some form of conduct. 'Morals' refers to those core values that are central to the maintenance of a free and democratic society. The morals of a child will be endangered by sexual immorality where: (1) the sexual conduct presents a real risk that the child will not develop an understanding that exploitive or non-consensual sexual activity is wrong; (2) the conduct degrades or dehumanizes women such that the child will not develop an understanding that all persons are equal and worthy of respect regardless of gender; (3) the conduct imperils the child's understanding of parents' responsibilities to protect and nurture their children; and (4) to the extent that the conduct actively involves the child, it may endanger the child's morals by leaving him or her without a proper sense of his or her own self-worth or autonomy: *R v. E.(B.)* (1999), 139 CCC (3d) 100, 29 CR (5th) 51 (Ont. CA)." (*Martin's Annual Criminal Code, 2005*)

"Although the offence of engaging in sexual immorality in the home of a child violates s. 2(b) of the Charter, it is a reasonable limit within the meaning of s. 1 and is therefore valid: *R v. E.(B.)* (1999), 139 CCC (3d) 100, 29 CR (5th) 51 (Ont. CA)." (*Martin's Annual Criminal Code, 2005*)

Sexual Assault

The offence of sexual assault does not include any age limitations.

SEXUAL ASSAULT: CRIMINAL CODE, SECTION 271(1)

Every one who commits a sexual assault is guilty of

(a) an indictable offence and is liable to imprisonment for a term not exceeding ten years; or

(b) an offence punishable on summary conviction and liable to imprisonment for a term not exceeding eighteen months.

The facts in issue that constitute assault, as set forth in s. 265 of the *Criminal Code*, must first be established before a charge of sexual assault can be pursued.

ASSAULT: CRIMINAL CODE, SECTION 265(1)

A person commits an assault when

> (a) without the consent of another person, he applies force intentionally to that other person, directly or indirectly;

> (b) he attempts or threatens, by an act or a gesture, to apply force to another person, if he has, or causes that other person to believe on reasonable grounds that he has, present ability to effect his purpose; or

> (c) while openly wearing or carrying a weapon or an imitation thereof, he accosts or impedes another person or begs.

APPLICATION: CRIMINAL CODE, SECTION 265(2)

This section applies to all forms of assault, including sexual assault, sexual assault with a weapon, threats to a third party or causing bodily harm and aggravated sexual assault.

CONSENT: CRIMINAL CODE, SECTION 265(3)

For the purposes of this section, no consent is obtained where the complainant submits or does not resist by reason of

> (a) the application of force to the complainant or to a person other than the complainant;

> (b) threats or fear of the application of force to the complainant or to a person other than the complainant;

> (c) fraud; or

> (d) the exercise of authority.

Once the facts in issue constituting assault have been established, the nature of the assault (sexual versus non-sexual) must be determined.

To establish that an assault is sexual in nature, certain tests must be met. The Supreme Court of Canada has addressed this question in *R v. Chase* and *R v. V.(K.B.)*.

"Sexual assault is an assault, within any one of the definitions of that concept in s. 265(1), which is committed in circumstances of a sexual nature such that the sexual integrity of the victim is violated. The test to be applied in determining whether the impugned conduct has the requisite sexual nature is an objective one: whether viewed in the light of all the circumstances the sexual or carnal context of the assault is visible to a reasonable observer. The part of the body touched, the nature of the contact, the situation in which it occurred, the words and gestures accompanying the act, and all other circumstances surrounding the conduct, including threats, which may or may not be accompanied by force, will be relevant. The intent or purpose of the person committing the act, to the extent that this may appear from the evidence, may also be a factor in considering whether the conduct is sexual. If the motive of the accused is sexual gratification, to the extent that this may appear from the evidence it may be a factor in determining whether the conduct is sexual. The existence of such a motive is, however, merely one of many factors to be considered: *R v. Chase*, [1987] 2 SCR 293, 37 CCC (3d) 97, 59 CR (3d) 193 (6:0)." (*Martin's Annual Criminal Code, 2005*)

"Sexual assault does not require proof of sexuality or sexual gratification, which are merely factors. The conduct of the accused in grabbing his young child's genitals as a form of 'discipline' was an aggressive act of domination which violated the sexual integrity of the child which could be found to be a sexual assault: *R v. V.(K.B.)* (1992), 71 CCC (3d) 65, 13 CR (4th) 87, 8 OR (3d) 20 (CA), aff'd. [1993] 2 SCR 857, 82 CCC (3d) 382, 22 CR (4th) 86." (*Martin's Annual Criminal Code, 2005*)

As the Supreme Court indicated, sexual gratification is not a necessary element in a charge of sexual assault. Touching of parts of the body that is deemed to violate sexual integrity appears to be enough to pursue a charge of sexual assault, particularly in light of the court's decision in *R v. V.(K.B.)*.

When the elements of a charge of sexual assault have been established, the degree of force used will determine the section of the *Criminal Code* that has been violated.

If there has been bodily harm or if a weapon has been used, the charge may be sexual assault with a weapon or sexual assault causing bodily harm, as defined in s. 272 of the *Criminal Code*.

SEXUAL ASSAULT WITH A WEAPON, THREATS TO A THIRD PARTY, OR CAUSING BODILY HARM: CRIMINAL CODE, SECTION 272(1)

Every person commits an offence who, in committing a sexual assault,

> (a) carries, uses or threatens to use a weapon or an imitation of a weapon;

> (b) threatens to cause bodily harm to a person other than the complainant;

> (c) causes bodily harm to the complainant; or

> (d) is a party to the offence with any other person.

PUNISHMENT: CRIMINAL CODE, SECTION 272(2)

Every person who commits an offence under subsection (1) is guilty of an indictable offence and liable

> (a) where a firearm is used in the commission of the offence, to imprisonment for a term not exceeding fourteen years and to a minimum punishment of imprisonment for a term of four years; and

> (b) in any other case, to imprisonment for a term not exceeding fourteen years.

An abuser's threats to harm a third party, covered by s. 272(1)(b), can impede the investigation of a child sexual abuse case. The child may be intimidated by the abuser's threats of harm to a person such as the child's mother. The seriousness with which the law views such threats is apparent in the fact that the punishment for making such threats during a sexual assault is the same as the punishment for using a weapon during a sexual assault.

AGGRAVATED SEXUAL ASSAULT: CRIMINAL CODE, SECTION 273

> (1) Every one commits an aggravated sexual assault who, in committing a sexual assault, wounds, maims, disfigures or endangers the life of the complainant.

(2) Every person who commits an aggravated sexual assault is guilty of an indictable offence and liable

> (a) where a firearm is used in the commission of the offence, to imprisonment for life and to a minimum punishment of imprisonment for a term of four years; and
>
> (b) in any other case, to imprisonment for life.

Sexual Offences Involving Children: Summary

The following list briefly describes common child-related sex offences in the *Criminal Code*.

- *Sexual interference.* Sexual interference is established when the accused directly or indirectly touches the complainant for a sexual purpose. The accused is usually 14 years old or older. See s. 150.1(3), which does not in most circumstances allow the charging of anyone under 14. A 12- or 13-year-old may be charged if either was in a position of trust or authority regarding the complainant. The complainant must be under 14 years old.

- *Invitation to sexual touching.* The offence is established when the accused: invites, counsels or incites, the complainant to touch the accused the complainant or any person for a sexual purpose. The accused is usually 14 years old or older. See s. 150.1(3), which does not in most circumstances allow the charging of anyone under 14. A 12- or 13-year-old may be charged if either was in a position of trust or authority toward the complainant. The complainant must be under 14 years old.

- *Sexual exploitation.* The offence is established when the accused invites himself or herself, counsels, or incites the complainant to touch himself or herself, the accused, or any other person for a sexual purpose or when the accused touches the complainant for a sexual purpose. The accused must be in a position of authority toward a young person between the ages of 14 and 17. The complainant must be 14 to 17 years old.

The *Criminal Code* offences that involve the sexual abuse of children may be divided into offences involving physical contact and offences where physical contact is not required.

Contact offences
- sexual interference (s. 151)
- sexual exploitation (contact) (s. 153(1)(a))
- incest (s. 155)
- sexual assault (s. 271)
- sexual assault with a weapon, threats to a third party, or causing bodily harm (s. 272)
- aggravated sexual assault (s. 273)

Non-contact offences
- invitation to sexual touching (s. 152)
- sexual exploitation (invitation) (s. 153(1)(b))

All of these offences may be considered indictable for the purpose of arrest. Other criminal offences may also apply, depending on the nature of the incident.

RULING OUT CHILD ABUSE: SUDDEN INFANT DEATH SYNDROME

Every year infants die suddenly, unexpectedly, and for no apparent reason in their sleep. Yet they all have something in common: they are all victims of **sudden infant death syndrome (SIDS)**. SIDS, sometimes called "crib death," is not preventable or predictable. These infant deaths remain unexplained after all known causes have been ruled out through autopsy, death scene investigation, and medical history. SIDS affects families of all races, religions, and income levels. Its victims appear to be healthy. Neither parents nor doctors can tell which infants will die. The first year of life is a time of rapid growth and development when any infant may be vulnerable to SIDS.

sudden infant death syndrome (SIDS)
the sudden, unexpected, and unexplained death of an infant during sleep

Most SIDS deaths occur when a infant is between two and four months of age. In fact, 95 percent of all SIDS victims are under six months of age. The risk of SIDS then diminishes during the first year of life. The diagnosis of SIDS is not used when the victim is more than one year old.

What Causes SIDS?

We do not yet know exactly how or why SIDS happens, although researchers are making great progress in identifying deficits, behaviours, and other factors that may put an infant at higher risk. Scientists are exploring the development and function of the nervous system, the brain, and the heart; breathing and sleep patterns; body chemical balances; autopsy findings; and environmental factors to determine the causes of SIDS. It is likely that SIDS is caused by some subtle developmental delay, an anatomical defect, or functional failure. SIDS, like many other medical disorders, may eventually be found to have more than one explanation and more than one means of prevention. This may explain why the characteristics of SIDS babies are so varied.

While no one knows what causes SIDS, we do know that

- of every 1,000 infants born, one will die of SIDS before the age of one year;

- 95 percent of infants who die of SIDS are younger than six months old, and the majority of them die between two and four months of age; and

- most infants who die of SIDS seem perfectly healthy before they die.

SIDS can be determined as the cause of death only after an autopsy, an examination of the death scene, and a review of the child's medical history.

Although researchers have not yet discovered the causes of SIDS, they do know that

- SIDS is not caused by vomiting and choking;

- SIDS is not contagious;

- SIDS is not child abuse;

- SIDS does not cause pain or suffering for the infant; and

- SIDS is not caused by routine immunizations.

Risk Factors

We do not know which infants will die of SIDS, but we do know that there are certain risk factors that make a SIDS death more likely:

- The mother used alcohol or drugs or smoked during pregnancy.
- The infant is exposed to cigarette smoke in the home.
- The infant sleeps on soft bedding surfaces, such as quilts, sheepskins, and pillows.
- The infant sleeps with soft pillows, a beanbag cushion, or stuffed animals.
- The infant sleeps on his or her belly.

Police Intervention

Police investigating the death of an infant should treat the scene as a sudden death of undetermined cause. The coroner must be notified as stated in s. 10(1) of the *Coroners Act*. As previously stated, only an autopsy can identify whether the cause of death was SIDS. The family will be going through an extremely emotional period and may be unable to provide information regarding the death. In substantiated SIDS cases, the family is not being uncooperative; instead, they probably do not have any information to provide.

Things can still go wrong even when parents do everything right. The fact is that many SIDS victims have no known risk factors; and most infants with one or more risk factors will not die of SIDS. Because the causes of SIDS remain unknown, police must refrain from concluding that childcare practices caused the infant's death. The investigating officers should treat the scene as they would a crime scene while trying to take into account the emotional distress of the family. The investigation is an integral part of a SIDS diagnosis: it rules out accidental, environmental, and unnatural causes of death.

But, there is always the possibility that the death was not caused by SIDS. Look for signs of suffocation or physical signs that indicate accidental, abusive, or environmental causes of death. Remember that a victim of SIDS will show no outward signs of abuse. Death occurs during sleep. There is no evidence that the victim suffers any pain or discomfort. There should not be any sign of a struggle. Only a small number of children die of SIDS. Far more die as a result of abuse, often at the hands of a parent.

SUDDEN UNEXPLAINED DEATH SYNDROME

Sudden unexplained death syndrome (SUDS) describes cases of sudden mortality for which a coroner has been unable to determine the exact cause of death. In incidents of SUDS, the coroner may find that there is a possibility that the person did not die of natural causes.

In making this diagnosis, the coroner will apply the criteria for SIDS, plus the following additional criteria:

- unexplained healed injury,
- unexplained toxicology, and
- history of abuse.

NEGLECT

Neglect is established by a pattern of behaviour over a period of time, which can make detection difficult for police officers. Note that the definition of neglect varies from one piece of legislation to the next. A general definition of **neglect** for the purposes of this chapter is caregiver omissions in providing adequate care that result in actual or potential harm to a child. The question arises: What is "adequate care"? The term is hard to define because it is subjective. This makes establishing a standard of adequate care difficult.

Neglect of a child may be devastating to his or her physical, emotional, and psychological well-being. The physical form of neglect, failing to provide the necessities of life (referred to as "necessaries of life" in the *Criminal Code*), may result in criminal prosecution. Anyone who has the responsibility to provide such necessaries and fails to do so can be charged with an offence under the *Criminal Code*. The sections of the *Criminal Code* pertaining to neglect are reproduced below.

neglect
for the purposes of this chapter, caregiver omissions in providing adequate care that result in actual or potential harm to a child

DUTY OF PERSONS TO PROVIDE NECESSARIES: CRIMINAL CODE, SECTION 215(1)

Every one is under a legal duty

(a) as a parent, foster parent, guardian or head of a family, to provide necessaries of life for a child under the age of sixteen years;

(b) as a married person, to provide necessaries of life to his spouse; and

(c) to provide necessaries of life to a person under his charge if that person

(i) is unable, by reason of detention, age, illness, mental disorder or other cause, to withdraw himself from that charge, and

(ii) is unable to provide himself with necessaries of life.

OFFENCE: CRIMINAL CODE, SECTION 215(2)

Every one commits an offence who, being under a legal duty within the meaning of subsection (1), fails without lawful excuse, the proof of which lies on him, to perform that duty, if

(a) with respect to a duty imposed by paragraph (1)(a) or (b),

(i) the person to whom the duty is owed is in destitute or necessitous circumstances, or

(ii) the failure to perform the duty endangers the life of the person to whom the duty is owed, or causes or is likely to cause the health of that person to be endangered permanently; or

(b) with respect to a duty imposed by paragraph (1)(c), the failure to perform the duty endangers the life of the person to whom the duty is owed or causes or is likely to cause the health of that person to be injured permanently.

PUNISHMENT: CRIMINAL CODE, SECTION 215(3)

Every one who commits an offence under subsection (2) is guilty of

(a) an indictable offence and is liable to imprisonment for a term not exceeding two years; or

(b) an offence punishable on summary conviction.

This section places a legal obligation on parents to provide the necessaries of life until a child reaches age 16. Necessaries include food, clothing, shelter, and medical treatment.

"This offence imposes liability on an objective basis. On a charge contrary to subsec. (2)(a)(ii), the Crown must prove a marked departure from the conduct of a reasonably prudent parent in circumstances where it was objectively foreseeable that the failure to provide the necessaries of life would lead to a risk of danger to the life, or a risk of permanent endangerment to the health, of the child: *R v. Naglik*, [1993] 3 SCR 122, 83 CCC (3d) 526, 23 CR (4th) 335." (*Martin's Annual Criminal Code, 2005*)

Neglect of a child is also identified in s. 37(2) of the CFSA as one of the situations where a child may be in need of protection:

A child is in need of protection where,

(a) the child has suffered physical harm, inflicted by the person having charge of the child or caused by or resulting from that person's,

(i) failure to adequately care for, provide for, supervise or protect the child, or

(ii) pattern of neglect in caring for, providing for, supervising or protecting the child;

(b) there is a risk that the child is likely to suffer physical harm inflicted by the person having charge of the child or caused by or resulting from that person's,

(i) failure to adequately care for, provide for, supervise or protect the child, or

(ii) pattern of neglect in caring for, providing for, supervising or protecting the child;

The need to establish a pattern of neglect probably removes the probability of police obtaining sufficient grounds to remove the child from the home. Patterns of neglect are more likely to be established through the observations and investigations of dedicated child protection workers.

Signs of Neglect

The following are some signs that may indicate neglect (Children's Aid Society of Algoma, 1998). These signs do not necessarily establish neglect and should be viewed in the context of the child's usual standard of care:

• The child is inappropriately dressed for the season.

• The child is extremely dirty.

- The child suffers from poor dental or medical care.

- The child is left with inappropriate caregivers or is left unattended for periods of time that are excessive in light of the child's age.

Section 79(3) of the *Child and Family Services Act* identifies the age at which a child may be left unattended. The section does not define what is reasonable care or an inappropriate caregiver. Investigating officers must use their judgment to determine whether reasonable care is being provided by an appropriate caregiver.

LEAVING CHILD UNATTENDED: CHILD AND FAMILY SERVICES ACT, SECTION 79(3)

No person having charge of a child less than sixteen years of age shall leave the child without making provision for his or her supervision and care that is reasonable in the circumstances.

Note that this section of the *Child and Family Services Act* discusses adequate supervision but does not define it. In fact, adequate supervision has not been objectively defined by legislation; instead, it is situationally established. Thus, the standard of adequate supervision will vary with the child's age, development, and behaviour. Also, the standard of adequate supervision will vary with the area in which the child lives. For example, the degree of supervision required for a child living in a rural area may differ from the degree of supervision required for a child in an urban area.

Parents must provide a basic level of care in order to meet any standard of "adequate supervision." Parents must take precautions that minimize the risk of moderate or serious harm to a child and ensure that the child's basic needs have been met: food, clothing, shelter, and medical treatment.

REVERSE ONUS: CHILD AND FAMILY SERVICES ACT, SECTION 79(4)

Where a person is charged with contravening subsection (3) and the child is less than ten years of age, the onus of establishing that the person made provision for the child's supervision and care that was reasonable in the circumstances rests with the person.

If the officer deems that the lack of care or the care provided is inadequate in the circumstances, the child may be considered to be a child in need of protection as defined in s. 37(2) of the CFSA.

Some signs of neglect may be more difficult for police officers to detect but come to police attention when reported by child protection workers or other concerned parties:

- The child lacks adequate shelter (including but not limited to unsafe, inadequately heated, or unsanitary living conditions).

- The child is malnourished. Signs include low body weight, an extremely low body fat to lean tissue ratio (in infants), sallow complexion, skin conditions caused by dehydration, and prolonged diarrhea.

- The child suffers from severe diaper rash or other skin disorders caused by lack of proper hygiene.

Behavioural signs of neglect include the following (Children's Aid Society of Algoma, 1998):

- Slowness in development of speech and motor skills, without any apparent physical cause.

- Lack of attachment to parents.

- Inappropriate attachment to other adults.

- Excessive demands for affection and attention.

- Poor school performance.

- Illegal activity or abuse of alcohol and drugs.

OTHER FORMS OF NEGLECT

There are other instances of neglect that require the intervention of police or child protection workers. CIS identified the following as being the most common forms of neglect: failure to supervise leading to physical harm; physical neglect; permitting criminal behaviour; abandonment; medical neglect; failure to supervise leading to sexual harm; and failure to provide necessary treatment.

Failure To Supervise Leading to Physical Harm

When this form of neglect exists, the child is in need of protection. Police or child protection workers may intervene.

CHILD IN NEED OF PROTECTION: CHILD AND FAMILY SERVICES ACT, SECTION 37(2)

A child is in need of protection where,

(a) the child has suffered physical harm, inflicted by the person having charge of the child or caused by or resulting from that person's,

(i) failure to adequately care for, provide for, supervise or protect the child, or

(ii) pattern of neglect in caring for, providing for, supervising or protecting the child;

Physical Neglect

Physical neglect includes not adhering to the duty to provide the necessities of life. The child is also in need of protection.

Permitting Criminal Behaviour

This type of neglect falls within the parameters of s. 37(2) of the CFSA. The child is in need of protection. Police may intervene. Under ss. 37(2)(j) and (k) of the CFSA, a child is in need of protection where

(j) the child is less than twelve years old and has killed or seriously injured another person or caused serious damage to another person's property, services or treatment are necessary to prevent a recurrence and the child's parent or the person having charge of the child does not provide, or refuses or is unavailable or unable to consent to, those services or treatment;

(k) the child is less than twelve years old and has on more than one occasion injured another person or caused loss or damage to another person's property, with the encouragement of the person having charge of the child or because of that person's failure or inability to supervise the child adequately.

Abandonment

A situation of abandonment could constitute neglect and is a criminal offence as defined in s. 218 of the *Criminal Code.*

ABANDONING CHILD: CRIMINAL CODE, SECTION 218

Every one who unlawfully abandons or exposes a child who is under the age of ten years, so that its life is or is likely to be endangered or its health is or is likely to be permanently injured, is guilty of an indictable offence and liable to imprisonment for a term not exceeding two years.

ABANDONMENT AND ENDANGERING A CHILD: R v. HOLZER

"While the Crown, to prove this offence, must prove not only that the child was abandoned but that, *inter alia*, its life was likely to be endangered, the offence was made out where the accused abandoned her child in a motor vehicle for an indefinite period of time in an environment which posed a threat to its life due to the cold temperatures and risk of abduction. It was no excuse that the accused intended to return several hours later at a time, when according to expert evidence, the child would still be alive. It is the act of endangering that constitutes the offence: *R v. Holzer* (1988), 63 CR (3d) 301 (Alta. QB)." (*Martin's Annual Criminal Code, 2005*)

ABANDONMENT UNDER THE CHILD AND FAMILY SERVICES ACT

The CFSA also includes abandonment as one of the situations where a child is in need of protection. While the *Criminal Code* specifies a child for the purpose of abandonment as being under 10 years of age, a child within the meaning of the CFSA is a person under 16 years of age. Police or child protection workers may intervene in situations of abandonment. According to s. 37(2)(i) of the CFSA, police or child protection workers may intervene where

(i) the child has been abandoned, the child's parent has died or is unavailable to exercise his or her custodial rights over the child and has not made adequate provision for the child's care and custody, or the child is in a residential placement and the parent refuses or is unable or unwilling to resume the child's care and custody.

Medical Neglect

A situation of medical neglect allows police or a child protection worked to apprehend the child due to the parent's neglect in providing medical treatment. Section 37(2)(e) of the CFSA allows police or child protection workers to apprehend the child where

> (e) the child requires medical treatment to cure, prevent or alleviate physical harm or suffering and the child's parent or the person having charge of the child does not provide, or refuses or is unavailable or unable to consent to, the treatment.

The *Criminal Code* refers to failure to provide medical treatment as a form of neglect. The *Child and Family Services Act* also refers to failure to provide medical treatment and describes it as a situation where a child could be in need of protection. The CFSA expands on the *Criminal Code* provisions by further stating that the parent must take steps to prevent physical harm or suffering.

The parent must provide adequate health care in the following respects:

- Reasonable efforts must be made to treat minor problems—for example, by cleaning a child's cut.

- Professional care must be obtained for moderate to severe problems, such as difficulty breathing.

- Preventive health care must be provided. This may be a contentious issue where the observer believes that preventive health care is necessary, but such care may not be economically feasible for the parent—for example, preventive dental care.

- The health care provided must meet accepted health care standards.

Failure To Supervise Leading to Sexual Harm

In this situation, a child has been or could be sexually abused, and the parent, due to neglect or wilful blindness, did nothing to stop the abuse. Section 37(2)(c) of the CFSA allows intervention where

> (c) the child has been sexually molested or sexually exploited, by the person having charge of the child or by another person where the person having charge of the child knows or should know of the possibility of sexual molestation or sexual exploitation and fails to protect the child.

Failure To Provide Necessary Treatment

In situations where the parent does not provide treatment to alleviate or prevent any emotional or psychological damage to the child, the child may be considered to be in need of protection. Under ss. 37(2)(f) to (h) of the CFSA, police and child protection workers have authority to intervene where

> (f) the child has suffered emotional harm, demonstrated by serious ...
>
> > (i) anxiety,
> >
> > (ii) depression,

(iii) withdrawal,

(iv) self-destructive or aggressive behaviour, or

(v) delayed development,

and there are reasonable grounds to believe that the emotional harm suffered by the child results from the actions, failure to act or pattern of neglect on the part of the child's parent or the person having charge of the child;

(f.1) the child has suffered emotional harm of the kind described in subclause (f)(i), (ii), (iii), (iv) or (v) and the child's parent or the person having charge of the child does not provide, or refuses or is unavailable or unable to consent to, services or treatment to remedy or alleviate the harm;

(g) there is a risk that the child is likely to suffer emotional harm of the kind described in subclause (f)(i), (ii), (iii), (iv) or (v) resulting from the actions, failure to act or pattern of neglect on the part of the child's parent or the person having charge of the child;

(g.1) there is a risk that the child is likely to suffer emotional harm of the kind described in subclause (f)(i), (ii), (iii), (iv) or (v) and that the child's parent or the person having charge of the child does not provide, or refuses or is unavailable or unable to consent to, services or treatment to prevent the harm;

(h) the child suffers from a mental, emotional or developmental condition that, if not remedied, could seriously impair the child's development and the child's parent or the person having charge of the child does not provide, or refuses or is unavailable or unable to consent to, treatment to remedy or alleviate the condition.

Protection of the Officer from Personal Liability

Neglect is often difficult for police officers to identify due to their limited interaction with the neglected child. If there is any risk of immediate danger to the child's well-being, the officer should apprehend the child and contact the appropriate child protection authorities. If the officer's actions are not malicious and are carried out in good faith, the CFSA protects the officer against any civil liability. This protection is congruent with the paramount purpose of the Act, child protection.

PROTECTION FROM PERSONAL LIABILITY: CHILD AND FAMILY SERVICES ACT, SECTION 40(14)

No action shall be instituted against a peace officer or child protection worker for any act done in good faith in the execution or intended execution of that person's duty under this section or for an alleged neglect or default in the execution in good faith of that duty.

INVESTIGATING CHILD ABUSE

Regulation 3/99 of the *Police Services Act* of Ontario requires that police services develop policies and procedures for investigating incidents of child abuse. Police officers must follow the policies of their police service. The following information is generic in content.

The role of the police in an investigation of child abuse is twofold. Police conduct the investigation to determine whether the child is in need of protection and to determine whether there are reasonable grounds to believe that a criminal offence has been committed.

The investigation involves gathering evidence in order to establish the facts, and preparing for criminal proceedings where appropriate. These activities include:

- preserving the crime scene,

- obtaining the child's account of events,

- obtaining a statement from the alleged offender,

- obtaining statements from other witnesses,

- arranging to obtain and preserve any physical evidence,

- obtaining medical and other expert opinions if needed, and

- determining the need to arrest a suspect.

The majority of assaults against children, defined as persons under the age of 18, are committed by non-family members. This changes substantially with the age of the child. A younger child is much more likely to be assaulted by a family member. Statistics Canada has found that family members are responsible for 70 percent of all assaults against children less than three years old. Within this group, parents are responsible for 85 percent of the assaults.

The perpetrator of physical and sexual abuse of children, statistically, is likely to be the father of the household. Statistics show that of reported cases where responsibility was determined, the father was responsible for 98 percent of sexual assaults and 71 percent of non-sexual assaults. Females were the victims of 80 percent of sexual assaults and 53 percent of non-sexual assaults (Statistics Canada, 1998). Females are most likely to be sexually assaulted by their fathers when they are between the ages of 12 and 14. Males are more likely to be sexually assaulted between the ages of 3 and 6. The instances of non-sexual assault perpetrated by the father increase in both females and males as their age increases.

Perpetrators of child abuse frequently share many of the following character traits and past experiences:

- *They abuse others.* Investigation will likely reveal that the child abuser has also carried out abusive acts or exhibited abusive behaviours toward others.

- *They like to have power and control.* The need to control his or her immediate environment may lead the abuser to violence or demeaning verbal abuse used as a method of maintaining control of his or her surroundings.

- *They live isolated from society.* The pattern of demeaning and abusive behaviour generally does not endear the abuser to society in general.

- *They have few friends or family connections.* The egocentric nature of the abuser's personality does not lend itself well to friendship or close family ties.

- *They are part of a cycle of child abuse.* The abuser was abused as a child. Childhood abuse may be a contributing factor but it is not present in all child abusers.

- *They abuse alcohol/drugs.* These are contributing factors but not the sole cause of the behaviour.

- *They suffer from severe postpartum depression.* This is a legally recognized mental disorder that affects a small number of females. Although it is a factor contributing to child abuse, statistically, based on the percentage of females who abuse children, it is not a very significant factor.

- *They have poor coping skills.* The abuser is unable to effectively deal with daily stressors.

- *They have low self-esteem, likely due to an abusive childhood.* Abusive mothers tend to be battered wives.

- *They are unable to effectively communicate with the child.* The abuser may believe that the child is not listening because the child does not understand the expectations of the abuser.

- *They believe in corporal punishment for children.* Abusive parents may believe that harsh physical punishment is necessary to control the child. (See the section entitled "Punishment Versus Abuse," above.)

Although statistics and identification of common character traits may help focus an investigation, officers must continue to think laterally and not rule out possible suspects until all available evidence is obtained. One of the most valuable sources of evidence is the victim. Evidence from this source is often difficult to obtain.

Maintaining Objectivity

Investigating child abuse can be very emotionally difficult for many police officers. Feelings of anger and disgust may emerge. But regardless of his or her emotions, the investigating officer has to be objective and gather the necessary information and evidence. Emotional reactions should not be allowed to interfere with an officer's professionalism or cause an officer to say or do anything that could harm the investigation. An officer may be outraged by what he or she learns, but must remain calm and in control. Loss of emotional control by the officer may have a negative effect on the child. The child has probably seen a substantial amount of anger and inappropriate behaviour in his or her life, and a display of police exasperation may lead the child to believe that he or she is the cause of the exasperation.

ACCESSING THE CHILD VICTIM

It may be difficult to gain access to a child one suspects of being abused. In many instances an immediate family member is the abuser and will deny the authorities access to protect himself or herself. If access is denied, an officer must use other means to establish contact with the child. The reporting requirements of the CFSA can be a starting point. If the suspected abuse has been reported by a person designated in s. 72 of the Act, that person may be able to provide evidence of abuse, allowing the officer to establish that the child is in need of protection as defined in s. 37(2) of the Act. If there is reason to believe that the child is in need of protection, the Children's Aid Society must be contacted.

The CFSA authorizes three methods of bringing a child before the court to determine whether the child is in need of protection. The following sections will address these methods sequentially from least to most invasive.

Section 40(4) of the CFSA, below, allows child protection workers, which includes police officers, as defined in s. 40(13), to apply to the court to have the person in charge of the child bring the child before the court. The court will determine whether the child is in need of protection.

This section may be used when the danger to the child is not immediate, but there is cause to believe that the child may be in need of protection.

ORDER TO PRODUCE OR APPREHEND CHILD: CHILD AND FAMILY SERVICES ACT, SECTION 40(4)

Where the court is satisfied, on a person's application upon notice to a society, that there are reasonable and probable grounds to believe that

(a) a child is in need of protection, the matter has been reported to the society, the society has not made an application under subsection (1), and no child protection worker has sought a warrant under subsection (2) or apprehended the child under subsection (7); and

(b) the child cannot be protected adequately otherwise than by being brought before the court, the court may order

(c) that the person having charge of the child produce him or her before the court at the time and place named in the order for a hearing under subsection 47(1) to determine whether he or she is in need of protection; or

(d) where the court is satisfied that an order under clause (c) would not protect the child adequately, that a child protection worker employed by the society bring the child to a place of safety.

If a child protection worker has reasonable grounds to believe that the danger to the child is not immediate but likely imminent, an application may be made to the court to have a warrant issued allowing the immediate apprehension of the child and delivery to a place of safety. The child will be brought before the court to determine if the child is in need of protection, and to determine the appropriate method of child protection.

WARRANT TO APPREHEND CHILD: CHILD AND FAMILY SERVICES ACT, SECTION 40(2)

A justice of the peace may issue a warrant authorizing a child protection worker to bring a child to a place of safety if the justice of the peace is satisfied on the basis of a child protection worker's sworn information that there are reasonable and probable grounds that

(a) the child is in need of protection; and

(b) a less restrictive course of action is not available or will not protect the child adequately.

The most invasive apprehension authority contained within the CFSA is the authorization of immediate, warrantless apprehension of a child in need of protection. Apprehension without a warrant is generally carried out by police officers in situations where the danger to the child is immediate. Due to the immediacy of circumstances, it would not be expeditious for the officer to apply for pre-authorization in the form of a warrant or court order.

APPREHENSION WITHOUT WARRANT: CHILD AND FAMILY SERVICES ACT, SECTION 40(7)

A child protection worker who believes on reasonable and probable grounds that

(a) a child is in need of protection; and

(b) there would be a substantial risk to the child's health or safety during the time necessary to bring the matter on for a hearing under subsection 47(1) or obtain a warrant under subsection (2),

may without a warrant bring the child to a place of safety.

Legislators have recognized that the immediate apprehension of a child without a warrant may be a situation in which the person in charge of the child may not be cooperative. Because the safety of the child is paramount, the legislation authorizes child protection workers to use force to enter and search for a child in need of protection.

RIGHT OF ENTRY, ETC.: CHILD AND FAMILY SERVICES ACT, SECTION 40(11)

A child protection worker who believes on reasonable and probable grounds that a child referred to in subsection (7) is on any premises may without a warrant enter the premises, by force, if necessary, and search for and remove the child.

The CFSA offers a degree of legal protection for persons carrying out their duty to protect children. If the child protection worker was acting in good faith, and without malicious intent, no legal action will be taken against the worker, even if the court finds that he or she lacked reasonable grounds to apprehend the child.

If, after investigation or apprehension, the child protection worker determines that the child is or may be in need of protection, the child must be brought before the court to determine how to best protect the child. "Court," for the purpose of the CFSA, means the Ontario Court of Justice or the Family Court of the Superior Court of Justice.

APPLICATION: CHILD AND FAMILY SERVICES ACT, SECTION 40(1)

A society may apply to the court to determine whether a child is in need of protection.

CHILD PROTECTION HEARING: CHILD AND FAMILY SERVICES ACT, SECTION 47(1)

Where an application is made under subsection 40(1) or a matter is brought before the court to determine whether the child is in need of protection, the court shall hold a hearing to determine the issue and make an order under section 57.

Where the court determines that the child is in need of protection, s. 57 of the CFSA, below, sets out the options available to the court. The court will select the option that will best protect the child in the circumstances.

ORDER WHERE CHILD IN NEED OF PROTECTION: CHILD AND FAMILY SERVICES ACT, SECTION 57(1)

Where the court finds that a child is in need of protection and is satisfied that intervention through a court order is necessary to protect the child in the future, the court shall make one of the following orders, in the child's best interests:

1. *Supervision order* That the child be placed with or returned to a parent or another person, subject to the supervision of the society, for a specified period of at least three and not more than twelve months.

2. *Society wardship* That the child be made a ward of the society and be placed in its care and custody for a specified period not exceeding twelve months.

3. *Crown wardship* That the child be made a ward of the Crown, until the wardship is terminated under section 65 or expires under subsection 71(1), and be placed in the care of the society.

4. *Consecutive orders of society of wardship and supervision* That the child be made a ward of the society under paragraph 2 for a specified period and then be returned to a parent or another person under paragraph 1, for a period or periods not exceeding an aggregate of twelve months.

In addition to the previous options, the court may also prohibit access to the child. These orders may prohibit access absolutely or may allow supervised access.

RESTRAINING ORDER: CHILD AND FAMILY SERVICES ACT, SECTION 80(1)

Where the court finds that a child is in need of protection, the court may, instead of or in addition to making an order under subsection 57(1), make an order in the child's best interests restraining or prohibiting a person's access to or contact with the child, and may include in the order such directions as the court considers appropriate for implementing the order and protecting the child.

Interviewing the Victim

The nature of child abuse and the likelihood that the abuse took place in the family home make investigation very difficult. There may be little physical evidence available. The child may not exhibit any visible sign of injury at the time of the interview. The abuser, being in complete control of the child, will generally ensure that the child's injuries are healed to the point of not being visible before the child is allowed to appear in public.

The lack of prominent physical evidence leaves the police only the interview with the child to try to determine whether abuse took place.

But the victim's young age and immaturity may hinder the police in obtaining information through an interview and may present the following problems:

- The concept of abuse may not be understood by the victim because of his or her trust in and dependence on the abuser, which may lead him or her to believe that the abuser did not do anything wrong.

- The victim may believe that he or she caused the abuse, or that no one will believe his or her story.

- The victim may not want to talk about the abuse. He or she may fear the abuser or be embarrassed to reveal the details to strangers.

- The victim may not be able to express himself or herself well and may be embarrassed about using slang or "bad" words.

- The victim may believe that everyone will be angry with him or her for revealing the abuse or, if the abuser is a family member, that the family will break up.

- The victim may feel worthless because of the abuse, and may believe that what happens to him or her does not matter.

Police services are required to have officers trained in child abuse response. If possible, an officer with this special training should conduct the interview. The interview may be carried out jointly by the officer and a child protection worker. Each may prompt the other in an unobtrusive manner to solicit pertinent information from the victim.

The same officer and child protection worker should conduct all the interviews. This allows the child to become acquainted with the interviewers. It also helps the police to piece together the fragments of information that may emerge over many sessions.

The interviewers must use language that is appropriate to the child's age and stage of development. The child's understanding of sexual touches or disciplinary spankings may be limited, and he or she may have no concept of right and wrong. For younger children, notions such as "good touches" and "bad touches" may be more suitable for interview use than advanced concepts such as right and wrong.

Treating the child sensitively is a priority. The interview should take place as soon as possible following the disclosure or report of abuse. Several brief interviews may be necessary to allow the child to overcome his or her fear and reluctance. Brief sessions also accommodate children's short attention spans. The number and duration of interviews should be confined to the minimum necessary. Where the child has difficulty communicating, the interviewers should make arrangements to have a competent and unbiased interpreter or communication specialist, or a person skilled in communicating with the particular child, present for the interview. The questions posed to the child should be simple enough for him or her to understand and respond to.

When interviewing witnesses or victims, interviewers should use open-ended questions. Open-ended questions are those that do not have simple "yes" or "no" answers. These questions are helpful in that they

- make no suggestions;

- invite witnesses or victims to talk in their own words;

- act as memory prompts;

- get people talking;

- encourage full answers;

- help to get accurate information; and

- let the witness or victim talk 80 percent of the time.

The interviewers should also paraphrase the victims' or witnesses' words when they ask subsequent questions. Also, when a conversation goes off topic, the interviewers should

- wait for a break;
- bring it back to the topic;
- use another open-ended question;
- not interrupt a statement;
- ask questions to confirm points later; and
- if possible, ask the witnesses or victims to write their own statements.

Interviewers should avoid closed-ended questions when interviewing witnesses or victims. Courts may consider them as leading questions. The interviewers must be careful not to use leading questions or a repetitive, badgering style of questioning when speaking with the child. The need to please may prompt the child to say what he or she thinks the interviewers want to hear. Closed-ended questions are often unproductive because they

- suggest an idea to the witness or victim;
- lead the witness or victim to repeat what the interviewers said; and
- elicit little information because they take only one word to answer.

The officer should make a verbatim record of the interview using videotape or audiotape.

The interview should take place in an area where the child feels safe and not intimidated, such as an interview room filled with toys or a similar neutral environment. The child's home is not the best interview environment, especially if it is suspected that the abuse occurred there.

Careful observation of the child's non-verbal language may alert the interviewers to potential areas of conflict or avenues of investigation. If, for example, mention of a specific place or person causes a negative non-verbal reaction from the child, further investigation may be indicated.

These interviews, due to the age of the victim and his or her lack of sophistication, require that the interviewing officers have an understanding of the thought and communication processes of children.

INTERVIEWING THE VICTIM OF A PEDOPHILE

The interview should be carried out in the same manner as any other investigation of child sexual abuse. There may be more hesitation on the part of the child if there has been an ongoing relationship with the offender. The offender is probably a person whom the child has seen regularly and with whom the child has developed a trust relationship. This relationship will have been fostered by the offender's constant reminders of the supposed need for secrecy. The child will naturally be hesitant about disclosing the private details of this relationship.

This hesitancy may be overcome through patient interviewing of the child. As in other child sexual abuse cases, several brief interviews may be necessary to obtain all the details. The child may be worrying about the safety of his or her family. Reassuring the child that the offender will not be allowed to harm him or her and the family may help alleviate the child's fear of reprisals.

Family support of the child is crucial to healing. If the family blames the child for the attention that his or her plight has attracted, the child may decide that silence is the best option and blame himself or herself for the family's troubles. When speaking with the child, the interviewing officer must clearly communicate the message that the abuser, not the child, was in the wrong, and that the child is in no way responsible for what has happened to the abuser or to the family. Others who seek to help the child must reinforce the same message.

STAGES OF CHILD DEVELOPMENT AND THEIR IMPLICATIONS FOR POLICING

How Children Learn

School curriculums have been based on an understanding of how children learn. Learning and understanding are a developmental process in human beings. Children learn at different rates, and often in different ways during their development. Experts in the field of education, however, have determined that certain characteristics in learning patterns can be generally related to the student's age and grade.

Teachers use different techniques and methodologies to instruct children at different ages. Children respond and learn better when the means of communicating is appropriate to their level of understanding. Thus, the language that teachers use must reflect what the child is capable of understanding.

These factors are important for police officers. Police must be aware that children not only express themselves differently from adults, but are incapable of grasping certain information and concepts at certain ages as well.

Interviewing children then, should be guided by this knowledge. In law, too, this factor has been recognized. Legal professionals stress the importance of explaining, in appropriate language, legal rights to young persons suspected of crimes. Children cannot be held legally accountable for their actions until the age of 12, a further recognition that a child's sense of personal responsibility for his or her actions develops slowly. The testimony of a child under the age of 14 is weighed in terms of whether the child understands his or her requirement to tell the truth.

Interviewing child victims, witnesses, and suspects, then, should be conducted using this understanding of how children learn, and where appropriate, using the techniques and methodologies that have proven effective in the classroom.

The following sections address the ability of specific age groups to understand situations and to convey their understanding. Knowledge of the child's abilities and age-related perspectives may help the officer formulate appropriate questions that will allow the child to relate his or her experiences clearly.

Age 2 to 5: Preschool-Aged Children

Children in this age group are highly dependent on their parents or guardians. They understand their parents and other adults much better than their peer group. They understand simple instructions, and tend to pick up general instructions more than specific details. Children this age are egocentric and unaware of the perspectives of others. Language is highly adaptive, sometimes only understood by the children themselves. Children learn at this stage by trial and error, and memory only gradually develops. They judge things on the basis of appearance. They do not have any true understanding of time. Time is understood as "now." Past, present, and future are not understood.

Age 5 to 7: Kindergarten, Grade 1

Children in this age group often have a well-developed vocabulary (20,000 words), although some "baby words" may linger in speech. Children this age are often highly imaginative, and enjoy telling stories. They will express ideas in loosely connected sentences and will have trouble with abstract terms such as ask/tell, more/less, and older/younger. These children like to imitate adults, and need praise, warmth, patience, and success. The also need supervision and guidance. Friendship with peers is important, but the source of authority comes from parents and other adults. Children this age idolize their favourite people.

Age 7 to 9: Grades 2, 3, 4

Children in this age group are more self-assured and outgoing. They communicate well with peers and adults, and are able to carry on organized conversations with both. They can assume responsibility for simple tasks. Although same-sex friendships flourish at this age, parents and parental approval are still very important. Concepts of time, distance, speed, size, shape, and quantity have meaning. These children have a developed ability to express themselves through pictures, words, and numbers.

Age 9 to 10: Grade 5

Children in this age group are able to use past experiences when considering their actions. Generally, however, they can handle only concrete concepts and their ability to perceive abstract ideas is limited. Their primary influence remains with their families. Children in this age group seek adults other than parents with whom to identify. They have a basic sense of right and wrong.

Age 10 to 11: Grade 6

Children at this age can understand some problem solving and decision making but generally only in concrete terms. They are developing a strong sense of loyalty and peer identity. They are beginning to show interest in their future options. Children at this stage are beginning to apply logical thinking.

Age 11 to 12: Grade 7

Children in this age group are now able to generalize about cause and effect, and can assume some responsibility for their actions. Twelve-year-old children are legally culpable for their actions according to law. They are intensely interested in themselves and in moral or value decisions. They are deeply concerned about fairness, and peer influence is becoming a powerful influence in their lives.

Age 12 to 13: Grade 8

Children in this age group experiment with ideas, fashions, etc. They usually work well within groups, teams, and clubs, and often look to their peers more than their families to provide support. They are at an age when they are vulnerable to role models, good and bad.

Age 13 to 14: Grade 9

Children at this age are able to absorb a wealth of information and are able to think in abstract terms. They tend to be argumentative with their families, their friends, and even with themselves. They are interested in personal relationships as well as peer groups. They are attempting to understand their place in the world, and have a deep-rooted desire for individual recognition.

Age 15 to 16: Grade 10

Generally, at this age, the young person has a good understanding of right and wrong and is able to express himself or herself in clearly understood language. These young people may be experimenting sexually and may be subject to peer pressure. They may be rebellious within the family group and may push their societal limits.

Clearly, very young children (under the age of seven) are difficult interview subjects, and often are ideal victims of such crimes as sexual abuse. The child's inability to determine time and space, or to describe incidents in detail make interviews difficult. Also, young children's state of dependency and trust in adults poses many problems.

Older children also have limitations—factors that the interviewers must be aware of if they are to be successful. Appropriate language, questioning techniques, props, guides, and anatomically correct dolls are useful aids when applied to the correct age groupings.

TESTIFYING

If the child is mature enough to understand that part of the process will involve testifying in court, the interviewers may explain, in appropriate language, the provisions of the *Criminal Code* that allow testimony to be given from a private location. This may assist in alleviating some of the child's fears of facing his or her abuser.

EVIDENCE OF COMPLAINANT OR WITNESS: CRIMINAL CODE, SECTION 715.1

In any proceeding relating to an offence under section 151, 152, 153, 155 or 159, subsection 160(2) or (3), or section 163.1, 170, 171, 172, 173, 210, 211, 212, 213, 266, 267, 268, 271, 272 or 273, in which the complainant or other witness was under the age of eighteen years at the time the offence is alleged to have been committed, a videotape made within a reasonable time after the alleged offence, in which the complainant or witness describes the acts complained of, is admissible in evidence if the complainant or witness, while testifying, adopts the contents of the videotape.

VIDEOTAPED STATEMENTS: R v. F.(C.C.)

"A statement is 'adopted' within the meaning of this section where the witness recalls giving the statement and testifies that they were attempting to be honest and truthful when they gave the statement. A videotaped statement is admissible even if a witness has an independent present memory of the events or if the witness cannot remember the events discussed in the videotape. In the latter case, there are several factors in this provision which guarantee the reliability of the videotaped statement including the requirement that the statement be made within a reasonable time, that the trier of fact will have an opportunity to observe the demeanour and assess the personality and intelligence of the child in the videotape, and that the child attest that she was attempting to be truthful at the time that the statement was made. The test for adoption is not a final determination of reliability, but rather a test for determining the threshold degree of reliability required for the admission of the video. Once a trial judge rules that the statement has been adopted, the videotaped statement together with the *viva voce* evidence given at trial comprises the whole of the evidence-in-chief. Even if evidence which contradicts the videotaped statement is elicited in cross-examination, this does not render those parts of the videotape inadmissible. The circumstances in which the video was made, the veracity of the witness's statements and the overall reliability of the evidence are factors which are relevant to weight rather than the admissibility of the statement: *R v. F.(C.C.)*, [[1997] 3 SCR 1183, 120 CCC (3d) 225, 11 CR (5th) 209]." (*Martin's Annual Criminal Code, 2005*)

EXCLUSION OF PUBLIC IN CERTAIN CASES: CRIMINAL CODE, SECTION 486(1)

> Any proceedings against an accused shall be held in open court, but where the presiding judge, provincial court judge or justice, as the case may be, is of the opinion that it is in the interest of public morals, the maintenance of order or the proper administration of justice, or that it is necessary to prevent injury to international relations or national defence or national security, to exclude all or any members of the public from the court room for all or part of the proceedings, he or she may so order.

PROTECTION OF CHILD WITNESSES: CRIMINAL CODE, SECTION 486(1.1)

> For the purposes of subsections (1) and (2.3) and for greater certainty, the "proper administration of justice" includes ensuring that the interests of witnesses under the age of eighteen years are safeguarded in proceedings in which the accused is charged with a sexual offence, an offence against any of sections 271, 272 and 273 or an offence in which violence against the person is alleged to have been used, threatened or attempted.

TESTIMONY OUTSIDE COURT ROOM: CRIMINAL CODE, SECTION 486(2.1)

Despite section 650, if an accused is charged with an offence under section 151, 152, 153, 153.1, 155 or 159, subsection 160(2) or (3) or section 163.1, 170, 171, 172, 173, 210, 211, 212, 213, 266, 267, 268, 271, 272 or 273 and the complainant or any witness, at the time of the trial or preliminary inquiry, is under the age of eighteen years or is able to communicate evidence but may have difficulty doing so by reason of a mental or physical disability, the presiding judge or justice, as the case may be, may order that the complainant or witness testify outside the court room or behind a screen or other device that would allow the complainant or witness not to see the accused, if the judge or justice is of the opinion that the exclusion is necessary to obtain a full and candid account of the acts complained of from the complainant or witness.

USE OF A SCREEN IN TESTIFYING: R v. LEVOGIANNIS

"The circumstances under which a judge may make an order under this subsection do not require that exceptional and inordinate stress be caused to the child. The trial judge has a substantial latitude in deciding whether the use of the screen should be permitted and the evidence in support of the application need not take any particular form. In exercising the discretion under this subsection, the trial judge may consider evidence of the capabilities and demeanour of the child, the nature of the allegations and the circumstances of the case. It may well be that the trial judge may also consider the fact that the accused is unrepresented in determining whether or not to permit the use of the screen: *R v. Levogiannis*, [1993] 4 SCR 475, 85 CCC (3d) 327, 25 CR (4th) 325 (9:0)." (*Martin's Annual Criminal Code, 2005*)

MISSING CHILDREN

Police services, as required by regulation 3/99 of the *Police Services Act*, will have specific policies and procedures that deal with missing children. Officers are required to follow the procedures of their respective police service.

Voluntarily Missing Children

In abusive situations there are instances where the child feels he or she has no choice but to leave the abusive home. This does not mean that all runaways are products of an abusive environment. The majority of runaways leave home for other reasons. Boredom may entice the child to seek excitement elsewhere or on the street. Refusal to abide by house rules is an often encountered reason for leaving. Users of illicit drugs may leave home to seek out areas where drugs are readily available.

Statistics compiled by the RCMP Missing Children's Registry indicate that in 2002 there were a total of 66,532 reported cases of missing children under the age of 18 in Canada. By far, the most common type of missing child reported is in the "runaway" category. For whatever reason, the child has chosen to leave the family home. This category accounted for 52,390 reported cases in 2002, or almost 79 percent of all reported cases of missing children.

The second most common type of missing child is in the "unknown" category. This label is applied to missing children when there was no previous indication that the child would leave the home. "Unknown" does not necessarily indicate foul play, but only that police have not definitively categorized the missing child as a runaway, or voluntarily missing. The "unknown" category accounted for 10,994 reported cases, or about 17 percent of all reported cases of missing children.

There are legislative avenues available to assist in the apprehension and returning of runaways. The CFSA contains provisions that allow the apprehension of runaway children. A child within the meaning of this legislative authority is a person under the age of 16.

APPLICATION: CHILD AND FAMILY SERVICES ACT, SECTION 43(1)

In this section, "parent" includes

(a) an approved agency that has custody of the child;

(b) a person who has care and control of the child.

Although the child may be voluntarily missing, the parent, as defined in s. 43(1) of the CFSA, has the option of appearing before a justice of the peace to obtain a warrant authorizing police to apprehend the missing child and return him or her to the parent. The parent must appear before a justice. Police cannot appear on behalf of the parent.

The conditions for obtaining the warrant are specific:

- the parent must swear an information before a justice using Form 10 of the CFSA (see appendix 3B at the end of this chapter);

- the child must be under the age of 16;

- the child must have left the custody of the parent without parental consent; and

- the parent must believe that the child's health and safety may be at risk.

If the justice accepts the information of the parent, a Warrant to Apprehend and Return a Child Who Has Withdrawn from a Parent's Control, Form 9 of the CFSA, will be issued (see appendix 3A at the end of this chapter). The warrant authorizes all police in the province of Ontario to apprehend the named child and return the child to the custody of the parent, or if not possible or immediately impractical, to a place of safety as defined in s. 37(1) of the CFSA.

WARRANT TO APPREHEND RUNAWAY CHILD: CHILD AND FAMILY SERVICES ACT, SECTION 43(2)

A justice of the peace may issue a warrant authorizing a peace officer or child protection worker to apprehend a child if the justice of the peace is satisfied on the basis of the sworn information of a parent of the child that,

(a) the child is under the age of sixteen years;

(b) the child has withdrawn from the parent's care and control without the parent's consent; and

(c) the parent believes on reasonable and probable grounds that the child's health or safety may be at risk if the child is not apprehended.

WARRANT TO APPREHEND RUNAWAY CHILD: CHILD AND FAMILY SERVICES ACT, SECTION 43(3)

A person who apprehends a child under subsection (2) shall return the child to the child's parent as soon as practicable and where it is not possible to return the child to the parent within a reasonable time, take the child to a place of safety.

NOTICE TO PARENT, ETC.: CHILD AND FAMILY SERVICES ACT, SECTION 43(4)

The person in charge of a place of safety to which a child is taken under subsection (3) shall make reasonable efforts to notify the child's parent that the child is in the place of safety so that the child may be returned to the parent.

WHERE CHILD NOT RETURNED TO PARENT WITHIN TWELVE HOURS: CHILD AND FAMILY SERVICES ACT, SECTION 43(5)

Where a child taken to a place of safety under subsection (3) cannot be returned to the child's parent within twelve hours of being taken to the place of safety, the child shall be dealt with as if the child had been taken to a place of safety under subsection 40(2) and not apprehended under subsection (2).

WHERE CUSTODY ENFORCEMENT PROCEEDINGS MORE APPROPRIATE: CHILD AND FAMILY SERVICES ACT, SECTION 43(6)

A justice of the peace shall not issue a warrant under subsection (2) where a child has withdrawn from the care and control of one parent with the consent of another parent under circumstances where a proceeding under section 36 of the *Children's Law Reform Act* would be more appropriate.

NO NEED TO SPECIFY PREMISES: CHILD AND FAMILY SERVICES ACT, SECTION 43(7)

It is not necessary in a warrant under subsection (2) to specify the premises where the child is located.

The legislation recognizes that the safety of the runaway child is at risk. The warrant (Form 9) allows police to enter any premises at any time, by force if necessary, to search for and remove the child.

AUTHORITY TO ENTER, ETC.: CHILD AND FAMILY SERVICES ACT, SECTION 44(1)

A person authorized to bring a child to a place of safety by a warrant issued under subsection 41(1) or 43(2) may at any time enter any premises specified in the warrant, by force, if necessary, and may search for and remove the child.

PROTECTION FROM PERSONAL LIABILITY: CHILD AND FAMILY SERVICES ACT, SECTION 44(7)

> No action shall be instituted against a peace officer or child protection worker for any act done in good faith in the execution or intended execution of that person's duty under this section or section 41, 42 or 43 or for an alleged neglect or default in the execution in good faith of that duty.

If, upon apprehension, police believe that the child may be in need of protection as defined in s. 37(2) of the CFSA, and the person presenting the possible danger is the parent, the child may be taken to a place of safety. In situations where the child is brought to a place of safety, s. 72 requires that police report their suspicion that the child may be in need of protection to the Children's Aid Society. Child protection workers will carry out an investigation, along with police if appropriate, to determine if the child may be in need of protection. If the investigation determines that the child may be in need of protection, court proceedings may be initiated to determine how to best protect the child. Police may conduct a parallel or subsequent investigation to determine possible offences.

CHILD PROTECTION PROCEEDINGS: CHILD AND FAMILY SERVICES ACT, SECTION 43(8)

> Where a peace officer or child protection worker believes on reasonable and probable grounds that a child apprehended under this section is in need of protection and there may be a substantial risk to the health or safety of the child if the child were returned to the parent,
>
> > (a) the peace officer or child protection worker may take the child to a place of safety under subsection 40(7); or
> >
> > (b) where the child has been taken to a place of safety under subsection (5), the child shall be dealt with as if the child had been taken there under subsection 40(7).

In situations where the child has left parental custody voluntarily and there is no reason to believe that the child is in need of protection, the child will be returned to the parent.

Abduction

Police services, as required by regulation 3/99 of the *Police Services Act*, will have specific policies and procedures that deal with abducted children. Officers are required to follow the procedures of their respective police service.

There are situations where a child is not voluntarily missing, such as in cases of abduction. Such situations, while often making headline news, are not common. Statistics compiled by the RCMP Missing Children's Registry indicate that in 2002 there were a total of 66,532 reported cases of missing children in Canada (Dalley, 2003). The most common category of missing child reported is in the "runaway" classification. For whatever reason, the child has chosen to leave the family home. This category accounted for 52,390 reported cases in 2002, or almost 79 percent of all reported cases of missing children.

The number of children abducted by a stranger in 2002 was 35. Parental abduction, in comparison, was significantly more common with 429 reported occurrences in 2002. Occurrences in the province of Ontario in 2002 accounted for approximately 40.4 percent or 173 reported cases of parental abduction in Canada.

Parental abduction is a criminal offence. The *Criminal Code* identifies the offences of parental abduction in cases where a custody order exists and in instances where no order exists.

ABDUCTION IN CONTRAVENTION OF CUSTODY ORDER: CRIMINAL CODE, SECTION 282(1)

> Every one who, being the parent, guardian or person having the lawful care or charge of a person under the age of fourteen years, takes, entices away, conceals, detains, receives or harbours that person, in contravention of the custody provisions of a custody order in relation to that person made by a court anywhere in Canada, with intent to deprive a parent or guardian, or any other person who has the lawful care or charge of that person, of the possession of that person is guilty of
>
> > (a) an indictable offence and is liable to imprisonment for a term not exceeding ten years; or
> >
> > (b) an offence punishable on summary conviction.

The decision in the case of *R v. McDougall* identifies the court's definition of "detain." This definition should be considered in determining whether the offence of parental abduction in contravention of a custody order has been established. The court determined that there must be a deliberate attempt to deprive the non-custodial parent of possession of the child. This does not mean that the person in custody of the child has not violated the terms of the custody order, but only that a criminal offence may not have been committed.

DETENTION AND POSSESSION: R v. McDOUGALL

"The term 'detain' in this section means 'withhold' and thus the mere fact that a parent keeps a child longer than the prescribed access period would not necessarily constitute a withholding and thus a detention of the child. Further, to prove the requisite intent for the offence, there must be proof that the act was done for the express purpose of depriving the other parent of possession of the child. Mere recklessness would not suffice. There must be an intention to somehow put the child beyond the reach of the other parent's custody or control. An intention not to assist or co-operate in the regaining of physical control of the child by the other parent cannot be equated with the intention to deprive that parent of possession of the child: *R v. McDougall* (1990), 62 CCC (3d) 174, 3 CR (4th) 112, 1 OR (3d) 247, 42 OAC 223 (CA)." (*Martin's Annual Criminal Code, 2005*)

Police should be careful when considering arrest for a breach of a custody order. The orders may be varied by the court and it may take time for the varied order to be obtained by the involved parties. Police may not have immediate access to the most recent variance of the custody order. The Ontario Provincial Court in *R v. McCoy* advised police to be cautious and make inquiries about the accuracy of the custody order.

ACCURACY OF THE CUSTODY ORDER: R v. McCOY

"Every custody order is subject to variation and particularly where the order is only an interim custody order, police officers before attempting to arrest a parent for abduction in contravention of such an order should take reasonable steps and make such inquiries as are appropriate and possible to ensure that the order accurately reflects the true legal relationship between the parties: *R v. McCoy* (1984), 17 CCC (3d) 114 (Ont. Prov. Ct.)." (*Martin's Annual Criminal Code, 2005*)

If there are reasonable grounds for believing that a child is being unlawfully withheld in violation of a custody order issued under the authority of the *Children's Law Reform Act* (CLRA), and there is no reason to believe that the child is in danger, the person having custody of the child may appear before the court and request an order to apprehend the child.

ORDER WHERE CHILD UNLAWFULLY WITHHELD: CHILDREN'S LAW REFORM ACT, SECTION 36(1)

Where a court is satisfied upon application by a person in whose favour an order has been made for custody of or access to a child that there are reasonable and probable grounds for believing that any person is unlawfully withholding the child from the applicant, the court by order may authorize the applicant or someone on his or her behalf to apprehend the child for the purpose of giving effect to the rights of the applicant to custody or access, as the case may be.

An order under CLRA s. 36(2) directs police to apprehend and deliver the child to the person named in the order.

ORDER TO LOCATE AND TAKE CHILD: CHILDREN'S LAW REFORM ACT, SECTION 36(2)

Where a court is satisfied upon application that there are reasonable and probable grounds for believing,

> (a) that any person is unlawfully withholding a child from a person entitled to custody of or access to the child;

> (b) that a person who is prohibited by court order or separation agreement from removing a child from Ontario proposes to remove the child or have the child removed from Ontario; or

> (c) that a person who is entitled to access to a child proposes to remove the child or to have the child removed from Ontario, and that the child is not likely to return,

the court by order may direct a police force, having jurisdiction in any area where it appears to the court that the child may be, to locate, apprehend and deliver the child to the person named in the order.

An order under CLRA s. 36(5) authorizes police to enter any place, by force if necessary and search for and remove the child.

ENTRY AND SEARCH: CHILDREN'S LAW REFORM ACT, SECTION 36(5)

For the purpose of locating and apprehending a child in accordance with an order under subsection (2), a member of a police force may enter and search any place where he or she has reasonable and probable grounds for believing that the child may be with such assistance and such force as are reasonable in the circumstances.

TIME: CHILDREN'S LAW REFORM ACT, SECTION 36(6)

An entry or a search referred to in subsection (5) shall be made only between 6 a.m. and 9 p.m. standard time unless the court, in the order, authorizes entry and search at another time.

ABDUCTION WHERE A CUSTODY ORDER IS NOT IN EFFECT

It is very difficult for police officers to ascertain the rightful custodial parent of a child without a court order. The *Criminal Code* addresses the issue of parental abduction of a child under 14 years of age through the provisions of s. 483.

ABDUCTION: CRIMINAL CODE, SECTION 283

(1) Every one who, being the parent, guardian or person having the lawful care or charge of a person under the age of fourteen years, takes, entices away, conceals, detains, receives or harbours that person, whether or not there is a custody order in relation to that person made by a court anywhere in Canada, with intent to deprive a parent or guardian, or any other person who has the lawful care or charge of that person, of the possession of that person, is guilty of

(a) an indictable offence and is liable to imprisonment for a term not exceeding ten years; or

(b) an offence punishable on summary conviction.

(2) No proceedings may be commenced under subsection (1) without the consent of the Attorney General or counsel instructed by him for that purpose.

Note that s. 283(2) directs that proceedings shall not be commenced without the permission of the Crown.

CRIMINAL CODE OFFENCES RELEVANT TO CHILD ABUSE: SUMMARY

Physical Abuse of Children

The *Criminal Code* contains numerous offences related to physical abuse of children, some of which apply to victims of all ages and others that are specific to children, including:

- assault (s. 266);

- assault causing bodily harm or with a weapon (s. 267);

- aggravated assault (s. 268);

- aggravated assault excision (s. 268(3)) (genital mutilation to a female child under 18);

- causing bodily harm with intent (ss. 244 to 244.1);

- unlawfully causing bodily harm (s. 269);

- administering a noxious thing (s. 245);

- criminal negligence (ss. 219 to 221);

- murder (ss. 229 to 231);

- manslaughter (s. 234);

- infanticide (s. 233) (child under 1 year);

- killing an unborn child in the act of birth (s. 238); and

- homicide from injury before/during birth (s. 223(2)) (child born alive who later dies).

Sexual Abuse of Children

Similar to offences related to physical abuse, the *Criminal Code* contains sexual offences that apply to victims of all ages as well as offences specific to children. In addition, there are significant differences in how offences in the former category apply to sexual activity among adults, between adults and children, and among children. The *Criminal Code* offences concerning the sexual abuse of children include:

- sexual interference (s. 151) (child under 14);

- invitation to sexual touching (s. 152) (child under 14);

- sexual exploitation (s. 153) (by adult in position of trust or authority; child between 14 and 18);

- sexual assault (ss. 271 to 273);

- incest (s. 155);

- exposure (ss. 173 and 173(2)) (of genitals for sexual purpose; child under 14);

- child pornography (s. 163.1);

- procuring (ss. 212(2), (2.1), and (4)) (child under 18);

- Parent or guardian procuring sexual activity (s. 170) (child under 18); and

- householder permitting sexual activity (s. 171) (child under 18).

Neglect of Children

Although the *Criminal Code* does not establish a specific criminal offence of child neglect, the criminal law recognizes the responsibility of parents and guardians to provide care and protection for children through several related offences, including:

- failure to provide necessaries of life (s. 215);

- criminal negligence (ss. 219 to 221) (child under 16);

- abandoning child (s. 218) (child under 10);

- neglect to obtain assistance in childbirth (s. 242); and

- corrupting children (s. 172) (child under 18).

Emotional and Psychological Abuse of Children

The *Criminal Code* does not include specific offences concerning emotional or psychological abuse of children. What it does include are several offences, applicable to victims of all ages, with respect to threatening or intimidating behaviour by others:

- criminal harassment (s. 264);

- conveying threats (s. 264.1);

- intimidation (s. 423);

- making indecent or harassing telephone calls (s. 372);

- extortion (s. 346); and

- culpable homicide (s. 222(5)) (causing death by wilfully frightening a human being, in the case of a child or sick person).

Kidnapping and Abduction of Children

The *Criminal Code* has specific offences addressing parental and non-parental abductions. These offences include:

- kidnapping and forcible confinement (s. 279) (any person);

- abduction of person under 16 (s. 280(1)) (by any person);

- abduction of person under 14 (s. 281) (by person not parent, guardian, or person having lawful charge of person under 14);

- abduction in contravention of custody order (s. 282(1)) (by parent or guardian; child under 14);

- abduction (s. 283) (by parent or guardian; child under 14); and

- removal of child from Canada (s. 273.3) (for the purpose of committing certain offences against the child; different provisions for specified offences against children under 14, 14 to 18, and under 18).

Other Criminal Code provisions

By virtue of s. 7(4.1) of the *Criminal Code*, sexual offences against children committed outside Canada by Canadian citizens or permanent residents are deemed to have been committed in Canada.

KEY TERMS

abuse

child

child sexual abuse

neglect

pedophile

sudden infant death syndrome (SIDS)

REFERENCES

Child and Family Services Act. (1990). RSO 1990, c. C.11.

Children's Aid Society of Algoma. (1998). *Handbook on child abuse.* Sault Ste. Marie, ON: Author.

Children's Law Reform Act. (1990). RSO 1990, c. C.12.

Coroners Act. (1990). RSO 1990, c. C.37.

Criminal Code. (1985). RSC 1985, c. C-46, as amended.

Dalley, M. (2003). *Canada's missing children 2002 annual report.* Ottawa: Minister of Public Works and Government Services.

Martin's Annual Criminal Code, 1999. (1999). Aurora, ON: Canada Law Book.

Martin's Annual Criminal Code, 2005. (2005). Aurora, ON: Canada Law Book.

Murphy, W.D. (1985). The dynamics and phases of sexual abuse. Sexual Abuse Treatment Project, Department of Human Services, University of Tennessee.

Police Services Act. (1990). RSO 1990, c. P.15.

Reporting suspicions of child abuse. (1999). *Dispatch, 13*(2), 6–7.

Stechey, F.M. (2001). PANDA: A dentist's introduction to recognizing child abuse. *Dental Practice Management* (Summer), 26–28.

EXERCISES

True or False

_____ 1. Physical contact between the abuser and the child must occur before the police can intervene in a case of child sexual abuse.

_____ 2. The colour of a bruise provides an exact way to determine when the bruising occurred.

_____ 3. A police officer cannot remove a "child in need of protection" under s. 37 of the CFSA without a warrant.

_____ 4. A victim of child abuse always wants to talk about the abuse he or she has endured.

_____ 5. Proving sexual assault requires proof that the assailant experienced sexual gratification.

_____ 6. Child neglect is not a criminal offence.

Short Answer

1. List the types of professionals who are required by the *Child and Family Services Act* to report reasonable suspicions of child abuse. What are the possible repercussions for failure to report?

2. List the types of situations under s. 37(2) of the *Child and Family Services Act* that may lead to a child being identified as "in need of protection."

3. Under what circumstances does a police officer have the right to bring a child in need of protection to a "place of safety" without the authority of a warrant?

4. What problems might a police officer encounter when trying to interview a child abuse victim? Be sure to discuss why it might be necessary to hold several brief interview sessions.

5. List four behavioural signs of possible child sexual abuse.

    a.

    b.

c.

d.

6. List four physical signs of possible child sexual abuse.

   a.

   b.

   c.

   d.

7. List two sexual offences that can involve children and do not require physical contact between the abuser and the victim to support a conviction.

    a.

    b.

8. List four behavioural signs of possible child physical abuse.

    a.

    b.

    c.

    d.

9. List four physical signs of possible child physical abuse.

    a.

    b.

    c.

    d.

10. List four signs of possible child neglect.

    a.

    b.

    c.

d.

11. Explain the circumstances under which the *Criminal Code* allows correction of a child by force (s. 43).

12. Summarize the circumstances under which the neglect provisions of s. 215 of the *Criminal Code* apply.

Case Analysis

Case 3.1

You are a police officer called to a local school regarding an abuse complaint. You speak to Ms. Smith, who tells you that one of her students, 10-year-old Jack, is being beaten by his parents. Jack confirms her account.

You then speak to Jack's parents, and discover that both have been drinking beer. They tell you that Jack misbehaves. They punish him by spanking him about five or six times a week. Just today they had to spank him because he kicked the cat. Jack tells you that his parents spank him almost every day for practically no reason at all.

What should you do? Can charges be laid? Be sure to refer to the *Criminal Code* in your answer.

Case 3.2

You are a police officer responding to a complaint of assault at a local school. You speak to the suspect, an 11-year-old named Joe. He tells you that his father, Joe Sr., told him to beat up Bill, an 8-year-old at the same school, because Bill's father got a promotion at work that Joe Sr. thought he himself deserved. Joe Sr. told Joe Jr. that beating up Bill was the only way to redeem their family's honour. He also said that Joe Jr. did not have to worry about the police because he was only 11 years old.

What should you do? Can charges be laid? Be sure to refer to the appropriate legislation in your answer.

Case 3.3

You are a police officer responding to a call for assistance at 135 Main Street. Upon arrival you are met by 13-year-old Sally Smith. She tells you that she is being abused by her father. He yells at her for the least little thing she does and won't allow her to go out with her friends. She is now grounded for two weeks for drinking beer and not allowed to leave the house except to go to school. She feels like she is being forcibly confined to the house like a prisoner. She hates her father and is thinking about running away or killing herself.

What will you do in this situation? Explain your authorities.

Case 3.4

You are a police officer. It is 11 p.m. when you receive information from Mrs. Noseworthy that her neighbours, the Simpsons, often leave their children alone when they go to work. Mrs. Noseworthy saw both parents leave the residence about two hours ago. They work the night shift at a factory. She heard some shouting and swearing coming from the Simpson residence. She asks you to attend the residence and see whether the children are all right.

You attend at the Simpson residence, where Amanda Simpson meets you at the door. She is 16 years old. She asks you to come into the house. You enter the living room where you notice a wine bottle on the coffee table. You tell her that you are there to determine whether everything is all right. She tells you that everything is fine. You ask whether her parents are at home. She tells you they work from 10 p.m. to 8:00 a.m. at the car plant. They are part of the cleaning staff. She looks after the house and her two brothers, 14-year-old John and 12-year-old Patrick, while her parents are at work.

You hear some shouting from the rear of the house. Amanda shouts: "Go back to sleep, you have to get up at six-thirty for school!" The voice tells her: "Shut up! Who made you the f'n queen!"

She shouts back, "The police are here, they are going to take you away if you keep swearing!"

Patrick Simpson, who is 12, enters the living room. He is in his underwear. He appears startled and exclaims, "Holy S#$%, it's the police!" Amanda tells him to watch his language. He apologizes and sits in a chair. The front door opens and a teenage male, later identified as 14-year-old John Simpson, walks into the living room. Amanda shouts at him, "Where were you? You are supposed to be in by ten-thirty. It's now twenty to twelve. You have school in the morning. You just wait until Mom and Dad are home. Now get to bed!"

John starts to say something but stops when he sees you. He asks, "Why are the police here?" Amanda tells him. John replies, "That nosy Mrs. Noseworthy! She is always spying on us!" Amanda tells the two boys to go to bed. They walk down the hallway, presumably to go to their bedrooms.

Amanda tells you that everything is all right. She has to make lunches for school tomorrow and finish her studying before going to bed. She tells you that she has to get up at 6 a.m. to make breakfast for the boys so that they will be ready to catch their bus at 7:15. She asks you if you would please leave now.

What will you do in this situation? Be sure to quote authorities.

Case 3.5

You are a police officer investigating a complaint of a child with a slingshot. You attend 67 Bruhau Street, the home of the child in question. You speak to Mr. Jones, the father of the child. A 10-year-old boy comes into the room.

Mr. Jones speaks to the boy: "Billy Jones, have you been shooting your slingshot at cars or windows?" The boy replies: "No sir, I shot a few birds and hung them in the barn with the rest, but I didn't hit no cars or houses!"

Mr. Jones asks you, "Exactly what is the problem, officer?" You tell him of the complaint, which was rather vague, and that you were concerned that the boy might inadvertently cause property damage. Mr. Jones tells you that he taught his son how to shoot a slingshot. He invites you to come to the barn to see his son's shooting abilities.

You attend the barn where you see approximately 100 birds hanging from the roof by strings. The birds are in varying states of decay and dismemberment. Mr. Jones proudly tells you that his son killed them all with his slingshot in just two weeks. He boasts that his son's skills are improving—Billy had killed only 50 in the previous two weeks.

Billy is holding a bird in his hand. He tells you, "I just shot this one while you were walking to the barn. See, still twitching!" Mr. Jones tells his son not to let the bird suffer. "Kill it the way I showed you." Billy then breaks the bird's neck by twisting its head.

Mr. Jones tells his son, "Hang it over in the corner with the others that you shot today. If you keep up the good shooting, today could be your record." He turns to you and states, "I'm real proud of that boy. A real killer. He'll be a great soldier, just like his old man."

What will you do in this situation? Be sure to quote authorities (if any). Your answer must demonstrate a thorough understanding of any pertinent legislation.

Case 3.6

You are a police officer responding to a call for assistance at a local shopping mall. Upon arrival you are met by security guard Jay Star. He tells you that there is a disturbance going on in front of a restaurant at the other end of the mall. While en route to the restaurant, Star tells you what he knows about the incident. He received a call from another security guard that two females were shouting at each other about an incident that happened in the restaurant. That is all the information he has to provide.

You arrive on the scene. There appears to be an argument between two females as described by Star. There are two other security guards present. They tell you that they have been keeping the females separated, but that they continue to shout and swear at each other. There are three small children beside one of the females. They are crying.

Security tells you that they told the females to leave the mall but one of them, identified as Linda Truman, refused to leave, telling them to call the police.

When you approach the females, Linda Truman tells you that she is glad to see you. She is angry and exclaims, "This bitch is abusing her children!" She is referring to the other female in the incident, identified as Sally Smith. Sally shouts, "Shut your f#$&* mouth! I wanted to leave, but that bitch threatened to call the Children's Aid Society and report that I was abusing my kid. I said I would stay until the police arrived because the CAS is a pain in the butt!" You tell them to stop shouting and ask them to explain what happened.

Linda tells you that she and Sally were in the restaurant drinking beer. Sally had her three children, ages three, four, and five, with her. Linda had about 6 or 7 bottles of beer. Sally had about 11 or 12 beers. One of the children asked for a glass of Pepsi. Sally said she wouldn't waste money on Pepsi and gave the child a drink of beer. The children complained that they were hungry and asked for some French fries. Smith again said she wouldn't waste money on restaurant food; there was food at home.

When one of the children began to cry, Sally slapped the child on the shoulder and told him to stop crying. Linda became upset and told Sally that she is not allowed to slap her children. She read something in a school policy that her child brought home from school about not being allowed to hit a child. Sally then called her a stupid cow, and said she didn't know anything about children. Sally added, "You have to hit them once in a while when they get out of line; not hard, just enough to let them know who's the boss!"

The two then began to argue. They were told to leave the restaurant, which they did. When security told them to leave the mall, Sally agreed but Linda refused, telling security to call the police. The security guards confirm that when Sally tried to leave, Linda threatened to call the Children's Aid Society and report the abuse. Sally said she would stay until the police arrived because the CAS is a pain in the butt.

Smith tells you that she did nothing wrong and that she wants to leave now.

What will you do in this situation? Explain your answer. Be sure to quote authorities.

APPENDIX 3A FORM 9, CHILD AND FAMILY SERVICES ACT

Form 9

Child and Family Services Act

WARRANT TO APPREHEND AND RETURN A CHILD WHO HAS WITHDRAWN FROM A PARENT'S CONTROL

Ontario Court   Court file no.
(Provincial Division)

at . . . .

. . . .

(address)

TO ALL CHILD PROTECTION WORKERS AND PEACE OFFICERS IN THE PROVINCE OF ONTARIO:

On the basis of an Information under subsection 43(2) of the *Child and Family Services Act*, which information is laid before me on oath of . . . .

❑   a parent of the child named or described on the back of this warrant,

❑   an authorized officer of an approved agency that has custody of the child,

❑   a person who has care and control of the child,

I am satisfied that the child is under sixteen years of age.

I am also satisfied, on the basis of that information, that the child has withdrawn from the care and control of a person described above without that person's consent. I am also satisfied, on the basis of that information, that the person described above believes on reasonable and probable grounds that the child's health or safety may be at risk if the child is not apprehended.

I am further satisfied, on the basis of that information, that the child has not withdrawn from the care and control of one parent with the consent of another parent in circumstances where a proceeding under section 36 of the *Children's Law Reform Act* would be more appropriate.

Check this box only if child's   ❑   I am further satisfied, on the basis of that Information, that the child may now
whereabouts are known   be found at (*Give a municipal address or a precise description of the premises where the child may be found.*)

. . . .

. . . .

. . . .

. . . .

I THEREFORE AUTHORIZE YOU to return the child to the child's parent

. . . . at . . . .

(name)   (address)

as soon as practicable and, where it is not possible to return the child to the parent within a reasonable time, to take the child to a place of safety as defined in the *Child and Family Services Act.*

This warrant further authorizes you to enter by force if necessary and to search . . . .

(Name and location of premises)

and to remove the child from it.

This warrant expires on the . . . . day of . . . . , 19 . . . .

. . . .

(Date)   (Signature of justice of the peace)

. . . .

(City, town, etc. where this Warrant signed)   (Print or type name of justice of the peace

Insert all available information

. . . .

Full name of child   Birth date (d,m,y)   Sex

. . . .

Aliases or nicknames

. . . .

Residential address   Telephone number

. . . .

Present location of child   Telephone number

. . . .

Height   Weight   Hair colour   Hair style   Eye colour   Complexion

. . . .

Other features

. . . .

Name and address of person to be contacted for further information   Telephone number

APPENDIX 3B   FORM 10, CHILD AND FAMILY SERVICES ACT

Form 10

Child and Family Services Act

INFORMATION IN SUPPORT OF A WARRANT TO APPREHEND AND RETURN A CHILD WHO HAS
WITHDRAWN FROM A PARENT'S CONTROL

Ontario Court   Court file no.
(Provincial Division)

at . . . .

. . . .

(address)

This is the Information of . . . . of

(Name of informant)

. . . .

(address)

1. I am   ❏ a parent of

❏ an authorized officer of an approved agency that has custody of

❏ a person who has care and control of

. . . . who was born on . . . .

(name of child)   (date)

2. On or about the . . . . day of . . . . , ...

(name of child)

withdrew from my care and control without consent by: . . . .

(describe circumstances)

3. I have reasonable and probable grounds to believe that if . . . . is not
apprehended his/her health or safety may be at risk, for the following reasons: (child's name)

(set out reasons) . . . .

. . . .

. . . .

. . . .

4. . . . . has not withdrawn from the care and

(name of child)

control of one parent with the consent of another parent in circumstances where a proceeding under section 36 of the *Children's
Law Reform Act* would be more appropriate.

(Do not complete if not applicable)

5. I have reasonable and probable grounds to believe that . . . .

(name of child)

may be found at . . . .

(address)   (street and number)   (municipality)

Sworn (or affirmed) before me this . . . . day
of   , 19   at

the . . . . of . . . .

(Signature of informant)

in the . . . . of

. . . .

. . . .

(A justice of the peace in and
for the Province of Ontario)

CHAPTER 4

Spousal Abuse

Chapter Objectives

After completing this chapter, you should be able to:

- Describe the types of spousal abuse.

- Identify the provisions of the *Criminal Code*, the *Family Law Act* of Ontario, and the *Children's Law Reform Act* of Ontario that apply to spousal abuse cases.

- Describe the various restraining orders available in situations of spousal abuse.

- Describe techniques for police intervention in spousal abuse situations.

- Describe criminal harassment and identify the provisions of the *Criminal Code* that apply to criminal harassment.

- Describe dating violence and identify drugs commonly used in dating violence.

INTRODUCTION

Spousal abuse is the physical, sexual, emotional/psychological, or financial abuse of one spouse by another. For the purposes of this chapter, **spouse** means any person involved in a relationship of cohabitation. Both women and men experience spousal abuse. Statistics Canada's *1999 General Social Survey on Victimization* (GSS) (Statistics Canada, 2000) indicates that 8 percent of women (690,000) and 7 percent of men in Canada (549,000) reported experiencing at least one incident of violence by a current or previous partner during the survey's five-year reporting period. Overall, this amounts to approximately 7 percent of adult Canadians.

spousal abuse
the physical, sexual, emotional/psychological, or financial abuse of one spouse by another

spouse
any person involved in a relationship of cohabitation

Abuse of Female Spouses

According to the GSS and Health Canada surveys, women and men experience similar rates of violent and emotional abuse in their relationships. However, the violence experienced by women tends to be more severe and is more likely to be repeated. For example, compared with men, women were

- six times more likely to report being sexually assaulted;

- five times more likely to report being choked;

- five times more likely to require medical attention as a result of an assault;

- three times more likely to be physically injured by an assault;

- more than twice as likely to report being beaten;

- almost twice as likely to report either being threatened with a gun or knife, or having a gun or knife used against them;

- much more likely to fear for their lives or be afraid for their children as a result of the violence;

- more likely to have sleeping problems, suffer depression or anxiety attacks, or have lowered self-esteem as a result of being abused; and

- more likely to report repeated victimization.

The surveys also found that women experience higher levels of certain types of emotional abuse than do men:

- Women were four times more likely to report being threatened, harmed, or having someone close to them threatened or harmed.

- Women were more than twice as likely to report having their property damaged or their possessions destroyed.

- Women reported a higher incidence of being isolated from family and friends.

- Women reported a higher rate of name-calling and put-downs.

Homicide data reveal that women are also at higher risk of being killed by their husbands. In the 10-year period of 1991–2000, homicides involving intimate partners accounted for 27 percent of all homicides in Canada. During that period, intimate partners killed 1,056 persons, but far more women were killed than men:

- Of the 846 women killed (80 percent of the total), 481 were killed by a current spouse, 185 by an estranged spouse, 177 by a boyfriend, and 3 by a same-sex partner.

- Of the 210 men killed (20 percent of the total), 161 were killed by a current spouse, 18 by an estranged spouse, 23 by a girlfriend, and 8 by a same-sex partner.

Abuse of Male Spouses

The abuse of the male partner in a heterosexual relationship has not received much attention. There have been only two regional surveys and one national survey conducted since 1989 on the problem of husband abuse in Canada. The results are compiled in *Husband Abuse: An Overview of Research and Perspectives* (Tutty, 1999). The findings of these surveys were consistent with Statistics Canada's findings that as many women admit to using violence as men.

However, front-line workers report seeing few men who have been harmed to the same extent as women who have been abused by men. This may be because men who may face violence in intimate relationships have few resources to access and because many do not report the abuse.

There are several possible reasons why men may not report being abused:

- *They fear that they won't be believed.* Men are stereotypically the abusers and it is difficult for many people, including the police, to believe that men can be the victims of their female partners.

- *They are ashamed.* Men are regarded as the physically stronger sex. Society sees a man who is beaten by his wife as weak.

- *They adopt a macho, "I can handle it" attitude.* Men who are abused by their intimate partners typically do not seek help in dealing with the emotional and physical impact of the violence because they feel that doing so is unmasculine.

- *They keep silent to avoid embarrassment and ridicule.* Not confiding in a friend, relative, or professional is a common reaction of both male and female victims of domestic abuse because it is embarrassing to be victimized. But men typically face a greater degree of disbelief and ridicule than do most women in this situation, which helps enforce the silence.

- *They cope by avoiding the abuser.* Men often escape a bad home life that they are afraid of by spending extra time at work, staying in "their" space at home (for example, the garage or den), or even sleeping in the car or at a friend's place.

- *They often have no place to go for help.* As of 1999–2000, there were no shelters in Canada that provided residential services exclusively to adult male victims of family abuse. In fact, 90 percent of facilities have a policy of not admitting males. There are a very limited number of shelters that provide services to men abused by their family.

Spousal Abuse Victims and Violent Offence Victims

A Statistics Canada report, *Family Violence in Canada: A Statistical Profile 2004* (Canadian Centre for Justice Statistics, 2004), indicates that spousal abuse victims represent roughly 1 in 5 (18 percent) of all violent offence victims. In 2002, women represented roughly 85 percent of victims who reported spousal abuse to police, while men represented approximately 15 percent of victims. These proportions have remained relatively stable since 1995, although the number of spousal assault cases reported to police increased for both women and men over this time period. The number of criminal harassment cases involving intimate partners has also increased since 1995.

More than 93 percent of charges related to spousal assault in Ontario are laid against men. Most charges laid against women are counter-charges laid by an assaultive partner or are charges that stem from acts of self-defence.

The Uniform Crime Reporting Survey (UCR2), a police-reported crime statistics survey, also found that women were more often the victims of violent assault than men (Canadian Centre for Justice Statistics, 2004). The survey found that

- for approximately two-thirds of women and men, the abuse was inflicted by current spouses;

- 39 percent of female victims and 32 percent of male victims in the 1999 GSS reported the occurrence of violence after separation;

- of those who reported post-separation violence, 24 percent stated that the assaults became more severe and 39 percent reported that the violence began only after separation; and

- female victims (59 percent) were three times more likely than male victims (20 percent) to report being physically injured during violent encounters with their former partners.

Discrepancies between victim survey and police data can be explained by the fact that women report more serious violence with more severe consequences and that women are more likely than men to report spousal violence to the police.

Table 4.1 affirms that women are far more likely to be the victims of spousal assault than men.

Characteristics of Spouses at Greater Risk of Abuse

There is no single, definitive class of persons that suffers from spousal abuse. But data from the 1999 GSS indicate that the following groups are at greater risk of experiencing spousal violence:

TABLE 4.1   Victims of Spousal Violence by Offence Type Reported to a Subset of Police Departments, 2002[1,2,3,4]

| | Total | | Sex of victim | | | |
| | | | Female | | Male | |
Type of offence	No.	%	No.	%	No.	%
Homicide/attempt	132	0	105	0	27	1
Sexual assault	521	2	514	2	7	0
Major assault (assault levels 2 & 3)	4,446	13	3,355	12	1,091	21
Common assault (assault level 1)	21,526	63	18,419	64	3,107	60
Criminal harassment	2,453	7	2,159	7	294	6
Uttering threats	4,167	12	3,592	12	575	11
Other violent offences[5]	862	3	809	3	53	1
Total offences	34,107	100	28,953	100	5,154	100

Note: Percentages may not add up to 100% due to rounding. 0 = true zero or a value rounded to zero.

1. Excludes incidents where the sex and/or the age of the victim was unknown.

2. Data are not nationally representative. Based on data from 94 police departments representing 56% of the national volume of crime in 2002.

3. Includes victims aged 15 to 89.

4. Spousal violence refers to violence committed by legally married, common-law, separated and divorced partners.

5. Other violent offences include robbery, unlawfully causing bodily harm, discharge firearm with intent, assault against peace-public officer, criminal negligence causing bodily harm, other assaults, kidnapping, hostage-taking, explosives causing death/bodily harm, arson, and other violent violations.

Source: Statistics Canada, Canadian Centre for Justice Statistics, *Incident-Based Uniform Crime Reporting (UCR2) Survey*. Catalogue no. 85-224-XIE, table 1.2.

- younger Canadians (15–24), particularly young women;

- persons living in common law relationships;

- persons whose partners abuse alcohol (indicated by periodic heavy drinking);

- persons living with very controlling and emotionally abusive partners;

- aboriginal women;

- women undergoing a separation; and

- pregnant women (the violence often starts during a first pregnancy).

Although the preceding persons may have a statistically higher risk of abuse, anyone—regardless of sex, age, race, ethnicity, education, socioeconomic status, occupation, religion, sexual orientation, physical or mental abilities, or personality—may be vulnerable to being abused.

National data on the prevalence of spousal abuse in same-sex relationships are not available.

CAUSES OF ABUSE

Explanations for the causes of abusive behaviour tend to fall into two main categories: psychopathological theory and social learning theory (O'Connor, 2004).

The key ideas of each theory are summarized below.

Psychopathological Theory

According to psychopathological theory, the offender is a mentally disturbed individual who also may be suffering from alcohol or drug addiction. The offender may be venting frustration or anger at a substitute target. The victim may be seen as mentally or emotionally disturbed through his or her tolerance of such behaviour. The victim may also be suffering from guilt, and may believe that he or she induced the spouse to inflict the abuse.

Two opponents of this theory, Richard M. Tolman and Larry W. Bennett (1992), reject the premise that the abuser is mentally disturbed:

> The psychological characteristics of batterers are extremely diverse, so much so that no one pathology can be linked to battering. Research shows that no personality traits or clinical factors set abusive men apart from the general population. This is supported by a recent study in which one in five Canadian men living with a woman admitted to using violence against his partner. Most men who assault their partners are not violent outside the home. They do not hit their bosses or colleagues. When abusive men hit their partners, they often aim the blows at parts of the body where bruises don't show. If [abusive] men were truly mentally ill, they could not selectively limit and control their violence.

Social Learning Theory

According to social learning theory. people learn social behaviours by observing the behaviours of others. Social learning theory addresses both the behaviour learned by the abuser and the behaviour learned by the victim. There are three variations of this theory: intergenerational transmission of violence, learned helplessness, and cycle of violence.

INTERGENERATIONAL TRANSMISSION OF VIOLENCE

The intergenerational transmission of violence version of learning theory asserts that adults learn violence by having seen abusive relationships as a child.

There are those who believe that statistical data does not support this version of social learning theory. For example, Margaret Cooper and Cathy Widom conducted research with the assistance of the Correctional Service of Canada (CSC) and found little support for the theory. Violent offenders were interviewed in an attempt to compile statistical data. The CSC, in its report *The Impact of Experiencing and Witnessing Family Violence During Childhood* (Alksnis & Taylor, 2002), refers to the findings of Cooper (1992):

> Based on the few prospective studies that do exist, numerous reviewers maintain that the majority of abused children do not continue the cycle of violence as adults. Even in childhood, the proportion of children who exhibit clinical levels of emotional/behavioural problems as a result of living with family violence is lower than one might expect: about one-third of boys and one-fifth of girls are in the clinical range.

The CSC report also discusses the finings of Widom (1989):

> Estimates of the proportion of abused children who then go on to abuse their own offspring are around 30 percent. Witnessing violence between parents is thought to be only modestly related to marital aggression in the second generation; about 16–17 percent of witnesses report aggression in their own intimate relationships.

LEARNED HELPLESSNESS

According to the learned helplessness version of social learning theory, the victim stays in the relationship because of perceived or real economic and emotional dependency.

CYCLE OF VIOLENCE

The cycle of violence version of social learning theory states that the victim makes excuses for the offender's behaviour and believes that the offender will change. The abuser promises that the abuse will never happen again, and the victim wants to believe that this is true. But because the victim does not adamantly condemn the behaviour, the abuser concludes that the behaviour will not lead to relationship breakdown. The abuser then continues the abuse (even though he or she may see the abuse as situationally wrong) and a cycle of violence is created.

CHARACTERISTICS OF ABUSIVE SPOUSES

Abusers come from all social groups and backgrounds, and from all personality profiles. However, some characteristics fit a general profile of an abusive spouse. Abusive spouses often

- are jealous—they imagine that the other spouse is having affairs;

- need to control the relationship and the other spouse;

- project personal faults onto the other spouse;

- have an explosive temper;

- seek to isolate the other spouse;

- tend not to trust other people and therefore tend not to share their inner world with others;

- have a limited or no social network (the partner is the closest person they know);

- are subject to depression, known only to the family;

- get their needs met by exerting control, often through violence and threats;

- may threaten suicide if their partner leaves;

- are frequently demanding and assaultive in sexual behaviour; and

- lack sympathy for their partner's physical and emotional pain.

A study by the Solicitor General of Canada, conducted through the Correctional Service of Canada, identified some additional common characteristics of abusers (Hanson & Wallace-Capretta, 2000):

1. *Traditional sex-role expectations.* The abuser holds very traditional, stereotyped views of male–female roles and relationships. The abuser tends to be preoccupied with a macho ideal of manhood. He feels a need to dominate and control women and often expects it as his right and privilege. He tends to associate weakness with femininity and fears intimacy, which makes him feel vulnerable.

2. *A tendency to objectify women.* The abuser does not see women as people. He sees women as property or sexual objects.

3. *Communication deficits.* The abuser is frequently lacking in assertive communication skills and is more inclined to resolve problems through violence.

4. *Poor impulse control.* The abuser tends to express all negative feelings as anger, which he initially suppresses. Finally, he "explodes" and releases his anger, primarily through violent behaviour.

5. *Low self-esteem.* Despite the bravado that many abusers display, abusers characteristically suffer from low self-esteem. The abuser often feels that he has not lived up to his concept of the male sex role and consequently overcompensates with hyper-masculinity. He becomes emotionally dependent on his partner and feels threatened by the possibility of his

partner's departure. This is often evident in his excessive jealousy and possessiveness.

6. *Alcohol and/or drug problems.* There is a high incidence of alcohol and drug abuse among abusers. The alcohol acts to reduce inhibitions, intensifying abusive incidents.

7. *Abusive childhood.* Often, the abuser has been exposed to abusive behaviour in the home at a young age. He may defend his behaviour as normal, although in most situations he tries to hide his actions.

8. Denial. The abuser tends to minimize and deny the abuse. Very much like the alcoholic, the abuser denies that there is a problem and refuses to accept responsibility for the abusive behaviour. The abuser blames everyone else for making him angry, thereby excusing his actions.

9. *False genuineness.* The abuser may be pleasant and charming to his partner between periods of violence, and is often seen as a nice guy to outsiders.

Some of these characteristics, such as poor communication skills, lack of impulse control, and alcohol/drug abuse, will often create problems for the abuser outside the spousal relationship. Abusers, for example, may have a history of brushes with the law because of their inability to control their anger. These brushes with the law are sometimes violent and can take the form of "disturbance incidents," in which the abuser is verbally and physically aggressive.

ASSESSING THE RISK OF ABUSE

Very few empirical studies have sought to distinguish risk markers for abuse—a particular set of characteristics that may be used to determine whether individuals are at risk of becoming abusive or becoming victims of domestic violence. Currently, there is no totally accurate assessment tool that can predict abusive behaviour.

However, studies have sought to identify the characteristics of individuals who are at risk of murdering their spouses. Jacquelyn Campbell (2001) has identified nine homicide risk factors, which a majority of domestic violence experts have acknowledged:

- access to or ownership of guns,

- use of weapons in prior abusive incidents,

- threats with weapons,

- infliction of serious injury in prior abusive incidents,

- threats of suicide,

- threats to kill,

- drug or alcohol abuse,

- forced sex with a female partner, and

- obsessive behaviour (such as extreme jealousy or dominance).

Campbell also developed a questionnaire to help individuals assess whether they are at risk of being killed by a current or former partner: the Danger Assessment Instrument (1985, 1988). It has been widely tested and forms the basis for many of the informal assessment methods currently used. One current risk assessment and management tool is that developed by Randall Kropp, Stephen D. Hart, Christopher D. Webster, and Derek Eaves (1995) at the BC Institute Against Family Violence. It is called the Spousal Assault Risk Assessment Guide (SARA).

The SARA is a clinical checklist of risk factors identified in research literature. It is intended to be an accessible tool for a full range of professionals, and contains what the authors consider a basic set of factors that should be considered when assessing risk of violence.

The SARA identifies a variety of important risk factors for offenders:

- a history of spousal assault,

- a criminal history,

- past assaults,

- jealousy,

- past use of weapons or death threats,

- recent escalation in the severity or frequency of the violence,

- violation of no-contact orders,

- minimization or denial of abusive behaviour,

- attitudes that support or condone assault,

- recent employment problems,

- substance abuse and dependence,

- recent suicidal or homicidal intent, and

- recent psychotic and/or manic symptoms or personality disorders.

The nature of the current offence can also indicate risk—for example, whether the assault was severe and/or involved sexual assault, whether weapons were used, or whether non-contact orders were violated. Importantly, considerations regarding risk must never be limited; factors unique to a particular case must always be considered. For example, has the individual shown violence toward animals? Does he come from a country where he has been the victim of political persecution?

Recognizing that police officers do not have ready access to much of this information, the Department of Justice Canada has initiated a contract with the British Columbia Institute Against Family Violence and Dr. P. Randall Kropp to create a risk-assessment tool called the Brief Spousal Assault Form for the Evaluation of Risk (B-Safer). This tool could be useful for criminal justice personnel in determining the degree of risk in cases of spousal violence. B-Safer is currently being tested by police officers at three sites: Vancouver, BC, Charlottetown, PEI, and Summerside, PEI.

TYPES OF ABUSE

As previously stated, there are four categories of abuse: physical abuse, sexual abuse, emotional/psychological abuse, and financial abuse. The following sections will describe these types of abuse.

Physical Abuse

physical abuse
the use of force in a way that injures a person or poses a risk of injury to a person

Although emotional and psychological abuse may be as destructive as, or more destructive than, physical abuse, physical abuse is the type most commonly responded to by the police. It may occur just once or it may happen repeatedly. **Physical abuse** is the use of physical force in a way that injures a person or poses a risk of injury to a person. It includes beating, hitting, shaking, pushing, choking, biting, burning, kicking, or assaulting with a weapon. Other forms of physical abuse may include rough handling, confinement, or any dangerous or harmful use of force or restraint. Below are types of abuse that constitute an offence under the *Criminal Code*:

- assault (s. 266),

- assault with a weapon or causing bodily harm (s. 267),

- aggravated assault (s. 268),

- forcible confinement (s. 279(2)).

Sexual Abuse

sexual abuse
engagement in any form of sexual activity with a person without the full consent of that person; includes all forms of sexual assault, sexual harassment, or sexual exploitation

Sexual abuse is engagement in any form of sexual activity with a person without the full consent of that person. It includes all forms of sexual assault, sexual harassment, or sexual exploitation. Forcing someone to participate in unwanted, unsafe, or degrading sexual activity, or using ridicule or other tactics to try to denigrate, control, or limit a person's sexuality is sexual abuse.

Sexual abuse includes:

- refusing to have sex with a spouse to get back at him or her;

- treating a spouse as a sex object;

- forcing a spouse to look at pornography;

- showing a lack of intimacy;

- being promiscuous, or sleeping around;

- being rough (may constitute an offence);

- forcing a spouse to engage in sexual activity in certain positions; and

- forcing a spouse to have sex (may constitute an offence).

Note that many of the above actions and behaviours do not constitute an offence.

POSSIBLE CRIMINAL OFFENCES: SEXUAL ABUSE

Some members of the public mistakenly believe that a person cannot be charged with sexual assault when the complainant is that person's spouse. Section 278 of the *Criminal Code* is very specific in addressing this issue.

SPOUSE MAY BE CHARGED: CRIMINAL CODE, SECTION 278

> A husband or wife may be charged with an offence under section 271, 272 or 273 in respect of his or her spouse, whether or not the spouses were living together at the time the activity that forms the subject-matter of the charge occurred.

Note that ss. 271, 272, and 273, cited in s. 278, describe the following offences: sexual assault; sexual assault causing bodily harm or with a weapon or third party threats; and aggravated sexual assault.

The issue of spousal consent is often raised in cases of sexual abuse, especially where the spouse did not adamantly refuse sexual advances. Under s. 265 of the *Criminal Code*, consent is not given if there is a threat or fear of harm. Further, the decision in *R v. Ewanchuk*, discussed below, affirms that consent is not given where there is a fear of physical violence.

NO CONSENT WHERE FEAR OF PHYSICAL VIOLENCE: R v. EWANCHUK

"There is no defence of implied consent to sexual assault. The absence of consent is subjective and must be determined by reference to the complainant's subjective internal state of mind towards the touching at the time it occurred. The complainant's statement that she did not consent is a matter of credibility to be weighed in light of all of the evidence including any ambiguous conduct. If the trier of fact accepts the complainant's testimony that she did not consent, no matter how strongly conduct may contradict her claim, the absence of consent is established. The trier of fact need only consider s. 265(3) if the complainant has chosen to participate in sexual activity or her ambiguous conduct or submission has given rise to doubt regarding the absence of consent. There is no consent where the complainant consents because she honestly believes that she will otherwise suffer physical violence. While the plausibility of the alleged fear and any overt expressions of it are relevant in assessing the complainant's credibility that she consented out of fear, the approach is subjective: *R v. Ewanchuk*, [1999], 1 SCR 330, 131 CCC (3d) 481, 22 CR (5th) 1." (*Martin's Annual Criminal Code*, 2005)

Emotional/Psychological Abuse

Emotional/psychological abuse is behaviour intended to control or instill fear in a person, cause a person to fear for his or her safety, or diminish a person's sense of self-worth. It can take the form of verbal attacks, verbal threats, criticism, social isolation, intimidation, or exploitation to dominate another person. Several examples of these abusive acts are listed below:

emotional/psychological abuse
behaviour intended to control or instill fear in a person, cause a person to fear for his or her safety, or diminish a person's sense of self-worth

- intimidating (may constitute an offence);

- ignoring (silence);

- name-calling;
- yelling;
- being sarcastic or critical;
- degrading a spouse and family;
- inappropriately expressing jealousy;
- lying;
- falsely accusing;
- walking away during a discussion;
- finding and verbalizing faults;
- commenting negatively about spouse's physical appearance;
- ignoring spouse's feelings;
- ridiculing spouse's beliefs;
- insulting or humiliating spouse in public;
- refusing to allow spouse's family and friends to visit;
- threatening to leave spouse;
- punishing children because of anger toward spouse (may constitute an offence);
- bragging to spouse about affairs;
- threatening suicide if spouse leaves;
- threatening to harm spouse (may constitute an offence);
- threatening to destroy property (may constitute an offence);
- threatening to take children if spouse leaves (may constitute an offence);
- engaging in actions intended to terrorize spouse, such as playing with firearms or knives and driving dangerously when the spouse and children are in the car (may constitute an offence);
- forcing spouse to perform degrading acts (may constitute an offence); and
- attempting to exert control over spouse—for example, by depriving spouse of sleep, food, or sex.

Note that many of the above actions and behaviours do not constitute an offence.

POSSIBLE CRIMINAL OFFENCES: EMOTIONAL/PSYCHOLOGICAL ABUSE

The actions listed below constitute emotional/psychological abuse, and the may be an offence under the *Criminal Code*:

- abduction (s. 283),
- assault (ss. 266, 267, and 268),

- sexual assault (ss. 271, 272, and 273),

- uttering threats (s. 264.1),

- intimidation (s. 423),

- criminal harassment (s. 264),

- mischief (s. 430),

- cruelty to animals (s. 446), and

- harassing or indecent phone calls (s. 372).

Financial Abuse

Financial abuse encompasses a wide range of activities that result in financial loss or harm to a person. Financial abuse includes stealing from or defrauding a partner; withholding money; manipulating or exploiting a person for financial gain; denying a person access to financial resources; or preventing a person from working.

financial abuse
actions that result in financial loss or financial harm to a person

POSSIBLE CRIMINAL OFFENCES: FINANCIAL ABUSE

The actions listed below constitute financial abuse, and they may be an offence under the *Criminal Code*:

- theft (s. 334),

- fraud (s. 380),

- false pretense (s. 362), and

- uttering a forged document (s. 368).

Other Possible Offences Relating to Spousal Abuse

The following is a list of other possible *Criminal Code* offences applicable to spousal abuse. The list is not exhaustive. The investigating officer must use his or her knowledge and judgment to identify which offences, if any, have been committed and determine an appropriate response:

- use of a firearm during the commission of an offence (s. 85),

- careless use of a firearm (s. 86),

- pointing a firearm (s. 87),

- possession of a weapon for a dangerous purpose (s. 88), and

- dangerous operation of motor vehicles, vessels, and aircraft (s. 249).

These offences are indictable for the purpose of arrest.

The abuse suffered by the victim is often a combination of abusive behaviours. Physical and sexual abuse is likely to be cyclical. Emotional/psychological abuse may be constant. The abusive situation generally follows the pattern described in the cycle of violence, discussed below.

THE CYCLE OF VIOLENCE

The cycle of violence is a model often used to describe the reoccurring situation of spousal abuse. The cycle is broken into the four stages, described below.

Stage One: The Occurrence

An abusive act has been carried out against the spouse. This act may not invoke police action—for example, emotional or psychological abuse. In the case of violence, the police will respond as directed by the solicitor general.

Stage Two: Reconciliation

The abuser will apologize to the victim. He or she may profess deep regrets about his or her actions. He or she may promise to never be abusive again. The abuser may be able to convince the victim that the abuse was the victim's fault. The victim may agree and promise not to provoke the abuser again. The abuser may also deny that any abuse took place or may claim that he or she doesn't remember committing the abuse.

Stage Three: The Calm or Honeymoon Period

The abuser and the victim put the incident behind them. The abuser has been forgiven for his or her actions or the victim has accepted responsibility, absolving the abuser of blame. The abuser will not be abusive during this stage. There may be romantic encounters and promises of a better life to come.

Stage Four: Tension-Building

The abuser begins to exhibit signs of abusive behaviour. Stress is building in the abuser's life. There has been no change in the abuser's psyche nor an intervention to address the initial problem of abuse. Whatever reason the abuser had for the previous abusive acts has not been dealt with. The abuser has not suffered any repercussions for his or her abusive behaviour. Minor incidents such as becoming upset over trivial matters may begin to occur. The tension (stress) begins to increase until the abuser lashes out and commits abuse again.

The cycle does not always go through all stages in all abusive relationships. There maybe continuous tension and abusive behaviour without any reconciliation or period of calm. This usually occurs in situations where the abuse has happened on several occasions and the abuser has not been held accountable. The cycle will perpetuate itself unless someone intervenes to stop it. Police intervention through arrest or the laying of charges is an effective way of telling the abuser that his or her actions will not be tolerated.

WHY DO WOMEN STAY?

Officers may find it difficult to understand why a spouse chooses to remain in the home with an abuser. But there are many explanations, ranging from fear of leaving to love for the spouse (Ochberg, 1998):

1. *Fear.* Many women fear that they will suffer even worse abuse if they leave their partner. Their fears are well founded. Women have a heightened risk of spousal homicide after marital separation.

2. *Shame.* Some women who bear the marks of physical abuse cannot bear to be seen in public. They would rather stay in the home than suffer the humiliation.

3. *Lack of resources.* Battered women often lack a support system due to isolation. Their family ties and friendships have been destroyed, leaving them psychologically and financially dependent on the abusive partner:

   a. Many women become isolated from friends and families. Either the jealous and possessive abuser isolates them, or the women avoid friends and family to hide the signs of the abuse. The isolation contributes to a sense that there is nowhere to turn.

   b. Many women have at least one dependent child. They stay in the abusive home for fear they will not be able to support the child on their own.

   c. Many women are not employed outside of the home. They fear not being able to support themselves.

   d. Many women have no property that is solely theirs. They fear they will not be able to find adequate housing.

   e. Some women lack access to cash or bank accounts. These women must depend on their spouse for the necessities of life.

   f. Many women fear that if they leave they will lose the children and joint assets.

   g. Many women fear they will face a decline in living standards for themselves and their children if they leave.

4. *Lack of finances/economic reality.* Economic dependence on the abuser is a very real reason for remaining in the relationship. Public assistance programs have been drastically reduced in some jurisdictions, and the programs that remain provide inadequate benefits.

5. *Lack of housing once the victim has to leave a shelter.* Although many women are able to escape immediate danger by fleeing to a shelter, this is not a permanent housing solution. Many women end up returning to their home and to the abuse because there is a real lack of housing available to them.

6. *Children.* Being a single parent can be a strenuous experience in the best of circumstances, and for most battered women, conditions are far from ideal. The enormous responsibility of raising children alone can be

overwhelming. Often, the abuser may threaten to take the children away from her if she even attempts to leave.

7. *Feelings of guilt.* Some abused women feel a sense of guilt:

   a. These women may believe that their husbands are sick or need their help. The idea of leaving produces feelings of guilt.

   b. Many battered women feel that the violence is their fault. They may feel that their behaviour somehow provokes the abuser's violence. If they would only be a better wife, they tell themselves, then he would change.

8. *Promises of reform.* The abuser promises that the abuse will never happen again, and the victim wants to believe that this is true.

9. *Sex-role conditioning.* Some women hold beliefs about sex roles that discourage them from leaving:

   a. Some women are taught to be passive and dependent on men.

   b. Some women do not believe that divorce is an appropriate alternative.

   c. Some women believe that a single-parent family is unacceptable. They choose to endure the abuse rather than deprive their children of a father in the home.

   d. The abuser rarely is abusive all the time. During the non-violent phases, he may fulfill the abused woman's dream of romantic love. She believes that he is basically a "good man." She may also rationalize that her abuser is basically good until something bad happens to him and he has to "let off steam."

10. *Religious beliefs.* Religious beliefs reinforce the commitment to marriage. Many faiths hold that the husband is head of the family and that it is a wife's duty to be submissive to him. This may be a powerful reason for staying in a destructive relationship.

11. *The sanctity of marriage.* Clergy and secular counsellors may see only the goal of saving the marriage at all costs, rather than the goal of stopping the violence.

12. *Societal acceptance/reinforcement of violence.* Many people turn a "deaf ear" to spousal abuse and believe that what goes on behind closed doors is a private matter.

13. *Love for spouse.* Most people enter a relationship for love, and that emotion does not simply vanish in the face of difficulty:

    a. After a battering, the abuser often is apologetic. The apologies and promises of reform are often perceived as the end of the abuse.

    b. Many women rationalize their abuser's behaviour by blaming stress, alcohol, problems at work, unemployment, or other factors.

Note that the above reasons for why women stay in abusive homes do not lessen the duty of police to intervene. An officer's duty is to assist the victim in any way legally possible. A victim's decision to stay in the home should have no bearing on an officer's response.

PARENTAL ABDUCTION OF CHILDREN AS A FORM OF PSYCHOLOGICAL ABUSE

In domestic disputes children are often used as pawns. Often, one partner will threaten to take the children away from the partner who has legal custody of them. Using children this way is a form of psychological abuse and may involve the commission of a criminal act, as described in ss. 283 and 282 of the *Criminal Code.*

ABDUCTION: CRIMINAL CODE, SECTION 283

(1) Every one who, being the parent, guardian, or person having the lawful care or charge of a person under the age of fourteen years, takes, entices away, conceals, detains, receives or harbours that person, whether or not there is a custody order in relation to that person made by a court anywhere in Canada with intent to deprive a parent or guardian, or any other person who has the lawful care or charge of that person, of the possession of that person, is guilty of

(a) an indictable offence and is liable to imprisonment for a term not exceeding ten years; or

(b) an offence punishable on summary conviction.

(2) No proceedings may be commenced under subsection (1) without the consent of the Attorney General or counsel instructed by him for that purpose.

"The intent to deprive of possession will exist whenever the taker knows or foresees that his or her actions would be certain or substantially certain to result in the parent being deprived of the ability to exercise control over the child. ... : *R v. Dawson,* [1996] 3 SCR 783, 111 CCC (3d) 1, 2 CR (5th) 121." (*Martin's Annual Criminal Code, 2005*)

ABDUCTION IN CONTRAVENTION OF CUSTODY ORDER: CRIMINAL CODE, SECTION 282

(1) Every one who, being the parent, guardian or person having the lawful care or charge of a person under the age of fourteen years, takes, entices away, conceals, detains, receives or harbours that person, in contravention of the custody provisions of a custody order in relation to that person made by a court anywhere in Canada, with intent to deprive a parent or guardian, or any other person who has the lawful care or charge of that person, of the possession of that person is guilty of

(a) an indictable offence and liable to imprisonment for a term not exceeding ten years; or

(b) an offence punishable on summary conviction.

(2) Where a count charges an offence under subsection (1) and the offence is not proven only because the accused did not believe that there was a valid custody order but the evidence does prove an offence under section 283, the accused may be convicted of an offence under section 283.

"The term 'detain' in this section means 'withhold' and thus the mere fact that a parent keeps a child longer than the prescribed access period would not necessarily constitute a withholding and thus a detention of the child. Further, to prove the requisite intent for the offence, there must be proof that the act was done for the express purpose of depriving the other parent of possession of the child. ... : *R v. McDougall* (1990), 62 CCC (3d) 174, 3 CR (4th) 112, 1 OR (3d) 247 (CA)." (*Martin's Annual Criminal Code, 2005*)

Defences for Abduction

Certain statutory and common law defences are available to the accused in parental abduction cases. Section 284 of the *Criminal Code* allows a defence based on the accused having obtained the permission of the custodial parent. However, s. 286 prohibits abduction based on the consent of the child.

Section 285 allows the defence of necessity (also a common law defence). The accused must establish that it was necessary to abduct the child in order to protect him or her from imminent harm, or that the accused was escaping imminent danger.

The officer investigating alleged parental abduction of children should try to establish whether a valid custody order is in place. It may be difficult to establish the order's validity because such orders are often amended and the complainant might fail to produce the amended copy. It is always possible that a complainant is trying to use the police to inflict damage on a former partner by maliciously reporting contravention of a custody order. This, of course, does not relieve the officer of his or her duty to ensure the safety and well-being of the child.

POLICE INTERVENTION IN SPOUSAL ABUSE SITUATIONS

In May 1982, the House of Commons Standing Committee on Health, Welfare and Social Affairs tabled its *Report on Violence in the Family: Wife Battering* (1982). In the report, the committee noted that police were being trained to generally avoid the arrest of a batterer unless he was found actually hitting the victim or unless the victim had suffered injuries that were severe and required a certain number of stitches.

Later that year, on July 8, 1982, the House of Commons unanimously adopted a motion encouraging all Canadian police forces to have their officers regularly lay charges in cases of wife beating.

Four years later, in 1986, the attorneys general and solicitors general of all jurisdictions in Canada issued directives or guidelines to police and Crown prosecutors concerning spousal abuse cases. These directives shared essentially the same objective: ensuring that spousal assaults were treated as a criminal matter. Police policies generally required officers to lay charges where they had reasonable grounds to believe that an assault had taken place. Crown policies generally required the prosecution of cases of spousal assault where sufficient evidence existed to support the prosecution. The victim's wishes were not considered.

The primary objectives of the charging policy for cases of spousal assault are:

- to remove from the victim the responsibility and blame for the decision to lay charges;

- to increase the number of charges that are laid in reported cases of spousal abuse;

- to increase the reporting of incidents where spousal abuse occurred; and

- to reduce the number of incidents of reoffence.

This directive included provisions requiring that police lay charges in incidents of spousal abuse if reasonable grounds existed. Further to this policy, the *Police Services Act* of Ontario requires that police services implement procedures regarding domestic violence.

REG. 3/99 OF THE POLICE SERVICES ACT OF ONTARIO

12(1) Every chief of police shall develop and maintain procedures on and processes for undertaking and managing general criminal investigations and investigations into ...

(d) domestic occurrences; ...

After the development of the directive in 1986, the Ministry of the Solicitor General of Ontario developed the Domestic Violence Justice Strategy (DVJS). It was developed in response to the inquest and 1998 recommendation of the May/Iles coroner's jury. The inquest dealt with the deaths of Randy Iles, who had a history of spousal violence, and his wife's cousin, Arlene May, with whom Iles had an intimate relationship. The DVJS includes a policing component, which sets out guidelines for the handling of domestic violence occurrences. These guidelines, contained in appendix 4A, supersede previous guidelines.

The DVJS, released in 2000, coordinates police response and the prosecution of domestic violence occurrences where offences have been identified. Not all of these strategies are yet implemented.

The policing component of the DVJS sets out guidelines that may enhance the effectiveness of police response to domestic violence occurrences. Within the content of the strategy is a requirement that police complete a Domestic Violence Supplementary Report (see appendix 4B at the end of this chapter). The report is used to identify risk factors for domestic violence and may be used to develop a risk assessment procedure, based on the circumstances of identified situations of domestic violence. This report is also used during a show-cause hearing as evidence to support pre-trial detention.

Note that police services are required to have domestic violence policies in place. Officers should follow the policies and procedures of their respective police services. The following information is general in content.

Public Safety

AUTHORITY TO ENTER A HOME: R v. GODOY

The following commentary on the Supreme Court of Canada decision in the case of *R v. Godoy* appears to give police officers the authority to enter a home by force if necessary if there is articulable cause to believe that a person's life is in danger.

"In *R v. Godoy*, [1999] 1 SCR 311, 131 CCC (3d) 129, 21 CR (5th) 205, 117 OAC 127, 235 NR 134 (SCC), the Supreme Court of Canada held that forced entry into a dwelling house in response to a disconnected 911 call did not violate s. 8. The common law duty of police to preserve life is engaged whenever it may be inferred that the 911 caller may be in distress. In this case, the accused had refused entry to the police responding to the 911 call. The forced entry of the apartment to locate the caller and determine the reason for the call constituted a justifiable use of police powers. The police do not, however, have a further authority to search the premises or otherwise intrude on a resident's privacy or property. The court did not consider the applicability of the plain view doctrine in such circumstances." (*Martin's Annual Criminal Code, 2005*)

Officer Safety

In cases of spousal abuse, the first priority of responding officers is their personal safety. The most dangerous aspect of the spousal abuse call is the approach and entry. Note that the brief discussion of officer safety presented here encompasses only the most elementary aspects of officer safety and does not provide sufficient information to ensure the safety of responding officers.

Ideally, two officers will attend domestic violence occurrences, but this is not always possible. For example, in remote OPP detachments, a back-up officer may not be available. Here, one officer will attend to protect the involved parties. However, the officer must assess the risk to his or her safety and determine whether he or she can safely intervene. In such cases, intervention beyond physical protection is generally not feasible.

Responding officers should assess the level of danger at each of the following phases of the response:

- *Approach.* Officers must ask themselves: Is backup available? How long until backup arrives? Officers must also watch the area for danger. Is the abuser outside the premises? Does the abuser possess a weapon? During the approach phase, officers must also consider issues of lighting, adapting to the dark, silhouetting, obstacles, and cover and concealment.

- *Entry.* Officers should use care in their positioning at doors. They should pay attention to windows, the roof, and any areas where someone could be concealed. Officers should not enter when directed by voice only; instead, they must wait for someone to come to the door. They must enter legally; observe the premises for dogs, weapons, and other dangers; be alert to the number of persons on the premises; and look for signs of alcohol and drug use (which can diminish inhibitions and increase the potential for violence). Officers should be aware that the potential for violence may increase because of their presence. The abused spouse may feel safer with the police around and lash out at the abuser because he or she knows that the police will not allow the abuser to retaliate.

- *Inside the premises.* Once inside, the officers should pay attention to the number of persons on the premises and their location. The officers should carefully observe their surroundings, looking for broken articles or other evidence of a struggle, potential weapons, and "blind" areas where someone could jump out at them. They must also check for injuries to any of the parties.

Other Concerns

Does the abused spouse require medical assistance? Does the abused spouse wish to leave the home? Also, the consumption of alcohol or drugs by one or both spouses may mean that the officer will not be able to engage the parties in rational discussion. Obtaining information from an emotionally traumatized victim of abuse or a victim who believes that he or she has caused the abuse can also be difficult.

THE INTERVENTION PROCESS

The following is an example of an intervention in a domestic dispute. It is an example only and may not apply to every situation. The intervening officer should be ready to improvise at any time. The officer can bring the process to a halt at any time by making an arrest.

The following guide is based on the assumption that the officer has safely and legally entered a residence where spousal abuse has been or is taking place. The intervention process has four parts: defusing the potential for violence, interviewing, mediating, and making a referral.

Defusing the Potential for Violence

The officer's first course of action is to defuse the potential for violence:

- The officer must use as little force as possible to intervene. Physical force and verbal commands directed toward one of the spouses may lead the other spouse to believe that the officer is on his or her side and may cause tempers to flare. (The officer also risks losing the image of impartiality that he or she may need to rely on at later stages of the intervention.)

- The spouse expressing the most anger should immediately be addressed. This may be an unpleasant task for the officer, but it will help defuse the situation more quickly.

- The parties must be separated and their eye contact with each other broken. The officer must not lose sight of his or her partner. The separation should be as brief as possible—simply long enough to gather the information required to understand the immediate problem. The parties may become agitated if separated too long, and this can exacerbate the situation. When separating the parties, the officer should avoid taking them to the kitchen (where weapons are available) or the bedroom (an intimate area where the abuse may have occurred). These are commonly recognized as the two most dangerous rooms in a residence for police officers to speak to disputing spouses.

- The officer should allow the parties to vent. Letting them shout or otherwise relieve their stress non-violently may assist at later stages when the parties are together. The officer should respond to their venting in a calm, reassuring manner. This shows them that the officer is in control and may be able to help.

When the threat of violence is no longer high, the parties should be brought back together. There is no particular time frame within which this should happen. The officer must use his or her judgment to determine whether the threat has sufficiently diminished. The parties should be brought within speaking and eye contact distance, but not allowed physical contact at this point, because violence is still a possibility.

The officer should remember that control of the situation, including the flow of conversation, can be influenced by his or her demeanour. Speaking to the parties in a calm, controlled manner will help give them confidence in the officer's abilities.

Interviewing

The potential for violence has been defused and the parties have been brought together to discuss their problem. The officer must remember that he or she is there to resolve a conflict as well as to gather information about a possible offence. This is where interviewing skills are important. The ability to defuse a situation and advise the parties of what resources are available to help them, and at the same time investigate a possible offence, is something that is learned through problem solving and lateral thinking. The following interview techniques may help the officer obtain the information necessary to decide on a course of action:

- *Direct the flow of conversation.* One officer should direct the flow of conversation. Who this will be should be decided before the interviewing starts. A prearranged signal will allow other officers at the interview to tell the interviewing officer that a detail is unclear, that further information is required, or that there are discrepancies in the information.

- *Control the conversation.* The interviewing officer should be firm and in control of the conversation, but not to the point of being authoritarian. If the officer treats the parties as suspects or tells them what they should be doing about their problem, they may feel as if they are being interrogated.

- *Place the more aggressive spouse in the most comfortable seat, with his or her hips below the knees if possible.* This makes it more difficult for the spouse to get up quickly, and thus enhances officer safety.

- *Set the rules of the conversation beforehand.* The officer should tell the parties that no interruptions or hostile words or actions will be tolerated.

- *Listen actively during the conversation* (see chapter 2, under the heading "Effective Listening"). The interviewing officer should speak only when necessary to direct the flow of the conversation or to clarify points that need immediate clarification. Care must be taken not to ask leading questions, which can damage the credibility of a statement that might later be needed as evidence. The interviewing officer must maintain absolute impartiality throughout the entire process.

- *Maintain the focus of the conversation on the problem.* The parties should direct their conversation toward solving their problem. The officers should politely decline to answer if asked for personal opinions.

- *Observe non-verbal communication.* Watching the body language of one spouse when the other is speaking can help an officer gauge the truthfulness of the spoken message or the degree of fear or intimidation that one spouse exerts over the other.

- *If the parties resume arguing, ensure that the situation does not become violent.* If it does, immediate arrest may be necessary.

Here are some tactics that can be used to interrupt an argument that threatens to escalate into violence. Most of these tactics rely on a temporary distraction.

- *Make a surprise request or comment.* Questions such as "May I have a glass of water?" or "What's cooking on the stove?" can focus the parties' attention on the officer.

- *Use eye contact to control the flow of conversation.* Through eye contact, the officer may be able to express displeasure with a spouse's conduct.

- *Consider shouting at the parties.* This tactic may work, but it is risky. They may see the officer's shouting as a loss of control and think that the situation is beyond help.

- *Interject with a summary of the problem.* When each party has had an opportunity to speak, the officer should summarize his or her understanding of the problem. The parties should then be asked whether the officer's understanding is accurate.

- *Do nothing.* Most people will expect the police to intervene. If the officer does nothing, the parties may feel uncomfortable arguing in front of an audience. The officer can use this tactic only if he or she is sure that neither party will assault the other. If the parties are separated, as described above, and properly positioned, they should not be able to make physical contact.

The officer must now decide whether the problem can be adequately addressed by the police or is beyond the scope of police intervention. The officer may decide to mediate if he or she believes that the problem can be satisfactorily handled on the spot.

Mediating

Many problems cannot be successfully mediated, but if the officer decides to use mediation, here are some suggestions that may help:

- *Use mediation when arrest is inappropriate or the problem is vague and the parties express an interest in resolving it.* Mediation can also be useful when the parties are still angry. It may not help resolve their problem, but it may give them time to get rid of their anger.

- *Remember that the parties caused the problem, and therefore they are the ones who must solve it.* The police can offer help, but cannot solve the problem. Police must not accept responsibility for the problem. It is possible that the parties will resist police attempts to get them to suggest their own solutions to their problem. There may be a perception that the police will solve the problem. The officer must therefore be persistent in advising the parties that they are responsible for arriving at a solution to their problem.

- *Address the less cooperative spouse.* This can be unpleasant but is more effective than devoting a lot of attention to the more cooperative spouse.

- *Accept the ideas proposed by the parties.* It is not the officer's place to criticize proposed solutions. The ideas may appear ludicrous, but at least the parties are talking.

- *Settle for partial agreement between the parties.* Total agreement between the parties is not necessary. A degree of compromise is at least a step in the right direction. Even if the officer cannot help the parties find a solution to their problem, they may still feel better because they have had an opportunity to discuss their problem.

Making a Referral

Mediation, whether successful or unsuccessful, is often followed by a referral to a community or social service agency. The officer should do the following before making a referral:

- *Determine whether the parties want assistance.* A forced referral is a waste of effort. The parties must genuinely want assistance if the agency is to be of any use.

- *Inform the parties about the agency's capabilities and limits.* The parties should be told that the agency may be able to help, not that the agency can solve their problem. If possible, the agency's address and telephone number should be provided, as well as information about any costs the parties might incur.

- *Obtain a commitment from the parties that they will seek help.* A commitment by the parties affirming that they will seek help places the onus on them to ensure that they do. It also corrects any perception they may have that it is the officer's responsibility to solve their problem.

When Mediation Is Not Appropriate

Many times, mediation is not the appropriate response. In situations where violent behaviour is evident, arrest is necessary. If arrest of the abuser is the appropriate response, the officer should explain to the abused spouse that removal of the abuser is a temporary reprieve. The abuser will be released from custody in the majority of cases. The abused spouse may use this temporary reprieve to make a decision. The officer should not offer legal advice, only information concerning criminal charges. Requests for an officer's opinion should be met with facts. For example, if the abused spouse asks, "Will he do it again?" an appropriate response is, "In most cases the abuser assaults the spouse again." It can be difficult to avoid becoming emotionally caught up in spousal abuse cases, but if the officer fails to be objective when assessing the situation and gathering evidence, the investigation may be hampered. It can be difficult to be objective and at the same time empathetic, but effective use of interpersonal skills makes this possible.

The abused spouse may not understand the process of charging the abuser. The abused spouse needs to be told that the police lay the charges and that the abused spouse does not have to initiate criminal proceedings. It is also important to mention that s. 4(5) of the *Canada Evidence Act* allows the abused spouse to be a competent witness for the Crown. The officer should explain that the abused spouse may have to testify in court if the abuser pleads not guilty. Sections 4(2) and (4) of the *Canada Evidence Act* identify situations where the wife or husband of a person charged with any of the identified offences is both a competent and compellable witness. The identified offences are offences of violence or offences against children.

The officer must ensure that he or she has gathered the necessary evidence to support the charges. Recording all pertinent information in the officer's notebook and having the abused spouse read and sign the notebook are one form of insurance against later recantation by the abused spouse. Obtaining a formal statement from the abused spouse after the abuser is in police custody is also desirable. Medical reports and photographs of injuries may be useful if the case goes to trial.

If charges are to be pursued, sometimes the abused spouse will contact the officer after a few days have passed to request that charges be withdrawn. This typically happens during the reconciliation stage or honeymoon period mentioned earlier, when the abuser may have said that the abuse will stop and never happen again. The officer will have a difficult and possibly unpopular decision to make. Recalling statistics on spousal abuse and homicide may assist the officer with his or her decision.

If there is sufficient evidence to substantiate a charge, the solicitor general's directive requires the police to lay an information.

If police are attending in situations where one spouse has decided to leave, their role is to ensure the safety of the involved parties. They may advise that the personal property of another may not be taken from the home. They may also recommend that only personal items be immediately removed and that the courts decide the legal entitlement to any joint property. The officers should not assist in the lawful removal of any personal property unless its removal is being interfered with. The officers' assistance should be rendered only to ensure the safety of all parties. The officers should not physically assist in the removal of any property. It may seem like the correct course of action to assist the distressed spouse but it is not. The officers should try to remain impartial and allow the parties to accept responsibility for their decisions. Physical assistance may be interpreted as confirmation of one spouse's decision and, therefore, as a loss of objectivity.

ENHANCING VICTIM SAFETY

The most effective method of stopping the abuser from causing further injury to the victim is to prevent the abuser from having contact with the victim. There are several court orders that can assist with this objective. Some require that both the victim and accused appear before the court. Such orders, although effective, may take some time to obtain.

"Protection orders," on the other hand, can be obtained immediately. Ontario's *Domestic Violence Protection Act* (DVPA) has provisions to obtain intervention orders in cases of domestic violence. These orders are issued under s. 3 of the DVPA, after a hearing.

Where the situation poses imminent danger to a person and would not allow time for the applicant to appear before the court, the DVPA has provisions for emergency intervention orders. Section 4(1) of the Act, below, describes the conditions that must be met before an emergency intervention order is issued. These orders may be issued by a designated judge or justice of the peace. Due to the urgent nature of the situation, the abuser is not required to be notified of the application.

EMERGENCY INTERVENTION ORDER: DOMESTIC VIOLENCE PROTECTION ACT, SECTION 4(1)

On application, without notice to the respondent, the court or a designated judge or justice may make an emergency intervention order if the court or designated judge or justice is satisfied on a balance of probabilities that,

> (a) domestic violence has occurred;

> (b) a person or property is at risk of harm or damage; and

> (c) the matter must be dealt with on an urgent and temporary basis for the protection of the person or property that is at risk of harm or damage.

The emergency order contains conditions that assist in protecting the applicant, which are described in s. 4(3) of the DVPA.

CONTENTS OF EMERGENCY INTERVENTION ORDER: DOMESTIC VIOLENCE PROTECTION ACT, SECTION 4(3)

An emergency intervention order may only contain a provision that the court could include in an intervention order under paragraph 1, 2, 3, 4, 5, 6 or 7 of subsection 3(2) which the court or designated judge or justice considers appropriate in the circumstances for the urgent protection of a person or property that is at risk of harm or damage.

Section 7(2) of the DVPA states that the court will prescribe the manner of service of the emergency order.

SERVICE: DOMESTIC VIOLENCE PROTECTION ACT, SECTION 7(2)

An emergency intervention order shall be served on the respondent in the prescribed manner.

The manner in which the order is served is set out in s. 7(1) of the DVPA (see page 153). Due to the urgent nature of the order, the contents of an emergency order will supersede other civil orders that may be in effect, as stated in s. 4(7) of the DVPA.

EMERGENCY INTERVENTION ORDER PREVAILS OVER CIVIL ORDERS: DOMESTIC VIOLENCE PROTECTION ACT, SECTION 4(7)

An emergency intervention order prevails over any order made under the *Children's Law Reform Act*, the *Divorce Act* (Canada) or the *Family Law Act* against or affecting the applicant or respondent or any child.

Other information concerning the emergency order is given is ss. 8(1) and 8(2) of the DVPA.

ORDERS IMMEDIATELY EFFECTIVE: DOMESTIC VIOLENCE PROTECTION ACT, SECTION 8(1)

An intervention order and an emergency intervention order are effective immediately upon being made.

NOT ENFORCEABLE WITHOUT SERVICE OR NOTICE: DOMESTIC VIOLENCE PROTECTION ACT, SECTION 8(2)

Despite subsection (1), an intervention order or an emergency intervention order is not enforceable against the respondent unless the respondent,

> (a) has been served with the order; or
>
> (b) has received notice of the order.

Under s. 4(8) of the DVPA, when either the applicant or the respondent requests a hearing to vary or terminate the order, the hearing will be conducted within 30 days of the request. The respondent will be notified and may be present.

RIGHT TO HEARING: DOMESTIC VIOLENCE PROTECTION ACT, SECTION 4(8)

Every emergency intervention order shall,

> (a) advise the applicant and the respondent that they are entitled to a hearing before the court for the purpose of asking for the variation or termination of the emergency intervention order if either one requests a hearing within 30 days after the respondent is served with the order; and
>
> (b) set out the procedures to be followed in order to make the request.

The applicant must be at least 16 years of age and falls into one of the categories listed in s. 2(1) of the DVPA.

APPLICANT: DOMESTIC VIOLENCE PROTECTION ACT, SECTION 2(1)

Subject to subsection (2), the following persons may apply for an intervention order or an emergency intervention order:

1. A spouse or former spouse, within the meaning of Part III of the *Family Law Act*, of the respondent.

2. A same-sex partner or former same-sex partner, within the meaning of Part III of the *Family Law Act*, of the respondent.

3. A person who is cohabiting with the respondent, or who has cohabited with the respondent for any period of time, whether or not they are cohabiting at the time of the application.

4. A person who is or was in a dating relationship with the respondent.

5. A relative of the respondent who resides with the respondent.

Upon application and finding of a situation of domestic violence as identified in s. 1(2) of the DVPA, the Superior Court of Justice may make a temporary or final intervention order. Section 3(2) describes what the order may include.

CONTENTS OF ORDER: DOMESTIC VIOLENCE PROTECTION ACT, SECTION 3(2)

An intervention order may contain any or all of the following provisions that the court considers appropriate in the circumstances for the protection of any person or property that may be at risk of harm or damage or for the assistance of the applicant or any child:

1. Restraining the respondent from attending at or near, or entering, any place that is attended regularly by the applicant, a relative of the applicant, any child or any other specified person, including a residence, property, business, school or place of employment.

2. Restraining the respondent from engaging in any specified conduct that is threatening, annoying or harassing to the applicant, a relative of the applicant, any child or any other specified person.

3. Requiring the respondent to vacate the applicant's residence, either immediately or within a specified period of time.

4. Requiring a peace officer, within a specified period of time, to accompany the applicant, respondent or a specified person to the applicant's residence and supervise the removal of that person's or another named person's belongings.

5. Restraining the respondent from contacting or communicating with the applicant or any other specified person, directly or indirectly.

6. Restraining the respondent from following the applicant or any other specified person from place to place, or from being within a specified distance of the applicant or other specified person.

7. Requiring a peace officer to seize,

    i.   any weapons where the weapons have been used or have been threatened to be used to commit domestic violence, and

    ii. any documents that authorize the respondent to own, possess or control a weapon described in subparagraph i.

8. Granting the applicant exclusive possession of the residence shared by the applicant and the respondent, regardless of ownership.

9. Requiring the respondent to pay the applicant compensation for monetary losses suffered by the applicant or any child as a direct result of the domestic violence, the amount of which may be summarily determined by the court, including loss of earnings or support, medical or dental expenses, out-of-pocket expenses for injuries sustained, moving and accommodation expenses and the costs, including legal fees, of an application under this Act.

10. Granting the applicant or respondent temporary possession and exclusive use of specified personal property.

11. Restraining the respondent from taking, converting, damaging or otherwise dealing with property in which the applicant has an interest.

12. Requiring the respondent to attend specified counselling.

13. Recommending that a child attend specified counselling at the respondent's expense.

Section 7(1) of the DVPA describes how the intervention order may be served.

SERVICE: DOMESTIC VIOLENCE PROTECTION ACT, SECTION 7(1)

An intervention order made by the court under section 3 or 6 shall be served on the respondent,

(a) by a peace officer, if the court so directs;

(b) by the applicant's counsel or agent;

(c) by the court, if the applicant was unrepresented before the court; or

(d) in any other prescribed manner.

There are other provincial orders available that may assist in protecting the victim. These are contained in the *Family Law Act* (FLA), *Children's Law Reform Act* (CLRA), and *Criminal Code*. The relevant sections of each of these acts are discussed below.

FAMILY LAW ACT

Orders Concerning Possession of the Home

One of the many concerns of an abused spouse is housing. The thought of leaving the family home may make the victim reluctant to leave the abusive environment. However, the courts have the ability to grant the victim interim possession of the home through the provisions of the FLA. By informing victims of this possibility, officers may be able to alleviate some of this fear. One of the factors that the court will consider in determining possession of the home is any occurrence of spousal or child abuse.

If spousal or child abuse has occurred, a court might give the applicant the exclusive right to live in the home. This order does not mean that the applicant now owns the home, only that he or she has the right to live there without the abusive partner until other arrangements are made.

Safety issues must be considered when contemplating a request for an interim possession order. The abuser will know where the victim lives. It may be advisable that the victim seek a non-contact order in conjunction with the interim possession order. The most common of these orders is a recognizance (also known as a peace bond), which is issued by a justice under the authority of s. 810 of the *Criminal Code*. This order is discussed below under the heading "Criminal Code."

ORDER FOR POSSESSION OF MATRIMONIAL HOME: FAMILY LAW ACT, SECTION 24(1)

Regardless of the ownership of a matrimonial home and its contents, and despite section 19 (spouse's right of possession), the court may on application, by order,

(a) provide for the delivering up, safekeeping and preservation of the matrimonial home and its contents;

(b) direct that one spouse be given exclusive possession of the matrimonial home or part of it for the period that the court directs and release other property that is a matrimonial home from the application of this Part;

(c) direct a spouse to whom exclusive possession of the matrimonial home is given to make periodic payments to the other spouse;

(d) direct that the contents of the matrimonial home, or any part of them,

(i) remain in the home for the use of the spouse given possession, or

(ii) be removed from the home for the use of a spouse or child;

(e) order a spouse to pay for all or part of the repair and maintenance of the matrimonial home and of other liabilities arising in respect of it, or to make periodic payments to the other spouse for those purposes;

(f) authorize the disposition or encumbrance of a spouse's interest in the matrimonial home, subject to the other spouse's right of exclusive possession as ordered; and

(g) where a false statement is made under subsection 21(3), direct,

(i) the person who made the false statement, or

(ii) a person who knew at the time he or she acquired an interest in the property that the statement was false and afterwards conveyed the interest,

to substitute other real property for the matrimonial home, or direct the person to set aside money or security to stand in place of it, subject to any conditions that the court considers appropriate.

TEMPORARY OR INTERIM ORDER: FAMILY LAW ACT, SECTION 24(2)

The court may, on motion, make a temporary or interim order under clause (1)(a), (b), (c), (d) or (e).

ORDER FOR EXCLUSIVE POSSESSION: CRITERIA—FAMILY LAW ACT, SECTION 24(3)

In determining whether to make an order for exclusive possession, the court shall consider,

(a) the best interests of the children affected;

(b) any existing orders under Part I (Family Property) and any existing support orders;

(c) the financial position of both spouses;

(d) any written agreement between the parties;

(e) the availability of other suitable and affordable accommodation; and

(f) any violence committed by a spouse against the other spouse or the children.

OFFENCE: FAMILY LAW ACT, SECTION 24(5)

A person who contravenes an order for exclusive possession is guilty of an offence and upon conviction is liable,

> (a) in the case of a first offence, to a fine of not more than $5,000 or to imprisonment for a term of not more than three months, or to both; and

> (b) in the case of a second or subsequent offence, to a fine of not more than $10,000 or to imprisonment for a term of not more than two years, or to both.

ARREST WITHOUT WARRANT: FAMILY LAW ACT, SECTION 24(6)

A police officer may arrest without warrant a person the police officer believes on reasonable and probable grounds to have contravened an order for exclusive possession.

Orders Concerning Harassment

The FLA also includes provisions allowing a spouse, former spouse, or same-sex partner to apply for an interim or final order prohibiting harassment.

"Court," in the sections of the FLA below, means the Ontario Court (Provincial Division) (Ontario Court of Justice), the Unified Family Court, or the Ontario Court (General Division) (Superior Court of Justice).

ORDER RESTRAINING HARASSMENT: FAMILY LAW ACT, SECTION 46(1)

On application, a court may make an interim or final order restraining the applicant's spouse, same-sex partner or former spouse or same-sex partner from molesting, annoying or harassing the applicant or children in the applicant's lawful custody, or from communicating with the applicant or children, except as the order provides, and may require the applicant's spouse or former spouse to enter into the recognizance that the court considers appropriate.

OFFENCE: FAMILY LAW ACT, SECTION 46(2)

A person who contravenes a restraining order is guilty of an offence and upon conviction is liable,

> (a) in the case of a first offence, to a fine of not more than $5,000 or to imprisonment for a term of not more than three months, or to both; and

> (b) in the case of a second or subsequent offence, to a fine of not more than $10,000 or to imprisonment for a term of not more than two years, or to both.

ARREST WITHOUT WARRANT: FAMILY LAW ACT, SECTION 46(3)

A police officer may arrest without warrant a person the police officer believes on reasonable and probable grounds to have contravened a restraining order.

CHILDREN'S LAW REFORM ACT

The CLRA has provisions to prohibit harassment in situations where child custody is at issue.

ORDER RESTRAINING HARASSMENT: CHILDREN'S LAW REFORM ACT, SECTION 35(1)

On application, a court may make an interim or final order restraining a person from molesting, annoying or harassing the applicant or children in the applicant's lawful custody and may require the person to enter into the recognizance or post the bond that the court considers appropriate.

OFFENCE: CHILDREN'S LAW REFORM ACT, SECTION 35(2)

A person who contravenes a restraining order is guilty of an offence and on conviction is liable to either or both a fine of $5,000 and imprisonment for a term of not more than three months for a first offence and not more than two years for a subsequent offence.

ARREST WITHOUT WARRANT: CHILDREN'S LAW REFORM ACT, SECTION 35(3)

A police officer may arrest without warrant a person the police officer believes on reasonable and probable grounds to have contravened a restraining order.

Upon arresting a person for a breach of any provincial orders under legislation such as the FLA or the CLRA police must follow the release provisions of s. 149(1) of the *Provincial Offences Act* (POA) of Ontario.

RELEASE AFTER ARREST BY OFFICER: PROVINCIAL OFFENCES ACT, SECTION 149(1)

Where a police officer, acting under a warrant or other power of arrest, arrests a person, the police officer shall, as soon as is practicable, release the person from custody after serving him or her with a summons or offence notice unless the officer has reasonable and probable grounds to believe that,

(a) it is necessary in the public interest for the person to be detained, having regard to all the circumstances including the need to,

(i) establish the identity of the person,

(ii) secure or preserve evidence of or relating to the offence, or

(iii) prevent the continuation or repetition of the offence or the commission of another offence; or

(b) the person arrested is ordinarily resident outside Ontario and will not respond to a summons or offence notice.

The POA allows police to detain an arrested person if the arresting officer has reasonable grounds to believe that the person will repeat the offence. If the arresting officer does not release the suspect, the suspect must be brought before the officer in charge according to s. 149(2) of the POA.

RELEASE BY OFFICER IN CHARGE: PROVINCIAL OFFENCES ACT, SECTION 149(2)

Where a defendant is not released from custody under subsection (1), the police officer shall deliver him or her to the officer in charge who shall, where in his or her opinion the conditions set out in clauses (1)(a) and (b) do not or no longer exist, release the defendant,

(a) upon serving the defendant with a summons or offence notice;

(b) upon the defendant entering into a recognizance in the prescribed form without sureties conditioned for his or her appearance in court.

The officer in charge may release after satisfying that release will not endanger any person or the public. If the officer in charge believes that the suspect poses a danger, or will repeat the offence, the suspect must be brought before a justice of the peace within 24 hours, as stated in s. 150(1) of the POA.

PERSON IN CUSTODY TO BE BROUGHT BEFORE JUSTICE: PROVINCIAL OFFENCES ACT, SECTION 150(1)

Where a defendant is not released from custody under section 149, the officer in charge shall, as soon as is practicable but in any event within twenty-four hours, bring the defendant before a justice and the justice shall, unless a plea of guilty is taken, order that the defendant be released upon giving his or her undertaking to appear unless the prosecutor having been given an opportunity to do so shows cause why the detention of the defendant is justified to ensure his or her appearance in court or why an order under subsection (2) is justified for the same purpose.

If the officer in charge believes the suspect poses a danger to the victim or the public, a "show cause" hearing must be held. In cases where a restraining order is violated, due diligence may require the Crown to ask the court to detain the suspect if it believes that there is any possibility of future violations of the order. This request for detention is made through a show-cause hearing, according to s. 150(4) of the POA, below. The Crown or officer in charge must present evidence to the justice that establishes that the suspect would pose a threat if he or she were released.

ORDER FOR DETENTION: PROVINCIAL OFFENCES ACT, SECTION 150(4)

Where the prosecutor shows cause why the detention of the defendant in custody is justified to ensure his or her appearance in court, the justice shall order the defendant to be detained in custody until he or she is dealt with according to law.

CRIMINAL CODE

Upon establishing reasonable grounds to believe that an assault has been committed, the officer will lay a criminal charge. If appropriate, the accused will be arrested. The accused will be released with conditions imposed within the authority of s. 515 of the *Criminal Code*, which deals with judicial interim release. These conditions may include non-harassment or non-communication provisions.

If the officer does not establish reasonable grounds, he or she will not pursue charges. However, if the victim fears harm from the abuser, the victim, or any person, may appear before a justice to request that a recognizance to keep the peace be issued. This recognizance is commonly referred to as a "peace bond."

Sworn testimony must be presented to the justice to establish the belief that harm will occur. When the information is accepted, the justice will issue a summons requiring that the accused appear before the court to answer to the allegations. Note that this is not a criminal proceeding. There is no determination of guilt or innocence of a criminal offence. The sections of the *Criminal Code* dealing with the recognizance and summons are reproduced below.

WHERE INJURY OR DAMAGE FEARED: CRIMINAL CODE, SECTION 810(1)

An information may be laid before a justice by or on behalf of any person who fears on reasonable grounds that another person will cause personal injury to him or her or to his or her spouse or common-law partner or child or will damage his or her property.

DUTY OF JUSTICE: CRIMINAL CODE, SECTION 810(2)

A justice who receives an information under subsection (1) shall cause the parties to appear before him or before a summary conviction court having jurisdiction in the same territorial division.

ADJUDICATION: CRIMINAL CODE, SECTION 810(3)

The justice or the summary conviction court before which the parties appear may, if satisfied by the evidence adduced that the person on whose behalf the information was laid has reasonable grounds for his or her fears,

(a) order that the defendant enter into a recognizance, with or without sureties, to keep the peace and be of good behaviour for any period that does not exceed twelve months, and comply with such other reasonable conditions prescribed in the recognizance, including the conditions set out in subsections (3.1) and (3.2), as the court considers desirable for securing the good conduct of the defendant; or

(b) commit the defendant to prison for a term not exceeding twelve months if he or she fails or refuses to enter into the recognizance.

CONDITIONS: CRIMINAL CODE, SECTIONS 810(3.1) AND 810(3.2)

(3.1) Before making an order under subsection (3), the justice or the summary conviction court shall consider whether it is desirable, in the interests of the safety of the defendant or of any other person, to include as a condition of the recognizance that the defendant be prohibited from possessing any firearm, cross-bow, prohibited weapon, restricted weapon, prohibited device, ammunition, prohibited ammunition or explosive substance, or all such things, for any period specified in the recognizance and, where the justice or summary conviction court decides that it is so desirable, the justice or summary conviction court shall add such a condition to the recognizance.

(3.2) Before making an order under subsection (3), the justice or the summary conviction court shall consider whether it is desirable, in the interests of the safety of the informant, of the person on whose behalf the information was laid or of that person's spouse or common-law partner or child, as the case may be, to add either or both of the following conditions to the recognizance, namely, a condition

> (a) prohibiting the defendant from being at, or within a distance specified in the recognizance from, a place specified in the recognizance where the person on whose behalf the information was laid or that person's spouse or common-law partner or child, as the case may be, is regularly found; and

> (b) prohibiting the defendant from communicating, in whole or in part, directly or indirectly, with the person on whose behalf the information was laid or that person's spouse or common-law partner or child, as the case may be.

BREACH OF RECOGNIZANCE: CRIMINAL CODE, SECTION 811

A person bound by a recognizance under section 83.3, 810, 810.01, 810.1 or 810.2 who commits a breach of the recognizance is guilty of

> (a) an indictable offence and liable to imprisonment for a term not exceeding two years; or

> (b) an offence punishable on summary conviction.

A breach of a recognizance issued under s. 810 of the *Criminal Code* is a dual procedure offence. For the purpose of arrest, the breach may be treated as an indictable offence. Under s. 495 of the *Criminal Code*, the accused may be arrested without a warrant. The release provisions of ss. 496 through 503 apply, as in any criminal offence.

Seizure of Firearms and Other Weapons

If the accused possesses firearms, and there are reasonable grounds to believe that the possession of firearms could pose a danger to the victim, and there is time to appear before a justice to obtain a warrant to seize the firearms, the provisions of s. 117.04(1) of the *Criminal Code* will apply.

APPLICATION FOR WARRANT TO SEARCH AND SEIZE: CRIMINAL CODE, SECTION 117.04(1)

> Where, pursuant to an application made by a peace officer with respect to any person, a justice is satisfied by information on oath that there are reasonable grounds to believe that the person possesses a weapon, a prohibited device, ammunition, prohibited ammunition or an explosive substance in a building, receptacle or place and that it is not desirable in the interests of the safety of the person, or of any other person, for the person to possess the weapon, prohibited device, ammunition, prohibited ammunition or explosive substance, the justice may issue a warrant authorizing a peace officer to search the building, receptacle or place and seize any such thing, and any authorization, licence or registration certificate relating to any such thing, that is held by or in the possession of the person.

Note also that if there is an immediate danger to the victim, police may seize the firearms without a warrant.

SEARCH AND SEIZURE WITHOUT WARRANT: CRIMINAL CODE, SECTION 117.04(2)

Where, with respect to any person, a peace officer is satisfied that there are reasonable grounds to believe that it is not desirable, in the interests of the safety of the person or any other person, for the person to possess any weapon, prohibited device, ammunition, prohibited ammunition or explosive substance, the peace officer may, where the grounds for obtaining a warrant under subsection (1) exist but, by reason of a possible danger to the safety of that person or any other person, it would not be practicable to obtain a warrant, search for and seize any such thing, and any authorization, licence or registration certificate relating to any such thing, that is held by or in the possession of the person.

In either situation, police must appear before a justice to determine the disposition of the items seized. If the seizure was made without a warrant, the officer must also establish the reasonable grounds for the seizure as set out in s. 117.04(3) of the *Criminal Code*.

RETURN TO JUSTICE: CRIMINAL CODE, SECTION 117.04(3)

A peace officer who executes a warrant referred to in subsection (1) or who conducts a search without a warrant under subsection (2) shall forthwith make a return to the justice who issued the warrant or, if no warrant was issued, to a justice who might otherwise have issued a warrant, showing

(a) in the case of an execution of a warrant, the things or documents, if any, seized and the date of execution of the warrant; and

(b) in the case of a search conducted without a warrant, the grounds on which it was concluded that the peace officer was entitled to conduct the search, and the things or documents, if any, seized.

If the suspect does not currently possess weapons and police want to prevent the suspect from obtaining them in the future, police can apply to a provincial court judge for an order under s. 111 of the *Criminal Code*, below. This order prohibits the person from possessing weapons where the court has reasonable grounds to believe that it is not in the interests of public safety for the person to possess weapons. This prohibition may last up to five years.

APPLICATION FOR PROHIBITION ORDER: CRIMINAL CODE, SECTION 111(1)

A peace officer, firearms officer or chief firearms officer may apply to a provincial court judge for an order prohibiting a person from possessing any firearm, crossbow, prohibited weapon, restricted weapon, prohibited device, ammunition, prohibited ammunition or explosive substance, or all such things, where the peace officer, firearms officer or chief firearms officer believes on reasonable grounds that it is not desirable in the interests of the safety of the person against whom the order is sought or of any other person that the person against whom the order is sought should possess any such thing.

Police may consider an application under s. 117.011(1) of the *Criminal Code*, below. When a person is prohibited from possessing weapons, this provision is designed to limit their access to weapons belonging to someone with whom they live or associate.

APPLICATION FOR ORDER: CRIMINAL CODE, SECTION 117.011(1)

A peace officer, firearms officer or chief firearms officer may apply to a provincial court judge for an order under this section where the peace officer, firearms officer or chief firearms officer believes on reasonable grounds that

(a) the person against whom the order is sought cohabits with, or is an associate of, another person who is prohibited by any order made under this Act or any other Act of Parliament from possessing any firearm, cross-bow, prohibited weapon, restricted weapon, prohibited device, ammunition, prohibited ammunition or explosive substance, or all such things; and

(b) the other person would or might have access to any such thing that is in the possession of the person against whom the order is sought.

In situations where the accused has been arrested and there is no immediate danger to the victim, police may ask that the accused be prohibited from possessing firearms as a condition of release. A justice, within the authority of s. 515(4.1) of the *Criminal Code*, may prohibit the accused from possessing firearms in situations where a violent offence has been committed.

CONDITION PROHIBITING POSSESSION OF FIREARMS, ETC.: CRIMINAL CODE, SECTION 515(4.1)

When making an order under subsection (2), in the case of an accused who is charged with

(a) an offence in the commission of which violence against a person was used, threatened or attempted,

(a.1) a terrorism offence,

(b) an offence under section 264 (criminal harassment),

(b.1) an offence under section 423.1 (intimidation of a justice system participant),

(c) an offence relating to the contravention of subsection 5(3) or (4), 6(3) or 7(2) of the *Controlled Drugs and Substances Act*,

(d) an offence that involves, or the subject-matter of which is, a firearm, a cross-bow, a prohibited weapon, a restricted weapon, a prohibited device, ammunition, prohibited ammunition or an explosive substance, or

(e) an offence under subsection 20(1) of the *Security of Information Act*, or an offence under subsection 21(1) or 22(1) or section 23 of that Act that is committed in relation to an offence under subsection 20(1) of that Act,

the justice shall add to the order a condition prohibiting the accused from possessing a firearm, cross-bow, prohibited weapon, restricted weapon, prohibited device, ammunition, prohibited ammunition or explosive substance, or all those things, until the accused is dealt with according to law unless the justice considers that such a condition is not required in the interests of the safety of the accused or the safety and security of a victim of the offence or of any other person.

COURT PROCESS

Although the victim may be initially relieved to know that police are required to lay charges, the prospect of facing their assailant in court may be daunting for some. This fear often manifests itself through the victim's hesitancy to testify. As the case moves into prosecution, the onus for successful prosecution is put on the shoulders of the victim. Because the courts consistently use a "best evidence rule," which requires that the most persuasive evidence available be used, most trials have relied on the victim's testimony. This practice has resulted in situations where, due to the pressures, threats, fear, and intimidation experienced by victims, many have refused to testify or have recanted their original story. Thus, although more assault charges have been laid by police since the introduction of provincial directives regarding domestic violence, increasing numbers of cases are being withdrawn by the Crown.

The Domestic Violence Court Process

To address the specific problems of prosecuting domestic violence cases, the Domestic Violence Court process was introduced. The process also allows the victim to have more input into the court's disposition of the offence.

This project first started in Toronto with the testing of two different specialized courts in an attempt to create a more effective criminal justice system response to spousal abuse. These courts have four objectives:

- to intervene early in domestic violence situations;

- to provide better support to victims throughout the criminal justice process;

- to more effectively prosecute domestic violence cases; and

- to hold offenders accountable for their behaviour.

There are two levels of court: a "plea court" and a criminal court. Which court will be used depends on the severity of the offence. Note: The term "levels" is for the purpose of this discussion only. It is not a legal term.

LEVEL 1: THE PLEA COURT

The plea court may be used where the offender and the victim wish to reconcile. A judge hears the domestic violence case in plea court if four conditions are met:

1. it is the first time that the accused has been charged with a domestic violence offence;

2. there are no visible injuries to the victim;

3. weapons were not used during the offence; and

4. the victim agrees to the court's disposition of mandatory treatment for the offender.

In the plea court process, a specialized Crown prosecutor does the screening. The Victim/Witness Assistance program consults with the victim and provides information and referrals to community resources. The accused then pleads guilty and is ordered to attend a Partner Assault Response (PAR) program. At the conclusion of the PAR program, a report is provided to the Crown. If satisfactory, that report can be considered as a mitigating factor in sentencing. But, the Crown usually recommends a conditional discharge. If the accused does not successfully complete the program, the criminal process is resumed.

LEVEL 2: THE CRIMINAL COURT

Level 2 is a regular criminal court. This court is used when any of the four conditions for participation in level 1 court have not been met, or when the offender did not satisfactorily complete the PAR program.

Expanding the Domestic Violence Court Process

Ontario has made a commitment to expand the Domestic Violence Court process. As of January 2005, 16 court jurisdictions had instituted specialized domestic violence processes. The provincial government has committed that all 54 court jurisdictions will have either a specialized court with designated staff to handle domestic violence cases or a regular court with a specialized process for doing so. All jurisdictions, regardless of size, will have a specialized process with the following components:

- a Domestic Violence Court Advisory Committee to support the work of the specialized domestic violence court process;

- interpreters to help non-English and non-French speakers communicate with police, Crown prosecutors, and victim support staff;

- enhanced investigative procedures for police (including use of a risk indicator tool, currently under development and initial testing);

- designated victim/witness assistance staff specially trained to give support and information to victims;

- designated Crown prosecutors specially trained in prosecuting domestic violence cases, to produce consistency and continuity;

- specialized counselling programs for abusive partners; and

- specialized processing to expedite cases and ensure coordination of services.

At medium-sized and small rural sites, these components may be implemented differently based on the volume of cases and the size of the jurisdiction. For example, rather than designated staff or a dedicated courtroom, specially trained staff may be used.

CRIMINAL HARASSMENT

Reports of **criminal harassment**, also known as stalking, should be taken seriously. The stalker has shown by his or her actions that he or she intends to intimidate, harass, or in some instances harm the person being stalked or that person's family or property. In cases of spousal abuse the stalker has already shown a propensity toward violence. Stalking behaviour should be treated as a serious threat to the well-being of the spouse. The abuser is expressing contempt for the spouse through premeditated criminal behaviour. He or she has constructed a plan of intimidation. Relevant sections of the *Criminal Code* concerning criminal harassment are set out below.

CRIMINAL HARASSMENT: CRIMINAL CODE, SECTION 264(1)

No person shall, without lawful authority and knowing that another person is harassed or recklessly as to whether the other person is harassed, engage in conduct referred to in subsection (2) that causes that other person reasonably, in all the circumstances, to fear for their safety or the safety of anyone known to them.

PROHIBITED CONDUCT: CRIMINAL CODE, SECTION 264(2)

The conduct mentioned in subsection (1) consists of

(a) repeatedly following from place to place the other person or anyone known to them;

(b) repeatedly communicating with, either directly or indirectly, the other person or anyone known to them;

(c) besetting or watching the dwelling-house, or place where the other person, or anyone known to them, resides, works, carries on business or happens to be; or

(d) engaging in threatening conduct directed at the other person or any member of their family.

PUNISHMENT: CRIMINAL CODE, SECTION 264(3)

Every person who contravenes this section is guilty of

(a) an indictable offence and is liable to imprisonment for a term not exceeding ten years; or

(b) an offence punishable on summary conviction.

Criminal harassment may be considered to be an indictable offence for the purpose of arrest.

Statistics on Criminal Harassment in Canada

The most current Statistics Canada police and court data relating to criminal harassment are given below:

- In total, 9,080 criminal harassment incidents were reported to a sample of 123 police forces in Canada in 2002. This number accounts for slightly over 4 percent of all violent incidents reported to those police forces that year.

- Of the victims, 76 percent were female.

- Female victims tended to be younger than male victims. Of the female victims, 42 percent were under 30 years of age; of the male victims, only 27 percent were under 30 years of age.

- Of the accused, 84 percent were male.

- Of the female victims, 31 percent were criminally harassed by a current or former intimate partner; slightly fewer female victims were harassed by an acquaintance or a friend (23 percent each).

- Of the male victims, 39 percent were criminally harassed by a casual acquaintance, while only 13 percent were stalked by a current or former intimate partner.

- 66 percent of all criminal harassment incidents occurred at the victim's home.

- Although victims almost always suffered emotional harm, physical injury was recorded by the police in less than 2 percent of all cases.

Types of Stalkers

Most stalkers fit into one of three broad categories: intimate partner stalkers, delusional stalkers, and vengeful stalkers (O'Connor, 2005).

INTIMATE PARTNER STALKERS.

The intimate partner stalker is usually the person who "can't let go." About 50 percent of all stalkers fall into this category. Most of these stalkers have been in some form of relationship with the victim. The contact may have been minimal, such as a blind date, but more commonly the contact involved a prolonged dating relationship, common law union, or marriage. These are people (usually male) who refuse to believe that a relationship has really ended. Often the victim feels sorry for them and unwittingly encourages them by trying to "let them down easy," or agreeing to talk "just one more time." This type of stalker mounts a campaign of harassment, intimidation, and psychological terror. In many respects, intimate partner stalking is an extension of domestic violence and relates to a desire to control a former partner.

DELUSIONAL STALKERS

Delusional stalkers frequently have little, if any, contact with their victims. They may be casual acquaintances (27.9 percent) or unknown to the victim (8 percent) (Statistics Canada, 2000). They may have a serious mental illnesses such as schizophrenia. Delusional stalkers hold tight to some false belief that keeps them tied to their victims.

The stalker may have come from a physically or emotionally abusive family background. Delusional stalkers are usually unmarried and socially immature loners, unable to establish or sustain close relationships with others. They rarely date and have had few, if any, sexual relationships. Because they are both threatened by and yearn for closeness, they often pick victims who are unattainable—for example, a married woman, a clergyman, a therapist, a doctor, or teacher. Those in the helping professions are particularly vulnerable to delusional stalkers. Any kindness may be converted into a delusion of intimacy.

Two forms of delusions experienced by this type of stalker are erotomania and love obsessional delusions. In erotomania stalking incidents, the majority of stalkers are male. The stalker's delusional belief is that the victim loves him and is having a relationship with him, although they might never have met. The person about whom this conviction is held is usually of a higher status than the stalker. The victim could be his supervisor at work, his child's pediatrician, his church minister, or the police officer who stopped him for a traffic violation but did not charge him. Sometimes it can be a complete stranger.

The love obsessional stalkers, on the other hand, can be obsessed in their love without possessing the belief that the victim loves them. These stalkers know they are not having a relationship with their victim, but firmly believe that if they pursue him or her hard enough and long enough, he or she will come to love them in return.

VENGEFUL STALKERS

Vengeful stalkers are angry with their victims over something, real or imagined. Politicians, for example, are harassed by many of these types of stalkers, who become angry over, say, some piece of legislation that the politician supports. Disgruntled ex-employees may stalk their former bosses, co-workers, or both. Some vengeful stalkers are psychopaths; others are delusional (and often paranoid), and all are convinced that they are the true victims. They stalk to "get even." In general, the less of a relationship that actually existed prior to the stalking, the more mentally disturbed the stalker.

Cyber-Stalking and Online Harassment

Criminal harassment can be conducted through the use of a computer. Not all such complaints of cyber-stalking fall within the definition of criminal harassment. For example, "cyber-stalking" or "online harassment" may refer to

- direct communication through email;
- Internet harassment, where the offender publishes offensive or threatening information about the victim; and
- unauthorized use, control, or sabotage of the victim's computer.

Cyber-stalking can include delivering threatening or harassing messages through one or more of the following online mediums:

- email,
- chat rooms,
- message boards,
- newsgroups, and
- forums.

Other variations of cyber-stalking include the following:

- sending inappropriate electronic greeting cards;

- posting personal advertisements in the victim's name;

- creating websites that contain threatening or harassing messages to the victim or that contain provocative or pornographic photographs, which the stalker relates in some way to the victim;

- sending viruses to the victim's computer;

- using spyware to track website visits or record keystrokes that the victim makes; or

- sending harassing messages to the victim's employer, co-workers, students, teachers, friends, customers, family, or place of worship, or sending harassing messages forged in the victim's name to others.

In some situations, criminal harassment charges may be appropriate. Depending on the activity involved, *Criminal Code* charges under ss. 342.1 (unauthorized use of a computer), s. 342.2 (possession of device to obtain computer service), and s. 430(1.1) (mischief in relation to data) should also be considered.

Harassing and Indecent Telephone Calls

Some stalkers use the telephone in their attempts to maintain control over their victim. Calling and then hanging up, making repeated calls, and making indecent calls can be criminal offences under ss. 372(2) and 372(3) of the *Criminal Code*.

INDECENT TELEPHONE CALLS: CRIMINAL CODE, SECTION 372(2)

Every one who, with intent to alarm or annoy any person, makes any indecent telephone call to that person is guilty of an offence punishable on summary conviction.

HARASSING TELEPHONE CALLS: CRIMINAL CODE, SECTION 372(3)

Every one who, without lawful excuse and with intent to harass any person, makes or causes to be made repeated telephone calls to that person is guilty of an offence punishable on summary conviction.

Because indecent and harassing telephone calls are both **summary conviction offences**, the police must find the suspect committing the offence before they can arrest, according to s. 495 at the *Criminal Code*. The frequency and content of the telephone calls determine what action the police will take. Calls can be traced, although this may be more difficult if the suspect is calling from a cellphone or pay phone. The victim should be asked to keep a record of calls received. Alternatively, the victim can change his or her telephone number or use a call display feature to screen calls. Any call that meets the definition of the **indictable offence** of threatening in s. 264.1 of the *Criminal Code* may provide a basis for arrest if there is proof of the identity of the person who conveyed the message or caused it to be conveyed.

summary conviction offence
a crime that is less serious than an indictable offence and that is tried without a jury or preliminary hearing

indictable offence
a crime that is more serious than a summary conviction offence, that carries heavier penalties, and that may be tried by a judge or a judge and jury

Intervention in Cases of Criminal Harassment

When deciding on a method of intervention, police must remember that the safety of the victim is paramount at all times and is a higher priority than evidence gathering (Department of Justice Canada, 2004). To determine the appropriate level or type of intervention in a given case, a threat assessment or risk assessment is first made.

A threat assessment assesses the risk of violence that the suspect poses to the victim and assesses the potential impact of the type of intervention on the victim's safety.

A risk assessment evaluates individuals to determine the risk that they will commit violent acts. The aim of research in this area is to develop intervention strategies to reduce this risk. Risk assessments are contextual and only relevant for a specific period of time. The absence of violence or threats of violent behaviour does not mean that violence will not occur in the future. Note that the terms "threat assessment" and "risk assessment" are often used interchangeably.

The assessment should include the following information: the type of stalker, and the history or nature of the relationship between the stalker and the victim (for example, a history that includes acts of violence, threats, and damage to property). A history of violent behaviour is a strong indicator of the stalker's potential for future violence. Threat assessments should consider all available evidence, as well as all records of police action.

After the threat assessment has been completed, an investigation and case management strategy should be devised and put into action. Several such stragegies are discussed below. Note that they can be used alone or in combination, depending on the specifics of the case.

(The Department of Justice Canada is currently supporting the development of a revised risk assessment tool, which will be piloted at three sites. This revised tool is designed to assess risk for spousal assault in criminal and civil justice settings, but it will likely also provide useful information for criminal harassment cases involving former domestic relationships.)

Intervention Options

POLICE WARNING

A police warning may consist of a face-to-face meeting with police and/or a written warning. A meeting with police may affect the suspect's state of mind, and the victim's safety. This type of intervention should be carried out only after police have considered all the facts and evidence, and only at the appropriate stage of the investigation. Warning the alleged offender serves two purposes: it shows the victim that the police have taken their complaint seriously, and it informs the offender that his or her behaviour is unacceptable. A warning also gives the offender an opportunity to explain his or her conduct at an early stage, so that police can make well-informed case management decisions in the future.

Stalkers are often deterred by a face-to-face meeting with police in which the police lay out the consequences of continuing the behaviour. In a small number of cases, particularly those involving mentally disordered stalkers, the best option may be to not take action and instead monitor the situation. In these cases, if the victim or police respond, the stalker may escalate his or her stalking behaviour.

When police are monitoring a situation, they must consider consulting mental health professionals, who may provide additional information and insight into possible behaviours that may emerge in the mentally ill person. Note that with this option police are not ignoring the situation. Instead, they have simply decided that a warning may not be the best option.

On the other hand, if a warning is to be used, the suspect should be cautioned before the interview and the interview documented so that the information is accessible to future investigators, should the warning prove to be ineffective. The interview can provide information about the suspect's thought processes and behaviour patterns. It can also provide admissions or corroboration. The most common psychological defences of a stalker involve minimization, denial, and projection of blame onto the victim. Investigators should keep this in mind as they develop interrogation themes and attempt to establish a rapport with the offender.

Whenever possible, the warnings should be written. Police must carefully consider the content of the warning. A written warning establishes boundaries for the offender and provides a record and evidence of the exact wording used to warn the accused. The written warning, although not legally binding, could be used to establish that the accused understood that the victim was harassed, or that the accused was reckless or wilfully blind to this fact.

PEACE BONDS AND CIVIL PROTECTION ORDERS

These non-contact orders were discussed previously in this chapter. In situations of criminal harassment, these orders may be an effective deterrent.

The seeking of peace bonds and civil protection orders as a method of intervention should be considered when the victim fears for his or her safety and the suspect poses a risk of physical violence, but there is insufficient evidence to charge the suspect. Peace bonds and civil protection orders are not substitutes for criminal charges. Charges should be laid where there is evidence to support the charges.

SEIZURE OF FIREARMS

Police may choose to intervene by seeking an order to seize any firearms that the harasser owns. With the safety of the victim being paramount, police should consider applying the same firearms prohibition and seizure provisions of the *Criminal Code* that are applicable in spousal abuse situations:

- s. 117.04,
- s. 111,
- s. 117.011, and
- s. 515(4.1) (if suspect is arrested).

ARREST AND CHARGES

A strong and consistent response to criminal harassment requires that all allegations of criminal harassment be taken seriously. If there are reasonable and probable grounds to believe that the suspect has committed the offence of criminal harassment, arrest and charges are applicable.

Where one or more of the incidents giving rise to the complaint of criminal harassment can be construed as a single criminal offence other than criminal harassment, police should consider laying both the separate charge and the inclusive count of criminal harassment. Examples of other criminal offences under the *Criminal Code* include, but are not limited to, the following:

- intimidation (s. 423),

- uttering threats (s. 264.1),

- mischief (s. 430),

- indecent or harassing telephone calls (section 372),

- trespassing at night (s. 177),

- assault (s. 265),

- sexual assault (s. 271),

- failure to comply with a condition of undertaking or recognizance (s. 145(3)),

- breach of recognizance (s. 811), and

- failure to comply with a probation order (s. 733.1).

An accused who has outstanding charges against him or her and has contravened, or was about to contravene, his or her form of release should be arrested for criminal harassment, and the provisions of s. 524(2) of the *Criminal Code* should also be applied.

ARREST OF ACCUSED WITHOUT WARRANT: CRIMINAL CODE, SECTION 524(2)

Notwithstanding anything in this Act, a peace officer who believes on reasonable grounds that an accused

(a) has contravened or is about to contravene any summons, appearance notice, promise to appear, undertaking or recognizance that was issued or given to him or entered into by him; or

(b) has committed an indictable offence after any summons, appearance notice, promise to appear, undertaking or recognizance was issued or given to him or entered into by him,

may arrest the accused without warrant.

The accused will be brought before a justice (generally) or judge, depending on the original offence, as described in s. 524(3) of the *Criminal Code*.

HEARING: CRIMINAL CODE, SECTION 524(3)

Where an accused who has been arrested with a warrant issued under subsection (1), or who has been arrested under subsection (2), is taken before a justice, the justice shall

(a) where the accused was released from custody pursuant to an order made under subsection 522(3) by a judge of the superior court of criminal jurisdiction of any province, order that the accused be taken before a judge of that court; or

(b) in any other case, hear the prosecutor and his witnesses, if any, and the accused and his witnesses, if any.

Under s. 524(8) of the *Criminal Code*, the justice will cancel the original release document and order that the accused be detained in custody unless the accused can show cause why he should be released (reverse onus).

POWERS OF JUSTICE AFTER HEARING: CRIMINAL CODE, SECTION 524(8)

Where an accused described in subsection (3), other than an accused to whom paragraph (a) of that subsection applies, is taken before the justice and the justice finds

(a) that the accused has contravened or had been about to contravene his summons, appearance notice, promise to appear, undertaking or recognizance; or

(b) that there are reasonable grounds to believe that the accused has committed an indictable offence after any summons, appearance notice, promise to appear, undertaking or recognizance was issued or given to him or entered into by him,

he shall cancel the summons, appearance notice, promise to appear, undertaking or recognizance and order that the accused be detained in custody unless the accused, having been given a reasonable opportunity to do so, shows cause why his detention in custody is not justified within the meaning of subsection 515(10).

This section may be useful in detaining the accused in custody, thus enhancing the pre-trial safety of the victim.

DATING VIOLENCE

Dating violence is any intentional physical, sexual, or psychological attack on one partner by the other in a dating relationship. Although both men and women may both be abusive, the abuse of women by men is more pervasive and usually more severe. Between 16 and 35 percent of women surveyed say they have experienced at least one physical assault by a male dating partner (Rodgers, 1994).

dating violence
any intentional physical, sexual, or psychological attack on one partner by the other in a dating relationship

Physical and Sexual Abuse in Dating

Physical abuse against a person includes shoving, slapping, choking, punching, kicking, biting, burning, hair pulling, using a weapon, threatening with a weapon, or forcibly confining.

Typically, men use physical force to assert control, whereas women use it to protect themselves, to retaliate, or to prevent an attack that they fear their partner is about to commit.

Sexual abuse includes unwanted sexual touching, using force or pressure to get a partner to consent to sexual activity, rape and attempted rape, and attempting or having intercourse with a person who, due to the influence of alcohol or drugs, cannot fully consent to the act. These kinds of abuse are more often directed at women.

Date Rape Drugs

Some sexual offenders use drugs to subdue a victim. The use of drugs to overcome the victim may make investigation of the offence more difficult. The victim may not recall much of the incident due to the amnesic effects of the drug. The following information describes some of the drugs used by sexual offenders.

"Date rape" drugs are substances such as Rohypnol (pill form), gamma-hydroxybutyrate (GHB) liquid form, and ketamine. They're usually slipped unnoticed into drinks at bars, clubs, and parties. The drugs are used to incapacitate or reduce the inhibitions of the victim. Some drugs leave the victim weakened, helpless, or unconscious—unable to escape or resist or to call for help. When the drug wears off, memory may be impaired.

The most commonly used drug is alcohol. Alcohol may be combined with other drugs to assist in overcoming any resistance by the victim.

These drugs are discussed in more detail below.

KETAMINE

Ketamine has many street names, including purple, Special K, kit kat, and Super K. The drug takes effect very soon after ingestion, and the effects last approximately six hours. It causes a dissociative state, which has been described as a "near death" experience. The drug also affects balance, judgment, and the ability to communicate. An overdose causes the victim to experience difficulty breathing. It can be fatal if mixed with alcohol or other drugs.

Ketamine is used as a veterinary and medical anesthetic. It comes as a clear liquid (like water), and it has been reported that it can also come in a white crystalline powder form.

During recovery, which may take as long as 48 hours, the individual may experience reactions such as vivid dreams, confusion, excitement, and, occasionally, hallucinations. He or she may also display irrational behaviour.

ROHYPNOL

Rohypnol is the brand name for flunitrazepam, a benzodiazepine drug—the same family of medications as Valium, Halcion, and Xanax. Benzodiazepines have been used for the treatment of anxiety and sleep disturbances and in anesthesia. It is illegal to make or sell Rohypnol in Canada or the United States.

The drug has no detectable taste or colour, and it takes effect within one hour of ingestion. The effects include feelings of intoxication and relaxation, visual disturbances, and loss of control.

As with most other illicit drugs, Rohypnol is known by several street names, including Ruffies, Roofies, Rophies, Roches, Roaches, La Rochas, Rib, Forget Pill, Poor Man's Quaalude, R-2s, Circles, Mind-Erasers, and Mexican Valium.

GHB

GHB is gamma-hydroxybutyrate. It is a powerful drug that acts as a depressant on the central nervous system. Because it is rapidly metabolized by the body, its effects can be felt within 15 minutes. It is a colourless, odourless liquid that has a salty taste.

GHB causes reduced inhibitions and drowsiness. Other side effects can include dizziness, nausea, vomiting, confusion, seizures, respiratory depression, and coma. In some cases, GHB can also cause amnesia. When GHB is taken with alcohol or other drugs, the consequences may be life-threatening.

Date Rape Drugs and the Criminal Code

Intentionally drugging a person to prevent or reduce the possibility of resistance to unwanted sexual activity is a criminal offence. Section 246 of the *Criminal Code*, below, sets out the offence. This offence appears to be more prevalent in dating situations than in spousal abuse situations.

OVERCOMING RESISTANCE TO COMMISSION OF OFFENCE: CRIMINAL CODE, SECTION 246

Every one who, with intent to enable or assist himself or another person to commit an indictable offence,

(a) attempts, by any means, to choke, suffocate or strangle another person, or by any means calculated to choke, suffocate or strangle, attempts to render another person insensible, unconscious or incapable of resistance, or

(b) administers or causes to be administered to any person, or attempts to administer to any person, or causes or attempts to cause any person to take a stupefying or overpowering drug, matter or thing,

is guilty of an indictable offence and liable to imprisonment for life.

Studies of the prevalence of sexual abuse in dating are less clear-cut than studies of the prevalence of other physical abuses. This is in part because the definition of sexual abuse varies within the general population. However, one 1994 survey that used the *Criminal Code* definitions of sexual assault found that 37 percent of Canadian women had experienced at least one sexual assault since the age of 16 (Roberts, 1994). Another survey reported that four out of five female undergraduates at Canadian universities said they had been victims of violence in a dating relationship. Of that number, 29 percent reported incidents of sexual assault (DeKeseredy and Kelly, 1993).

Police should intervene in dating violence as in any act of violence. Charges should be laid and measures taken to enhance the victim's safety.

Emotional Abuse in Dating

Emotional abuse may occur in dating relationships. It can include insults, profanity, belittling remarks, and threats. It may also include destroying a dating partner's property or possessions, isolating him or her from relatives and friends, and treating him or her with extreme possessiveness or jealousy. Emotional abuse reflects the abuser's desire to control the dating partner's behaviour. The abuser seeks to erode the partner's self-confidence and thereby lessen his or her ability to act independently (Thorne-Finch, 1992).

Both women and men may use emotional abuse to control their dating partners. Men, however, are more likely to escalate the abuse if they believe that they are losing control. When the emotional abuse is no longer effective, abusers will sometimes turn to physical violence in an attempt to reassert control.

KEY TERMS

criminal harassment   physical abuse

dating violence   sexual abuse

emotional/psychological abuse   spousal abuse

financial abuse   spouse

indictable offence   summary conviction offence

REFERENCES

Alksnis, C., & Taylor, J. (2002). *The Impact of experiencing and witnessing family violence during childhood: Child and adult behavioural outcomes.* http://www.csc-scc.gc.ca/text/pblct/fv/fv04/toce_e.shtml.

Campbell, J. (1985, 1988). Danger assessment instrument. http://www.vawprevention.org/research/instrument.shtml.

Campbell, J. (2001). Issues in risk assessment in the field of intimate partner violence: What practitioners need to know. Paper presented at an International Conference on Children Exposed to Domestic Violence, Our Children Our Future: A Call to Action, London, ON.

Canada. House of Commons. Standing Committee on Health, Welfare and Social Affairs. (1982). *Report on violence in the family: Wife battering.* Ottawa: Author.

Canada Evidence Act. (1985). RSC 1985, c. C-5.

Canadian Centre for Justice Statistics. (2004). *Family violence in Canada: A statistical profile 2004* (catalogue no. 85-224-XIE). Ottawa: Statistics Canada.

Canadian Centre for Justice Statistics. (2004). *Uniform crime reporting survey.* Ottawa: Statistics Canada.

Children's Law Reform Act. (1990). RSO 1990, c. C.12.

Cooper, M. (1992). *Current and future effects on children witnessing parental violence: An overview and annotated bibliography series on interpersonal violence report no. 1.* Vancouver: BC Institute Against Family Violence.

Criminal Code. (1985). RSC 1985, c. C-46, as amended.

Department of Justice Canada. (2004). *Criminal harassment: A handbook for police and crown prosecutors.* http://canada.justice.gc.ca/en/ps/fm/pub/harassment/index.html.

Domestic Violence Protection Act, 2000. (2000). SO 2000, c. 33.

Family Law Act. (1990). RSO 1990, c. F.3.

Hanson, R.K., & Wallace-Capretta, S. (2000). *A multi-site study of treatment for abusive men. User report 2000-05.* Ottawa: Department of the Solicitor General of Canada.

Kropp, P.R., Hart, S.D. , Webster, C.D., & Eaves, D. (1995). *Manual for the spousal assault risk assessment guide,* 2nd ed. Vancouver: BC Institute Against Family Violence.

Martin's Annual Criminal Code, 2005. (2005). Aurora, ON: Canada Law Book.

Ochberg, F. (1998). *Understanding the victims of spousal abuse.* http://www.giftfromwithin.org/html/spousal.html.

O'Connor, T.R. (2004). *Intimate violence.* http://faculty.ncwc.edu/toconnor/300/300lect05.htm.

O'Connor, T.R. (2005). *The psychology of violence, intimidation and hate.* http://faculty.ncwc.edu/toconnor/psy/psylect08.htm.

Ontario. Ministry of the Solicitor General and Correctional Services. (1994). *Policing standards manual.* Toronto: Author.

Police Services Act. (1990). RSO 1990, c. P.15.

Provincial Offences Act. (1990). RSO 1990, c. P.33.

Roberts, J. (1994). Criminal justice processing of sexual assault cases. *Juristat: Service bulletin, 14*(7), 1. Ottawa: Canadian Centre for Justice Statistics.

Rodgers, K. (1994). Wife assault: The findings of a national survey. *Juristat: Service Bulletin, 14*(9), 3. Ottawa: Canadian Centre for Justice Statistics.

Statistics Canada. (2000). *1999 general social survey on victimization.* Ottawa: Author.

Thorne-Finch, R. (1992). *Ending the silence: The origins and treatment of male violence against women.* Toronto: University of Toronto Press.

Tolman, R.M., & Bennett, L.W. (1992). A review of quantitative research on men who batter. In R.K. Hanson and L. Hart (Eds.), *Evaluation of treatment programs for male batterers: Conference.* Ottawa: Ministry of Solicitor General.

Tutty, L. (1999). *Husband abuse: An overview of research and perspectives.* Ottawa: Health Canada, Family Violence Prevention Unit.

Widom, C.S. (1989). Does violence beget violence? A critical examination of the literature. *Psychological Bulletin, 106,* 3–28.

EXERCISES

True or False

_____ 1. The majority of abused spouses call the police the first time they are abused.

_____ 2. Psychological spousal abuse is not as damaging as physical spousal abuse.

_____ 3. Abusive spouses are unlikely to stop their abusive behaviour without police intervention.

_____ 4. A person cannot be convicted of sexually assaulting his or her spouse.

_____ 5. Within the provisions of the _Family Law Act_, a police officer may apply for a restraining order on behalf of an abused spouse.

_____ 6. The arrival of the police on the scene of a domestic dispute can trigger an escalation of violence between the spouses.

_____ 7. The _Family Law Act_ authorizes restraining orders only for those who are legally married.

Multiple Choice

1. Section 265 of the _Criminal Code_ relates to the following type or types of abuse:

    a. physical

    b. emotional

    c. psychological

    d. all of the above

2. A restraining order under s. 46 of the _Family Law Act_ of Ontario may be obtained by:

    a. the officer investigating the case

    b. the accused

    c. the victim

    d. a social worker on behalf of the victim

3. A restraining order under s. 35 of the _Children's Law Reform Act_ of Ontario may be obtained by:

    a. the officer investigating the case

    b. the accused

    c. the victim

    d. a social worker on behalf of the victim

4. A "peace bond" under s. 810 of the *Criminal Code* may be obtained by:

    a. the officer investigating the case

    b. the victim

    c. a social worker on behalf of the victim

    d. all of the above

5. A violation of s. 810 of the *Criminal Code* is an offence of the following kind for arrest purposes:

    a. summary conviction

    b. indictable

    c. dual

    d. provincial

Short Answer

1. What are some common characteristics of abusive spouses?

2. List three actions characteristic of persons who commit emotional spousal abuse.

3. List three actions characteristic of persons who commit psychological spousal abuse.

4. Explain the four stages of the cycle of violence in cases of spousal abuse.

5. When there is insufficient evidence to pursue criminal charges in a case of spousal abuse, what possible alternatives does the justice system offer?

6. Describe the tools provided by the *Criminal Code* and other statutes for halting the actions of stalkers.

7. Explain the directive of the solicitor general regarding the laying of charges by police in domestic violence situations.

Case Analysis

Case 4.1

You are a police officer responding to a complaint of harassment. You attend the residence of Maggie Jones, who tells you that her boyfriend, Don Smith, has been harassing her. Don was living with her until three days ago, when, during an argument about her teenage daughter, he struck her in the face several times. Maggie called her brothers, who threw Don out of the house and told him not to return. Since then Don has been calling her constantly. During the past two days he has called her about 50 times to ask her forgiveness and tell her that he wants them to be together again. Maggie also tells you that Don has been sitting in his car outside her house on several occasions, but drives away when she comes out of the house. She is afraid that Don is unstable and may try to hurt her or her daughter.

Using the CAPRA system, describe what you would do in this situation.

Case 4.2

You are a police officer responding to a disturbance call at 123 Robie Street. The call was placed by an anonymous person from a nearby pay phone. On arrival, you find that the residence is quiet. You go to the door, and a teenage boy who identifies himself as Chris Wilson answers and invites you inside. You ask whether there is any problem, but before Chris can answer, a man who identifies himself as Chris's father, Tex, shouts, "What the hell are you doing here? How did you get in? Leave the boy alone!" Chris remains silent and walks away as his father approaches.

Tex appears extremely agitated. You ask whether anything is wrong. He tells you, "Everything is fine. What the hell are you doing here?" You explain that you received a disturbance call. He becomes enraged and begins shouting at you, "Get the hell out! I don't want you in my house! Damn police! Who the hell do you think you are! I'm going to sue you! Get out! Get out!" Tex crosses the room and opens the front door, telling you to "get the hell out of my house and don't come back! I can look after my family!"

What do you do in this situation? Explain your obligations as a police officer and be sure to mention the relevant laws.

Case 4.3

John and Jane have divorced. A custody order has been issued allowing Jane visitations with their daughter, Jill, on Saturdays from 10 a.m. to 6 p.m.

You, a police officer, receive a call at 7 p.m. on Saturday from John. Jane has not returned with Jill. You attend the scene. Upon your arrival at 9:15 p.m., Jane is just pulling into the driveway. John is incensed and wants Jane charged with child abduction in contravention of a custody order. Jane tells you that she knows she is late, but the service at the pizza place where they had dinner was slow. She tells you that the child prefers to be with her anyway.

What will you do in this situation? Be sure to quote authorities.

Case 4.4

You are a police officer responding to a call for assistance at 456 Perth Street, the residence of Ruthie and George Smith. You are met by Ruthie Smith and Hazel Taylor. Ruthie tells you that her husband, George Smith, is in the living room and that she wants him to leave. You enter the living room, where you meet two males, later identified as George Smith and Harry Wesson.

George appears to be very upset; he asks you why you are there and says that he doesn't want any trouble. You ask about the situation. George tells you that Ruthie is leaving him for Hazel. Hazel interjects: "Ruthie and I have been together for two years. He knew and didn't care!" George replies: "I don't care what you both do, I just want my boys!"

Hazel tells George that she and Ruthie are going to raise his sons. George replies: "There is no way I am going to allow my sons to be raised in a homosexual home!"

Harry then begins to shout at Hazel, telling her that what she is doing is immoral and unnatural and that she is going to hell.

George tells Ruthie that she can have the house, the cars, all their retirement money, and whatever else she wants. All he wants is to have his sons with him. Ruthie tells him that he can't have the children and that she and Hazel will give them a good home. He can come and visit when all the support details have been ironed out. She tells him that there is nothing wrong with a homosexual relationship and that she loves Hazel more than she ever loved him. George doesn't reply. But Harry does. He tells Ruthie that she is sick and that she disgusts him.

George then asks Ruthie: "Where are the boys?" She tells him that they are safe and that he can see them when they get the support payments sorted out and she is granted custody. George replies; "You are never going to get custody! Where are the boys?" Ruthie refuses to tell him, saying only that they are in a safe place. George is extremely upset and says, "You sent them to your mother's, didn't you?" Ruthie again replies: "They are in a safe place." George turns to you and states: "Her mother lives in England. She must have sent the boys to England!"

You ask Ruthie about the location of the children. Ruthie replies: "I can't tell you until we settle some legal matters such as support. Also, George hits the kids. I can't protect them if he knows their location."

George protests: "I never hit my sons!"

Harry shouts, "You're a liar! George never hit the boys!"

Explain what you will do in this situation. Be sure to quote authorities.

Case 4.5

You are a police officer. You have been dispatched to 123A Portage Street regarding a call of possible domestic violence. The information was received from a neighbour in the adjoining townhouse at 123B Portage Street. The caller reported that she heard screaming and what sounded like furniture being overturned.

Upon arrival at 123A Portage Street, you are unable to hear anything out of the ordinary. All is quiet except for the sound of a television. You ring the doorbell. Mr. James MacKinnon answers the door.

You ask whether there is anything wrong. He tells you that nothing is going on and tells you to "go away."

You ask to speak with Mrs. MacKinnon.

He tells you, "She doesn't want to speak with any cops. Now get out of here!"

What will you do in this situation? Be sure to quote authorities.

Case 4.6

You are a police officer responding to a domestic dispute at 789 Main Street, the Furr residence. An OMPPAC check reveals that police have attended the residence regarding similar complaints nine times in the past six months; no one has been charged.

Upon arrival you hear shouting and swearing from inside the residence. You knock on the door but receive no answer; the shouting and swearing continue. You again knock on the door, this time a male, later identified as Jack Furr, answers the door. He appears to be highly intoxicated. His speech is slurred when he asks you: "What the hell do you want?" You tell him that you received a call for assistance from this residence. He replies, "Nobody from this house called the police. Now get the F#$%* off my property!"

You hear a voice in the background asking, "Who is at the door?"

Jack replies, "It's the F#$%* police. They said that someone called." The voice, later identified as Lucy Furr, replies, "I called, let them in!" Jack says to you, "Then come on in, you F#$%* pig!"

You enter the home. The living room is a mess. There are beer bottles and cans everywhere. Pizza and takeout food containers are littered across the floor and furniture. Sitting in the corner of the room is Lucy. She beckons you to come and speak with her.

As you speak with Lucy, it becomes obvious that she is highly intoxicated. She asks you to come and sit beside her. You decline and ask her why she called. She tells you that her husband, Jack, is abusing her. He shouts and swears at her and calls her "a lazy bitch." She is sick of it and wants him out. Jack interjects, saying that all she does is sit around drinking and ordering takeout food. He adds, "She's a lazy bitch."

The two begin to argue. You interrupt and tell Lucy that you are not going to take her husband from the home because no offence has taken place. She replies that Jack is abusing her. You explain that what has happened is not a police matter, because insulting someone is not illegal. She replies, "Well then. He slapped me across the face a couple of weeks ago!" Jack protests: "I never hit you!"

What will you do in this situation? Be sure to quote authorities.

Case 4.7

Joe Smiley moved to a small community to retire. While buying groceries, he met Janice Burke, a cashier at the store. During the course of their conversation at the checkout, Burke told Smiley that she lived in a farmhouse approximately 20 kilometres from town. He commented about how frightening it must be to live alone, but not to worry, he was not a stalker.

Three days later Smiley again spoke with Burke while paying for groceries. They met again at a community breakfast event two days later. That same afternoon, Smiley arrived at Burke's house. She was alone, preparing to go out for the evening. Burke invited Smiley in, but told him that she had to leave soon.

Smiley talked about his repeated visits to the farmhouse when she was not there, and how glad he was to have found her at home. He spoke again of her isolated setting and her vulnerability to attack. He accurately described her activities with her friends that day.

After approximately one-half hour, Burke told Smiley that he had to leave because she was going out. Smiley left the house. Burke noticed that he did not take his jacket. Burke then went to the home of Joan Paul, a friend. She told Paul that Smiley was "creeping her out" and that she felt uncomfortable when he was around her.

That evening, while attending a community gathering, Paul met Smiley. She told him that Burke was upset by his visit.

The following morning, Smiley showed up at Burke's home. He knocked on the door but received no answer. Burke was at home but was afraid to answer the door. She hid in an area away from the windows until he departed. Smiley began to depart, then stopped and parked his vehicle behind Burke's car. He returned and banged loudly on the door. After approximately 10 minutes, he drove off. Burke then called the police.

Police then interviewed Smiley. He provided a statement indicating that he was new in town, single, and lonely, and that Burke was friendly. He had run into her accidentally at the store, and later at a community event. When he came to visit, she invited him in for a drink. He believed that they were "getting along quite well." When he left Burke's home, there was no indication that she was upset. He was quite puzzled when he later heard that she was upset with him.

He explained in his statement that he had gone to her house the next day to find out why she was upset and to retrieve his jacket. He knocked on the door a couple of times, but it appeared that no one was at home. As he was leaving, he saw a curtain move. He stopped his vehicle and ran back to see if she was at home and if anything was wrong. After receiving no answer, he left.

You are the investigating officer. What will you do? Explain your rationale.

APPENDIX 4A   POLICING STANDARDS MANUAL (2000): DOMESTIC VIOLENCE OCCURRENCES

February 2000 LE-024 1/12
Ontario Ministry of the Solicitor General

Legislative/Regulatory Requirements

Section 29 of the Adequacy Standards Regulation requires a police services board to have a policy on investigations into domestic violence occurrences. In addition, section 12(1)(d) requires the Chief of Police to develop and maintain procedures on and processes for undertaking and managing investigations into domestic violence occurrences.

The focus of these policies and procedures should be on domestic violence occurrences. For the purposes of this guideline, domestic violence occurrence means:

Domestic violence is any use of physical or sexual force, actual or threatened, in an intimate relationship, including emotional/psychological abuse or harassing behaviour. Although both women and men can be victims of domestic violence, the overwhelming majority of this violence involves men abusing women.

Intimate relationships include those between the opposite-sex and same-sex partners. These relationships vary in duration and legal formality, and include current and former dating, common-law and married couples.

Criminal Code offences include, but are not limited to homicide, assault, sexual assault, threatening death or bodily harm, forcible confinement, harassment/stalking, abduction, breaches of court orders and property-related offences.

These crimes are often committed in a context where there is a pattern of assaultive and/or controlling behaviour. This violence may include physical assault, and emotional, psychological and sexual abuse. It can include threats to harm children, other family members, pets and property. The violence is used to intimidate, humiliate or frighten victims, or to make them powerless. Domestic violence may include a single act of abuse. It may also include a number of acts that may appear minor or trivial when viewed in isolation, but collectively form a pattern that amounts to abuse.

Sample Board Policy

Board Policy #_____

It is the policy of the _____ Police Services Board with respect to domestic violence occurrences that the Chief of Police will:

    a) in partnership with the police service's local Crown, Probation and Parole Services, Victim/Witness Assistance Programme (VWAP), Victim Crisis and Referral Service (VCARS), municipalities, local Children's Aid Societies and other local service providers and community representatives responsible for issues related to domestic violence, including women's shelters, work to establish and maintain one or more domestic violence coordinating committees that cover the geographic areas that fall within the jurisdiction of the police service;

b) implement one or more of the models set out in Ministry guidelines for the investigation of domestic violence occurrences and ensure that the police service has access to trained domestic violence investigators;

c) develop and maintain procedures for undertaking and managing investigations into domestic violence occurrences that address:

   i) communications and dispatch;

   ii) initial response;

   iii) enhanced investigative procedures;

   iv) the mandatory laying of charges where there are reasonable grounds to do so, including in cases where there is a breach of a bail condition, probation, parole or a restraining order;

   v) the use of a risk indicators tool;

   vi) children at risk;

   vii) high risk cases and repeat offenders;

   viii) occurrences involving members of a police service;

   ix) post-arrest procedures;

   x) victim assistance; and

   xi) safety planning;

d) ensure that the police service's response to domestic violence occurrences are monitored and evaluated; and

e) ensure that officers and other appropriate members receive the appropriate Ministry accredited training.

Police Service Guidelines

1. Every Chief of Police, in partnership with the local Crown, Probation and Parole Services, VWAP, VCARS, local Children's Aid Society, municipalities, and other local service providers and community representatives responsible for issues related to domestic violence, including women's shelters, should work to establish one or more domestic violence coordinating committees that cover the geographic areas that fall within the jurisdiction of the police service. The suggested terms of reference for the domestic violence coordinating committee include:

   a) establishing a protocol for the operation of the committee;

   b) establishing criteria for case and/or systems review;

   c) reviewing cases that meet the established criteria, and subject to confidentiality requirements, sharing case specific information among relevant member organizations in order to provide a coordinated response;

    d) monitoring and evaluating the response to cases by organizations participating on the domestic violence coordinating committee;

    e) reviewing the availability of services to victims of domestic violence, including the provision of safety planning;

    f) coordinating the development of local written protocols on domestic violence that address:

        i) the roles and responsibilities of organizations involved in providing services to victims, including notifying and informing the victim about release of the accused, bail conditions, and the criminal justice process;

        ii) information sharing among the organizations; and

        iii) referrals for service, including the provision of assistance to victims and children in cases which do not proceed to court, or where no charges have been laid;

    g) developing local community strategies and responses to address and prevent repeat victimization, including promoting and supporting follow-up with victims of domestic violence; and

    h) developing initiatives/programs for the prevention and early intervention, including:

        i) Domestic Violence Emergency Response System (DVERS), where practical;

        ii) addressing the needs of child witnesses of violence; and

        iii) awareness and information programs on domestic violence occurrences for students and other service providers.

2. Every police service should ensure that it has access to trained domestic violence investigators.

3. Domestic violence investigators will have the primary responsibility for undertaking, managing or reviewing the investigation of domestic violence occurrences, except where the type of occurrence involves an offence which is addressed by the police service's criminal investigation management plan established pursuant to section 11 of the *Regulation on the Adequacy and Effectiveness of Police Services* or is a threshold major case as defined in the *Ontario Major Case Management Manual*.

4. A Chief of Police should not designate a person as a domestic violence investigator unless that person is a police officer and has successfully completed the required training accredited by the Ministry or has equivalent qualifications and skills as designated by the Ministry.

5. A police service may meet its obligations under paragraph 2 by either:

    a) ensuring that an adequate number of patrol officers are designated as domestic violence investigators;

    b) establishing a specialized unit of domestic violence investigators that will be responsible for undertaking, managing or reviewing the investigation of domestic violence occurrences;

c) designating a domestic violence occurrence as a threshold occurrence under the police service's criminal investigation management plan, thereby requiring that the investigation be undertaken or managed by a criminal investigator; or

d) designating patrol supervisors as domestic violence investigators who will be responsible for undertaking, managing or reviewing all domestic violence occurrence investigations.

6. Where a police service decides to meet its obligations under paragraph 2 by one of the methods set out in paragraph 5(b)-(d), it should also ensure that its patrol officers receive the required training accredited by the Ministry on the police response to domestic violence occurrences.

7. Every police service, in conjunction with the domestic violence coordinating committee and local community and social service agencies, should consider the need for, and the feasibility of, implementing a multi-disciplinary follow-up support for victims of domestic violence in the their jurisdiction. This support could focus on victims' assistance, counselling, attendance at court, children who witness violence, and intervention strategies, such as safety planning, in cases where there is repeat victimization or high risk to the victim.

8. Every police service's procedures should:

a) require that all domestic violence occurrence calls be responded to as a priority call for service even if the call is withdrawn, including calls relating to a possible breach of a bail, parole or probation condition, peace bond or a restraining order;

b) require that when a call is received and the suspect has threatened violence and there is reason to believe that the suspect intends to go to the victim's location the police will go to the victim's location;

c) set out the number of police officers to attend at the scene, with two as a minimum;

d) indicate the type of information to be gathered by communications and dispatch personnel and provided to responding officers, including at minimum:

   i) caller's name, address, telephone number and relation to the incident (e. g., witness, victim);

   ii) information about the suspect (e.g., relationship to victim, current location, description, any known mental illnesses, suicidal threats, history of abuse/violence);

   iii) extent of injuries, if known;

   iv) whether the suspect or other residents of the household are under the influence of drugs or alcohol;

   v) whether firearms or other weapons are known to be present at the scene or accessible to the suspect from some other location;

vi) whether the suspect or anyone in the household has been issued or refused an authorization to acquire a firearm, Firearms Licence or registration certificate;

vii) whether the suspect is known to have access to firearms;

viii) whether children or other persons are present in the household and their location within the dwelling;

ix) whether there has been one or more previous domestic violence occurrence calls to the address, the nature of previous incidents and whether weapons have been involved; and

x) whether a current peace bond/restraining order or bail/probation condition exists against anyone in the household or suspect; and

e) require communications and dispatch personnel to be provided with a checklist or reference sheet that sets out the information to be gathered and provided to responding officers.

9. The procedures should provide that whenever possible at least one of the minimum two officers responding to a domestic violence occurrence should be a patrol officer who has received training on the police response to domestic violence occurrences or a domestic violence investigator.

10. The procedures should provide that upon arrival at the scene the officers should:

a) try to quickly separate the parties;

b) assist any party in obtaining medical assistance, if necessary;

c) ensure that any children at the scene are provided with appropriate support/assistance; and

d) gather and preserve evidence in accordance with the police service's procedures on the collection, preservation and control of evidence and property.

11. The procedures should provide that:

a) all officers responding to a domestic violence occurrence should make detailed notes, including on the actions and utterances of the parties; and

b) a detailed occurrence report should be completed for every domestic violence occurrence regardless of whether any charges were laid or an offence alleged.

12. The procedures should address the interviewing of the victim(s), suspect and witnesses, including:

a) where available, practical and appropriate, the use of audio or video taping of statements in accordance with the *R. v. KGB* guidelines;

b) separate interviews where practical and safe for officers and the parties;

c) if required, the use of an interpreter by a person outside the family where practical;

d) that the officers should ask the victim and other witnesses direct questions about:

   i) any history of abuse/violence and stalking/criminal harassment;

   ii) any history of personal threats, including threats to life;

   iii) any concerns over the safety of the victim;

   iv) the presence of, or access to, firearms and registration certificates;

   v) the previous use of weapons;

   vi) any history of drug or alcohol abuse; and

   vii) any history of mental health or stability issues;

e) the processes and considerations for interviewing child witnesses, including the appropriateness of asking the child any of the questions set out in (d);

f) that the officer should ask the victim any other questions relevant to the completion of the risk indicators part of the domestic violence supplementary report form;

g) requesting that the victim review and sign the officer's record of their statement, or any other statement that has been provided, and the statements should include the date; and

h) interviewing third party witnesses, including neighbours, other emergency personnel who have responded to the scene and medical personnel who treat the victim.

13. The procedures should address the gathering and documenting of evidence, including:

   a) asking whether the victim was physically assaulted and whether any internal or external injuries occurred and noting their response (including where possible on a diagram);

   b) photographing the crime scene (e.g., overturned furniture or destroyed property), including the use of video taping, where available and practical;

   c) with the victim's consent, photographing the victim's injuries and taking additional photographs within 24-48 hours of the initial occurrence when the injuries are more visibly apparent (if possible by a member of the same gender; consideration should be given to using Polaroid photographs when appropriate);

   d) gathering any other evidence, including answering machine tapes, hospital records, torn and/or blood stained clothing, or fingerprint evidence if the suspect has broken into the victim's residence (including any evidence obtained for a Sexual Assault Treatment Centre whose mandate has been expanded to include domestic violence);

   e) the review and preserving of 911 tapes that record the call for service;

f)   the names and date of birth of all children present, or who normally reside, in the home; and

g)   the use of search warrants to obtain relevant evidence.

14. The procedures should provide that in any domestic violence occurrence, which is a threshold major case, the investigation will be in accordance with the Ministry's designated *Ontario Major Case Management Manual.*

15. The procedures should provide that in all domestic violence occurrences an officer is to lay a charge where there are reasonable grounds to do so, including:

a)   where a person has breached a condition of bail, parole, probation or a peace bond;

b)   for any offence committed under the *Criminal Code,* including obstruction of justice (i.e., dissuading the victim from testifying); or

c)   when there is a contravention of a valid order under sections 24 and 46 of the *Family Law Act* and section 35 of the *Children's Law Reform Act.*

16. A decision to lay charges should not be influenced by any of the following factors:

a)   marital status/cohabitation of the parties;

b)   disposition of previous police calls involving the same victim and suspect;

c)   the victim's unwillingness to attend court proceedings or the officer's belief that the victim will not cooperate;

d)   likelihood of obtaining a conviction in court;

e)   verbal assurances by either party that the violence will cease;

f)   denial by either party that the violence occurred;

g)   the officer's concern about reprisals against the victim by the suspect; or

h)   gender, race, ethnicity, disability, socioeconomic status or occupation of the victim and suspect.

17. The procedures should provide that an officer should explain to both the victim and the suspect that it is their duty to lay a charge when there are reasonable grounds to believe that an offence has been committed, and that only a Crown can withdraw the charge.

18. The procedures should address the use of warrants to enter a dwelling house for the purpose of arrest or apprehension in accordance with the relevant sections of the *Criminal Code.*

19. The procedures should provide that if the suspect is not present when officers arrive, and reasonable grounds exist to lay a charge, a warrant for the arrest of the accused should be obtained as soon as possible. Once obtained, a warrant should be entered on CPIC as soon as practicable and

no later than within 24 hours. Every reasonable effort should be made to locate and apprehend the suspect.

20. The procedures should address dual arrest, as well as the laying of counter-charges, and highlight the importance of determining the primary offender in order to distinguish assault from defensive self-protection.

21. The procedures should provide that in all domestic violence occurrences, officers should consider whether there is any evidence of criminal harassment, and should also follow the police service's procedures on criminal harassment investigations.

22. The procedures should provide that in all domestic violence occurrences the officers involved will:

    a) follow the police service's procedures on preventing/responding to occurrences involving firearms, regardless of whether any charges are laid; and

    b) where appropriate, determine whether there is compliance with the sections of the *Criminal Code* and *Firearms Act* relating to safe storage of firearms.

23. The procedures should provide that, as soon as possible, whenever a charge is laid in a domestic violence occurrence, the domestic violence supplementary report form will also be completed, including the part of the report relating to the risk indicators checklist. Where a suspect has been arrested, the procedures should provide that the risk indicators part of the report will be completed prior to any decision to release the suspect or detain for a bail hearing, and will be included with the Crown brief/ show cause report.

24. The procedures should address the use of behavioural science services in domestic violence occurrences if the circumstances of the case require a risk assessment, and how these services can be accessed in accordance with the requirements of the *Regulation on the Adequacy and Effectiveness of Police Services.*

25. The domestic violence supplementary report should be based on the Ministry's designated report form and should include, at minimum, the risk indicators set out by the Ministry.

26. The procedures should require police officers to address issues relating to children, who are under 16, in accordance with the police service's procedures on child abuse and neglect and the police service's protocol with the local Children's Aid Societies.

27. The procedures should address the investigative supports that may be available to assist in cases determined to be high risk, or where there is a repeat offender with a history of domestic violence with the same or multiple victims, including:

    a) the use of physical surveillance;

    b) electronic interception;

c)   video and photographic surveillance; and

d)   victim/witness protection services.

28. The procedures should provide that in cases involving high risk, or where there is a repeat offender, that the offender should be entered into the 'SIP' category on CPIC as soon as possible, and no later than within 24 hours.

29. The procedures should provide that where an offender has engaged in a pattern of offending that may indicate hate/bias motivation towards women, that the domestic violence investigator raise with the Crown the possibility of introducing evidence of hate/bias motivation as an aggravating factor for the purposes of sentencing the offender if convicted.

30. The procedures should set out the steps to be followed when a domestic violence occurrence involves a member of its police service or another police service.

31. The procedures should provide that in all domestic violence occurrences officers will comply with the police service's procedures relating to bail and violent crime.

32. The procedures should provide that in all domestic violence occurrences where there has been a breach of bail, or there is about to be a breach, officers will comply with the police service's procedures relating to breach of bail.

33. Consistent with local protocols, the procedures should set out the roles and responsibilities for notifying and informing the victim as soon as possible about the release of the accused, time and location of bail hearing, bail conditions and the criminal justice process.

34. The procedures should provide that officers who respond to domestic violence occurrences will provide assistance to the victim based on the police service's local procedures, including:

a)   assisting the victim in obtaining medical assistance, if necessary;

b)   remaining at the scene until they are satisfied that there is no further immediate threat to the victim;

c)   addressing any special needs of the victim (e.g., dealing with communication barriers);

d)   addressing the needs of child witnesses of domestic violence occurrences, including encouraging the child's primary caregiver to consider obtaining assistance for the child from a counsellor with experience in assisting child witnesses of domestic violence;

e)   if requested by the victim, attending the residence of the victim to ensure peaceful entry when the victim or accused returns to take possession of personal belongings and when concerns for the victim's safety exist because of the presence of the accused in the residence, unless peaceful entry of the residence cannot be achieved, or the removal of certain property is contested by either party, in which case the officers should advise the parties of the need to seek a civil remedy;

    f)   arranging for transportation to a shelter or place of safety, if necessary, with the location remaining confidential to the suspect/accused and third parties; and

    g)   providing information to the victim on services that are available, and offer to make initial contact with victims' services.

35. Police services should provide, in conjunction with local victims' services, a localized pamphlet on domestic violence that includes information on local resources to assist victims.

36. The procedures should provide that officers who respond to domestic violence occurrences should ensure that issues surrounding the victim's safety are addressed, including directly providing the victim with information on safety planning or providing information to the victim on the availability of safety planning information and assistance within the community.

37. The procedures should provide in cases where it is determined that there is a high risk, or repeat victimization, a domestic violence investigator or another member of the police service, should warn the victim about the potential risk to the victim or any children, and offer to meet with the victim to assist in developing or reviewing the victim's safety plan and to identify other measures that may be taken to help safeguard the victim and any children.

38. Every police service shall require supervisors to monitor, and ensure, compliance with the police service's procedures related to domestic violence occurrences.

39. Every police service should designate a domestic violence coordinator who will be responsible for:

    a)   monitoring the response to, and investigation of domestic violence occurrences, including compliance with the police service's procedures by supervisors, officers and other members;

    b)   monitoring and evaluating follow-up to domestic violence cases;

    c)   liaising with the Crown, Probation and Parole Services, VWAP, VCARS, the local Children's Aid Society, and other local services and community representatives responsible for responding to issues related to domestic violence occurrences;

    d)   informing the public and media about the police service's domestic violence occurrences procedures; and

    e)   ensuring that statistical data are kept on domestic violence occurrences and provided to the Ministry in the form designated by the Ministry.

40. Every police service should periodically review the police service's procedures to ensure consistency with legislative and case law changes.

41. Every police service should ensure that persons who provide communications and dispatch functions are trained regarding domestic violence occurrence calls for service.

42. Every police service should ensure that its domestic violence investigators have successfully completed Ministry accredited training, or have the equivalent qualifications and skills designated by the Ministry, that addresses:

   a) the dynamics of abusive relationships including the effects of physical assault and psychological abuse;

   b) the initial police response to domestic violence occurrences, including officer safety;

   c) interviewing, including interviewing child witnesses;

   d) collection, care and handling of evidence;

   e) search, seizure and warrants;

   f) firearms seizures and legislation;

   g) the mandatory charge policy, dual arrest and counter-charging;

   h) court orders (e.g., restraining orders), judicial interim release orders, parole certificates, other relevant legislation and probation;

   i) victim assistance and local victim services, as well as victims with special needs;

   j) risk indicators and assessment, including the completion of the domestic violence supplementary report form;

   k) procedures relating to post-arrest;

   l) strategies for addressing repeat victimization and high risk cases;

   m) safety planning; and

   n) issues relating to children who witness violence.

43. Where a police service decides to meet its obligations under paragraph 2 by one of the methods set out in paragraph 5(b)-(d), it should also ensure that an adequate number of its patrol officers have received Ministry accredited training on the police response to domestic violence occurrences that addresses:

   a) the dynamics of abusive relationships including the effects of physical assault and psychological abuse;

   b) the initial police response to domestic violence occurrences, including officer safety;

   c) preservation of the crime scene, and initial collection of evidence and interviewing;

   d) court orders (e.g., restraining orders), judicial interim release orders, parole certificates, other relevant legislation and probation;

   e) firearms seizures and legislation;

   f) the role of the domestic violence investigator;

   g) procedures relating to children at risk;

h) the completion of the domestic violence supplementary report, including risk indicators;

i) procedures relating to post-arrest;

j) victims' assistance and local victim services, as well as victims with special needs; and

k) issues relating to children who witness violence.

APPENDIX 4B   DOMESTIC VIOLENCE SUPPLEMENTARY REPORT

DOMESTIC VIOLENCE SUPPLEMENTARY REPORT
To be completed by investigating officer where there are charges laid and an occurrence report submitted.
Also to be attached to the Show Cause Report

Date of This Report _____ Time: _____ Occurrence # _____
                    (yy / mm / dd)   (24 hr. clock)

Date of Incident _____ Time: _____
                 (yy / mm / dd)   (24 hr. clock

Investigating Officer: _____   Division/
                                                                    Detachment:

VICTIM: _____
            (Surname, First Name)(to include birth name)

Relationship to Accused   ☐ Married   ☐ Common-Law   ☐ Separated (includes dating, common-law)
(check all that apply)
                             ☐ Child in Common   ☐ Dating   ☐ Divorced   ☐ Same gender couple   ☐ By Marriage

Condition of Victim at time of interview (duration of time passed since incident occurred: _____)
☐ Crying   ☐ Angry   ☐ Nervous ☐ Hysterical   ☐ Upset ☐ Calm
☐ Drugs   ☐ Alcohol   ☐ Afraid   ☐ Other / Specify:

Victim Vulnerability   ☐ Immigration Status ☐ geographic/community isolation   ☐ children   ☐ language
                        ☐ lack of access to telephone/other means of communication ☐ other considerations

Medical Treatment   ☐ Not Required   ☐ Refused ☐ Will Seek Own   ☐ To Hospital by Ambulance   ☐ Other

Medical Release Signed ☐ YES   ☐ NO   ☐ Refused/Specify:

Describe all injuries   *(Include part of body injured and appearance, and date of observations)*

Children Present ☐ YES ☐ NO   AGES: Violence   ☐ Directly Assaulted ☐ Witnessed ☐ Heard

CAS Notified   ☐ YES ☐ NO   Notified by: _____   Name of CAS Contact: _____

ACCUSED: _____   Telephone _____
             (Surname, First Name, alias if applicable)

Address

Charge(s) Laid _____

Condition of Accused   ☐ Drugs ☐ Alcohol ☐ Angry ☐ Threatening ☐ Apologetic ☐ Upset ☐ Nervous ☐ Crying ☐ Calm Other / Specify:

Medical Treatment   ☐ Not Required   ☐ Refused ☐ Will Seek Own   ☐ To Hospital by Ambulance   ☐ Other

Describe all injuries   *(Include part of body injured and appearance and date of observations)*

HISTORY (ACCUSED)   Checked by: Criminal Record NO ☐ ☐ YES (attach)
CPIC checked: ☐ On File   ☐ Not on File   _____   ☐ 810 Peace Bond   ☐ Probation
                                                                        ☐ Parole   ☐ Breach of Parole Certificate
Local RMS checked: ☐ On File   ☐ Not on File   ☐ Conditional Sentence
☐ Bail release with ☐ FAC/PAL   ☐ FAC/PAL   ☐ Possesses Firearms,   Storage location: ☐ Other Current Court Orders
  conditions   Refused/ Revoked ☐ Other weapons   _____   ☐ Breach of any Court Orders

☐ Driver's License ☐ Vehicle access _____
Outstanding Charges file attached: ☐   Name of Probation Officer and Probation and Parole Officer contacted (if applicable): _____
☐ Previous occurrences related to domestic violence: ☐ Yes ☐ No

Previous Incidents Reported To:	No. of Incidents	Brief Details *(include date and nature of injuries)*
☐ Regional Police Service		
☐ Municipal Police Service		
☐ OPP (including previous org. #)		
☐ Another Police Service		
☐ Victim Services		
☐ Hospital		
☐ Other Agency		
☐ Unreported		

EVIDENCE:

Statements:

1

VICTIM: ☐ None ☐ Written ☐ Audio ☐ Video KGB warned: ☐ YES ☐ NO
☐ other corroborating evidence _____

Children: ☐ None ☐ Written ☐ Audio ☐ Video

Caller: ☐ None ☐ Written ☐ Audio ☐ Video

Witness (es): ☐ None ☐ Written ☐ Audio ☐ Video

Police witness (es) ☐ None ☐ Written ☐ Audio ☐ Video

Accused: ☐ None ☐ Written ☐ Audio ☐ Video ☐ Utterance

Photographs: *Videotaping:*

☐ Scene _____   ☐ Scene _____ Tape No.: _____

☐ Relating to Victim: ☐ at the time ☐ 48 hrs later   ☐ relating to Victim _____ Tape No.: _____

☐ Relating to Accused   ☐ Relating to Accused Tape No.:

Incident Information:

☐ 9-1-1- Call   ☐ Non-Emergency Call   ☐ None Tape Ordered: ☐ YES ☐ NO
Caller: ☐ Victim ☐ Child (ren)   ☐ Accused ☐ Other (specify)

Weapons: Involved in incident ☐ YES ☐ No Seized: ☐ YES ☐ No FAC/PAL seized ☐ YES ☐ No Ammunition Seized ☐ YES ☐ No

Type of Weapon: _____

Investigative follow-up required: ☐ Yes ☐ No Action Required: _____

Date Required by: _____

RISK FACTORS:
To be completed by the investigating officer. Where there are multiple choices circle all that apply!

		YES	NO	U/K
a)	Does the victim fear that the accused will continue the assaults, seriously injure or kill her/him or the children?	☐	☐	☐
b)	Has there been a recent escalation in frequency or severity of assaults/threats against the victim?	☐	☐	☐
c)	Has there been a recent separation or change in the relationship between the victim and the accused?	☐	☐	☐
d)	Has there been a recent change in the contact between the children and the accused?	☐	☐	☐
e)	Has the accused experienced any unusually high stress recently, e.g. financial, loss of job, health problem?	☐	☐	☐
f)	Does the accused have any known mental health problems, or exhibits a loss of touch with reality or bizarre behaviour?	☐	☐	☐
g)	Has the accused ever demonstrated jealousy or obsessive behaviour towards the victim and/or previous partner?	☐	☐	☐
h)	Has the accused demonstrated any stalking behaviour towards (a) the victim? (b) Family? or (c) any other person? (e.g. harassing phone calls, watching, threatened or has destroyed the victim's personal property, sending unwanted letters, following/contacting through third party, frequenting workplace etc.)	☐	☐	☐
i)	Does the accused abuse drugs and/or alcohol?	☐	☐	☐
j)	Has there been a noticeable increase in the abuse of drugs and/or alcohol?	☐	☐	☐
k)	Is the accused more angry or violent when using drugs and/or alcohol?	☐	☐	☐
l)	Has the accused ever sexually abused the victim and/or a previous partner?	☐	☐	☐
m)	Has the accused threatened/attempted suicide?	☐	☐	☐
n)	Has the accused threatened to harm/kill the victim or any other family members/acquaintances?	☐	☐	☐
o)	Has the accused threatened to or destroyed any of the victim's personal property?	☐	☐	☐
p)	Has the accused injured or killed a pet owned by the victim?	☐	☐	☐
q)	Does the accuser's personality feature anger, impulsiveness or poor behaviour control?	☐	☐	☐
r)	Does the accused own/have access to firearms or weapons including a license for the firearm?	☐	☐	☐
s)	Has the accused used or threatened the use of firearms or weapons against the victim/children or any other person?	☐	☐	☐

ADDITIONAL INFORMATION:
_____

Offered to Contact VSA ☐ Yes ☐ No   Did Victim Accept Offer ☐ Yes ☐ No

Place of Safety provided/Women's Shelter ☐ Yes ☐ No   Third Party Contact Available ☐ Yes ☐ No

Information on safety planning provided ☐ Yes ☐ No

REPORT COMPLETED BY: _____   **CHECKED BY SUPERVISOR:** _____
                        (please print)   (please print)

Date of Completion: _____ (Rank, Badge #) _____   Date: _____ (Rank, Badge #) _____

FOLLOW-UP/BAIL CONDITIONS:

2

CHAPTER 5

Elder Abuse

Chapter Objectives

After completing this chapter, you should be able to:

- Describe the types of elder abuse.

- Describe techniques for police intervention in elder abuse situations.

- Identify some of the mental health problems faced by the elderly and explain how they can complicate police intervention in elder abuse situations.

- Identify and provide for the needs of the abuse victim.

INTRODUCTION

Elder abuse is the term for any violence or mistreatment directed toward an elderly person by someone on whom the elderly person depends for food, shelter, or other aid. An **elderly person**, for the purpose of this chapter and most of the studies discussed in this chapter, is a person over the age of 60.

A common feature of elder abuse is isolation of the victim by the abuser. Isolation allows the abuser to exert his or her power over the victim without fear of repercussions.

It is not possible to know the full extent of abuse of elderly adults. Elder abuse is usually not reported by the victims themselves, but rather by others, or comes to light when the police investigate some other matter.

According to the Department of Justice (2003), elderly persons who are being abused may be unwilling, or unable, to report it for any of the following reasons:

- dependence on the abuser (emotional, physical, or economic);

- fear of being put in an institution;

- fear of retaliation or abandonment;

- fear of outside intervention (and loss of independence and control);

- fear of not being believed;

- pressure to maintain the family/community reputation;

elder abuse
any violence or mistreatment directed toward an elderly person by someone on whom the elderly person depends for food, shelter, or other aid

elderly person
a person over the age of 60

- beliefs about importance of marriage and family;

- cognitive impairment or disability, including dementia or Alzheimer's;

- physical frailty or disability;

- social or geographic isolation;

- literacy, language, or cultural barriers; and

- shame or stigma.

SURVEYS ON ELDER ABUSE IN CANADA

The surveys described below provide data on the prevalence of elder abuse in Canada.

The 1999 General Social Survey on Victimization (GSS) reported that approximately 7 percent of the more than 4,000 Canadian adults 65 years of age and older who responded had experienced some form of emotional or financial abuse by an adult child, spouse, or caregiver in the five years prior to the survey (Statistics Canada, 2000).

Emotional abuse was the most frequently reported type of abuse. Approximately 7 percent of respondents reported that they had been emotionally abused. The two most common forms of emotional abuse reported were (1) being insulted or called names or (2) being allowed limited contact with family and friends.

Financial abuse was reported by 1 percent of respondents.

Only 1 percent of respondents reported experiencing physical or sexual abuse. Nearly 2 percent of respondents said that they had suffered more than one type of abuse.

The incidence-based Uniform Crime Reporting Survey (UCR2) also provides information on elder abuse. The survey found that in 2000 the largest category of police-reported violent crime committed against older adults by family members was assault. Usually, the crime was common assault, which includes slapping, pushing, punching, and threats to apply force. The three most frequent offences inflicted on older adults by family members were common assault (54 percent), uttering threats (21 percent), and assault with a weapon or causing bodily harm (13 percent).

Where family violence was reported to the police forces that participated in the survey, it was found that adult children and spouses accounted for 71 percent of individuals responsible for victimizing older adults. Survey data showed that 80 percent of those accused of violently victimizing an older family member in 2000 were male. In 2000, family members killed three out of every one million seniors (for a total of 10 older adults), which represents 26 percent of all older adult homicides in Canada. From 1974 to 2000, older adult homicides committed by family members were most commonly committed by spouses (39 percent), adult children (37 percent), and members or the extended family (24 percent).

According to the Department of Justice Canada (2003), national data indicates that gender is a factor in elder abuse:

- Nearly 65 percent of all older adult victims of family violence in 2000 were female.

- Between 1974 and 2000, older women were at higher risk of spousal homicide than were older men. The data indicate that 52 percent of the older women who were victims of family homicide were killed by their spouses, compared with 25 percent of older men.

- Older male victims were almost twice as likely as older female victims to be killed by their adult sons (42 percent versus 24 percent).

- More older men (9 percent) than older women (6 percent) reported being victims of financial or emotional abuse by adult children, caregivers, or spouses in the 1999 GSS.

Elder Abuse in Institutions

Older adults who are either physically frail or disabled, and those who are cognitively impaired, may be more vulnerable to abuse, especially if they are residents of long-term care facilities. These individuals may be more vulnerable to elder abuse because they already require the protective environment of an institution.

There are no available national studies on the prevalence of institutional abuse in Canada. However, in 1997, the College of Nurses of Ontario conducted a survey of nurses that provided some anecdotal evidence of the prevalence of abuse in elder care institutions (College of Nurses of Ontario, 1997).

The survey identified that 56 percent of nurses working in community care witnessed or heard about at least one incident of abuse by a nurse since 1993. The survey found that over 90 percent of these incidents were personally witnessed by the respondent. The most commonly mentioned types of abuse witnessed were roughness (31 percent); yelling and swearing (28 percent); offensive/embarrassing comments (28 percent); and hitting/shoving (10 percent).

SIGNS OF ELDER ABUSE

There are some behaviours and signs that may indicate elder abuse. However, the majority of these indicators are generally not observed by police. Police must rely on reports of abuse by concerned individuals before they can intervene. This poses a quandary because the persons most able to report these indicators of abuse are, statistically, likely to be the abusers.

Indicators of elder abuse include the following (Winnipeg Police Service, 2000):

- repeated occurrences of unexplained physical injuries or accidents;

- a history of changing hospitals and/or doctors;

- dehydration and/or malnutrition;

- unexplained delays in seeking treatment for injuries;

- rent, mortgage, or utility bills that are unpaid or in arrears;

- bedsores, worsening personal hygiene, untreated wounds, and absence of wound dressings;

- insufficient money to purchase clothing, food, medications, or other necessities even though income appears adequate;

- feelings of hopelessness and resignation, withdrawal, and suicidal thoughts;

- depression, fearfulness, anxiety, and low self-esteem in the older person;

- inappropriate use of medication, withholding of needed medications, and oversedation; and

- an occurrence of unusual activity in the older person's bank account, including a change in the amount or frequency of withdrawals, many withdrawals being made by bank card rather than at the teller, and the opening of joint bank accounts.

AGE AS AN AGGRAVATING FACTOR AT SENTENCING

Note that s. 718.2 of the *Criminal Code* recognizes that in crimes committed against elderly persons where the perpetrator of the crime was motivated by bias or prejudice based on age or physical or mental disability, the bias or prejudice will be considered to be an aggravating factor at sentencing. This principle applies to all types of criminal offences.

OTHER SENTENCING PRINCIPLES: CRIMINAL CODE, SECTION 718.2

A court that imposes a sentence shall also take into consideration the following principles:

(a) a sentence should be increased or reduced to account for any relevant aggravating or mitigating circumstances relating to the offence or the offender, and, without limiting the generality of the foregoing,

(i) evidence that the offence was motivated by bias, prejudice or hate based on race, national or ethnic origin, language, colour, religion, sex, age, mental or physical disability, sexual orientation or any other similar factor, ...

shall be deemed to be aggravating circumstances.

TYPES OF ELDER ABUSE

There are five specific types of elder abuse: physical abuse, sexual abuse, financial abuse, neglect, and emotional/psychological abuse.

Physical Abuse

Physical abuse includes any violent act, even if it does not result in physical injury. Physical coercion, such as forced feeding and the use of restraints, also constitutes physical abuse.

Physical abuse includes the following (Department of Justice Canada, 2003):

- scalding or burning,

- spitting,

- beating,

- shoving or pushing,

- handling roughly, and

- slapping or hitting.

Physical abuse against elderly persons may also include the following actions (Department of Justice Canada, 2003):

- confining them to chairs or beds;

- confining them to rooms, including locking them in;

- tying them to pieces of furniture;

- using and misusing physical restraints; and

- using tranquillizers, alcohol, or medication as a means of making them more manageable or subduing them.

SIGNS OF PHYSICAL ABUSE

Signs that a person might be experiencing physical abuse include:

- physical injuries such as bruises, welts, cuts, or burns, or head injuries that cannot be explained, or where the explanation seems unlikely;

- confusion or tiredness, which may be due to overmedication;

- loss of mobility, which may be a result of being restrained;

- marks on furniture where restraints might have been used;

- locks on entrance/room doors; and

- locks in areas where food is kept.

CRIMINAL OFFENCES RELATED TO PHYSICAL ABUSE

As with any unauthorized application of force, there are criminal offences under the *Criminal Code* that may apply. The offence will depend on the nature of the application of force:

- criminal negligence causing bodily harm or death (ss. 220 to 221),

- unlawfully causing bodily harm (s. 269),

- manslaughter (ss. 234 and 236),

- murder (ss. 229 to 231 and s. 235), and

- assault (ss. 265 to 268).

The act of overmedicating the elderly person with the intent to overcome resistance is a criminal offence as defined in s. 246 of the *Criminal Code.*

OVERCOMING RESISTANCE TO COMMISSION OF OFFENCE: CRIMINAL CODE, SECTION 246

Every one who, with intent to enable or assist himself or another person to commit an indictable offence, …

> (b) administers or causes to be administered to any person, or attempts to administer to any person, or causes or attempts to cause any person to take a stupefying or overpowering drug, matter or thing,

is guilty of an indictable offence and liable to imprisonment for life.

Forcible confinement is another criminal offence that can arise when the elderly are under the care of others, as described in s. 279(2) of the *Criminal Code.*

FORCIBLE CONFINEMENT: CRIMINAL CODE, SECTION 279(2)

Every one who, without lawful authority, confines, imprisons or forcibly seizes another person is guilty of

> (a) an indictable offence and liable to imprisonment for a term not exceeding ten years; or

> (b) an offence punishable on summary conviction and liable to imprisonment for a term not exceeding eighteen months.

"The offence under this subsection does not require proof of total physical restraint of the victim: *R v. Gratton* (1985), 18 CCC (3d) 462 (Ont. CA), leave to appeal to SCC refused [1985] 1 SCR viii." (*Martin's Annual Criminal Code, 2005*)

Illegal restraint of the elderly can include being locked in a room or tied to a bed, chair, or other object. The elderly person's physical condition may prevent him or her from calling for assistance or escaping. Note that a charge of forcible confinement is sustainable even if the victim offered no resistance, as stated in s. 279(3) of the *Criminal Code.*

NON-RESISTANCE: CRIMINAL CODE, SECTION 279(3)

In proceedings under this section, the fact that the person in relation to whom the offence is alleged to have been committed did not resist is not a defence unless the accused proves that the failure to resist was not caused by threats, duress, force or exhibition of force.

Counselling or helping an elderly person to commit suicide is also an offence that may be considered physical (and possibly psychological) abuse, as stated in s. 241 of the *Criminal Code.*

COUNSELLING OR AIDING SUICIDE: CRIMINAL CODE, SECTION 241

Every one who

> (a) counsels a person to commit suicide, or

> (b) aids or abets a person to commit suicide,

whether suicide ensues or not, is guilty of an indictable offence and liable to imprisonment for a term not exceeding fourteen years.

Sexual Abuse

Sexual abuse is any form of engaging in sexual activity with a person without the full consent of that person. The elderly person may not have the ability to give consent due to dementia or the effects of prescription drugs. Or consent may have been obtained through fear of repercussions, in which case it is invalid, as was shown in the case of *R v. Ewanchuk*, discussed below.

Sexual abuse includes unwanted sexual touching; sexual relations without voluntary consent; or the forcing or coercing of degrading, humiliating, or painful sexual acts. It also includes incidents of sexual exploitation and sexual harassment.

Regardless of the type of sexual abuse, the key issue in determining whether abuse has occurred is consent, as discussed in ss. 273.1(1) and 273.(2) of the *Criminal Code*.

MEANING OF "CONSENT": CRIMINAL CODE, SECTION 273.1(1)

Subject to subsection (2) and subsection 265(3), "consent" means, for the purposes of sections 271, 272 and 273, the voluntary agreement of the complainant to engage in the sexual activity in question.

WHERE NO CONSENT OBTAINED: CRIMINAL CODE, SECTION 273.1(2)

No consent is obtained, for the purposes of sections 271, 272 and 273, where

(a) the agreement is expressed by the words or conduct of a person other than the complainant;

(b) the complainant is incapable of consenting to the activity;

(c) the accused induces the complainant to engage in the activity by abusing a position of trust, power or authority;

(d) the complainant expresses, by words or conduct, a lack of agreement to engage in the activity; or

(e) the complainant, having consented to engage in sexual activity, expresses, by words or conduct, a lack of agreement to continue to engage in the activity.

NO CONSENT WHERE FEAR OF HARM: R v. EWANCHUK

"There is no consent where the complainant consents because she honestly believes that she will otherwise suffer physical violence. While the plausibility of the alleged fear and any overt expressions of it are relevant in assessing the complainant's credibility that she consented out of fear, the approach is subjective: *R v. Ewanchuk*, [1999] 1 SCR 330, 131 CCC (3d) 481, 22 CR (5th) 1." (*Martin's Annual Criminal Code, 2005)*

Sexual abuse may also include the following activities (Winnipeg Police Service, 2000):

- engaging in acts that are physically intrusive, including sexualized kissing and/or fondling, oral and/or genital contact, digital penetration, and vaginal and/or anal intercourse;

- engaging in exhibitionist and voyeuristic behaviour or engaging in offensive verbal and non-verbal sexual behaviours;

- forcing an unwilling person to view pornographic materials;

- involving the victim in the production of pornographic materials; and

- allowing other people sexual access to the individual.

There may be *Criminal Code* offences that apply in cases of sexual abuse of elderly persons, including sexual assault (ss. 271 to 273) and sexual exploitation of a person with a disability (s. 153.1).

SEXUAL EXPLOITATION OF PERSON WITH DISABILITY: CRIMINAL CODE, SECTION 153.1(1)

Every person who is in a position of trust or authority towards a person with a mental or physical disability or who is a person with whom a person with a mental or physical disability is in a relationship of dependency and who, for a sexual purpose, counsels or incites that person to touch, without that person's consent, his or her own body, the body of the person who so counsels or incites, or the body of any other person, directly or indirectly, with a part of the body or with an object, the body of any person, including the body of the person who so invites, counsels or incites and the body of the person with the disability, is guilty of

(a) an indictable offence and liable to imprisonment for a term not exceeding five years; or

(b) an offence punishable on summary conviction and liable to imprisonment for a term not exceeding eighteen months.

DEFINITION OF "CONSENT": CRIMINAL CODE, SECTION 153.1(2)

Subject to subsection (3), "consent" means, for the purposes of this section, the voluntary agreement of the complainant to engage in the sexual activity in question.

WHEN NO CONSENT OBTAINED: CRIMINAL CODE, SECTION 153.1(3)

No consent is obtained, for the purposes of this section, if

(a) the agreement is expressed by the words or conduct of a person other than the complainant;

(b) the complainant is incapable of consenting to the activity;

(c) the accused counsels or incites the complainant to engage in the activity by abusing a position of trust, power or authority;

(d) the complainant expresses, by words or conduct, a lack of agreement to engage in the activity; or

(e) the complainant, having consented to engage in sexual activity, expresses, by words or conduct, a lack of agreement to continue to engage in the activity.

The definition of consent in s. 153.1 and the limits of the defence of belief in consent are similar to the provisions of ss. 273.1 and 273.2 of the *Criminal Code* (respecting sexual assault). Therefore, reference should be made to the notes in *Martin's Annual Criminal Code* under those sections. See, in particular, the discussion of *R v. Ewanchuk*, which is given under both sections.

SIGNS OF SEXUAL ABUSE

The following signs may indicate sexual abuse:

- presence of a sexually transmitted disease in an elderly person who is not known to be sexually active;

- bleeding, pain, or bruises in the genital area; or

- depression, fear, anxiety, withdrawal, or passivity (these signs may also indicate other kinds of abuse).

Financial Abuse

Financial abuse includes financial manipulation or exploitation through fraud, theft, forgery, or extortion. It means using elderly people's property or money dishonestly. It could also mean failing to use elderly people's assets for their welfare. When someone acts without consent in a manner that financially benefits one person at the expense of another, financial abuse has occurred.

Common forms of financial abuse of the elderly are theft or misuse of money; extortion of money or property; and forcing someone to sell his or her property. Any of these actions can lead to criminal charges.

Caregivers, because of their power over the elderly, often have the opportunity to extort money or property from their charges. For example, a caregiver might threaten to withdraw care from an elderly person unless title to real estate is signed over. Using an elderly person's property without his or her permission (as in appropriating an elderly person's vehicle for one's own use) is another form of financial abuse.

Financial abuse can also include wrongful use of a power of attorney. A **power of attorney** is a legal instrument that authorizes a person to carry out specific acts on behalf of another person. Elderly people who have difficulty managing their financial affairs often grant a power of attorney to a family member. Typically, the power of attorney gives the family member access to bank accounts, investment property, and so forth, which can create the potential for abuse.

power of attorney
legal instrument that authorizes a person to carry out specific acts on behalf of another person

Some other examples of financial abuse include:

- stealing possessions;

- selling property without permission;

- refusing to pay back borrowed money when requested;

- charging exorbitant prices for goods or services;

- refusing to move out of the elderly person's home when asked;

- sharing a home with an elderly person without paying a fair share of the household expenses; and

- unduly pressuring the elderly person to buy drugs or alcohol.

There are several *Criminal Code* offences that may be present in situations of financial abuse. These offences include:

- theft (ss. 323, 328 to 332, and 334);

- criminal breach of trust (s. 336);

- extortion (s. 346);

- forgery (s. 366);

- theft, forgery, etc., of credit card (s. 342);

- uttering a forged document (s. 368); and

- fraud (s. 380).

Neglect

neglect
failing to care for or meet the needs of elderly persons who are dependent and cannot meet their own needs

Neglect is failing to care for or meet the needs of elderly persons who are dependent and cannot meet their own needs. Neglect can be intentional or unintentional. Unintentional neglect may occur when a caregiver does not meet the needs of an elderly person because of a lack of skill or information.

Neglect may include failing to provide the following (Department of Justice Canada, 2003):

- adequate personal care (for example, failing to turn over a bedridden elderly person frequently to prevent bedsores);

- comfortable and safe living conditions;

- a clean home environment;

- items essential for personal cleanliness;

- transportation to required appointments;

- adequate clothing, nutrition, and other necessities; and

- prescribed or other medications necessary to maintain health.

Although the first five examples above do not constitute criminal offences, the final two examples—failing to provide necessities—may be an offence.

Withholding the necessaries of life (food, shelter, clothing, health care, etc.) from an elderly person can be an offence under s. 215(1) of the *Criminal Code*.

DUTY OF PERSONS TO PROVIDE NECESSARIES: CRIMINAL CODE, SECTION 215(1)

Every one is under a legal duty ...

(c) to provide necessaries of life to a person under his charge if that person

(i) is unable, by reason of detention, age, illness, mental disorder or other cause, to withdraw himself from that charge, and

(ii) is unable to provide himself with necessaries of life.

SIGNS OF NEGLECT

Signs of neglect can include the following (University of Alberta, Legal Studies Program, 2003a):

- dry lips, pale complexion, or unhealthy weight loss, which may indicate malnourishment;

- clothing that is dirty or inappropriate for the weather;

- an absence of dentures, glasses, or hearing aids, when these items are needed;

- physical appearance that indicates infrequent bathing (for example, matted, oily hair);

- untreated incontinence;

- mental or physical deterioration with no apparent medical reason;

- confinement;

- wandering;

- lack of food items in the house;

- inadequate medication or overmedication; and

- meal preparation or housekeeping standards that could cause illness or accident.

It is important to distinguish between neglect and self-neglect. Neglect is caused by someone else, whereas self-neglect is caused by the older person not taking care of himself or herself.

Emotional/Psychological Abuse

Emotional or psychological abuse may be defined as behaviour intended to control a person, instill fear in a person, cause a person to fear for his or her safety, or diminish a person's sense of self-worth (Nova Scotia Department of Community Services, 2002a). It may include frequent verbal aggression; social isolation (for example, refusing to allow access to family members or friends); humiliation; degradation; threats to institutionalize the person; and actions that deliberately frighten the victim.

Emotional/psychological abuse can also include the removal of decision-making power; the removal of or refusal to provide aids for mobility (for example, wheelchair or cane); the use of restraints or threats to use restraints; and the infantilization of the elderly person (treating the elder like a child).

Although it is not a criminal action to humiliate, insult, or belittle someone, threatening can be a criminal offence under s. 264.1 of the *Criminal Code*.

UTTERING THREATS: CRIMINAL CODE, SECTION 264.1

Every one commits an offence who, in any manner, knowingly utters, conveys or causes any person to receive a threat

(a) to cause death or bodily harm to any person;

(b) to burn, destroy or damage real or personal property; or

(c) to kill, poison or injure an animal or bird that is the property of any person.

Emotional/psychological abuse may involve other offences under the *Criminal Code*: criminal harassment (s. 264); harassing phone calls (s. 372); and intimidation (s. 423).

SIGNS OF EMOTIONAL/PSYCHOLOGICAL ABUSE

Signs that an elderly person might be experiencing emotional/psychological abuse include the following (University of Alberta, Legal Studies Program, 2003b):

- apathy, withdrawal, or depressed state without any apparent reason;

- physical indicators of imposed isolation (for example, locks on doors and no phone, television, or radio);

- evidence that the older person is being consistently ignored, treated passively, or treated like an infant by a caregiver; and

- fear of particular family members, friends, or caregivers.

REASONS FOR ELDER ABUSE

Elder abuse occurs because the elderly are often vulnerable. Some abusers suffer from psychological or emotional problems that contribute to their actions, but others simply act out of greed, self-indulgence, or the desire to exert control.

Abuse can be inflicted by family members, professional caregivers, and any other person in a caregiving role.

In home care settings where the elderly person is ill, primary care is often provided by the family, with limited assistance from part-time professionals. The stress of looking after an ill parent or other relative can trigger abuse by the family member.

Financial dependence can lead to elder abuse. The caregiver may be financially dependent on the elderly person because of unemployment or other problems. Financial dependence can cause the caregiver to attempt to dominate a vulnerable elderly relative who is no longer able to look after himself or herself. Domination may take the form of the caregiver having the elderly person turn over total control of his or her bank account, with the threat of withdrawal of care if the elderly person does not comply.

Abuse can take place in institutional settings as well. Abusive acts by staff may be caused by stress. The abuse may include assault and theft, although institutional abuse more commonly takes the form of neglect, substandard care, and lack of respect for the elderly.

There are some common factors that appear to contribute to elder abuse (Nova Scotia Department of Community Services, 2002b). Although these factors may contribute to abusive behaviour, they are not reasons to excuse the behaviour.

1. Stress:

    Abuse can stem from stresses in a caregiver's life. Adult children who care for their parents often face the additional demands of careers, children, and the financial burden of providing for an adult in their home. Note, however, that the majority of caregivers are not abusive no matter how stressful their lives are.

2. Substance abuse/psychological problems:

    Some caregivers may suffer from substance abuse, poor impulse control, and other issues that affect their ability to care for the elderly. These behavioural problems are likely to manifest themselves in other areas of their life, including their care of an elderly person.

3. Unresolved family conflict/abusive behaviour patterns:

    If an adult child was abused at a young age, he or she may simply repeat the abuse. Homicide data from 1997 to 2000 indicate that 43 percent of individuals accused of committing a homicide against an older adult family member had a history of family violence with that victim. Although this may be a contributing factor, the majority of abused children are not abusive in adulthood.

4. Increased vulnerability:

    As adults age, they may increasingly have to rely on a caregiver for daily care and emotional support if they suffer from physical or cognitive impairment, or if they lack mobility. Elderly persons who become increasingly powerless, vulnerable, and dependent on their caregivers may be at higher risk for abuse.

5. Societal factors:

    Canadian and American cultures in general have been conditioned to have negative social attitudes about aging.

    Many members of the public perceive that the elderly are generally frail, dependent, sick, and unproductive. This belief, called **ageism**, could lead to discrimination against older adults and may contribute to abuse.

ageism
discriminatory belief that the elderly are generally frail, dependent, sick, and unproductive

POLICE INTERVENTION

The goals of police intervention are to stop the abuse and improve the quality of life of the victim. With those goals in mind, police should ask themselves the following questions before beginning the intervention:

- In what way will the intervention empower the victim?

- In what way will the intervention deprive the victim of power?

- In what way will the intervention enhance the victim's safety?

- In what way will the intervention reduce the safety of the victim?

With these points in mind, the officer must intercede in a manner that meets the victim's needs but also fulfills his or her duty to investigate possible offences. The abuse complaint will probably not have been initiated by the victim, and the victim may hesitate to provide information.

Officers should not become exasperated in situations where the abused elder does not wish to cooperate. If the person is not suffering from a mental disorder and is able to make logical decisions, he or she may choose to do nothing.

Seniors are adults, not children. Because they are adults, they have the right to choose how they live. However unlikely it may seem to the officer that anyone would want to live in an abusive situation, the choice belongs to the victim. Officers must allow victims of elder abuse to choose the form of help, and the degree of help, that they want. Some victims will choose to live in abusive situations even after the officer explains their options for leaving or getting out of the abusive situation.

Where the victim may be relying on the abuser for daily care and charges have been laid, alternative care arrangements will be necessary. The need for alternative care should not prevent the officer from charging the abuser if charges are warranted, for the abuser must not be allowed to continue his or her abusive behaviour. If the officer fails to act, this may reinforce the abuser's control over the victim. Alternative care may involve removing the abuser from the home and making arrangements with a community agency. This may be against the wishes of the victim.

Communicating with the Elderly Victim

If the victim is hesitant to speak, but does wish to provide a statement, there are a few suggestions that may be helpful:

- Reassure the victim that you are there to help and that you will do everything possible to assist him or her.

- Talk with the victim alone. The victim is not likely to talk about possible abuse when there is a chance that the abuser could overhear.

- Don't rush the victim. Allow the victim time to get his or her thoughts together and respond to your questions before you speak again.

Officers can also facilitate communication by being sensitive to the victim's feelings:

- Empathy and kindness must be displayed. If the allegations of abuse are true, the elderly victim has reason not to trust persons who claim that they want to help. The victim may have led a fearful, isolated life for a long time and have lost faith in the idea that things can get better. An officer who responds with courtesy, empathy, and kindness may be able to reduce the victim's level of distrust.

- The officer should not assume that all elderly persons have physical difficulties. Assuming, for example, that the elderly are always hard of hearing can embarrass both parties if an officer speaks too loudly to someone with normal hearing.

- If a radio or television is on in the room, the elderly person should be asked whether it may be turned off. The officer should not turn it off without permission, for this may lead the person to believe that the officer is trying to control his or her environment, which in turn will reinforce the person's feelings of helplessness.

Communication with the victim may be difficult if he or she has health problems such as diminished eyesight or hearing. In such situations the following approaches can help:

- On first encountering an elderly person, the officer should speak normally but look for any signs of hearing difficulty such as a puzzled facial expression, leaning to one side to favour a "good" ear, and responding to questions in a way that indicates the questions were not properly understood. If there is a question of this or any other physical disability, the officer should ask the victim if indeed there is a problem.

- The officer should speak directly to the elderly person. This may enhance the accuracy of communication. If the person is wearing a hearing aid, the officer can politely ask whether it is properly adjusted.

- If the elderly person has eyesight problems, the officer should try to ensure that any written information provided to the person is in large print.

With the permission of the victim, the officer should obtain statements from neighbours, family, and others with pertinent information. A thorough investigation may include consulting medical records (with the permission of the victim) and speaking with health care professionals to obtain information on possible previous abuse.

PERSONS WITH ALZHEIMER'S DISEASE

As with many other elderly persons who depend on others for their care, people with Alzheimer's are at risk for elder abuse. **Alzheimer's disease** is a progressive, degenerative disease that destroys brain cells and causes dementia. It can strike adults at any age, but it is most common in persons 65 and older. Some of the signs of Alzheimer's disease include the following (Alzheimer Society, 2005):

Alzheimer's disease
a progressive, degenerative disease that destroys brain cells and causes dementia

- memory loss that affects day-to-day functioning;

- difficulty performing familiar tasks;

- problems with language;

- chronological and spatial disorientation;

- decreased powers of judgment;

- problems with abstract thinking;

- misplacement of possessions;

- changes in mood or behaviour;

- changes in personality; and

- loss of initiative.

Conversing with a person with Alzheimer's disease to determine whether he or she has been abused may be difficult. The officer should use communication techniques that enhance the person's ability to understand the situation. The following techniques may be helpful:

- *Get the person's attention.* Approach slowly and if possible from the front. Gently touch the person to get his or her attention if the person appears unresponsive. Although the person's cognitive abilities may be greatly reduced, he or she may still be able to communicate by touch, emotion, or facial expression.

- *Make eye contact.* Making eye contact will help the person know who is speaking and may help the person concentrate on the message. Be aware of your body and facial expressions. Your non-verbal language may convey messages more powerfully than your verbal communication.

- *Speak slowly and clearly.* Use simple words and short sentences. Take your time and allow the person time to respond. Interrupting may discourage further communication.

- *Communicate one message at a time.* Keep the conversation simple. Too many thoughts or ideas may be confusing. Try to limit your questions to those that can be answered with a "yes" or a "no."

- *Pay attention to the person's reactions and body language.* Remember, although the person's cognitive abilities may be diminished, he or she may still be able to express emotions that convey meaning. Respond to the person's body language and emotions, even if they do not appear to match the person's verbal communications.

- *Use actions to illustrate your message.* Examples include pointing to a door or showing the person an article of his or her clothing to illustrate what you mean.

Although it may be frustrating to try to communicate with a person suffering from Alzheimer's disease, if the disease has not progressed to the later stages, the victim may be able to identify possible abusive behaviours.

THE MENTAL HEALTH OF THE ELDERLY

The mental health of any individual is difficult to assess during a short conversation. Common mental disorders of the elderly such as depression, dementia, and Alzheimer's disease make assessing the mental health of an elderly person much more difficult for police officers. Not only may the person be unaware of his or her disorder, the disorder itself may cause communication difficulty. Or, the person may be aware that he or she has a mental disorder but try to hide that fact because he or she fears social stigmatization or removal from the home.

Depression

depression
an illness involving one's body, mood, and thoughts; characterized by persistent feelings of sadness and loss of interest

Depression is an illness involving one's body, mood, and thoughts, and is characterized by persistent feelings of sadness and loss of interest. Depression is not the same as having a bad day. The feeling of being "down" may last for days, weeks, months, or years.

A 2002 Statistics Canada report identifies approximately 1.9 percent (72,390) of all Canadians over the age of 65 as having symptoms of a major depressive episode (Statistics Canada, 2003). A major depressive episode requires at least one episode of two weeks or more with persistent depressed mood and loss of interest or pleasure in normal activities, accompanied by problems such as decreased energy, changes in sleep and appetite, impaired concentration, feelings of guilt or hopelessness, and suicidal thoughts. This percentage may be higher because many people with depression, fearing social stigmatization or lack of understanding, do not seek treatment.

The symptoms of depression include the following (Canadian Mental Health Association, 1992):

- feelings of worthlessness, helplessness, or hopelessness;

- cognitive problems such as confusion, loss of memory, and inability to concentrate;

- prolonged sadness or unexplained crying spells;

- loss of interest in formerly enjoyable activities;

- withdrawal from friends;

- loss of or increase in appetite;

- persistent fatigue and lethargy;

- insomnia or need for increased sleep;

- aches and pains that cannot otherwise be explained; and

- suicidal thoughts.

The officer responding to a complaint of abuse may not recognize these symptoms and not understand that the elderly person is too depressed to recognize the abuse. The elderly person may fail to recognize that the abuser has contributed to the depression. (In some cases the depression is not the result of abuse, but the abuser takes advantage of the person's depressed state.)

Dementia

Dementia is characterized by confusion, memory loss, and disorientation (American Psychiatric Association, 2004). Most kinds of dementia are caused by Alzheimer's disease. Other causes include chronic high blood pressure, stroke, Parkinson's disease, and Huntington's disease. Dementia-like symptoms can be caused by adverse drug interactions, which are more common among the elderly. The possibility that an elderly abuse victim may be suffering the effects of overmedication by his or her caregiver should be considered, although it can be difficult to substantiate. The symptoms of dementia can also be mimicked by the symptoms of malnutrition (possibly caused by caregiver neglect) or insufficient blood flow or blood oxygenation related to heart disease, lung disease, or other conditions.

The investigating officer may have difficulty communicating with a victim of abuse who is also suffering from dementia. The victim may be withdrawn, unable to concentrate, and confused. The officer's ability to obtain clear and concise information in such circumstances will be greatly diminished. The officer should place all of what he or she observes into context.

dementia
mental deterioration characterized by confusion, memory loss, and disorientation

It may not be possible to obtain concise or even intelligible answers from a person suffering from dementia. This creates a difficult situation for police officers. The victim may not be able to recognize that he or she is being abused. Physical indications of abuse such as bruises, lacerations, bedsores, emaciation, and lack of cleanliness may be the only evidence an officer can obtain.

If possible, the names of any medications in plain sight should be recorded. It may be possible that the dementia has been induced intentionally through medication.

The officer must use his or her judgment to determine whether the apparent dementia is the result of abuse or simply of physical or mental conditions unrelated to improper treatment. The officer's lateral thinking skills should enhance his or her ability to arrive at a decision.

COMMUNITY SERVICES

Stopping the abuse is the best long-term solution for the elderly victim. However, because ending the abuse may mean removing the primary caregiver, the elderly person may be faced with the immediate problem of having no one to look after him or her. As a result, the victim's fears of institutionalization may be realized, prompting him or her to ask that charges not be laid or withdrawn. This request may or may not be granted. There is no directive or legislation that requires police to lay charges in cases of elder abuse, nor is there a policy requiring the Crown prosecutor to prosecute the accused.

In seeking to solve these problems, the Department of Justice Canada, through the National Crime Prevention Strategy and the Justice Partnership and Innovation Fund, now supports community-based initiatives to address the issue of elder abuse. These projects focus on awareness-raising activities, peer counselling programs, advocacy programs, and the establishment of community-based networks to consult and take action on the issue of abuse of elderly persons.

Police can contact local seniors' advocacy groups to obtain information about how to receive in-home care, which they can then pass on to the victims to allay their concerns. Police can inform victims that there are provincial programs in place that provide in-home care for seniors depending on the level of care needed. In most communities, homemaking services that assist the elderly person with cooking, cleaning, and personal care are available, as are home health care services that assist with in-home medical treatment.

KEY TERMS

ageism

Alzheimer's disease

dementia

depression

elder abuse

elderly person

neglect

power of attorney

REFERENCES

Alzheimer Society. (2005). *Alzheimer disease: 10 warning signs.*
http://www.alzheimer.ca/english/disease/warningsigns.htm.

American Psychiatric Association. (2004). *Mental health of the elderly.*
http://www.psych.org/public_info/elderly.cfm.

Canadian Centre for Justice Statistics. (2004). *Uniform crime reporting survey.*
Ottawa: Statistics Canada.

Canadian Mental Health Association. (1992). *1992 COMPAS survey of Canadians
about mental health, mental illness and depression.* Toronto: Author.

College of Nurses of Ontario. (1997). *Abuse of clients by RNs and RNAs: Report to
council on result of Canada Health Monitor Survey of Registrants.* Toronto:
Author.

Criminal Code. (1985). RSC 1985, c. C-46, as amended.

Department of Justice Canada. (2003). *Abuse of older adults: A fact sheet from the
Department of Justice Canada.* http://canada.justice.gc.ca/en/ps/fm/
adultsfs.html.

Martin's Annual Criminal Code, 2005. (2005). Aurora, ON: Canada Law Book.

Nova Scotia Department of Community Services. (2002a). *Fact sheet 7: Elder
abuse.* http://www.gov.ns.ca/coms/files/facts7.asp.

Nova Scotia Department of Community Services. (2002b). *Fact sheet 8: Abuse of
persons with disabilities.* http://www.gov.ns.ca/coms/files/facts8.asp.

Podnieks, E., et al. (1990). *National survey on abuse of the elderly in Canada: The
Ryerson study.* Toronto: Ryerson Polytechnical Institute.

Statistics Canada. (1995). *Causes of death.* Ottawa: Author.

Statistics Canada. (2000). *1999 general social survey on victimization.* Ottawa:
Author.

Statistics Canada. (2003). *Canadian community health survey: Mental health and
well-being.* Ottawa: Author.

University of Alberta. Legal Studies Program. (2003a). *Abuse of older adults—
Neglect and self-neglect FAQs.* http://www.law-faqs.org/elder/
eld-negl02.htm.

University of Alberta. Legal Studies Program. (2003b). *Abuse of older adults—
Emotional abuse FAQs.* http://www.law-faqs.org/elder/eld-emot02.htm.

Winnipeg Police Service. (2000). *Elder abuse.* http://www.winnipeg.ca/police/
TakeAction/elder%20abuse.htm.

EXERCISES

True or False

_____   1. Abusers of the elderly are often family members.

_____   2. Elder abuse is often reported by the victim.

_____   3. Isolation from friends and family is common in elder abuse.

_____   4. When attempting to communicate with a possible victim of elder abuse, police officers should always assume that the elderly person will be unable to communicate properly because of physical disabilities such as hearing loss.

_____   5. The elderly rarely suffer from depression.

_____   6. Withholding the necessaries of life from an elderly person can be a *Criminal Code* offence.

_____   7. The victim of elder abuse must initiate a complaint before the police can investigate.

Short Answer

1. Briefly define elder abuse.

2. Identify the five types of elder abuse discussed in this chapter and give an example of each.

   a.

   b.

   c.

d.

e.

3. Explain why victims of elder abuse seldom report being abused.

4. List four signs of possible physical elder abuse.

a.

b.

c.

d.

5. List two signs of possible sexual elder abuse.

   a.

   b.

6. List four signs of possible financial abuse of elders.

   a.

   b.

   c.

   d.

7. List four signs of possible neglect of elders.

   a.

b.

c.

d.

8. List four signs of possible emotional/psychological abuse of elders.

a.

b.

c.

d.

9. Describe five factors that may contribute to the abuse of elders.

   a.

   b.

   c.

   d.

   e.

10. Summarize the problems a police officer can face in obtaining information from a suspected victim of elder abuse. Be sure to mention depression and dementia in your answer. What approaches can the officer adopt to facilitate communication?

Case Analysis

Case 5.1

You are a police officer. You have received a complaint of elder abuse from a health care agency. The complaint alleges that a client is being abused by her son, the primary caregiver. The agency provides in-home care for the alleged victim, an 80-year-old woman. The alleged victim has had a stroke and is unable to care for herself. The agency reports that when one of its employees went to the client's house, the son refused to allow her in. He told the agency employee that his mother was too sick to see anyone and that he would look after her. The agency also reports that its employees have suspected on previous occasions that the son is emotionally abusing the mother.

Using the CAPRA system discussed in chapter 2, describe what you will do in this situation.

Case 5.2

You are a police officer. You have just stopped at a convenience store to buy a package of chewing gum. In front of you is an elderly man buying a package of pipe tobacco. He is dressed in dirty clothes and smells of urine. He does not produce any money but tells the clerk to put it on his tab. He then walks out. You approach the clerk to pay for your gum. He begins a conversation with you about the old man. The clerk, a male in his sixties, tells you that he used to work for the old man, Mr. Todd. Todd was once a successful businessman and is quite wealthy, but for the past three years he has never seemed to have any money. His sister is looking after him; she comes in and pays his tab three or four times a year.

Another older gentleman, Mr. Pitt, who has been listening to the conversation, interrupts. He tells you that he is a friend of Todd. He went to visit Todd last week after being unable to reach him by telephone. He found some notices informing Todd that his telephone service would be cut off if he did not pay an outstanding bill of $65. The notices indicated that Todd's cable service had already been cut off for non-payment. Pitt says that there was no food in the house and that the entire house was filthy. According to Pitt, Todd suffers from dementia and has difficulty carrying on a conversation. Pitt tells you that he is concerned about the well-being of his friend. He asks you to look into the matter and see whether anything can be done.

Using the CAPRA system discussed in chapter 2, describe what you will do in this situation.

Case 5.3

You are a police officer. You have been called to a residence regarding possible abuse of an elderly person. You speak to Mr. Smith, who tells you that there is nothing wrong and that no abuse has taken place. You hear someone call from another room, "Who is there?" Mr. Smith yells, "Be quiet!" You ask who is in the other room.

Smith replies, "My grandfather." You ask to speak to the grandfather. Smith replies, "Sure."

You enter the room where you find an elderly gentleman, identified as Mr. George Jacobs, 88 years old. He is tied to a large chair with a bed sheet. The bed sheet has been put around him under his arms and tied at the back of the chair. Jacobs begins shouting at his grandson, "Now you are in trouble, the police are here!"

You ask Smith why Jacobs is tied to the chair. Smith tells you that his grandfather has Alzheimer's disease and has trouble with his hips and knees. If he doesn't tie him to the chair, he wanders around the house. Smith explains that he can't watch him all the time and he fears that his grandfather will fall and hurt himself. He ties him to the chair for a few hours each afternoon so that he can get the housework done and prepare dinner for his grandfather.

Smith assures you that the sheet does not hurt his grandfather. The chair is very comfortable and Jacobs has the remote for the television, so he can watch whatever he wants. Smith assures you that he provides him with drinks and snacks in case he gets hungry or thirsty. As well, he puts the telephone beside the chair so that Jacobs can call anyone he wants.

Jacobs confirms that the sheet does not hurt, but he says that he doesn't want to be tied. He tells you that he does have some problems with his memory, but his knees and hips work most of the time.

Using the CAPRA system discussed in chapter 2, explain what you will do in this situation.

CHAPTER 6

Mental Illness and Psychological Disorders

Chapter Objectives

After completing this chapter, you should be able to:

- Identify mental illness from a policing perspective.

- Identify some of the common symptoms of mental illnesses.

- Identify and apply pertinent provisions of the *Mental Health Act* of Ontario.

- Identify personality disorders commonly encountered in policing.

- Identify and apply effective techniques for intervening with mentally ill persons.

- Identify symptoms of excited delirium.

INTRODUCTION

Since 1995, the Ontario government has undertaken major initiatives to update Ontario's mental health system to reflect modern practices and philosophies of hospital and community care. One of these initiatives involved a decrease in the proportion of funding for hospital-based treatment and an increase in the proportion of funding for community-based treatment. In 1994–95, 75 percent of these funds went to hospital-based treatment and 25 percent went to community-based treatment. But in 1999–2000, only 60 percent of these funds went to hospital-based treatment while 40 percent went to community-based treatment. This trend has continued in recent years.

The Canadian Mental Health Association has identified that waiting lists for services across the province of Ontario have grown significantly. Thousands of people in Ontario have no access to mental health services, possibly because funding for community mental health services has not been significantly increased over the past 10 years (Canadian Mental Health Association, 2005a). Complicating these problems is the government's policy of deinstitutionalization, begun in the late 1960s, in which hospital beds were closed and mentally ill patients were discharged into the community.

Deinstitutionalization, along with no significant increase in community care funding, may be why there has been an apparent increase in the frequency of interactions between police and mentally ill persons. Police are having to stand in as front-line mental health care workers. People with mental illness are increasingly coming into contact with police for minor nuisance crimes because of an apparent lack of mental health care.

For example, a study of the London, Ontario police department showed that between 1998 and 2001, the number of hours uniformed police spent dealing with people with serious mental illness doubled from 5,000 to 10,000 (Canadian Mental Health Association, 2005b). The study also showed that the increase in calls was for minor nuisance crimes or no crime at all, and that violent crime among people with serious mental illness was in fact decreasing. The same study showed that calls involving people with mental illness required up to $3.7 million of the $43 million London police department's 2001 budget.

The likelihood of contact with mentally ill persons has substantially increased for police. It is therefore important that police officers be able to recognize the symptoms and behaviours that may indicate mental illness. A basic understanding of mental illness may help officers decide which response option they choose.

This chapter will examine mental illness from the perspective of police intervention. It will show how officers can identify mental illness, and it will discuss intervention strategies.

FACTS ABOUT MENTAL ILLNESS

The following are facts about mental illness in Ontario (Canadian Mental Health Association, 2005b).

- 1 percent of Ontarians suffer from schizophrenia.

- 3 percent of Ontarians suffer from bipolar disorder.

- 5 to 12 percent of men and 10 to 25 percent of women in Ontario will have at least one episode of major depressive disorder in their lifetime.

- More than 90 percent of suicide victims have a diagnosable psychiatric illness.

- Persons who have depressive illness carry out 80 percent of all suicides.

- Both major depression and bipolar disorder account for 15 to 25 percent of all deaths by suicide in patients with severe mood disorders.

- Suicide is the most common cause of death for people with schizophrenia.

- 15 percent of people who have significant depressive illness commit suicide.

Statistics Canada reports that 70,557 Ontarians were hospitalized in 2000–1 due to mental disorders (Statistics Canada, 2001). Disorders requiring hospitalization included psychoses of varying causes such as bipolar disorder, schizophrenia, and personality disorders. These accounted for 72 percent of admissions.

IDENTIFYING MENTAL ILLNESS

Note: The information presented below is sufficient only to identify that a mental illness may be present and must not be used to attempt to diagnose specific disorders.

Bipolar Disorder

Bipolar disorder (also called manic-depression) is an illness characterized by alternating periods of mania and depression. A chemical imbalance in the brain is believed to be the cause of this illness. Mood swings may be mild, moderate, or severe. Not all people experience only the extremes of depression or mania; they may have one episode of mania and then have many periods of depression interspersed with periods of normal mood. Many people who suffer from bipolar disorder are able to control the illness with the assistance of medication.

bipolar disorder
illness characterized by alternating periods of mania and depression

In the manic phase, the person may feel "on top of the world" and believe that he or she does not require sleep. Thought processes may be accelerated, and the person may perceive that he or she is in a highly productive state. This perceived productivity may lead the person to maintain that nothing is wrong. The person may show dangerous lapses in judgment, experience feelings of invincibility, or display impulsive behaviour, potentially leading him or her to take chances or make decisions that may be injurious. Other symptoms include an exaggerated sense of self-esteem, continual talking, or an inability to concentrate. In its most severe form, the manic stage of the illness could involve extreme agitation and loss of reason (psychosis), delusions, or hallucinations.

In the depressed phase, the person suffers from feelings of sadness, hopelessness, and helplessness and experiences many other debilitating symptoms (described below). Suicide is a real threat, especially during an episode of depression.

Recognition of Bipolar Disorder

The following sections provide a brief description of some of the signs and symptoms that may be displayed by a person with bipolar disorder.

Note: These descriptions must not be used by a layperson to suggest or diagnose that any person may have bipolar disorder. They indicate only that the person may have a mental illness.

MANIC OR "HIGH" PHASE

Persons with bipolar disorder may show the following signs and symptoms when in the manic phase of the illness (Patient Health International, 2005):

- excessively high or euphoric feelings;

- extreme irritability;

- unrealistic belief in capabilities and powers;

- increased libido;

- uncharacteristically bad judgment;

- decreased need for sleep;

- refusal to admit that anything is wrong;

- intrusive, provocative, or aggressive behaviour;

- increased energy, restlessness, activity, racing thoughts, rapid speech; and

- drug abuse.

DEPRESSED OR "LOW" PHASE

Persons with bipolar disorder may show the following signs and symptoms when in the depressed phase of the illness (Patient Health International, 2005):

- persistent anxious, sad, or empty mood;

- feelings of hopelessness or pessimism;

- withdrawal from social contacts such as family and friends;

- preoccupation with failure or inadequacies;

- feelings of guilt, worthlessness, or helplessness;

- loss of interest in ordinary activities, including sex;

- decreased energy, feelings of fatigue;

- difficulty concentrating, remembering, making decisions;

- restlessness or irritability;

- sleep disturbances (too little or too much);

- loss of appetite, and weight loss or weight gain;

- chronic pain; and

- thoughts of death or suicide, or occasionally thoughts of homicide.

A person with bipolar disorder may slowly cycle through the mood phases or may rapidly cycle through the phases, causing severe mood changes in a short time period. The intervals between episodes and duration of manic or depressed stages may last for days, months, or, in rare cases, for years. This cycling of moods, extended depressed state, feelings of invincibility, and risk-taking behaviour may increase the risk of accidental death or injury or of suicide. There does not appear to be a significant risk of increased violent behaviour toward others, although the possibility exists.

Depressive Disorders

Depression is a mood disorder—a medical condition that is common and treatable. Depression occurs in all economic, geographic, social, and cultural settings.

Statistics Canada's *National Population Health Survey* (1997) reported that the total number of people that felt sad, blue, or depressed, or had lost interest in ordinary activities was 1,314,000.

Approximately 15 percent of the population suffer from moderate to severe depression during some time in their life. It is often difficult to predict when a depressive episode will occur, how long it will last, or what will trigger it.

Clinical depression (also called major depression or unipolar disorder) is an illness that is characterized by continually low, sad, and depressed mood that interferes with the individual's ability to work, sleep, eat, and enjoy once-pleasurable activities. Disabling episodes of depression can occur once, twice, or several times in a lifetime. Approximately 1 percent of Canadian men and 2 percent of Canadian women are clinically depressed at any one point in time, and about 5 percent of men and 10 percent of women experience clinical depression at some point in their life. Regardless of gender, once a person has had one experience of clinical depression, they are at a higher risk for repeated experiences.

A chronic illness, a severe loss, a difficult relationship, a financial problem, or any unwelcome change in life patterns can trigger a depressive episode. Depression may be related to dysfunctional regulation of the brain's chemistry, causing it to send "depressed" signals. Very often, a combination of genetic, psychological, and environmental factors is involved in the onset of a depressive disorder. Psychological makeup also plays a role in depression. People who have low self-esteem, who consistently view the world with pessimism, or who are easily overwhelmed by stress may be prone to depression.

The social stigma of having a mental illness prevents many people from seeking help, although a variety of effective treatments are available. When a proper diagnosis is made and effective treatment and advice are followed, most people recover. It is imperative that someone experiencing depression seek help. Without effective treatment, approximately 30 percent of persons with severe depressive disorders will attempt suicide. Of these, 15 percent will eventually take their life. This group accounts for almost 80 percent of all suicides.

There does not appear to be a substantial risk of violent behaviour toward others, although as with all police–public interactions, police officers must consider their own safety.

clinical depression
an illness that is characterized by a continually low, sad, and depressed mood and that interferes with the individual's ability to work, sleep, eat, and enjoy once-pleasurable activities

SYMPTOMS

The symptoms of depression may be difficult for police officers to identify given time constraints and the nature of the symptoms associated with the illness. Even so, officers should be aware that depressed individuals may show the following symptoms (Depression and Manic Depression Association of Alberta, 2005):

- a marked decrease in interest in usual activities, and often withdrawal from activities;

- feelings of sadness, emptiness, hopelessness, and anxiety;

- difficulty falling asleep and/or early awakening;

- thoughts about suicide;

- fatigue and energy loss;

- irritability;

- changes in eating habits; and

- difficulty with concentration, decision making, and memory.

Children and adolescents can also develop depression, often resulting in learning problems, school failure, disturbed relationships with other people, tendency to illness or psychosomatic disorders, or suicidal thoughts. Symptoms are similar to those in adult depression but children express them through different behaviours such as disruptiveness, fighting, delinquency, bed wetting, and substance abuse.

Postpartum Depression

Many women experience symptoms of depression after childbirth. These symptoms can range from a brief attack of the "baby blues" to clinical depression. This experience is referred to as **postpartum depression**. About 80 percent of new mothers will experience a mild form of postpartum depression, usually within a few days or weeks after giving birth (MediResource Inc., 2005). These feelings will usually disappear in a few weeks.

postpartum depression symptoms of depression that can range from a brief attack of the "baby blues" to clinical depression

Women who experience the baby blues commonly feel sad, angry, irritable, and insecure. They may experience self-doubts about being a competent mother, which may contribute to these feelings. They may burst into tears, often without apparent reason. Baby blues may also trigger the occasional negative thought about the baby. Although these feelings are upsetting to the mother, they are normal.

A more severe form of postpartum depression will affect about 20 percent of new mothers. This type of depression is more common with first pregnancies, and can affect women who were not previously depressed. Approximately 20 to 40 percent of women will also experience postpartum depression with subsequent births.

Severe postpartum depression is longer lasting than the baby blues. It includes the symptoms described above, as well as more serious symptoms. Postpartum depression resembles other forms of depression but has a somewhat unusual combination of symptoms that often include confusion and sometimes features of schizophrenia.

Some of the more common indicators of severe postpartum depression include:

- constant fatigue,
- a lack of interest in daily activities,
- withdrawal from friends and family,
- a lack of concern or overconcern for self and baby,
- insomnia,
- a lack of sexual responsiveness,
- severe mood swings, and
- a sense of failure and inadequacy.

There is no single definable cause of postpartum depression, although there are several possible contributing factors:

- hormonal changes,
- disappointment in the birth experience,
- a sense of loss from no longer being pregnant,
- marital dissatisfaction,

- the stress of caring for a demanding baby,

- a lack of family and social support,

- physical and mental exhaustion, and

- a family history of postpartum depression.

Although a few women may have a more persisting experience with postpartum depression, about 95 percent of women will improve within two to three months.

The most severe form of postpartum depression is postpartum psychosis. Postpartum psychosis usually develops within a few weeks after childbirth. A woman experiencing this form of depression becomes severely depressed and may experience hallucinations, acute anxiety, paranoia, and hysteria. She may have thoughts related to harming herself or the baby. Postpartum psychosis is relatively rare but requires immediate treatment by a qualified health care provider.

The *Criminal Code* recognizes the significant impact that postpartum depression may have upon the psyche of the sufferer. In some instances a new mother may behave violently toward her newborn child. (Section 2 of the *Criminal Code* defines a newborn child as being less than one year old.)

According to the *Criminal Code*, if a mother's actions cause the death of her child and at the time she was not fully recovered from the effects of childbirth (which includes postpartum depression), she should not be subjected to as severe a penalty as would otherwise be imposed. Section 233 of the *Criminal Code* acknowledges that the effects of childbirth are a mitigating factor in cases where a mother has caused the death of her newborn, and s. 237 describes the punishment for this offence.

INFANTICIDE: CRIMINAL CODE, SECTION 233

A female person commits infanticide when by a wilful act or omission she causes the death of her newly-born child, if at the time of the act or omission she is not fully recovered from the effects of giving birth to the child and by reason thereof or of the effect of lactation consequent on the birth of the child her mind is then disturbed.

PUNISHMENT: CRIMINAL CODE, SECTION 237

Every female person who commits infanticide is guilty of an indictable offence and liable to imprisonment for a term not exceeding five years.

Schizophrenia

The term "schizophrenia" comes from two Greek words: "schizo," which means split, and "phrenia," which means mind (Schizophrenia Society of Ontario, 2005). People who suffer from this illness do not, however, have a split or multiple personality, which is an entirely different condition. The term **schizophrenia** describes a family of psychological disorders characterized by psychotic thoughts, feelings, perceptions, and actions.

The cause of schizophrenia is unknown. It may be caused by a chemical imbalance within the brain, but these chemicals have not been specifically identified. Schizophrenia is often described as the most chronic and disabling of the mental illnesses.

schizophrenia
a family of psychological disorders characterized by psychotic thoughts, feelings, perceptions, and actions

Schizophrenia affects 1 in every 100 Canadians. There are approximately 300,000 people who suffer from schizophrenia in Canada, of whom 100,000 live in Ontario. The symptoms appear in late adolescence and early adulthood. In males the average age of onset is 18; in women it is 25. It is not possible to accurately describe all the symptoms that may be exhibited by persons diagnosed with schizophrenia, although some generalized symptoms may be observed.

The most dramatic and disabling symptoms involve reality distortion and disorganization of thinking. These symptoms can appear rapidly and include delusions of persecution or grandiosity, and hallucinations. These symptoms are usually treatable with medication.

The initial symptoms of schizophrenia usually appear well before the person's first psychotic episode. Parents may notice that a child who was once ambitious and outgoing has become withdrawn from friends and family, has lost interest in his or her usual activities, and has become unfeeling. Parents may find it difficult to decide whether something is really wrong with their child. The adolescent experience that all teenagers go through can involve similar periods of moodiness and withdrawal.

Psychotic episodes, with their attendant distortion of reality and altered brain function, often result in the psychotic person being hospitalized because they are deemed to be a danger to themselves and possibly to others. Someone experiencing a psychotic episode can be unpredictable and dangerous, especially when he or she has a concurrent substance abuse problem. Approximately 50 percent of persons diagnosed with schizophrenia develop a substance abuse problem that requires medical attention at some point in their life. The substance abuse may develop as the symptoms of schizophrenia worsen, perhaps as an escape for the sufferer or a way to deal with the fear of what he or she is beginning to experience.

The psychotic episodes that the schizophrenic person experiences may take the form of unusual realities, hallucinations, and delusions. Each type of psychotic episode is discussed below.

UNUSUAL REALITIES

unusual realities
perceptions of reality and views of the world that are sharply different from those of people who are not mentally ill and that may cause anxiety and confusion

To the person experiencing **unusual realities**, the world may appear distorted or changeable, possibly causing anxiety and confusion. This person may seem detached, distant, or preoccupied and may even sit without moving for hours, not uttering a sound. Alternatively, the person may be constantly moving, wide awake, vigilant, and alert.

HALLUCINATIONS

hallucination
sensory perception that is real only to the person experiencing it

Hallucinations are sensory perceptions that are real only to the person experiencing them. They may be experienced through all five senses: hearing, sight, smell, touch, and taste. The person may sense things that do not exist, such as imaginary voices that direct them to carry out certain actions. He or she may see persons or objects that do not exist or believe that things are touching them. The most common type of hallucination is the auditory hallucination (hearing voices). Attempts to convince the individual that his or her hallucination is unreal are generally futile. Still, it may be possible to appeal to the person's logic if he or she is not yet totally immersed in the hallucination.

To determine an appropriate response in dealing with a hallucinating person, officers should calmly ask the person whether he or she is seeing or hearing anything. Even if the person cannot respond logically, the officer can determine the nature and substance of the hallucination. Doing so is important because the hallucination could be directing the person to hurt someone, including the officer. Knowledge of the person's perception of their surroundings may assist the officer in choosing an appropriate response and in alleviating confusion about the person's apparently illogical display of agitation or fear.

DELUSIONS

Delusions are defects in belief or thought processes that are not reasonable. They are common to schizophrenia and usually involve themes of persecution and grandeur. Persons experiencing delusions of grandeur are not trying to convince others of their superiority—they sincerely believe that they are superior or have extraordinary powers. They may believe that they are an important person of the past, present, or future. Not all people suffering from delusions pose problems for police. For example, the delusional person could believe that he or she is a significant religious figure and behave virtuously. However, police should still exercise caution when dealing with these individuals. A person experiencing a religious delusion could also believe that he or she is superior to the police and thus not required to take direction from "inferior" persons. These delusions may develop into a state of paranoia.

delusion
defect in belief or thought processes that is not reasonable

More serious are **delusions of persecution**, which are common to paranoid schizophrenia. These are false and irrational beliefs that a person is being harassed, cheated, poisoned, or conspired against. Persons suffering from this type of delusion may become hostile, suspicious, reclusive, and uncooperative. They may also be dangerous. If they are convinced that they are about to be harmed, they may respond violently in an attempt to protect themselves. Therefore, officers must exercise extreme caution when dealing with these individuals. The officers' actions should be slow, and prior warning should be given before an action is taken—for example, "I am moving across the room. I am not going to hurt you." Officers should ensure that they do not touch the person or invade his or her personal space unless they need to apprehend the individual or protect themselves.

delusions of persecution
false and irrational beliefs that a person is being harassed, cheated, poisoned, or conspired against

Most schizophrenic individuals, however, are not violent. Some acutely disturbed persons may become violent, but this is relatively infrequent. Persons experiencing a psychotic episode may show an increased propensity toward violence.

Suicide is a potential danger for those with schizophrenia. There appears to be a higher suicide rate among schizophrenics than among the general population. But assessment of suicide risk is difficult because it is often difficult to predict the behaviour of persons with schizophrenia.

OTHER SYMPTOMS OF SCHIZOPHRENIA

The other major group of schizophrenic symptoms are deficits in the person's social and/or cognitive abilities. These symptoms may involve a decrease in motivation, initiative, and emotional response. The symptoms resemble those of clinical depression. Approximately 40 percent of people diagnosed with schizophrenia also experience depression, which can go untreated because of the similarity of the symptoms.

Cognitive deficit symptoms are generally distinct from negative symptoms. Cognitive deficits may impair memory, abstract thinking, vigilance, and other brain functions essential for most employment and social situations. These symptoms usually precede the onset of the first psychotic symptoms.

Some of these cognitive symptoms include disordered thinking and inappropriate emotional expression, which are discussed below.

Disordered Thinking

The person may endure hours of being unable to think straight. Thoughts may come and go so rapidly that it is impossible to "catch them." The person may not be able to concentrate on one thought for very long, may be easily distracted, and may be unable to focus. The person may be unable to order thoughts into logical sequences. The person's thoughts may become disorganized and fragmented, making conversation difficult.

Inappropriate Emotional Expression

People with schizophrenia sometimes exhibit what is called "inappropriate affect." This means showing emotion that is inconsistent with the person's speech or thoughts—for example, giggling while verbally expressing extreme despair.

Often people with schizophrenia show "blunted" or "flat" affect. They may not show the signs of normal emotion. Instead, they speak in a monotonous tone of voice and show little facial expression.

TREATING SCHIZOPHRENIA

One of the major difficulties in treating schizophrenia is that the affected individual rarely recognizes his or her symptoms as a disease process. Treatment often depends on the individual recognizing these symptoms as being those of schizophrenia. Without an awareness of his or her illness, the sufferer does not have any motivation to take medication to treat the illness. This poses a perplexing situation. During a delusional or hallucinatory episode, the person does not perceive that anything is out of the ordinary with his or her thought patterns. The delusion or hallucination is perceived as reality. The schizophrenic person finds no reason to believe that medication is needed to control his or her allegedly abnormal thoughts and perceptions.

Relapse is a common problem among schizophrenic people who are receiving treatment. The rate of relapse requiring hospitalization to treat psychotic episodes is about 80 percent in the first year of treatment. The major factor contributing to the relapse is the failure of the person to take his or her prescribed medication.

COMMUNITY TREATMENT ORDERS

With the objective of preventing recurrence of psychotic episodes, the *Mental Health Act* (MHA) was amended in 2000 to include the use of community treatment orders. Community treatment orders may assist in ensuring that the mentally ill person follows his or her prescribed treatment plan (see appendix 6D at the end of this chapter: Form 45, MHA). Community treatment orders may be useful in helping physicians provide treatment for patients who are unwilling to submit themselves for treatment. Such orders are legal documents that outline the conditions under which individuals with a serious mental illness may be treated within the community.

The purpose of community treatment orders is described in s. 33.1(3) of the MHA:

> The purpose of a community treatment order is to provide a person who suffers from a serious mental disorder with a comprehensive plan of community-based treatment or care and supervision that is less restrictive than being detained in a psychiatric facility. Without limiting the generality of the foregoing, a purpose is to provide such a plan for a person who, as a result of his or her serious mental disorder, experiences this pattern: The person is admitted to a psychiatric facility where his or her condition is usually stabilized; after being released from the facility, the person often stops the treatment or care and supervision; the person's condition changes and, as a result, the person must be re-admitted to a psychiatric facility.

These orders are somewhat controversial in that the person named in the order may be seen as not voluntarily submitting to therapy, but agreeing to the conditions of the order so that he or she will not be hospitalized, or so that he or she will be released from a psychiatric facility. Specific criteria must be met before authorization to issue a community treatment order is granted. These conditions are set out in s. 33.1(4) of the MHA.

CRITERIA FOR ORDER: MENTAL HEALTH ACT, SECTION 33.1(4)

A physician may issue or renew a community treatment order under this section if,

(a) during the previous three-year period, the person,

(i) has been a patient in a psychiatric facility on two or more separate occasions or for a cumulative period of 30 days or more during that three-year period, or

(ii) has been the subject of a previous community treatment order under this section;

(b) the person or his or her substitute decision-maker [see appendix 6G at the end of this chapter: *Health Care Consent Act, 1996*], the physician who is considering issuing or renewing the community treatment order and any other health practitioner or person involved in the person's treatment or care and supervision have developed a community treatment plan for the person;

(c) within the 72-hour period before entering into the community treatment plan, the physician has examined the person and is of the opinion, based on the examination and any other relevant facts communicated to the physician, that,

(i) the person is suffering from mental disorder such that he or she needs continuing treatment or care and continuing supervision while living in the community,

(ii) the person meets the criteria for the completion of an application for psychiatric assessment under subsection 15(1) or (1.1) where the person is not currently a patient in a psychiatric facility,

(iii) if the person does not receive continuing treatment or care and continuing supervision while living in the community, he or she is likely, because of mental disorder, to cause serious bodily harm to himself or herself or to another person or to suffer substantial mental or physical deterioration of the person or serious physical impairment of the person,

(iv) the person is able to comply with the community treatment plan contained in the community treatment order, and

(v) the treatment or care and supervision required under the terms of the community treatment order are available in the community;

(d) the physician has consulted with the health practitioners or other persons proposed to be named in the community treatment plan;

(e) subject to subsection (5), the physician is satisfied that the person subject to the order and his or her substitute decision-maker, if any, have consulted with a rights adviser and have been advised of their legal rights; and

(f) the person or his or her substitute decision-maker consents to the community treatment plan in accordance with the rules for consent under the *Health Care Consent Act, 1996.*

The order may be used as an alternative to institutionalization for individuals who suffer from a serious mental disorder, who have a history of repeated hospitalizations, and who meet the criteria for committal as set out in the MHA.

Involuntarily institutionalized psychiatric patients who agree to a treatment plan may enter into a community treatment order as a condition of their release from a psychiatric facility. The *Health Care Consent Act* (see appendix 6G at the end of this chapter) allows a substitute decision maker to accept the conditions of the order on behalf of the patient if the substitute decision maker believes that he or she can provide the necessary care.

A community treatment order may be issued by a physician where the following conditions are met (Ministry of Health and Long-Term Care, 2005):

1. the individual may be committed under the committal criteria;

2. it will benefit the person subject to the community treatment order;

3. appropriate supports exist in the community to meet the conditions of the community treatment order;

4. it is less restrictive and less intrusive to provide treatment/supervision for the individual in the community rather than in a psychiatric facility; and

5. consent has been obtained from the individual or substitute decision maker, if the individual is found incapable with respect to treatment.

Community treatment orders are initiated for a period of six months and are thereafter renewable for six-month intervals. They include a treatment plan as well as review, appeal, and cancellation mechanisms.

Safeguards for Patients

Community treatment orders may be seen as a form of coercive treatment and as such must have safeguards to protect the interests of the patient. A number of rights flow from the designation of a community treatment order, including:

- a right of review by the Consent and Capacity Board with appeal to the courts each time a community treatment order is issued;

- a right to request additional reviews by the Consent and Capacity Board in the event of a material change;

- a right to request a re-examination by the issuing physician to determine whether the community treatment order is still necessary for the person to live in the community;

- a right of review of findings of incapacity to consent to treatment; and

- provision for rights advice and an entitlement to counsel appointed by the board.

A person entering into a community treatment order has an obligation to follow the conditions of the order. Failure to follow the conditions may result in the examining physician issuing an order for examination (see appendix 6E at the end of this chapter: Form 47, MHA). Section 33.3(3) of the MHA states that the order is valid for 30 days and directs police to apprehend the named person and escort the person to the issuing physician for examination.

RETURN TO PHYSICIAN: MENTAL HEALTH ACT, SECTION 33.3(3)

An order for examination issued under subsection (1) is sufficient authority, for 30 days after it is issued, for a police officer to take the person named in it into custody and then promptly to the physician who issued the order.

Where a community treatment order is not in force and the person has displayed behaviours, due to a mental illness, that have caused or are likely to cause serious bodily harm to the person or to others, the physician may issue an application by physician for psychiatric assessment (see appendix 6A at the end of this chapter: Form 1, MHA). Foreknowledge of this behaviour should alert the police that officer safety must be a primary consideration when apprehending a person under the authority of an order for examination.

Once the person is apprehended, police are required to bring him or her to the issuing physician for assessment. Under s. 33.4(5) of the MHA, the issuing physician is required to examine the named person and decide whether a psychiatric assessment should be made, another community treatment order should be issued, or the person should be released.

ASSESSMENT ON RETURN: MENTAL HEALTH ACT, SECTION 33.4(5)

The physician shall promptly examine the person to determine whether,

> (a) the physician should make an application for a psychiatric assessment of the person under section 15;

> (b) the physician should issue another community treatment order where the person, or his or her substitute decision-maker, consents to the community treatment plan; or

> (c) the person should be released without being subject to a community treatment order.

If the physician requires a psychiatric assessment authorized by s. 15 of the MHA, police are required by s. 33 to remain with the person until the person is admitted to the psychiatric facility.

PERSONALITY DISORDERS

Personality disorders, although not classified as a mental illness, should be of concern to police officers. Knowledge of personality disorders may assist in officer safety, although it must be remembered that any personality type may present a danger. Caution must always be taken when dealing with any individual—regardless of apparent compliance. There are situations, such as repeated domestic disputes and execution of arrest warrants, where officers are called to the scene, or are engaged in circumstances in which they have prior knowledge of the type of person they will be encountering. Such information may help officers identify whether the person has a personality disorder, and allow the officer to approach the situation accordingly.

The two most frequently encountered personality disorders are the antisocial and the dependent personalities. There disorders, as well as other, less frequently encountered disorders, are discussed below. (Note that the material presented below is for information purposes only and must not be used to attempt to diagnose any specific disorder.)

Antisocial Personality Disorder

antisocial personality disorder
condition characterized by a disregard for the moral and legal rules of society and for other people's rights

Antisocial personality disorder is a condition characterized by a disregard for the moral and legal rules of society and other people's rights. The vast majority of persons with antisocial personality disorders are male (American Psychiatric Association, 1987).

The terms "sociopath" and "psychopath" are often used to describe antisocial personality disorders. The term "sociopath" stresses a pathological relationship with society. The sociopath is not only alienated from society, but also engaged in a negative relationship with members of the smaller social relationships of family and acquaintances. The term "psychopath" suggests that the psyche of the person is pathological. This is made evident through the psychopath's lack of conscience and lack of positive regard or feeling for others.

Regardless of the term used, it must be stressed that persons with an antisocial personality (ASP) are not insane. These individuals may want others to believe that their behaviour is beyond their control—that they act only because of their inability to control their behaviours—but this is a deception. Such a belief may allow them to continue their antisocial behaviour without having to accept responsibility or to face any repercussions for their conduct. The antisocial personality knows that much of what he or she does is considered both inappropriate and wrong by society. However, the person does not incorporate what society judges to be correct into his or her behaviour. He or she knows right from wrong, but chooses not to conform to socially accepted behaviours. The person's judgment as to what is appropriate behaviour is guided only by his or her need for immediate gratification.

Antisocial personality types tend to project upon others the negative consequences of their behaviour. This may include blaming individuals, groups, or society at large for their antisocial conduct. Rarely will they concede that they are responsible for their actions. Another noteworthy aspect of this personality is the propensity for high levels of aggression along with a low tolerance for frustration—a potentially violent mix.

Typically, antisocial personality traits also include a disregard for social obligations. These individuals easily enter into relationships if they perceive that the relationship may be advantageous for them. As soon as the relationship becomes inconvenient, or there is no gain to be had, or they no longer receive the behavioural reinforcement, they terminate the relationship. The relationships may last days or years, but nonetheless will be immediately and callously discontinued when either the relationship no longer provides benefit, or another person gains their attention.

Knowledge of some of the characteristics of the antisocial personality may be useful beyond safety considerations. Knowing the personality type may assist officers in directing the way in which the individual is questioned and treated. As with any investigation, certain approaches may be more effective in eliciting information.

DESCRIPTION OF THE ANTISOCIAL PERSONALITY

Note: Antisocial behaviour may occur during the course of schizophrenia or during manic episodes. Such occurrences do not indicate that the person has an antisocial personality disorder, but are symptoms of the person's illness.

The following is a brief description of some of the characteristics that may be displayed by an antisocial personality.

The person, generally male, is at least 18 years old. Evidence of disorderly conduct is exhibited before age 15, including truancy, initiation of physical confrontations, physical cruelty to people or animals, and acts of vandalism. There is also evidence of irresponsible and antisocial behaviour after the age of 15, including the inability to maintain consistent employment, repeated criminal acts, aggressive or assaultive acts including spousal and/or child abuse, repeatedly failing to honour financial obligations, impulsive behaviour including the inability to maintain a consistent address, no specific immediate goals, reckless regard for personal safety, non-committed personal relationships, and a lack of remorse for wrongs committed.

INTERVIEWING ANTISOCIAL PERSONALITY TYPES

The major obstacle in interviewing the antisocial personality is his or her need to control the conversation (US Department of Justice, FBI Uniform Crime Reports, 1992). At the beginning of the interview, the ASP may be testing his or her limits, observing the reaction of the interviewer, and internally establishing that he or she has control over the interview. Clearly, control of the conversation must always be securely located with the interviewer. However, it may be advantageous for the interviewer to consciously relinquish a small amount of control to the interviewee. This may be accomplished by allowing the ASP to vent his or her feelings about law enforcement, society in general, or whatever group he or she believes is responsible for his or her behaviour. Any lashing out, or show of distaste for the comments of the ASP or the inappropriateness of his or her behaviour, is likely to be based on societal norms and should be avoided: the interviewer must recognize that the ASP does not consider societal normalcy in his or her decision-making process. Such displays may lead the ASP to conclude that, due the interviewer's lack of under-standing and intelligence, further discussion would be meaningless.

It is always a balancing routine with the ASP as to where the "locus of control" rests within the interview process. One of the more successful ways to create an effective rapport is to let the ASP know early in the interview process that he or she is assisting the interviewer. The interviewer should convey to the ASP that with his or her help, the interviewer will obtain information that he or she otherwise could not obtain. This is, in all likelihood, not true, but it establishes in the mind of the ASP his or her importance. Compliance thereafter is more easily received.

Dependent Personality

dependent personality
person who is overreliant on others for his or her physical and emotional needs

Dependent personalities (DPs) are people who are overreliant on others for their physical and emotional needs. These individuals have a history of poor social interaction. They may be described as "weak and ineffective, passive, lacking energy, compliant to a fault, nice but totally inadequate." Typically, these individuals have maintained a relationship well into adulthood with a significant member of their immediate family. These relationships are often identified as "uncomfortable" by the dependent personality—but they maintained the relationship nonetheless. The DP often feels some animosity toward this significant family member. In most instances this family member has made most, if not all, decisions for the DP.

The mental status of the DP reflects the patterns of behaviour one would suspect, including dependency, submissiveness, anxiety, and an overall need to please others. During interviews, the low self-esteem of DP offenders will be apparent. Also noteworthy is the inability of the DP to deal with his or her anger, frustration, and hostility.

The emotional life of these types of individuals can be described using the analogy of a coiled spring. This coil, at the time of birth, begins to be compressed within the person. As he or she experiences situations in which frustration, anger, and hostility are involved, the "spring" compresses more and more. Each time the person is involved in situations that cause stress and anxiety, the tension of this emotional coil increases. Accompanying this increase, a trigger develops that can release the emotional turmoil. Once the trigger has developed, the person is at risk of an explosive episode. There is little or no way to anticipate exactly what will trigger this release. The individual will reach a point when "they have had enough." All the hostility and rage that had been repressed during previous years are vented.

DESCRIPTION

The following is a brief description of some of the characteristics that may be displayed by a dependent personality.

People with dependent personalities show a pervasive pattern of dependent and submissive behaviour beginning in early adulthood. Some indicators include the following:

- the inability to make everyday decisions without reassurance;

- allowing others to make major decisions for them;

- agreeing with others through fear of rejection;

- difficulty doing things by themselves;

- volunteering to do unpleasant or demeaning tasks to get people to like them;

- going to great lengths to avoid being alone;

- feelings of devastation when close relationships end;

- frequent preoccupation with fears of abandonment; and

- susceptibility to emotional injury from criticism.

INTERVIEWING DEPENDENT PERSONALITY TYPES

The interviewer must keep in mind that the DP will not generally take initiative throughout the interview process. This individual has a history of following commands and deferring to the wishes of others. If the correct approach is used, it will be relatively easy to elicit responses from him or her—with one caveat. Although the individual has been conditioned to be compliant, he or she has also developed a resentment to individuals representing authority. Under the apparent calm and docile surface, the dependent personality is a storm of anxiety and fear. His or her inability to deal with years of feelings concerning his or her sense of inadequacy and low self-worth has resulted in inordinate levels of anxiety. This level of anxiety must be reduced in the initial stages of the interview for the interview be productive.

The first technique used to alleviate the DP's fears and anxiety is for the interviewer to state at the beginning of the questioning that he or she understands that the process can sometimes cause anxiety. This allows the DP to consciously recognize his or her anxious feelings. The second technique used to reduce anxiety is to tell the person that the interviewer is not there to pass judgment, only to obtain information. Once the DP's level of anxiety is diminished, the interview can proceed with material directly related to the occurrence in question.

The interviewer must use caution when giving weight to the responses of DPs. In an interview, DPs may demonstrate the same psychological dynamics that they employ when interacting with others outside the interview setting. Consequently, they may sometimes do and say things they feel they should do and say rather than what they actually want to do and say. Therefore, the interviewer must continually verify and corroborate their statements.

OTHER PERSONALITY DISORDERS

This section will give a brief overview of four other personality disorders that are less frequently encountered in policing. The following information must not be used to diagnose any specific disorder.

Borderline Personality Disorder

People with borderline personality disorder display a pervasive pattern of instability of mood (not to be confused with bipolar disorder), interpersonal relationships, and self-image. The disorder begins in early adulthood and expresses itself in a variety of ways:

- a pattern of unstable and intense interpersonal relationships characterized by extremes of excess idealization and devaluation;

- potentially self-damaging behaviour;

- inappropriate, intense anger;

- self-mutilating behaviour;

- uncertainty of self (sexual orientation, goals, friends, etc.); and

- chronic feelings of boredom.

Narcissistic Personality Disorder

Narcissistic personality disorder is characterized by a pervasive pattern of grandiosity in thought or behaviour. The disorder begins in early adulthood. The narcissistic personality exhibits the following traits:

- reacts to criticism with feelings of rage or shame;

- is interpersonally exploitive;

- has an exaggerated sense of self-importance;

- believes that his or her problems are unique and can only be understood by "special" people;

- is preoccupied with fantasies of unlimited success, power, or brilliance;

- has a sense of entitlement; and

- requires constant attention and admiration.

The narcissistic personality is also egocentric, will display a lack of empathy, and is hypersensitive to the evaluation of others.

Passive–Aggressive Disorder

Beginning in early adulthood, the passive–aggressive personality displays a general pattern of passive resistance to demands for adequate social and occupational performance. This pattern is displayed in a variety of ways:

- procrastination;

- becoming sulky, irritable, or argumentative when asked to do something they do not want to do;

- working extremely and deliberately slowly on tasks they do not enjoy;

- protesting when others make demands of them;

- avoiding obligations by claiming to have forgotten them;

- believing that they are doing a much better job than others think they are doing;

- resenting suggestions from others about being more productive; and

- being highly critical of those in authority.

DETERMINING MENTAL ILLNESS: POLICE INTERVENTION

The following information may be used in determining whether a person is likely to be suffering from a mental illness within the meaning of the MHA of Ontario.

Mental illness, for the purpose of police intervention, may be defined as a departure from "normal" thinking that affects a person's ability to interact with his or her environment. There are two general categories of mental disorders encompassed by this definition: those that cause psychotic symptoms (for example, hallucinations and delusions) and those that do not (for example, depression, neuroses, and phobias). Both kinds of mental disorder may be equally debilitating.

In deciding whether to apprehend a person who appears to be mentally ill, the officer must form reasonable grounds to believe that the person is suffering from a mental disorder and that as a result of the disorder is or will be a danger to himself or herself or to others. The officer also has grounds to apprehend if he or she concludes that the person is unable to care for himself or herself due to a mental disorder.

The MHA recognizes that it is unlikely that the attending officer will have the time or the necessary expertise to diagnose a specific mental illness. Police need only conclude that, on the basis of the actions of the person, the person is likely suffering from a mental illness.

mental illness
for the purpose of police intervention, a departure from "normal" thinking that affects a person's ability to interact with his or her environment

Interacting with Persons in a Hallucinatory/ Delusional State

Delusions and hallucinations may be experienced simultaneously by the subject. Interaction with a person in a delusional/hallucinatory state may prove difficult for police. The following are some suggestions to ensure the safety of the officer and the subject during such interactions.

- *Remain aware that the delusion or hallucination is perceived as real to the subject.* The person believes that he or she is experiencing everything he or she sees or feels in the hallucination. If the person is delusional, the departure from normal, rational thought processes convinces the person that the delusion is real. Trying to convince the person otherwise will likely be unproductive.

- *Tell the person that you are there to help.* The person is attempting to interact within separate realities. Allow for delays in responses. If the person asks whether you are experiencing the hallucination or delusion, do not mislead the person by telling him or her that you are. This will reinforce the reality of the experience or lead the person to believe that you are deceiving him or her when you are unable to interact with the imaginary persons or objects in the hallucination. This loss of credibility will hamper your ability to positively interact with the subject.

- *Always make officer safety a major consideration.* Do not become complacent. It is unlikely that the presence of police officers will calm the person. More likely, if the person is delusional or paranoid, he or she will interpret the presence of police officers as evidence of conspiracies against him or her.

- *Watch for rapid movement of the eyes or head, which could indicate that the person is visually hallucinating.* Ask the person whether he or she is seeing or hearing anything or anyone. If so, ask what he or she is seeing or hearing. Try to determine the "message" that the person is receiving. Ask yourself: Is the person likely to react violently to the message?

- *Ask the person what type of assistance he or she requires.* Reassure the subject that police are there to help, provided that the person is not so deeply involved in the delusion that such reassurance will be ineffective. If the person indicates that he or she cannot control his or her actions, explain that police can help if required. If requests for assistance are not forthcoming, offer suggestions such as seeing a doctor or other persons that may assist.

- *If the person begins to speak rapidly, request that he or she slow down.* Such a request may reinforce delusions of intellectual superiority, but it is necessary to try to ascertain the direction of the person's thoughts. If the person does not respond to the request, ask specific questions such as his or her name, address, date of birth, or other questions that require specific answers. The purpose of such questioning is to try to force the person to slow down and think about the question.

- *Pay particular attention to the person's non-verbal messages.* Clenched fists, clenched teeth, and stiff or rapid movements may be indicators of potential violence. Or, if the person is non-responsive, he or she may display passive behaviour, not speak, and may stand motionless.

- *If the decision is made to apprehend the person under the authority of s. 17 of the MHA, tell the person of your intention.* There is the possibility of a violent reaction or refusal to cooperate. If safety precautions have been adhered to, such as removing access to weapons, and ensuring the availability of backup, the level of potential violence should be more easily managed. If the person is unwilling to accompany police to the hospital, explain that the issue is not debatable. Police may allow the person to retain some semblance of control by allowing them to make non-crucial decisions such as the choice of transportation by ambulance or police vehicle.

If the individual is not exhibiting the more obvious psychotic symptoms such as hallucinations and delusions, detecting mental illness may be more difficult. Speaking with the person may assist in determining whether a mental disorder is present. As you speak with the person, ask yourself the following questions:

- Is the person able to conduct a conversation, or are speech and thought patterns disjointed and confused? Is the person able to focus on the question posed?

- Is the person aware of his or her surroundings? Can he or she provide his or her name and address, provide the date, or answer common-knowledge questions?

Interacting with Psychotic Persons

Police may be called by concerned family members or other persons when someone is experiencing a psychotic episode.

When attempting to interact with a subject in a state of psychosis, most notably found in persons with bipolar disorder or schizophrenia, officers should give consideration to other possible causes of the behaviour. Psychotic episodes may be caused by medical conditions such as brain tumours, severe fevers, or epilepsy. Reactions to alcohol or other drugs, head injuries, or acute stress could also induce psychotic behaviour.

Hallucinations and delusions are the most frequently encountered symptoms of psychosis, although there are several others, including:

- extreme anxiety, fear, or panic for no apparent reason;

- withdrawal from family or friends;

- rapid mood swings (also a symptom of bipolar disorder);

- loss of ability to verbally interact;

- disordered, fragmented speech;

- loss of logical reasoning;

- flat emotional responses; and

- agitation.

Effective verbal interaction with a psychotic person may be extremely difficult due to his or her loss of ability to reason or think logically. The officer should try to listen to the person empathetically and respond in a calm, reassuring manner. The officer must also be aware of his or her proximity to the person. Invading the psychotic person's personal space can escalate the situation.

If the psychotic person becomes aggressive, it is in the best interest of all concerned to isolate and contain the person. Isolation and containment will reduce the likelihood that other persons will become involved or injured during any possible aggressive actions. It also increases the response options available to officers by limiting the actions of the aggressor through removal of access to weapons and actual confinement of area. Removal of any distractions, including persons, and deliberate, calm interaction may assist in de-escalating the situation. However, the subject may also react negatively to isolation and containment by becoming more aggressive, particularly if the psychosis is accompanied by paranoia. If such behaviour is exhibited and the scene is safely contained, officers may consider the option of disengagement.

It is unlikely that psychotic behaviour induced through means other than a mental illness will be identified by non-mental health professionals. Within the provisions of the MHA, an officer who has reasonable grounds to believe that the psychotic behaviour was caused by a mental illness would be justified in apprehending the person if he or she displayed violent behaviours. Section 17 refers to behaviours caused by an apparent mental disorder. The use of the word "apparently" in this section removes the requirement for police to prove a specific mental illness causing the identified behaviour.

RESPONSE OPTIONS

Regulation 3/99 of the *Police Services Act*, s. 13, requires police services to establish procedures on dealing with persons who are emotionally disturbed or have a mental illness. Police officers will follow the procedures of their respective police services.

The following information identifies some possible response options for police officers dealing with mentally disturbed persons. This section is to be used for information purposes only.

No Further Police Action

This may occur in situations where the reported behaviour was disturbing but not dangerous, such as a person walking on the sidewalk calmly talking to imaginary persons. Such people appear to be mentally disturbed but do not pose a danger to themselves or the public and are able to care for themselves. The officer forms the opinion that the person is not likely to pose any danger.

Release to Family or Friends

This may be an option where the officer is somewhat concerned about the ability of the subject to care for himself or herself. The person has not displayed any dangerous behaviour, but may be somewhat hindered in his or her ability to interact effectively. The person may show signs of confusion, such as not knowing where he or she is, or not knowing the time, date, year, etc. These signs could lead the officer to believe that the person's ability to care for himself or herself is compromised but that he or she poses no immediate physical danger. Release to the person's family or friends may be a viable option if the officer is able to obtain the information required to contact a family member.

In this situation, the person may not be suffering from a mental illness but may be suffering from a condition such as Alzheimer's disease (see chapter 5 and discussion below). The person may exhibit many of the same symptoms and behaviours as a person with a mental illness, but not be suffering from a mental illness within the meaning of the MHA.

Response Where Person Has Alzheimer's

Alzheimer's disease is a progressive, degenerative disease that destroys brain cells and causes dementia. It can strike adults at any age, but is most common in persons 65 and older. Some of the signs of Alzheimer's disease include:

- memory loss that affects day-to-day functioning,

- difficulty performing familiar tasks,

- problems with language,

- chronological and spatial disorientation,

- decreased powers of judgment,

- problems with abstract thinking,

- misplacement of possessions,

- changes in mood or behaviour,

- changes in personality, and

- loss of initiative.

The officer should check to see whether the person is registered in the Alzheimer Wandering Registry (see appendix 6F at the end of this chapter). The registry, which is stored in the Canadian Police Information Centre (CPIC) database, contains the names, addresses, physical descriptions, and contact information of the registrants. Each registrant is issued an identification bracelet and card on which pertinent information is recorded.

Voluntary Admittance

If a person is displaying indicators that lead the officer to suspect that a psychiatric assessment may be needed, but the person is not exhibiting behaviours that would allow the officer to use the authorities of s. 17 of the MHA, the officer could ask the person to voluntarily submit to a psychiatric assessment. This option may be applicable in situations where the officer does not believe that an immediate danger exists but is unable to release the person into the custody of family or friends. If the person agrees, he or she may be transported to a medical facility to be examined by a physician. The physician will make the determination whether or not the person should have a psychiatric evaluation.

Under s. 12 of the MHA, the subject may agree and be admitted for evaluation as an informal or voluntary patient.

ADMISSION OF INFORMAL OR VOLUNTARY PATIENTS: MENTAL HEALTH ACT, SECTION 12

Any person who is believed to be in need of the observation, care and treatment provided in a psychiatric facility may be admitted thereto as an informal or voluntary patient upon the recommendation of a physician.

As a voluntary patient, the person may leave the psychiatric facility at any time, according to s. 14 of the MHA.

INFORMAL OR VOLUNTARY PATIENT: MENTAL HEALTH ACT, SECTION 14

Nothing in this Act authorizes a psychiatric facility to detain or to restrain an informal or voluntary patient.

A problem occurs where the person refuses to be admitted and family or friends are not available. With no other legal options available, the officer must unconditionally release the person. Detailed notes of the interaction should be kept.

Order for Examination Issued by a Justice

An order for examination may be applicable in instances of unconditional release to family or friends. If the family or any person believes, on the basis of their observations, that as a result of a mental disorder, the person poses a danger to himself or herself or the public, or has caused, or is causing a person to fear for their safety, or is unable to care for themselves, the person may appear before a justice seeking an order for psychiatric evaluation. This order is used in situations where the subject will not voluntarily submit himself or herself to a physician for evaluation and the police have not formed reasonable grounds to believe that the person is an immediate danger or is unable to care for himself or herself.

The justice will hear sworn information from the concerned parties and decide, based on the information presented, whether the subject should be brought to a physician to determine whether a psychiatric evaluation is necessary.

A Form 2, MHA, Order for Examination (see appendix 6B at the end of this chapter), is issued by the justice authorizing police to apprehend the named person within seven days and bring him or her to a physician for assessment, as set out in ss. 16(1) and 16(3) of the MHA.

JUSTICE OF THE PEACE'S ORDER FOR PSYCHIATRIC EXAMINATION: MENTAL HEALTH ACT, SECTION 16(1)

Where information upon oath is brought before a justice of the peace that a person within the limits of the jurisdiction of the justice,

(a) has threatened or attempted or is threatening or attempting to cause bodily harm to himself or herself;

(b) has behaved or is behaving violently towards another person or has caused or is causing another person to fear bodily harm from him or her; or

(c) has shown or is showing a lack of competence to care for himself or herself, and in addition based upon the information before him or her the justice of the peace has reasonable cause to believe that the person is apparently suffering from mental disorder of a nature or quality that likely will result in,

(d) serious bodily harm to the person;

(e) serious bodily harm to another person; or

(f) serious physical impairment of the person,

the justice of the peace may issue an order in the prescribed form for the examination of the person by a physician.

AUTHORITY OF ORDER: MENTAL HEALTH ACT, SECTION 16(3)

An order under this section shall direct, and, for a period not to exceed seven days from and including the day that it is made, is sufficient authority for any police officer to whom it is addressed to take the person named or described therein in custody forthwith to an appropriate place where he or she may be detained for examination by a physician.

The examining physician will determine whether the person needs to have a psychiatric evaluation. If an evaluation is deemed necessary, the person may voluntarily submit to the evaluation or be required to submit to evaluation. Section 15 of the MHA, below, authorizes the examining physician to order the person to be evaluated at a psychiatric facility.

The order is issued as a Form 1, MHA, Physician's Order for Assessment (see appendix 6A at the end of this chapter). The order authorizes police to apprehend the named person within seven days and bring him or her to a psychiatric facility for evaluation.

APPLICATION FOR PSYCHIATRIC ASSESSMENT: MENTAL HEALTH ACT, SECTION 15(1)

Where a physician examines a person and has reasonable cause to believe that the person,

(a) has threatened or attempted or is threatening or attempting to cause bodily harm to himself or herself;

(b) has behaved or is behaving violently towards another person or has caused or is causing another person to fear bodily harm from him or her; or

(c) has shown or is showing a lack of competence to care for himself or herself,

and if in addition the physician is of the opinion that the person is apparently suffering from mental disorder of a nature or quality that likely will result in,

(d) serious bodily harm to the person;

(e) serious bodily harm to another person; or

(f) serious physical impairment of the person,

the physician may make application in the prescribed form for a psychiatric assessment of the person.

Section 33 of the MHA requires that police stay with the person until the person is admitted to the facility.

DUTY TO REMAIN AND RETAIN CUSTODY: MENTAL HEALTH ACT, SECTION 33

A police officer or other person who takes a person in custody to a psychiatric facility shall remain at the facility and retain custody of the person until the facility takes custody of him or her in the prescribed manner.

Immediate Apprehension

In some situations, the immediate apprehension of a mentally disturbed person is necessary—for example, where he or she is suicidal or violent. The person may be experiencing episodes of psychosis, as described earlier. Such persons may pose a risk to the safety of intervening officers. Refer to the previously discussed guidelines for dealing with these occurrences.

Apprehension of a person without prior judicial authorization is allowable only in situations where the safety of the individual or another person is, or is likely to be, in imminent jeopardy. Section 17 of the MHA allows for the immediate apprehension of the person only in circumstances where the officer does not have time to apply for judicial authorization through the provisions of s. 16 of the MHA, due to the immediacy of the danger.

ACTION BY POLICE OFFICER: MENTAL HEALTH ACT, SECTION 17

Where a police officer has reasonable and probable grounds to believe that a person is acting or has acted in a disorderly manner and has reasonable cause to believe that the person,

> (a) has threatened or attempted or is threatening or attempting to cause bodily harm to himself or herself;

> (b) has behaved or is behaving violently towards another person or has caused or is causing another person to fear bodily harm from him or her; or

> (c) has shown or is showing a lack of competence to care for himself or herself,

and in addition the police officer is of the opinion that the person is apparently suffering from mental disorder of a nature or quality that likely will result in,

> (d) serious bodily harm to the person;

> (e) serious bodily harm to another person; or

> (f) serious physical impairment of the person,

and that it would be dangerous to proceed under section 16, the police officer may take the person in custody to an appropriate place for examination by a physician.

Disengagement

Officers may use disengagement when the situation needs to be reassessed after initial contact with the mentally ill person. This option is available when the subject has been isolated and poses no danger to himself or herself or to the public. If possible, removal of potential weapons will assist in officer safety when the subject is to be removed or other options used. While awaiting backup, officers should make containment of the person their primary concern. The negative behaviour of a person experiencing a psychotic episode is unlikely to diminish while the officers wait for backup to arrive. A detailed description of the behaviour of the subject should be provided to other officers upon their arrival. The sharing of information is crucial in determining the next course of action.

EXCITED DELIRIUM

Excited delirium is sometimes encountered when dealing with emotionally disturbed or mentally ill persons. Persons experiencing **excited delirium** are in a state of acute agitation and hyperactivity, usually accompanied by violent behaviour. There has not yet been a definitive cause identified, but persons experiencing psychotic episodes and persons under the influence of drugs, most notably cocaine, appear to be at greater risk. In other instances, there are no identifiable contributing factors. There are some signs and symptoms that may indicate excited delirium:

excited delirium
state of acute agitation and hyperactivity, usually accompanied by violent behaviour

- violent/aggressive behaviour;

- disorientation;

- hallucinations;

- panic;

- paranoia;

- impaired thinking;

- diminished sense of pain;

- unexpected physical strength;

- apparent ineffectiveness of oleoresin capsicum (OC) spray, or pepper spray (a second application may be detrimental to the subject);

- profuse sweating; and

- sudden tranquility after aggressive actions.

The final six of these symptoms appear to be common in individuals deemed to be experiencing excited delirium.

In 1998, the Ontario Coroner's Office published a retrospective study of 21 cases of unexpected death in people with excited delirium that occurred between 1988 and 1995 within the province of Ontario (Pollanen et al., 1998). Of the cases reported, 18 deaths occurred while the subject was in police custody. In all 21 cases, Dr. Pollanen found that "many deaths related to excited delirium are associated with restraint in the prone position" (p. 1607) and that all of the subjects who died had lapsed into "tranquility" shortly after being restrained. The study also found that

- 12 subjects (57 percent) experienced excited delirium caused by a psychiatric disorder;

- 8 subjects (38 percent) experienced cocaine-induced psychosis;

- 18 of the deaths (86 percent) happened while the subject was in police custody and that efforts to resuscitate were unsuccessful;

- 8 of the 18 subjects (44 percent) restrained in the prone position also suffered chest compression from the body weight of the one to five people who were restraining them;

- 4 subjects (19 percent) had been pepper-sprayed;

- 4 subjects (19 percent) had heart disease at the time of death;

- 2 (10 percent) of the deaths happened in hospital after the subject was in a coma for several days;

- 6 subjects (29 percent) with cocaine-excited delirium had cocaine levels similar to those of recreational users and lower than those of people who actually died from cocaine intoxication; and

- levels of cocaine associated with recreational use may be sufficient to cause excited delirium.

Police officers should be aware that manias specific to psychiatric illness and drug-induced psychosis often present the same symptoms and behaviours as excited delirium. It is therefore almost impossible to accurately determine causation during an encounter.

The reasons for sudden and unexpected excited delirium deaths due to restraint are complex. Chris Lawrence (Ontario Police College), working with other medical experts such as Wanda Mohr (Associate Professor, Psychiatric Mental Health Nursing, University of Medicine and Dentistry of New Jersey), has been conducting groundbreaking research into the medical literature associated with excited delirium.

According to the medical literature reviewed for the report *Investigator Protocol: Sudden In-Custody Death*, there appear to be three specific groups of people who are most prone to sudden and unexpected death attributed to excited delirium (Lawrence & Mohr, 2004):

1. Individuals who are suffering from psychiatric illness, specifically bipolar disorders and schizophrenia. This is also noted in a study where both agitated and non-agitated subjects suffering from schizophrenia died suddenly and unexpectedly (Rosh, Sampson, & Hirsch, 2003).

2. Individuals who are chronic illicit stimulant users.

3. Individuals who combine the two previous risk factors.

The deaths of some individuals while in police custody have been attributed to excited delirium. Evidence, while inconclusive, suggests that physical restraint in certain positions may contribute to such deaths. The use of OC spray may also be a contributing factor in some of these deaths.

The greatest controllable factor contributing to the death of these persons appears to be the position in which they are restrained. In June 1998, the *Canadian Medical Association Journal* published a study of 21 persons who died after apparently experiencing excited delirium while in police custody in Ontario between 1988 and 1995. All subjects had been restrained after a violent struggle. The greatest number of incidents (18 percent) involved restraining the subject in the prone position. In 3 of the cases, the person had pressure applied to his neck. OC spray had been used on 4 of the subjects. All 21 persons lapsed into a state of tranquility after being restrained.

In most instances, excited delirium was likely due to a pre-existing psychiatric illness; in a significant number of cases, it resulted from recent use of cocaine. Other factors contributing to death during excited delirium include heart disease and obesity.

Police should consider the option of disengaging from the scene to assess or reassess the situation. This may be an option only if safety of the subject or others is not an issue.

If restraint of the individual is the only viable option, positioning the person in such a way that his or her breathing is not restricted may be the most significant aspect of excited delirium over which the police have some control.

It may be that people in a state of excited delirium have a greater oxygen requirement, predisposing them to rapid asphyxiation if placed in a position that inhibits their breathing, such as the prone position. This belief has been reinforced through coroners' rulings of positional asphyxiation as the cause of death in suspected cases of excited delirium. Positional or postural holds are the restraints most frequently associated with unexpected death in persons susceptible to excited delirium.

The position that appears to be most detrimental is face down with feet and hands cuffed together behind the person (commonly referred to as "hog-tying"). If possible, police should not use this restraint method to control persons showing signs of excited delirium. Positioning the restrained person in a manner that allows unrestricted breathing, such as sitting, may be helpful in preventing unanticipated death.

Excited delirium should be treated as a medical emergency. The subject should be provided with medical assistance as soon as possible. Police should tell attending medical personnel that they believe that the subject may be suffering from excited delirium based on their observations of the subject's actions and symptoms.

KEY TERMS

antisocial personality disorder

bipolar disorder

clinical depression

delusion

delusions of persecution

dependent personality

excited delirium

hallucination

mental illness

postpartum depression

schizophrenia

unusual realities

REFERENCES

American Psychiatric Association. (1987). *Diagnostic and statistical manual of mental disorders* (3rd Rev. ed.). Washington, DC: Author.

Canadian Mental Health Association. (2005a). *CAMIMH—Canadian Alliance on Mental Illness and Mental Health: Frequently asked questions.* http://www.cmha.ca/english/research/camimh/faq.htm.

Canadian Mental Health Association. (2005b). *Mental health system.* http://www.ontario.cmha.ca/content/mental_health_system/ ontario_election/fact_sheets.asp?cID=4125.

Criminal Code. (1985). RSC 1985, c. C-46, as amended.

Depression and Manic Depression Association of Alberta. (2005). *Primary unipolar recurrent type of depression.* http://www.incentre.net/dmdaa/.

Lawrence, C.W., & Mohr, W.K. (2004). Investigator protocol: Sudden in-custody death. *The Police Chief, 71*(1), 44–52.

MediResource Inc. (2005). *Women's health: Disease information.* http://mediresource.sympatico.ca/channel_disease_detail.asp? disease_id=106&channel_id=7&menu_item_id=1.

Mental Health Act. (1990). RSO 1990, c. M.7.

Ministry of Health and Long-Term Care. (2005). *Mental health: The next steps— Strengthening Ontario's mental health system.* http://www.health.gov.on.ca/ english/public/pub/mental/consultation.html.

Patient Health International. (2005). *Bipolar disorder.* http://www.patienthealthinternational.com/article/501886.aspx.

Police Services Act. (1990). RSO 1990, c. P.15.

Pollanen, M.S., Chiasson, D.A., Cairns, J.T., & Young, J.G. (1998). Unexpected death related to restraint for excited delirium: A retrospective study of deaths in police custody and in the community. *Canadian Medical Association Journal, 158*(12), 1603–1607.

Rosh, A., Sampson, B.A., & Hirsch, C.S. (2003). Schizophrenia as a cause of death. *Journal of Forensic Sciences, 48*(1), 164–167.

Schizophrenia Society of Ontario. (2004). *What is schizophrenia.* http://www.schizophrenia.on.ca/schiz.html.

Statistics Canada. (1997). *National population health survey.* Ottawa: Author.

Statistics Canada. (2001). *Hospitalizations for mental disorders, by provinces and territories.* http://www.statcan.ca/english/Pgdb/health57a.htm.

U.S. Department of Justice. FBI Uniform Crime Reports. (1992). *Killed in the line of duty: A study of felonious killings of law enforcement officers.* Washington, DC: Author.

EXERCISES

Short Answer

1. Define "mental illness" for the purpose of police intervention.

2. Identify some common symptoms of mental illness.

3. Describe the authorities of a Form 1, MHA from the perspective of police intervention.

4. Identify the authorities contained in a Form 2, MHA.

5. Describe the authorities contained in s. 17 of the MHA.

6. Explain excited delirium and list some of the common symptoms.

Case Analysis

Case 6.1

You are a police officer responding to a call of a disturbance in a shopping mall. Upon arrival you are met by mall security guard, Jane Star.

She tells you that she has received a complaint about a male sitting on one of the public benches. He keeps staring at everyone who passes. The store owners are complaining that he is bad for business. Star walks with you to the person's location. She points to the male in question, later identified as Rob Allan, sitting on a bench in front of a ladies' clothing store. You speak to Mr. Allan.

He tells you that he is just sitting on the bench talking to his friend and "checking out the ladies." He continues: "If you sit right here, you can see into the back changing area. Sometimes ladies come out wearing only their underwear! Look, Robert, there's one now!" It appears as if he is speaking to an unseen person to his right.

You ask, "Who is Robert?" Allan replies: "He is my friend, my best friend."

He then introduces you to Robert: "Robert this is … Sorry I didn't get your name." You tell him that you are Constable Steeves. He continues: "Robert, this is Constable Steeves. Constable Steeves, this is my best friend, Robert."

He then begins a conversation with his unseen friend. The conversation focuses on where they should go next to see some ladies.

What will you do in this situation? Explain your authorities.

Case 6.2

You are a police officer responding to a call for assistance at 789 Main Street. Upon arrival you are met by Pete Herman and Wendy Herman. Pete is very emotional and is crying.

Wendy tells you that she is scared of Pete. He has been having delusions and hallucinations for the past three days.

You speak to Pete.

He explains to you that he sometimes sees a black dog. The dog talks to him and tells him that he should be having sex with children. He is confused because the dog has never lied to him before, but he doesn't think it is right for adults to have sex with children. Pete tells you that he went to Dr. Kay about a year ago to get help. He told Dr. Kay about his hallucinations and that he believed that he may have sexually touched his two-year-old daughter.

Dr. Kay began counselling Pete and prescribed anti-psychotic drugs for him.

Pete tells you that it has been almost a year and nothing has changed. The therapies aren't working. The dog is around more than ever. It won't shut up.

What will you do in this situation? Explain your authorities.

Case 6.3

You are a police officer on foot patrol of the downtown area of the city. It is 5 p.m. You observe a person lying beside a dumpster behind a restaurant. As you approach the person, you recognize him as Joe Keith. Keith is homeless and an alcoholic. You shout to get his attention. He sits up. You ask him what he is doing.

He tells you that sometimes restaurants throw away their empty liquor bottles. If you can find a few of them and pour the liquor that is still in the bottom of the bottle together with the liquor in the other bottles, you can get a good drink. He tells you that the most beautiful sight he has seen was a half bottle of wine he found last week when he was checking dumpsters.

You ask him to stand up. He tells you that he has a bad leg and can't stand or walk very well. He pulls up his pant leg and shows you a large cut on his calf. He tells you that a rat told him that blood was just like red wine, so he cut himself to find out. He tells you that the "eff'n rat was lying!"

You ask if he wants to go to the hospital to get his leg checked. He replies: "Maybe in a few days. It's Friday night, the best night of the week to get booze. I don't want to go to the hospital tonight." He asks you if you can lend him a few dollars to get a drink. He hasn't had a drink since last night and is feeling pretty rough. He just needs a couple of drinks to "take the edge off."

What will you do in this situation? Explain your answer. Be sure to quote authorities.

APPENDIX 6A   FORM 1, MENTAL HEALTH ACT

Form 1

APPLICATION BY PHYSICIAN FOR PSYCHIATRIC ASSESSMENT

Mental Health Act

Name of Physician: ....

Physician Address: ....

Telephone Number: ( ) .... Fax Number: ( ) ....

On ...., I personally examined ....
                       (date)   (print first and last name of person)

whose address is: ....

You may only sign this FORM 1 if you have personally examined the person within the past seven days. In deciding if a Form 1 is appropriate, you must complete either Box A (serious harm test) or Box B (persons who are incapable of consenting to treatment and meet the specified criteria test) below.

BOX A — SUBSECTION 15 (1) OF THE *MENTAL HEALTH ACT*
SERIOUS HARM TEST

The Past/Present Test (Check one or more)

I have reasonable cause to believe that the person:

    [ ]   has threatened or is threatening to cause bodily harm to himself or herself,

    [ ]   has attempted or is attempting to cause bodily harm to himself or herself,

    [ ]   has behaved or is behaving violently towards another person,

    [ ]   has caused or is causing another person to fear bodily harm from him or her, or

    [ ]   has shown or is showing a lack of competence to care for himself or herself.

I base this belief on the following information (you may, as appropriate in the circumstances, rely on any combination of your own observations and information communicated to you by others):

My own observations:

....

....

Facts communicated to me by others:

....

....

The Future Test (Check one or more)

I am of the opinion that the person is apparently suffering from mental disorder of a nature or quality that likely will result in:

    [ ]   serious bodily harm to himself or herself

    [ ]   serious bodily harm to another person,

    [ ]   serious physical impairment of himself or herself.

I base this opinion on the following information (you may, as appropriate in the circumstances, rely on any combination of your own observations and information communicated to you by others):

My own observations:

....

....

Facts communicated to me by others:

....

....

BOX B — SUBSECTION 15 (1.1) OF THE *MENTAL HEALTH ACT*

PATIENTS WHO ARE INCAPABLE OF CONSENTING TO TREATMENT AND MEET THE SPECIFIED CRITERIA

Note: The patient must meet the criteria set out in each of the following conditions.

I have reasonable cause to believe that the person:

1. Has previously received treatment for mental disorder of an ongoing or recurring nature that, when not treated, is of a nature or quality that likely will result in one or more of the following: (please indicate one or more)

    [ ]   serious bodily harm to himself or herself,

    [ ]   serious bodily harm to another person,

    [ ]   substantial mental or physical deterioration of himself or herself, or

    [ ]   serious physical impairment of himself or herself;

AND

2. Has shown clinical improvement as a result of the treatment;

AND

I am of the opinion that the person,

3. Is incapable, within the meaning of the *Health Care Consent Act, 1996*, of consenting to his or her treatment in a psychiatric facility and the consent of his or her substitute decision-maker has been obtained;

AND

4. Is apparently suffering from the same mental disorder as the one for which he or she previously received treatment or from a mental disorder that is similar to the previous one;

AND

5. Given the person's history of mental disorder and current mental or physical condition, is likely to: (choose one or more of the following)

    [ ]   cause serious bodily harm to himself or herself, OR

    [ ]   cause serious bodily harm to another person, OR

    [ ]   suffer substantial mental or physical deterioration, OR

    [ ]   suffer serious physical impairment.

I base this opinion on the following information (you may, as appropriate in the circumstances, rely on any combination of your own observations and information communicated to you by others):

My own observations:

. . . .

. . . .

Facts communicated by others:

. . . .

. . . .

I have made careful inquiry into all the facts necessary for me to form my opinion as to the nature and quality of the person's mental disorder. I hereby make application for a psychiatric assessment of the person named.

Today's Date: . . . .   Today's Time: . . . .

Examining Physician's Signature: . . . .

This form authorizes, for a period of seven days including the date of signature, the apprehension of the person named and his or her detention in a psychiatric facility for a maximum of 72 hours.

for use at the psychiatric facility

Once the period of detention at the psychiatric facility begins, the attending physician should note the date and time this occurs and must promptly give the person a Form 42.

Date and Time detention commences: . . . .   Physician's Signature: . . . .

Date and Time Form 42 delivered . . . .   Physician's Signature: . . . .

APPENDIX 6B   FORM 2, MENTAL HEALTH ACT

Form 2
ORDER FOR EXAMINATION (Section 16)
Mental Health Act

To the police officers of Ontario:

Whereas information upon oath has been brought before me, a justice of the peace in and for the province of Ontario

by ....
(print full name of person bringing information)

of ....
(address of person bringing information)

in respect of ....
(print full name or other description of person to be examined)

of ....
(home address, if known)

PART A OR PART B MUST BE COMPLETED

PART A — SUBSECTION 16 (1)

Information has been brought before me that such person:

[ ]   has threatened or attempted or is threatening or attempting to cause bodily harm to himself or herself;

[ ]   has behaved or is behaving violently towards another person or has caused or is causing another person to fear bodily harm from him or her; or

[ ]   has shown or is showing a lack of competence to care for himself or herself.

In addition, based upon the information before me I have reasonable cause to believe that the person is apparently suffering from mental disorder of a nature or quality that likely will result in,

[ ]   serious bodily harm to the person;

[ ]   serious bodily harm to another person; or

[ ]   serious physical impairment of the person.

PART B — SUBSECTION 16 (1.1)

Information has been brought before me that such person:

(a) has previously received treatment for mental disorder of an ongoing or recurring nature that, when not treated, is of a nature or quality that likely will result in serious bodily harm to the person or to another person or substantial mental or physical deterioration of the person or serious physical impairment of the person; and

(b) has shown clinical improvement as a result of the treatment;

In addition, based upon the information before me I have reasonable cause to believe that the person:

(c) is apparently suffering from the same mental disorder as the one for which he or she previously received treatment or from a mental disorder that is similar to the previous one;

(d) given the person's history of mental disorder and current mental or physical condition, is likely to,

[ ]   cause serious bodily harm to himself or herself,

[ ]   cause serious bodily harm to another person,

[ ]   suffer substantial mental or physical deterioration of the person, or

[ ]   suffer serious physical impairment of the person; and

(e) is apparently incapable within the meaning of the *Health Care Consent Act, 1996* of consenting to his or her treatment in a psychiatric facility and the consent of his or her substitute decision-maker has been obtained.

Now therefore, I order you, the said police officers, or any of you, to take the said person in custody forthwith to an appropriate place for examination by a physician.

. . . .
(Date of Signature)

. . . .
(Municipality where order signed)

            . . . .
            (Signature of Justice of the Peace)

            . . . .
            (Print name of Justice of the Peace)

notes for applicant/informant

1. You may wish to provide your telephone number on this form so that you can be contacted by the police or the examining physician after this order is issued. This is entirely voluntary. You are not required to give this information for the order to be issued or for the order to be legally valid.

   Name: . . . .   Telephone Number: . . . .

2. You may wish to seek legal advice concerning this order, including the effect of this order and your legal rights.

3. You may wish to inform the police, the examining physician and/or an appropriate health care professional of the evidence you gave to the justice of the peace, if you consider it appropriate in all the circumstances to do so. If you decide to do so, please use the space provided below. Use the back of this form if necessary. You are not required to give this information for the order to be issued or for the order to be legally valid.

. . . .

. . . .

APPENDIX 6C   FORM 3, MENTAL HEALTH ACT

Form 3
CERTIFICATE OF INVOLUNTARY ADMISSION
Mental Health Act

Name of patient:

. . . .

Name of physician:

. . . .

Name of psychiatric facility:

. . . .

Date of examination:

. . . .

I hereby certify that the following three pieces of information are correct:

1. I personally examined the patient on the date set out above.

2. I am of the opinion that the patient named above is not suitable for voluntary or informal status.

3. Complete one or more boxes as appropriate.

    [ ] I am of the opinion that the patient named above meets the criteria set out in Box A.
    (Please complete Box A below.)

    [ ] I am of the opinion that the patient named above meets each of the criteria set out in Box B.
    (Please complete Box B below.)

BOX A — RISK OF SERIOUS HARM

Note: Check one or more boxes as appropriate.

The patient is suffering from mental disorder of a nature or quality that likely will result in:

    [ ] serious bodily harm to the patient,

    [ ] serious bodily harm to another person,

    [ ] serious physical impairment of the patient,

unless he or she remains in the custody of a psychiatric facility.

BOX B — PATIENTS WHO ARE INCAPABLE OF CONSENTING TO TREATMENT AND MEET THE SPECIFIED CRITERIA

Note: The patient must meet all of the following five criteria.

1. The patient has been found incapable, within the meaning of the *Health Care Consent Act, 1996* of consenting to his or her treatment in a psychiatric facility and the consent of his or her substitute decision-maker has been obtained.

2. The patient has previously received treatment for mental disorder of an ongoing or recurring nature that, when not treated, is of a nature or quality that likely will result in one or more of the following: (please indicate one or more)

    [ ] serious bodily harm to the patient,

    [ ] serious bodily harm to another person,

    [ ] substantial mental or physical deterioration of the patient, or

    [ ] serious physical impairment of the patient.

3. The patient has shown clinical improvement as a result of the treatment.

4. The patient is suffering from the same mental disorder as the one for which he or she previously received treatment or from a mental disorder that is similar to the previous one.

5. Given the patient's history of mental disorder and current mental or physical condition, the patient is likely to: (please indicate one or more)

    [ ]   cause serious bodily harm to himself or herself,

    [ ]   cause serious bodily harm to another person,

    [ ]   suffer substantial mental or physical deterioration, or

    [ ]   suffer serious physical impairment.

Date of signature: . . . .

Signature of attending physician: . . . .

NOTES

(1) This certificate is valid for 14 calendar days, including the day upon which it was signed.

(2) The following actions must be taken promptly after this form is signed:

    (a) The signing physician must give the patient a properly executed Form 30 notice and notify a rights adviser.

    (b) The rights adviser must meet with the patient and explain to him or her the significance of the certificate and the right to have it reviewed by the Consent and Capacity Board.

APPENDIX 6D   FORM 45, MENTAL HEALTH ACT

Form 45
COMMUNITY TREATMENT ORDER
Mental Health Act

PART 1 — TO BE FILLED OUT BY EXAMINING PHYSICIAN

Name of person: . . . .

Name of physician: . . . .

Name of substitute decision-maker (if applicable): . . . .

Name of psychiatric facility (if applicable): . . . .

Date of examination: . . . .

This community treatment order for the above named person is the:

    [ ]   first for this person

    [ ]   . . . . renewal
                              (number of times CTO has been renewed)

Date of issue of previous community treatment order (if applicable): . . . .

Date of expiry of previous community treatment order (if applicable): . . . .

During the previous three-year period, the person named above:

    [ ]   has been a patient in a psychiatric facility on two or more separate occasions or for a cumulative period of 30 days or more during that three-year period, OR

    [ ]   has been the subject of a previous community treatment order.

Criteria for Community Treatment Order

(Note: All the criteria set out below must be met for this order to be valid.)

I am of the opinion that,

(a) the person is suffering from mental disorder such that he or she needs continuing treatment or care and continuing supervision while living in the community; AND

(b) if the person does not receive continuing treatment or care and continuing supervision while living in the community, he or she is likely, because of mental disorder, to: (choose one or more of the following)

    [ ]   cause serious bodily harm to himself or herself, OR

    [ ]   cause serious bodily harm to another person, OR

    [ ]   suffer substantial mental deterioration of the person, OR

    [ ]   suffer substantial physical deterioration of the person, OR

    [ ]   suffer serious physical impairment of the person; AND

(c) the person is able to comply with the community treatment plan contained in the community treatment order; AND

(d) the treatment or care and supervision required under the terms of the community treatment order are available in the community; AND

(e) if the person is not currently a patient in a psychiatric facility, the person meets the criteria for the completion of an application for psychiatric assessment under subsection 15 (1) or (1.1).

The facts on which I formed the above opinion are as follows:

. . . .

. . . .

Rights Advice

Note: The person and his or her substitute decision-maker, if applicable, must receive rights advice before the order is issued.

I am satisfied that the substitute decision-maker of the person, if applicable, has consulted with a rights adviser and been advised of his or her legal rights, AND

I am satisfied that the person:

[ ]   has consulted with a rights adviser and been advised of his or her legal rights, OR

[ ]   has not consulted with a rights adviser because he or she has refused to consult a rights adviser.

Community Treatment Plan

Note: A copy of the community treatment plan must be attached to this order.

I am satisfied that a community treatment plan has been devised for the person.

I have consulted with all the persons named in the community treatment plan.

I am satisfied that:

[ ]   the person, OR

[ ]   the person's substitute decision-maker, if the person is incapable, consents to the community treatment plan.

The community treatment plan for the person is:

(Describe the community treatment plan. Use back of this form if necessary. The community treatment plan must be attached to this order.)

. . . .

. . . .

PART 2 — TO BE FILLED OUT BY THE PERSON OR THE PERSON'S SUBSTITUTE DECISION-MAKER

Undertaking of Person or Person's Substitute Decision-Maker
(to be completed by the person or the person's substitute decision maker, if applicable)

I am:

[ ]   the person named above. I promise to comply with all my obligations as set out in the community treatment plan, OR

[ ]   the person's substitute decision-maker. I promise to use my best efforts to ensure that the person named above complies with all the obligations as set out in the community treatment plan.

By my signature at the bottom of this order, I signify that I consent to the community treatment plan, and I consent to, and am assuming my undertakings as stated in, the community treatment plan.

PART 3 — TIME IN FORCE — TO BE COMPLETED BY THE EXAMINING PHYSICIAN

This community treatment order is in force for six months, including the day upon which it is signed, and expires at midnight on the . . . . day of . . . . 2 . . . . unless it is terminated at an earlier date.

PART 4 — PATIENT RIGHT TO APPLY TO CONSENT AND CAPACITY BOARD

A person who is subject to a community treatment order, or any person on his or her behalf, may apply to the Board using a Form 48 to inquire into whether or not the criteria for issuing or renewing this community treatment order have been met.

Signed at . . . .
         (name of psychiatric facility, or name of place [e.g., doctor's office, hospital] where community treatment order signed)

Date . . . .

                                        . . . .
                                                         (signature of physician)
                                        . . . .
                                                         (signature of person)
                                        . . . .
                                        (signature of substitute decision-maker [if applicable])

NOTES:

The following actions must be taken by the physician who signs this order immediately after the order is signed:

1.   A copy of this order, including the community treatment plan must be given to:

   (a) the person;

   (b) the person's substitute decision-maker, if applicable;

   (c) the officer in charge of a psychiatric facility, if applicable;

   (d) any other health practitioner or other person named in the community treatment plan.

2.   A notice in the approved form (**Form 46**) must be given to the person that he or she is entitled to a hearing before the Consent and Capacity Board.

APPENDIX 6E   FORM 47, MENTAL HEALTH ACT

Form 47

ORDER FOR EXAMINATION (Subsections 33.3 (1)and 33.4 (3))

Mental Health Act

To the police officers of Ontario:

Whereas ....
(name of person subject to a community treatment order)

of ....
(address of person subject to community treatment order)

is subject to a community treatment order issued or renewed on ....
(date of order)

by ....
(name of issuing or renewing physician)

of, ... , and
(business address of issuing or renewing physician)

Whereas such person has:

[ ]   failed to attend appointments or comply with treatment in accordance with subsection 33.1 (9) of the *Mental Health Act*, or

[ ]   failed to permit .... to
(name of physician)

review his/her condition, in accordance with subsection 33.4 (2) of the *Mental Health Act*; and

Whereas I have reasonable cause to believe that such person:

(i)   is suffering from mental disorder such that he/she needs continuing treatment or care and continuing supervision while living in the community;

(ii)   meets the criteria for the completion of a Form 1 (an application for psychiatric assessment under subsection 15 (1) or (1.1) of the *Mental Health Act*) and is not currently a patient in a psychiatric facility; and

(iii) if the person does not receive continuing treatment or care and continuing supervision while living in the community, he/she is likely, because of mental disorder, to: (choose one or more of the following):

[ ]   cause serious bodily harm to himself/herself,

[ ]   cause serious bodily harm to another person,

[ ]   suffer substantial mental or physical deterioration of the person,

[ ]   suffer serious physical impairment of the person.

Now therefore, I hereby issue this Order for Examination for any of you to take such person in custody forthwith to

....
(address of physician, agency or psychiatric facility where the person will be examined)

for an examination by me or by a physician named below appointed to carry out this responsibility in accordance with subsection 33.5 (2) of the *Mental Health Act*.

....
(name of physician, agency or psychiatric facility responsible for examination of the person)

This order is in force for 30 days after the date upon which it is issued and will expire at midnight on ....
(date order will expire)

Dated at .... ,
(name of municipality/city/town)

this ...... day of .... , 2 ......

....
(signature of physician)

....
(print name of physician)

Notes

1. The physician who issues an order for examination shall ensure that the police have complete and up-to-date information about the name, address and telephone number of the physician responsible for completing the examination required under an order for examination and shall ensure that the police have such information at all times that the order for examination is in force.

2. The physician who issues an order for examination shall ensure that the police are immediately notified if the person who is subject to the order for examination voluntarily attends for an examination or, for any other reason, the order for examination is cancelled prior to its expiry date.

3. The police may need a physical description of the person named in your Order for Examination so that the person may be located and returned to you for an examination. Please use the space below to provide the police with relevant information about the person's physical description.

4. The police may ask you for information about the person's physical description, in addition to the information you have provided below.

. . . .

. . . .

APPENDIX 6F   MISSING PERSON REPORT

Alzheimer **Wandering Registry**

REGISTRATION FORM

To register: 1. Please complete this form to the best of your ability. If you require assistance, please call your local Alzheimer Society at: ▶

or the National Office at 1-800-616-8816

2. **The form must be signed by the individual who is being registered or by the person who has been officially designated to make decisions on his/her behalf.**

3. Is the registrant a Veteran currently receiving benefits from Veterans Affairs Canada?

❑ Yes (If yes, **do not** enclose payment. Please note that the name and address will be verified with Veterans Affairs for accounting purposes)

❑ No   (see #4)

4. Write a $25 cheque for the one-time registration fee, **payable to the Alzheimer Society of Canada**.

5. Prepare now by keeping a current photo of the individual in your home.

6. Forward the completed form and cheque to your local Alzheimer Society or mail to:
    Alzheimer Society of Canada
    Safely Home - Alzheimer Wandering Registry
    20 Eglinton Avenue West, Suite 1200
    Toronto, Ontario   M4R 1K8

<u>Please allow 3 - 4 weeks for delivery.</u>

The information on this form is being collected by the Alzheimer Society of Canada and its affiliates. Information will be shared with the Royal Canadian Mounted Police, only for the purpose of locating missing persons. Information retained by the RCMP will be retained in the Personal Information Bank CMP PPU-005 in accordance with the Privacy Act and made available to law enforcement agencies through CPIC.

Office Use Only
ID Number

— **PLEASE PRINT CLEARLY** —

IDENTIFICATION OF PERSON

Surname

First Name (name engraved on bracelet)   Middle Name

Sex   Date of Birth (Year-Month-Day)   or   Age   Health Card Number
     M or F

RCMP GRC 3454 eng (2003-07)

Alzheimer *Society*
C A N A D A

Canadä

LIVING ARRANGEMENT OF THE REGISTRANT

☐ Alone   ☐ Institution   _____

☐ With Family   ☐ Other   _____

Street No. and Street Name   Apt. No.

City   Province   Postal Code

Home Phone No.   Business Phone No.

(___) _____   (___) _____

DESCRIPTION OF THE REGISTRANT

Height
Feet   Inches   or   CM

Weight
Lbs.   or   KG.

Race
W = White
NW = Non White

Hair Colour

BLD = Bald
BLK = Black
BLO = Blond
BRN = Brown
GRY = Grey
RED = Red
WHI = White

Hair Description

A = Curly
B = Wavy
C = Short
D = Long
E = Dyed
F = Ponytail
G = Brush Cut
H = Toupee/Wig
I = Other

Eye Colour

Left	Right

BLU = Blue
BRN = Brown
GRN = Green
HAZ = Hazel
BLK = Black
MRN = Maroon
GRY = Grey

Complexion

A = Dark
B = Light/Fair
C = Sallow
D = Ruddy
E = Freckled
F = Moles
G = Pimples/Pockmarked
H = Other

Language(s) spoken   Preferred

Walking Aid
(if yes, describe)   _____

Hearing Aid(s)   **Visual Aid(s)**   **Dentures(s)**
☐ Left ☐ Right   ☐ Glasses ☐ Contacts   ☐ Upper ☐ Lower

VISIBLE MARKS

Example:

Tattoo Scar Deformity Mark Amputation   Location (see "Body Location Table below)

□ □ □ ☑ □ | 1 | 6 | 0 |

Description:

| B | I | R | T | H | | M | A | R | K | | O | N | | C | H | E | E | K | |

Mark#1 (check only one)

Tattoo Scar Deformity Mark Amputation   Location (see "Body Location Table" below)

□ □ □ □ □ | | | |

Description:

| | | | | | | | | | | | | | | | | | | | | | | | |

Mark#2 (check only one)

Tattoo Scar Deformity Mark Amputation   Location (see "Body Location Table" below)

□ □ □ □ □ | | | |

Description:

| | | | | | | | | | | | | | | | | | | | | | | | |

BODY LOCATION TABLE

100 HEAD	200 RIGHT ARM	300 LEFT ARM	400 FRONT TORSO	500 LEFT LEG	600 RIGHT LEG	700 BACK TORSO
110 Forehead	211 Upper Arm	311 Upper Arm	410 Shoulders	511 Thigh	611 Thigh	720 Upper Back
120 Eyes	213 Elbow	313 Elbow	420 Chest	513 Knee	613 Knee	730 Middle Back
130 Ears	215 Forearm	315 Forearm	430 Abdomen	515 Calf	615 Calf	
140 Nose	220 Wrist	320 Wrist	440 Waist	520 Ankle	620 Ankle	740 Lower Back
150 Mouth	230 Hand	330 Hand	450 Hips	530 Foot	630 Foot	760 Buttocks
160 Cheek	241 Thumb	341 Thumb	460 Pelvis	541 Large Toe	641 Large Toe	761 Rectal
170 Chin	242 Index Finger	342 Index Finger	461 Genitals	542 Toe	642 Toe	
175 Jaw	243 Middle Finger	343 Middle Finger		543 Toe	643 Toe	
180 Neck	244 Ring Finger	344 Ring Finger		544 Toe	644 Toe	
	245 Little Finger	345 Little Finger		545 Small Toe	645 Small Toe	

BRACELET ORDER INFORMATION

Measure wrist and check box above appropriate size for bracelet
Please allow an extra half-inch for comfort

5"	5.5"	6"	6.5"	7"	7.5"	8"	8.5"	9"	9.5"	10"

Language preferred for engraving: □ English   □ French

WANDERING HISTORY

☐ None   ☐ Repeated   ☐ Habitual (Over 4 times)

Possible Locations: Places where this person may wander to, for example: Previous addresses, previous employment, favourite stores, nearby mall, post office, etc.

1. _____
2. _____
3. _____

HEALTH CONCERNS (allergies, medical conditions)

_____

_____

CAREGIVERS
(All correspondence will be mailed to the individual identified as the FIRST CONTACT)

Please ensure that ALL contacts are aware that the individual is registered.

FIRST CONTACT

Name		Relationship	
Address	City/Province		Postal Code
Tel. No. (Home)	Tel. No. (Business)	Cell Phone No.	Language of Preference ☐ Eng. ☐ Fr.

SECOND CONTACT

Name		Relationship	
Address	City/Province		Postal Code
Tel. No. (Home)	Tel. No. (Business)	Cell Phone No.	Language of Preference ☐ Eng. ☐ Fr.

THIRD CONTACT

Name		Relationship	
Address	City/Province		Postal Code
Tel. No. (Home)	Tel. No. (Business)	Cell Phone No.	Language of Preference ☐ Eng. ☐ Fr.

ACKNOWLEDGEMENT (Must be signed)

This information is provided voluntarily on the understanding that it shall be kept confidential at all times and only released to health care personnel and law enforcement agencies if the person is found wandering or reported missing.

Acknowledged by:
(Please print name) _____   Relationship: _____

Signature: _____   Date (Y-M-D): _____

- 4 -

Alzheimer Society of Canada, *Alzheimer Wandering Registry* Registration Form (Toronto: Author, 1997).

APPENDIX 6G   EXCERPTS FROM THE HEALTH CARE CONSENT ACT, 1996

Meaning of "substitute decision-maker"

9. In this Part,

"substitute decision-maker" means a person who is authorized under section 20 to give or refuse consent to a treatment on behalf of a person who is incapable with respect to the treatment.

List of persons who may give or refuse consent

20(1) If a person is incapable with respect to a treatment, consent may be given or refused on his or her behalf by a person described in one of the following paragraphs:

1. The incapable person's guardian of the person, if the guardian has authority to give or refuse consent to the treatment.

2. The incapable person's attorney for personal care, if the power of attorney confers authority to give or refuse consent to the treatment.

3. The incapable person's representative appointed by the Board under section 33, if the representative has authority to give or refuse consent to the treatment.

4. The incapable person's spouse or partner.

5. A child or parent of the incapable person, or a children's aid society or other person who is lawfully entitled to give or refuse consent to the treatment in the place of the parent. This paragraph does not include a parent who has only a right of access. If a children's aid society or other person is lawfully entitled to give or refuse consent to the treatment in the place of the parent, this paragraph does not include the parent.

6. A parent of the incapable person who has only a right of access.

7. A brother or sister of the incapable person.

8. Any other relative of the incapable person.

Requirements

20(2) A person described in subsection (1) may give or refuse consent only if he or she,

(a) is capable with respect to the treatment;

(b) is at least 16 years old, unless he or she is the incapable person's parent;

(c) is not prohibited by court order or separation agreement from having access to the incapable person or giving or refusing consent on his or her behalf;

(d) is available; and

(e) is willing to assume the responsibility of giving or refusing consent.

Meaning of "spouse"

20(7) Subject to subsection (8), two persons are spouses for the purpose of this section if,

(a) they are married to each other; or

(b) they are living in a conjugal relationship outside marriage and,

(i) have cohabited for at least one year,

(ii) are together the parents of a child, or

(iii) have together entered into a cohabitation agreement under section 53 of the *Family Law Act.*

Not spouse

(8) persons are not spouses for the purpose of this section if they are living separate and apart as a result of a breakdown of their relationship.

Meaning of "partner"

20(9) For the purpose of this section,

"partner" means,

(a) Repealed.

(b) either of two persons who have lived together for at least one year and have a close personal relationship that is of primary importance in both persons' lives.

Meaning of "relative"

20(10) Two persons are relatives for the purpose of this section if they are related by blood, marriage or adoption.

Meaning of "available"

20(11) For the purpose of clause (2)(d), a person is available if it is possible, within a time that is reasonable in the circumstances, to communicate with the person and obtain a consent or refusal.

Principles for giving or refusing consent

21(1) A person who gives or refuses consent to a treatment on an incapable person's behalf shall do so in accordance with the following principles:

1. If the person knows of a wish applicable to the circumstances that the incapable person expressed while capable and after attaining 16 years of age, the person shall give or refuse consent in accordance with the wish.

2. If the person does not know of a wish applicable to the circumstances that the incapable person expressed while capable and after attaining 16 years of age, or if it is impossible to comply with the wish, the person shall act in the incapable person's best interests.

Best interests

21(2) In deciding what the incapable person's best interests are, the person who gives or refuses consent on his or her behalf shall take into consideration,

(a) the values and beliefs that the person knows the incapable person held when capable and believes he or she would still act on if capable;

(b) any wishes expressed by the incapable person with respect to the treatment that are not required to be followed under paragraph 1 of subsection (1); and

(c) the following factors:

1. Whether the treatment is likely to,

    i. improve the incapable person's condition or well-being,

    ii. prevent the incapable person's condition or well-being from deteriorating, or

    iii. reduce the extent to which, or the rate at which, the incapable person's condition or well-being is likely to deteriorate.

2. Whether the incapable person's condition or well-being is likely to improve, remain the same or deteriorate without the treatment.

3. Whether the benefit the incapable person is expected to obtain from the treatment outweighs the risk of harm to him or her.

4. Whether a less restrictive or less intrusive treatment would be as beneficial as the treatment that is proposed.

Information

22(1) Before giving or refusing consent to a treatment on an incapable person's behalf, a substitute decision-maker is entitled to receive all the information required for an informed consent as described in subsection 11(2).

Conflict

22(2) Subsection (1) prevails despite anything to the contrary in the *Personal Health Information Protection Act, 2004.*

CHAPTER 7

Suicide

Chapter Objectives

After completing this chapter, you should be able to:

- Explain how age, gender, and other factors affect suicidal behaviour.

- Identify the provisions of the *Criminal Code* and *Mental Health Act* of Ontario that apply to suicide.

- Describe techniques for police intervention in suicide situations.

INTRODUCTION

A police officer will answer many calls for assistance in his or her career. Suicide calls can be some of the most emotionally difficult for an officer, whether the calls involve someone threatening suicide or someone who has already committed the act. The emotions felt, and sometimes repressed, by officers are real, and can affect their judgment and behaviour on suicide calls. It is therefore necessary for prospective officers to understand their own views on suicide before they become involved in suicide calls.

The task of police officers is to intervene when necessary to save lives. With the proper intervention, one-half to two-thirds of all suicide attempts are probably preventable. Police officers, however, are usually not psychiatrists or psychologists. However, they are typically the first individuals offering assistance that a suicidal person encounters. Knowing the signs of suicide, being able to assess a person's risk of suicide, knowing who commits suicide, and understanding why goes a long way toward ensuring that police intervention is successful.

WHO COMMITS SUICIDE?

Statistics Canada reports that suicide is the 11th leading cause of death in Canada. The suicide rate for Canadians, as measured by the World Health Organization (WHO), is 15 per 100,000 people. Between 1997 and 1999, there was a 10 percent increase in suicides across Canada, from 3,681 to 4,074. In Ontario, suicides rose from 930 in 1997 to 1,032 in 2001. It has been estimated that for every successful suicide up to 10 suicide attempts are made each year. In addition, an unknown number of deaths attributed to other causes (such as motor vehicle accidents) are in fact suicides.

Suicide, of course, is not restricted to particular age, race, gender, or income group, although the statistics indicate that some persons are at higher risk than others.

Men commit suicide at a rate four times that of women. According to a report by the Canadian Institute for Health Information, more men in Ontario committed suicide in the past 10 years than died in car crashes. Approximately 590 men committed suicide in Ontario between 1990 and 2000, while 558 men died in car crashes. Women, however, make three to four times more suicide attempts than men. Women are hospitalized for attempted suicide at 1.5 times the rate of men. Studies indicate that there is a significant correlation between a history of sexual abuse and the lifetime number of suicide attempts, and this correlation is twice as strong for women as for men. Aboriginal persons commit suicide at a rate seven times the national average—91 per 100,000 population (Royal Commission on Aboriginal Peoples, 1995). The suicide rate is believed to be higher among homosexuals than among the general population, although there are no statistics to substantiate this belief because death records are not categorized by sexual orientation. The risk seems to be higher when homosexuals first identify their sexual preference, possibly because of lack of acceptance by their families and society.

In Canada, suicide accounts for 24 percent of all deaths among 15- to 24-year-olds and 16 percent of all deaths among 16- to 44-year-olds. Suicide is the second leading cause of death for Canadians between the ages of 10 and 24. Seventy-three percent of hospital admissions for attempted suicide are for people between the ages of 15 and 44.

People with mood disorders are at a particularly high risk of suicide. Studies indicate that more than 90 percent of suicide victims have a diagnosable psychiatric illness. Nearly 80 percent of those who commit suicide are suffering from a serious depressive illness (Depressive and Manic Depressive Association of Ontario, 1994). Suicide is the most common cause of death for people with schizophrenia. Both major depression and bipolar disorder account for 15 to 25 percent of all deaths by suicide in patients with severe mood disorders.

The following are some additional facts about who commits suicide:

- During the period 1993–1997, 229 children aged 5 to 14 committed suicide.

- In 1997, there were 261 deaths by suicide in Canada by youth aged 15 to 19 years (207 males and 54 females).

- Suicide is the second most common cause of death among college students.

- Adolescent males are particularly vulnerable to impulsive suicide after suffering an academic or relationship setback or a conflict with authority.

- For those aged 20 to 24 years, there were 293 suicides in 1997, including 257 males and 36 females, showing an even higher male to female ratio (7:1) compared with the general population.

- The suicide rate among males increases substantially after age 65.

- Suicide accounts for 18 percent of deaths among alcoholics (87 percent of the victims are male).

- Alcoholism is a factor in 30 percent of all suicide attempts.

- People with AIDS have a suicide risk 20 times greater than that of the general population.

- In more than half of all suicides involving persons 50 and older, physical illness is an important contributing factor (American Foundation for Suicide Prevention, 1996).

WHY DO PEOPLE COMMIT SUICIDE?

Suicide is usually an act of desperation carried out by a person who believes that there is no other way to cope with unbearable emotional or sometimes physical pain. The emotional pain can be caused by a variety of problems, both real and perceived. The problem giving rise to the emotional pain may seem insignificant to others, but not to the sufferer. Money or relationship problems, loss of enthusiasm for life, debilitating diseases, and other troubles can all create what the sufferer perceives as insurmountable problems, with no resolution other than suicide.

Although this may sound absurd to someone with good coping skills, everyone has a stress threshold beyond which the ability to cope is lost. Suicide can seem like an attractive option to someone who believes that life will not get better. Police officers usually have stable personalities, and may find it difficult to understand why someone would go to such an extreme to escape what others might view as an insignificant problem.

It is difficult to gauge another person's stress threshold, even when one is intimately familiar with the other's thoughts and feelings. Moreover, different people react differently to the same stressors. The latter point is illustrated by the following story:

> Four people were imprisoned for their political views. The conditions of their incarceration were deplorable. Each was kept in solitary confinement. Food and water were scarce. There was no toilet and no sunlight. Hours, days, weeks, and months went by. There was no way for any of the four to know how long they had been imprisoned.
>
> Two committed suicide by hanging themselves with their shoelaces. A third went insane, never to recover. The fourth decided that no matter what cards life dealt him, he would prevail.
>
> When he was released, he emerged with a book about the experience. Using a pencil stub and writing on scraps of paper to record his thoughts, he was able to draw on his positive attitude to do something constructive during his months of imprisonment.

Why was one man able to endure when the others were not? No one can give a complete answer to this question. Everyone has his or her stress threshold.

A police officer must not allow personal views and prejudices to hamper his or her duty toward suicidal persons, most of whom are looking for help, not death. The officer is often the first ray of hope they encounter. The officer needs to put aside any prejudices about suicide and intervene in an unbiased, constructive manner. Familiarity with the intervention techniques and risk assessment procedures discussed later in this chapter can help the officer develop the proper attitude.

Commonalities Among Suicidal Persons

There appear to be some common traits, behaviours, and experiences among suicidal persons (Shneidman, 1996).

1. *They see suicide as a solution.* Suicide is not a random act. It is a way out of a dilemma, a problem, a bind, a crisis, or a situation that is unbearable. Suicide becomes the answer to the problem of suffering. It answers the questions: "How can I get out of this situation? What can I do?"

2. *They seek cessation of consciousness.* Suicidal people want to end consciousness and unendurable pain. Doing so is seen by the suffering person as the solution to life's painful and unsolvable problems.

3. *They see suicide as a way to escape from psychological pain.* Suicide is a combined movement away from unbearable psychological pain, intolerable emotion, and mental anguish.

4. *They have frustrated psychological needs.* Suicide stems from thwarted or unrealized psychological needs. These unfulfilled needs are what cause the pain and push the suicidal person to act. All suicidal acts reflect a specific psychological need that has not been fulfilled.

5. *They feel hopeless/helpless.* Suicidal people experience pervasive feelings of helplessness and/or hopelessness: "Things will never get better. There is no one who can help me."

6. *Their cognitive state in suicide is ambivalence.* People who commit suicide are ambivalent about living and dying, even as they are committing the act. They both want to die, and wish to be saved. For example, an individual might cut his throat and cry for help at the same time.

7. *Their perceptual state in suicide is constriction.* Suicidal people have a narrow or constricted view of their options: "There is nothing else I can do but kill myself. The only way out is death."

8. *They use suicide to egress, or escape.* To egress means to depart from a region. In the case of suicidal people, they attempt to escape from a region of distress: "I'll get out by killing myself." Suicide is the final egression.

9. *They communicate their intention to commit suicide.* Many individuals intent on committing suicide emit clues of intention, consciously or unconsciously—signs of distress, pleas for intervention, or whimpers of helplessness.

10. *Their decision to commit suicide is consistent with their lifelong styles of coping.* People react consistently to certain aspects of life throughout its span. There is a connection between an individual's decision to commit suicide, how that individual has coped with previous setbacks, and the

individual's capacity to endure psychological pain. For example, suicidal persons may show a tendency toward constriction or a tendency to throw in the towel.

The main thrust of these commonalities is that suicidal persons are unable to deal with their psychological pain and choose suicide as a means to end their pain. This "surcease" type of suicide is generally accepted as the most common type of suicide involving police intervention.

There are several factors that can challenge a person's will to live and precipitate his or her suicide. The most common of these factors are discussed below.

Relationships

Loss of a close emotional attachment can increase suicide risk. Moreover, some people try to change the nature of an existing relationship through threats of suicide. This sort of manipulative behaviour can have disastrous consequences when actions merely intended to mimic suicide and frighten the other partner in the relationship accidentally cause death.

Revenge and Expression of Anger

Suicide can be a means of teaching others a lesson, a hostile act intended to make others sorry for a perceived insult or injury.

Control

Someone who feels that his or her life is spinning out of control may see suicide as the only remaining option. Self-injury can be an attempt to regain control. This need for control sometimes expresses itself as murder-suicide or as seemingly random murder. The perpetrator of such acts has an intense need to control his or her life and possibly the lives of others.

Avoidance

Some people do not cope well with life's pressures. Built-up tension may find its release in self-destructive behaviour. Generally this takes the form of non-fatal self-mutilation—a cry for help—although the result is sometimes unintentional death.

Exit

A person plagued by a terminal illness, chronic pain, depression, feelings of guilt, or other seemingly intolerable afflictions may choose death as his or her means of escape.

Mental Illness and Psychological Disorders

Persons experiencing debilitating symptoms of mental illness are at risk of committing suicide. Recall that more than 90 percent of suicide victims have diagnosable psychiatric illness. (See also chapter 6, Mental Illness and Psychological Disorders.)

The risk increases with the delay in receiving assistance, more so if the person is experiencing a psychotic episode. The suicide usually occurs through the person's efforts to stop the psychotic episode. This is referred to as "psychotic suicide."

SUICIDE METHODS

The relative prevalence of various suicide methods differs among gender and age groups (Hafen and Frandsen, 1985).

Children

Children 14 and younger are most likely to use poison or prescription drugs to commit suicide. Poisons are obviously more easily obtainable than prescription drugs. They can be found at home—under the kitchen sink, in a storage shed or garage, and so on—and their labelling makes it easy for the child to identify them as poisons and to comprehend their effect.

Other methods are available to children, such as running in front of a moving vehicle or swallowing foreign objects. The method used is usually one of convenience with no discernible difference in the sexes.

Adolescents

Gender differences are readily apparent in the suicide methods used by young people aged 15 to 18. Females usually ingest drugs. The preferred methods for adolescent males are usually more violent and often dramatic.

Males Versus Females

In 2001, 3,692 Canadians died by suicide. By gender, 2,870 were males and 822 were females. Table 7.1 shows the the methods of suicide used and the percentage of males and females that used each method.

Suicide by Cop

suicide by cop
the use of police to commit suicide, achieved by challenging police with a lethal or apparently lethal weapon, giving them no choice but to use lethal force to stop the threat

A relatively new phenomenon is the use of police officers as a means of death. This method is referred to as **suicide by cop** or "victim-precipitated homicide."

Traditional methods of suicide, such as jumping from a high structure, crashing a speeding vehicle, or causing a self-inflicted wound, require a decision and commitment on the part of the victim. In victim-precipitated homicides, the difficult decision to end one's life is made by someone else. The disturbed or distraught individual, with a lethal or apparently lethal weapon, challenges law enforcement officers in a manner that leaves the officers no choice but to use lethal force to stop the threat.

Van Zandt (1993) states that the police are specifically singled out because they are the only community agency equipped with firearms and the training to react to potentially life-threatening situations with accurate and deadly force. In addition, persons who commit suicide by cop may feel that the stigma and social taboos associated with suicide can be absolved if they are killed by an external mechanism

TABLE 7.1   Methods of Suicide in Canada, by Gender

Method	Males (% of deaths)	Females (% of deaths)
Self-poisoning	10.3	36.9
Gases	10.7	7.7
Hanging	42.9	33.9
Drowning	2.5	4.0
Firearms	21.5	4.3
Burning	0.7	0.6
Cutting	2.9	1.5
Jumping	6.8	8.4
Motor vehicle	0.9	0.6
Other	0.9	2.2

Source: Statistics Canada. *Causes of death, shelf tables. Data Year—2001. ICD-10 X60-X84 and Y87.0.* Ottawa: Author.

such as the police. Police officers, as agents of the state, may represent to them a faceless means of ending their life in a somewhat dignified manner.

Gerberth (1993) has theorized that the police can symbolically represent the social conscience. Gerberth notes that, at times, suicidal individuals may have feelings of guilt, real or imagined. Police officers traditionally represent law and order within society. A guilt-ridden, suicidal individual may enter into an interaction with the police in an attempt to relieve his or her guilt-ridden conscience through punishment that may include death.

In other instances, the suicidal individual may not have the determination to end his or her own life. In these cases, the suicidal individual cannot "pull the trigger" and, therefore, seeks assistance in accomplishing his or her death.

Richard Parent, a leading expert in the field, estimates that at least one-third of police shootings across the continent are precipitated by the victim. Parent's research is based on examinations of more than 400 police shootings in Canada and more than 400 others in the United States between 1980 and 2002. Parent's research also involved interviews with police officers who used deadly force, and prison inmates who survived police shootings.

HOSTAGE-TAKING

Suicidal individuals may use hostage-taking incidents to bring about their demise. In these situations, the suicidal individual may adopt a confrontational posture with the police. They will often announce their intention to die. In addition, these individuals may set a deadline for their own death or begin talking about people who are dead as if they are still alive. In following this course of action, the individual accomplishes his or her own self-destruction while going out in a "blaze of glory."

The person may believe that being shot by the police will bring them notoriety they did not have in life. Even if the police shoot, but do not kill the person, the objective of notoriety has been achieved. This may sound absurd, but remember that the person has decided that his or her life is worthless; what does he or she have to lose?

COMMONALITIES AMONG PERSONS SEEKING SUICIDE BY COP

There appear to be some commonalities in incidents of victim-precipitated homicide:

- The person may make requests/demands such as "Kill me!" or "Shoot me!"

- The person may give a deadline for his or her death. The officer should ignore the deadline and not allow the person to control the situation.

- The person may refuse to listen to any requests from police and refuse to discuss the issue.

- The person may verbally communicate that he or she no longer wants to live but is unwilling to take his or her own life.

RESPONSE OPTIONS

When deciding on a response option in situations of victim-precipitated homicides, the responding officer should refer to the Use of Force Continuum and select an appropriate response based on the danger posed by the subject.

If forced to use a firearm to control the person, the officer may experience feelings of remorse or may feel anger at knowing that the person has manipulated him or her into using a firearm. These feelings can be addressed through critical incident stress debriefings, where officers are able talk about stressful incidents with the knowledge that anything they say will remain confidential.

LEGISLATION REGARDING SUICIDE

Suicide and attempted suicide are not viewed as a criminal matter in Canadian law. The aim of legislation, both federally and provincially, is to prevent the act of suicide from occurring.

There have been many ethical and philosophical debates about the appropriateness of the state intervening in situations where a person has chosen to end his or her life. Yet without police intervention, the suicidal person might make a rash and ill-considered decision. The majority of suicidal persons dealt with by police are irrational and seeking immediate relief from a short-term problem. Most have not considered the finality of their actions due to their emotional and psychological imbalance. Police intervention may stop an irreversible mistake.

Criminal Code

Counselling or assisting a person to commit suicide is a criminal act. Section 241 of the *Criminal Code* sets out the offence.

COUNSELLING OR AIDING SUICIDE: CRIMINAL CODE, SECTION 241

Every one who

      (a) counsels a person to commit suicide, or

      (b) aids or abets a person to commit suicide,

whether suicide ensues or not, is guilty of an indictable offence and liable to imprisonment for a term not exceeding fourteen years.

Section 14 of the *Criminal Code* identifies that no person may consent to allow another to take their life.

CONSENT TO DEATH: CRIMINAL CODE, SECTION 14

No person is entitled to consent to have death inflicted on him, and such consent does not affect the criminal responsibility of any person by whom death may be inflicted on the person by whom consent is given.

Mental Health Act of Ontario

The *Mental Health Act* (MHA) of Ontario, ss. 15, 16, and 17, authorizes that a person who poses a danger to himself or herself or others, due to a mental disorder, may be apprehended and brought to the appropriate medical facility for assistance.

The Act appears to presume that any person wishing to commit suicide is not mentally stable and should be apprehended for his or her protection.

Section 15(1) of the MHA sets out the authority for a physician to compel a person to submit to psychiatric examination if the physician believes that the person may be a danger to himself or herself or others.

APPLICATION FOR PSYCHIATRIC ASSESSMENT: MENTAL HEALTH ACT, SECTION 15(1)

Where a physician examines a person and has reasonable cause to believe that the person,

(a) has threatened or attempted or is threatening or attempting to cause bodily harm to himself or herself;

(b) has behaved or is behaving violently towards another person or has caused or is causing another person to fear bodily harm from him or her; or

(c) has shown or is showing a lack of competence to care for himself or herself,

and if in addition the physician is of the opinion that the person is apparently suffering from mental disorder of a nature or quality that likely will result in,

(d) serious bodily harm to the person;

(e) serious bodily harm to another person; or

(f) serious physical impairment of the person,

the physician may make application in the prescribed form for a psychiatric assessment of the person.

The prescribed form is referred to as a Form 1 MHA (reproduced in chapter 6, appendix 6A). A Form 1 directs police to apprehend the named person and bring him or her to a psychiatric facility for assessment.

Section 16(1) of the MHA sets out the authority of a justice of the peace to issue an order for examination.

JUSTICE OF THE PEACE'S ORDER FOR PSYCHIATRIC EXAMINATION: MENTAL HEALTH ACT, SECTION 16(1)

Where information upon oath is brought before a justice of the peace that a person within the limits of the jurisdiction of the justice,

(a) has threatened or attempted or is threatening or attempting to cause bodily harm to himself or herself;

(b) has behaved or is behaving violently towards another person or has caused or is causing another person to fear bodily harm from him or her; or

(c) has shown or is showing a lack of competence to care for himself or herself,

and in addition based upon the information before him or her the justice of the peace has reasonable cause to believe that the person is apparently suffering from mental disorder of a nature or quality that likely will result in,

(d) serious bodily harm to the person;

(e) serious bodily harm to another person; or

(f) serious physical impairment of the person,

the justice of the peace may issue an order in the prescribed form for the examination of the person by a physician.

This order is referred to as a Form 2 MHA (reproduced in chapter 6, appendix 6B). Any person may appear before a justice and provide sworn testimony that establishes reasonable grounds to believe the named person is a danger to himself or herself or others. The justice may issue an order for examination, Form 2, authorizing police to apprehend the named person and bring him or her to a physician for examination. The examining physician will determine whether the person needs a psychiatric assessment.

Section 17 of the MHA sets out the authority for police to apprehend a person without previous authorization.

ACTION BY POLICE OFFICER: MENTAL HEALTH ACT, SECTION 17

Where a police officer has reasonable and probable grounds to believe that a person is acting or has acted in a disorderly manner and has reasonable cause to believe that the person,

(a) has threatened or attempted or is threatening or attempting to cause bodily harm to himself or herself;

(b) has behaved or is behaving violently towards another person or has caused or is causing another person to fear bodily harm from him or her; or

(c) has shown or is showing a lack of competence to care for himself or herself,

and in addition the police officer is of the opinion that the person is apparently suffering from mental disorder of a nature or quality that likely will result in,

(d) serious bodily harm to the person;

  (e) serious bodily harm to another person; or

  (f) serious physical impairment of the person,

and that it would be dangerous to proceed under section 16, the police officer may take the person in custody to an appropriate place for examination by a physician.

This section authorizes police to immediately apprehend a person. Apprehension is authorized where reasonable grounds exist to believe that the person is a danger to himself or herself or others due to a mental disorder.

Upon apprehension, the person is brought to a physician for examination. The physician will decide whether further assessment is required.

SUICIDE AND POLICE INTERVENTION

For a police officer, intervening in a situation where a person believes that he or she has no reason to live is extremely dangerous and stressful. A suicidal person can be extremely unpredictable and is usually very irrational. Police officers must therefore follow guidelines designed to minimize the risk to their safety and expedite getting help for the suicide attempter.

The following information may be useful in assisting police officers to effectively and safely intervene with suicidal persons (improvisation may be necessary, however).

Officer Safety

It is the duty of the police to help persons in crisis, but a more pressing duty is returning home at the end of the shift. An injured officer is a liability on the scene and cannot assist anyone. Safety precautions must be foremost in the officer's mind.

A successful intervention begins with the officer taking proper precautions to ensure his or her own safety. Persons contemplating suicide can be dangerous. Most will be thinking and acting irrationally. In most interventions the person is looking for help, but there are some circumstances where the person is intent on self-destruction and possibly on eliminating those around him or her.

Suicidal behaviour involving weapons or assaultive actions obviously poses a threat to officer safety, but there are other dangers as well. A suicidal person with a blood-borne pathogen, such as HIV or hepatitis B or C, poses a substantial risk to anyone who has direct contact with that person's blood or, less dangerously, other bodily fluids.

Some suicidal persons will be drug abusers. An intravenous drug user may be carrying a number of harmful viruses in his or her body. The combination of drug abuse and suicidal behaviour presents serious health risks to officers.

There are other, less obvious dangers such as the possibility of an officer being attacked by a dog that is trying to protect its master. Or, a family member or friend may attempt to prevent police interference with a suicidal person's desire to die.

Suicide intervention is therefore a dangerous situation for police officers. Observing and quickly assessing the suicidal person and his or her surroundings are imperative for an effective intervention.

Obtaining Background Information

The information obtained before encountering the suicidal person is possibly more important than the information obtained on the scene. However, owing to time constraints or lack of information sources, it is not always possible to obtain background information.

The officers must use their discretion to determine whether (1) their response at the scene must be immediate or (2) the person can be better helped by obtaining a history of the situation. The circumstances surrounding the original call for assistance may help determine the degree of urgency. A few minutes spent speaking with someone who is knowledgeable about the situation may help the officers identify the suicidal person's problem and increase officer safety by giving the officers more preliminary information. In many cases the person's suicidal thoughts are a manifestation of his or her need for help. If the person calls someone to say that he or she is considering suicide, he or she may be crying out for help.

Interviewing relatives and friends of the suicidal person can be extremely helpful in determining the seriousness of the situation. But the information obtained should not be relied on exclusively, especially when safety concerns such as the availability of weapons arise. However, the information can be used to help plan a course of action.

Interviews with relatives and friends can provide information on changes in the person's behaviour. These behavioural changes can provide clues as to how the person is feeling and serve as warning signs of possible suicidal action, as shown in the table below:

Feelings	Warning signs
Desperation	Giving away possessions
Anger	Loss of interest in physical appearance, sexual activity, and life itself
Loneliness	Self-mutilation
Worthlessness	Reckless behaviour
Irritability	Negative comments about self
Depression	Change from depression to a feeling of being at peace (as a result of deciding to commit suicide)

The list in the table above is far from comprehensive. Many other warning signs may exist. Occasionally, a suicidal person provides no warning signs at all.

There are some questions that may help officers assess the person's risk of suicide:

- *How old is the person?* Certain age groups are more suicide prone than others.

- *Has the person previously attempted suicide?* Subsequent suicide attempts are more likely to be successful than first-time suicide attempts.

- *Has a family member or friend previously attempted or completed suicide?* The suicidal person may have a positive or negative reaction to this incident.

- *Has there recently been a death in the family?* The suicidal person may want to join a loved one.

- *Has the person recently suffered a significant loss?* The loss of a job, a home, or a romantic partner may make the person feel abandoned, without hope, or depressed.

- *Does the person have any religious beliefs?* Religious persons are less likely to commit suicide.

- *Is the person an alcoholic?* Alcoholics are more likely than non-alcoholics to commit suicide.

- *Is the person under the influence of drugs?* Drugs are involved in many suicides.

- *Does the person have a history of depression?* Depression is a major contributor to suicidal behaviour.

- *Is the person involved in a stable romantic relationship?* Where marital status is concerned, single persons are the highest-risk group, whereas married persons with children face the lowest risk.

Entry

Entry into public places should not pose a legal problem for officers. While legality of entry is an important consideration, officer safety should be the foremost consideration.

In situations where the suicidal person is armed or where a hostage is involved, responding officers shall adhere to the direction given by regulation 3/99 of the *Police Services Act.*

Section 22 of regulation 3/99, below, states that officers shall not enter an area where the situation requires the use of a tactical unit, unless it is necessary to prevent the loss of life or serious bodily harm.

22(1) Every chief of police shall establish procedures on preliminary perimeter control and containment.

(2) A police force may include a containment team using police officers and, if it does, the chief of police shall develop procedures for it.

(3) Police officers who are not members of a tactical unit and who are deployed in a containment function, including members of a containment team, shall not, before the arrival of members of a tactical unit, employ offensive tactics unless the police officers believe, on reasonable grounds, that to do so is necessary to protect against the loss of life or serious bodily harm.

Section 23 of regulation 3/99, below, identifies the composition and duties of a tactical unit.

23(1) A tactical unit or hostage rescue team, whether provided by a police force or on a combined or regional or co-operative basis, shall consist of a minimum of 12 full-time tactical officers, including the supervisor.

(2) A tactical unit shall be able to perform the following functions:

1. Containment.

2. Apprehension of an armed barricaded person.

(3) A tactical unit may perform explosive forced entry if it uses the services of a police explosive forced entry technician.

(4) A hostage rescue team shall be able to perform the functions set out in subsection (2) and hostage rescue.

(5) The functions of a tactical unit and hostage rescue team may be provided by one unit or team that is capable of performing the functions of both a tactical unit and a hostage rescue team.

(6) For the purposes of this section,

"full-time tactical officer" means a police officer assigned and dedicated to the tactical unit or hostage rescue team, but who, when not training or undertaking tactical or hostage rescue activities, may undertake community patrol.

As previously stated, officer safety is the first concern when entering a place where a suicidal person may be. The officers must use approach-and-entry techniques that will ensure safe access. The next concern should be legality of entry. The information received by the police may be incorrect, although in most circumstances the police should respond as if the information is accurate, especially if the information cannot be verified. It is possible that there may not be anyone in crisis, and therefore the legality of the entry must be considered. Entering a place other than a dwelling should not pose any legal difficulty. Legal entry into a dwelling is more complicated. If circumstances and safety considerations permit, the easiest method of entry is to knock on the door and ask permission to enter.

If invited entry is unsafe or otherwise unfeasible, officers should ensure, whenever possible, that entry is legally justified. The *Criminal Code* provides a right of entry under certain circumstances. Section 117.04(2) permits officers to enter to search and seize.

APPLICATION FOR WARRANT TO SEARCH AND SEIZE: CRIMINAL CODE, SECTION 117.04(2)

Where, with respect to any person, a peace officer is satisfied that there are reasonable grounds to believe that it is not desirable, in the interests of the safety of the person or any other person, for the person to possess any weapon, prohibited device, ammunition, prohibited ammunition or explosive substance, the peace officer may, where the grounds for obtaining a warrant under subsection (1) exist but, by reason of a possible danger to the safety of that person or any other person, it would not be practicable to obtain a warrant, search for and seize any such thing, and any authorization, licence or registration certificate relating to any such thing, that is held by or in the possession of the person.

To rely on this section, one needs to establish reasonable grounds that a person has a weapon and that there is a danger that the person will use the weapon to harm himself or herself or others. There also must be such an urgent need for entry that there is no time to obtain a warrant. The search should be used only to find the person and the weapon or weapons in question. Once the objects of the search have been found, the search must cease. This section cannot be used as an all-embracing authority to enter. Reasonable grounds must be ascertained in every situation, and one cannot automatically assume that a person who possesses a weapon does so in a manner that jeopardizes safety.

Extreme caution must be used when it has been reasonably established that a person possesses a weapon and is a danger to himself or herself or others. A simple precaution that can enhance officer safety is to have dispatch call the person and if possible keep him or her on the telephone while the premises are being entered.

A judicial decision on s. 103(2), the predecessor to s. 117.04(2), stated that s. 103(2) did not infringe s. 8 of the *Charter of Rights and Freedoms*: *R v. Smith* (1988), 5 WCB 164 (Ont. Prov. Ct.).

If the suicidal person poses a threat to anyone other than himself or herself, entry may be gained under the authority of s. 27 of the *Criminal Code*.

USE OF FORCE TO PREVENT COMMISSION OF OFFENCE: CRIMINAL CODE, SECTION 27

Every one is justified in using as much force as is reasonably necessary

(a) to prevent the commission of an offence

(i) for which, if it were committed, the person who committed it might be arrested without warrant, and

(ii) that would be likely to cause immediate and serious injury to the person or property of anyone; or

(b) to prevent anything being done that, on reasonable grounds, he believes would, if it were done, be an offence mentioned in paragraph (a).

This section can be used to justify the use of force to prevent the suicidal person from harming anyone else on the premises. The authority to use as much force as is reasonably necessary can include forcible entry into a dwelling to prevent an offence that would likely cause immediate and serious harm to a person. This authority applies only to an offence for which a person can be arrested without a warrant. Because attempting suicide is not illegal, s. 27 cannot be relied on as providing authority to enter when it has not been established that the suicidal person is a danger to someone other than himself or herself.

R v. Custer appears to give police officers the authority to forcibly enter private premises when there are reasonable grounds to believe that a person's life is in danger. Although this is a provincial court decision, and therefore not binding authority, it has been relied upon for many years without legal repercussions.

An officer would be in the execution of his duty in forcibly entering private premises where he believes on reasonable and probable grounds that he is confronted with an emergency situation involving the preservation of life of a person in the dwelling-house, or the prevention of serious injury to that person, and if a proper announcement is made prior to entry: *R v. Custer* (1984), 12 CCC (3d) 372, [1984] 4 WWR 133 (Sask. CA). (*Martin's Annual Criminal Code, 2005*)

The authority allowed by the Saskatchewan court seems to go beyond that of s. 27 of the *Criminal Code* by stating that it is the duty of a police officer to intervene in a situation involving the preservation of life. Apparently this applies to persons who may be a danger to themselves. The permission is given to officers only after proper announcement of their intentions has been made.

Similarly, the Supreme Court of Canada's decision in *R v. Godoy* appears to give police officers the authority to enter a home by force if necessary if there is

articulable cause
suspicion based on some
discernible fact

articulable cause to believe that a person's life is in danger. Articulable cause means suspicion based on some discernible fact. *R v. Simpson* addresses the issue of articulable cause:

> In the absence of statutory authority to stop a vehicle, the stopping and detention of the occupants for the purpose of determining whether they were involved in criminal activity can only be justified if the detaining officer has some articulable cause for the detention. There must be a constellation of objectively discernible facts which give the detaining officer reasonable cause to suspect that the detainee is implicated in the activity under investigation. A "hunch" based entirely on intuition gained by experience cannot suffice: *R v. Simpson* (1993), 79 CCC (3d) 482, 20 CR (4th) 1, 43 MVR (2d) 1, 12 OR (3d) 182 (Ont. CA). (*Martin's Annual Criminal Code, 2005*)

Articulable cause appears to be referred to in *R v. Godoy* as well:

> In *R v. Godoy*, [1999] 1 SCR 311, 131 CCC (3d) 129, 21 CR (5th) 205, 117 OAC 127, 235 NR 134 (SCC), the Supreme Court of Canada held that forced entry into a dwelling house in response to a disconnected 911 call did not violate s. 8. The common law duty of police to preserve life is engaged whenever it may be inferred that the 911 caller may be in distress. In this case, the accused had refused entry to the police responding to the 911 call. The forced entry of the apartment to locate the caller and determine the reason for the call constituted a justifiable use of police powers. The police do not, however, have a further authority to search the premises or otherwise intrude on a resident's privacy or property. The court did not consider the applicability of the plain view doctrine in such circumstances. (*Martin's Annual Criminal Code, 2005*)

In *R v. Godoy*, the officers did not have reasonable grounds to enter the dwelling house but did have articulable cause based on the phone call from the residence. The court cited the duty of police to preserve life and ruled that the forced entry was legal.

In situations where legal authority appears to be absent, the officer must use ingenuity to determine a method of entry. In some circumstances, possibly involving the elderly or persons with infirmities, there may be a person with power of attorney who can be contacted for permission to enter the residence. The legality of this approach can be questionable, however. The person contemplating suicide may consider himself or herself to be competent and able to make rational decisions, and think that the attorney does not have the authority to make decisions on his or her behalf. The *Mental Health Act* considers all persons contemplating or attempting suicide to be incompetent and acting irrationally. It does not make allowances for persons who possibly may be making an informed and, in the person's eyes, reasonable choice. The *Mental Health Act* does not contain provisions that allow police officers to enter a dwelling for investigative purposes.

In some cases, relatives or neighbours will have keys to the residence and the authority to use them in times of emergency. It can be argued that allowing the police to enter exceeds the authority granted by the homeowner, but it helps establish that the police made reasonable efforts to enter the residence without using force.

If no other recourse is readily available, it may be necessary to forcibly enter the home. The officers should enter in a manner that causes the least amount of property damage. If all other options have been exhausted and the officers are acting under a good faith belief that the person is in danger, there is little chance of prosecution.

Intervention After Entry

Once entry has been gained, the officers must establish whether the person is a danger to himself or herself or others. As always, officer safety is a primary concern.

UNCONSCIOUS PERSON

If the person is obviously injured and is unconscious, the first priority is medical assistance. The officers must be careful to avoid direct contact with blood-borne pathogens if administering first aid. The use of safety equipment such as latex gloves and barrier devices used when giving artificial respiration is necessary.

DECEASED PERSON

If on arrival at the scene the officers find that the person is obviously dead, they should not move or touch the body. The signs of obvious death are decomposition, decapitation, and rigor mortis. Each is discussed below.

DECOMPOSITION

If the body has begun to decompose, medical assistance is obviously not required. Decomposition may be determined visually or through a very distinct smell that will emanate from the body.

Decay of the body takes place through two processes. In the first process, the body's own enzymes break down tissue. In the second process, bacteria breaks down tissue. The bacteria may be present in the body or the surrounding environment. Bacterial decomposition is usually accompanied by the liquefaction of body tissues and the production of large volumes of gases. The body becomes bloated, which results in the expulsion of fluids, usually from body orifices.

Analyzing the rate of decomposition as a means of establishing time of death is not very accurate. High environmental temperatures may accelerate the process to the degree that decomposition may be advanced to a stage where time of death is indeterminable. Decomposition tends to occur rapidly in areas of the body that are engorged with blood at the time of death. Decay may also be unusually rapid in cases where bacteria are present in the blood at the time of death.

DECAPITATION

When a human body has been decapitated, the head is severed from the body. There is no possibility of providing any effective medical assistance in cases of decapitation.

RIGOR MORTIS

Rigor mortis is the stiffening of the body after death. It results from a chemical reaction that takes place in muscle tissue. Consequently, rigor mortis appears sooner and lasts longer in muscular, well-developed males. Conversely, it may develop more slowly in a person with less muscle mass. Infants show the effects of rigor mortis sooner than adults.

Investigation Where Person Is Deceased

Immediately upon discovery of a dead body, the scene must be secured for investigation. If the responding officers are not in charge of crime scene investigation, their duty is to secure the scene for the police investigators and the coroner. No one may enter the area and nothing must be removed from the scene until responsibility for the investigation is handed over to the officers who will be in charge.

Section 10(1) of the *Coroners Act* of Ontario requires that police officers immediately notify the coroner in all cases of "unexpected or sudden death."

DUTY TO GIVE INFORMATION: CORONERS ACT, SECTION 10(1)

Every person who has reason to believe that a deceased person died ...

(d) suddenly and unexpectedly ...

shall immediately notify a coroner or a police officer of the facts and circumstances relating to the death, and where a police officer is notified he or she shall in turn immediately notify the coroner of such facts and circumstances.

The coroner or designate will generally attend the scene. On the basis of his or her observations and the information provided by the investigating officer(s), the coroner will determine whether it is necessary to continue an investigation, called an **inquest**, separate from a police investigation.

inquest
investigation by a coroner into the cause of a unexpected or sudden death

The purposes of a coroner's inquest are set out in s. 31(1) of the *Coroners Act* and are quite specific.

PURPOSES OF INQUEST: CORONERS ACT, SECTION 31(1)

Where an inquest is held, it shall inquire into the circumstances of the death and determine,

(a) who the deceased was;

(b) how the deceased came to his or her death;

(c) when the deceased came to his or her death;

(d) where the deceased came to his or her death; and

(e) by what means the deceased came to his or her death.

The inquest cannot be used to determine criminal culpability, as stated in s. 31(2) of the *Coroners Act*.

PURPOSES OF INQUEST: CORONERS ACT, SECTION 31(2)

The jury shall not make any finding of legal responsibility or express any conclusion of law on any matter referred to in subsection (1).

Homicide or Suicide?

If the cause and nature of death are not readily apparent or if there are some unanswered questions regarding the circumstances of death, officers should treat the death as a homicide, the worst-case scenario. This entails treating the scene of death as a crime scene, which reduces the likelihood that potential evidence will be contaminated or that a possible homicide will not be investigated. The hypothesis that the death is a homicide allows the investigators the opportunity to establish evidence that supports the hypothesis. If the evidence does not support homicidal death, other avenues may be investigated.

There are several indicators that should arouse an officer's suspicion that a sudden death may be a homicide:

- multiple wounds;

- the absence of a weapon that caused the wounds;

- wounds on areas of the body not easily accessible to the victim (for example, a stab wound in the back is unlikely to be self-inflicted);

- signs of a struggle (for example, overturned furniture);

- signs of forcible entry to a home or room;

- body found outdoors, inappropriately dressed for the season, or a considerable distance from home; or

- missing wallet, jewellery, or other effects that are usually carried or worn.

There may be other situational indicators that appear to be out of context with circumstances of suicide or natural death.

The investigating officer must carefully examine the evidence before concluding that the sudden death was a suicide. It is possible that the deceased is the victim of a carefully crafted homicide. Using the worst-case scenario context, the investigator must find evidence at the scene to support the theory that death was the result of action taken by the victim, and not the result of the actions of another person. This evidence may include:

- handwritten notes explaining the suicide that are consistent in content with the opinions of others who knew the person. Mechanically produced documents are less reliable.

- information, obtained through interviews with persons having knowledge of the deceased, confirming that the victim had a problem that may have led to suicide.

- the manner of death, position of weapons used, position of the body, and bloodstain patterns.

- post-mortem lividity, which refers to the changes in skin colour that appear where blood has pooled. This pooling of blood can be used to determine whether the body has been moved and an approximate, although not very accurate, time of death. The colour of the area of lividity may be useful in initially identifying the cause of death. In instances of heart failure, the area of lividity is bluish-grey in colour. Carbon monoxide poisoning produces a pinkish-red colour. Cyanide poisoning produces a similar but more reddish colour.

Conscious Person

If the person is conscious, the officer must use verbal intervention techniques and his or her powers of observation to determine whether a danger of suicide or serious bodily harm exists. A conversation with the person may help. The officer must remember that the person is not a suspect in an investigation. As such, the tone of the conversation should not be that used in an interrogation.

The goals of intervention are to reduce the person's feeling of isolation through the use of effective communication, and to assess the seriousness of the threat to the person.

At this stage the officer should attempt to make contact with the suicidal person. From a position of safety, the officer should let the person know that he or she is not alone and help is available. The officer's demeanour and the degree of understanding and empathy he or she displays have an important influence on the outcome of the intervention. Officers should keep in mind the following tips for dealing with a potentially suicidal person:

- Try to be non-judgmental, non-threatening, non-critical, calm, sympathetic, and helpful.

- Show empathy for how the person feels. Ask: "How do you feel about things right now? What thoughts are you having?"

- Engage the subject in conversation if possible. Remarks should be kept short and simple.

- Try to address one key problem. Ask: "What is the one problem that is overwhelming right now?" Focus on the ability to manage the problem.

- Try to get the person to identify the problem and put it in perspective.

The officer should be direct and ask whether the person intends to hurt or kill himself or herself. This is important because such questioning immediately establishes the seriousness of the dialogue and possibly allows the officer to make an immediate decision about the nature of his or her intervention. The question should be succinct—for example, "Do you intend to kill yourself?" A question of this kind will not lead the person to entertain fresh thoughts of suicide. If the person indicates that he or she does wish to commit suicide, the officer may decide to rely on the arrest provisions of s. 17 of the MHA.

The Act authorizes the officer to take into custody a person who is a danger to himself or herself or others because of a mental illness.

However, the MHA does not address the manner in which such apprehensions are carried out. Use of force authorities pertaining to all provincial legislation of Ontario, including the MHA, are found in s. 146 of the *Provincial Offences Act* of Ontario.

USE OF FORCE: PROVINCIAL OFFENCES ACT, SECTION 146(1)

Every police officer is, if he or she acts on reasonable and probable grounds, justified in using as much force as is necessary to do what the officer is required or authorized by law to do.

If the person answers no to suicide or is noncommittal, further conversation with the person is essential for assessing the risk of suicide.

While speaking to the suicidal person, the officer should not lecture, criticize, or preach. The pros and cons of suicide should not be discussed, and the person's beliefs and rationale should not be challenged, because his or her reaction can be unpredictable.

The problem that caused the suicidal person to consider suicide is real to that person, and the officer must not express ridicule or deny that the problem exists. Above all, officers must remain calm and in control. The suicidal person has lost control of his or her life and may believe that his or her world is crumbling. The officer's calm reassurance may help the person put the problem into perspective.

Strategies for Verbal Intervention

The following 10 strategies, below, may assist with officer safety and reduce the risk to the suicidal person. Points 1 and 2 deal with building a rapport and making the area safer. Points 3 through 8 involve helping the person identify his or her problems, developing solutions, and settling on a method of assisting the person with his or her problems. Points 9 and 10 involve making a referral and evaluating suicide potential. Assistance could be provided through community agencies, mental health care facilities, or family. Note the reference to "his or her problems." Police officers should not allow the person's problems to become their problems. Empathy is necessary but the officers' emotional health demands that the problems remain with the suicidal person.

1. Build a rapport.

   - Let the person know that you are there to help.

   - Tell the person that you take the threat seriously.

   - Listen actively (see chapter 2 under the heading "Effective Listening").

   - Do not argue about the person's reason for contemplating suicide.

   - Talk about the suicide plan.

   - Remember that negotiation is not an option. The person does not have anything to offer. Offering options in exchange for the person's agreement to not end his or her life may not be effective. (The person may believe that his or her life is worthless.)

   - Carefully consider requests made by a suicidal person before fulfilling them. Requests for alcohol or other drugs that interfere with the person's ability to reason should be refused.

   - If you are the officer in charge of the scene, carefully consider requests to talk to a relative, friend, or clergy. The request may be a legitimate cry for help, or the person may be planning to apologize for the hardship he or she is about to impose—and then commit suicide.

2. Make the area safer.

    • Remove any readily accessible weapons.

    • If the person is holding a weapon, ask him or her to put it down.

3. Try to have the person identify the problem(s).

4. Focus the conversation on the problem(s).

5. Ask the person what he or she has done to address the problem(s).

6. Try to assist in helping or offering a solution to the problem(s).

7. Be positive when discussing solutions. Try to instill a sense of hope in the person.

8. Ask the person for an agreement to try the proposed solution(s).

9. If the person ceases his or her suicidal actions, provide immediate medical or psychological assistance through the appropriate referrals.

10. Evaluate suicide potential.

    • Evaluate background information and risk factors.

    • Use the three Ps (plan, past, partners) to determine immediate risk. The three Ps will be explained in the next section of this chapter.

Assessing the Risk of Suicide

three Ps (plan, past, and partners)
a risk assessment tool that determines whether there is a plan for suicide, a past history of suicide attempts, and partners who can reduce the risk of suicide by helping the person solve his or her problems

The next step, after acquiring information from conversations with the suicidal person and possibly friends and relatives, is to assess the risk of suicide. Using the **three Ps (plan, past, and partners)** to analyze the situation may help officers determine whether there is an immediate risk of suicide:

• *Plan.* How does the person plan to commit suicide? Does he or she have the means to carry out the plan? A plan suggests that the person is serious about ending his or her life. If there is a plan and steps have been taken to obtain the resources necessary to carry it out, the situation is serious. If the person has implemented a time frame, the situation needs immediate attention.

• *Past.* Has the person tried suicide before? A history of suicide attempts greatly increases the likelihood that the person will achieve the desired end. First-time attempts are less likely to end in death.

• *Partners.* Who is available to help the suicidal person overcome his or her personal difficulties? Are friends, family, and community and social service agencies available? Although police officers provide the initial intervention, long-term assistance is required. A network of these partners greatly reduces the risk that the person will commit suicide in the future.

If there is a plan, the risk is high. If the person has taken steps to carry out the plan, the risk has escalated. A combination of a developed plan and a history of suicide attempts creates a very high risk that the person will kill himself or herself. When the first two Ps are present and the third is unavailable, either literally or according to the accused's perception, the person is in extreme danger. Officers faced with these circumstances should take the person into custody and deliver him or her to an appropriate medical or psychiatric facility.

The first two Ps do not have to be present for an officer to take a person into custody. The provisions of s. 17 of the MHA allow an officer to use his or her judgment. In arriving at a decision, the officer needs to consider how the safety of the person and of society itself can best be protected.

Officers must take the following factors into consideration when trying to determine the risk of suicide:

- *Age.* Persons older than 50 (and especially males older than 65) are at higher risk.

- *Gender.* Males are more likely than females to kill themselves.

- *Stress.* The amount of real or perceived stress in a person's life influences the degree of risk. The more stress, the greater the risk.

- *Signs.* The more signs of suicidal tendencies displayed, the greater the risk.

If it is determined that the person is not at immediate risk of committing suicide, the officers should refer him or her to an appropriate community or social service agency. Ideally, the officers should provide the address, telephone number, and name of a contact person at the agency. One officer should make a followup call the next day to let the person know that the police are concerned and are available to help. If instead an immediate threat is identified, the provisions of s. 17 of the MHA may be applicable.

In situations where a person is experiencing a psychotic episode, officers will be unable to reason with him or her. Although the psychotic person is not rational, it may be possible to reach the person at some cognitive level. The person may be able to recognize that police are there to help even though he or she is unable to interact rationally. In such cases, the use of non-lethal force may be a viable last option to prevent the psychotic person from harming himself or herself. Anecdotal evidence appears to confirm that the use of conductive energy devices such as the Taser, which causes temporary paralysis, may be a more effective non-lethal control option than oleoresin capsicum (OC) spray. The use of OC spray appears to be less effective on persons experiencing psychosis and may contribute to excited delirium.

Some recent controversy has arisen regarding the use of the Taser to control violent, mentally ill persons. There have been reports of 60 deaths in Canada and the United States where a Taser has been used. It should be noted that in none of these deaths was the Taser ruled to be the cause of death. In all, the subjects were mentally ill and/or under the influence of a drug when they were "tasered."

The president of the BC Schizophrenia Society, Fred Dawe, has endorsed the use of Tasers by police as a method of saving lives. "The schizophrenia movement across this country believes in the Taser," he said. "We support the appropriate use of the Taser as a life-saving means of force in emergency police interventions."

If the situation escalates and the suicidal person becomes violent, disengagement from the scene may be a viable option. Although the safety of the person is an important concern, officer safety is foremost.

If the intervention is not successful and the person takes his or her life, the intervening officers must not consider their actions to be unsuccessful. The act of attempting to render assistance is all that can be expected. The police had, at the least, offered some solace to the person in their final moments.

Intervention Summary

1. Officer Safety

   - *First* priority.

   - Persons contemplating suicide may be dangerous due to irrational/self-destructive thinking.

   - Weapons may be present.

   - There is a risk of the intervening officer contacting bodily fluids that may contain blood-borne pathogens.

2. Obtaining Background Information

   - The officer should try to obtain as much background information about the person as is possible.

   - Time constraints may not allow the gathering of much information, but any information obtained is helpful.

   - If time is an issue, the officer should immediately check for the presence of weapons and any history of suicide attempts.

   - If time permits, the officer then may obtain information regarding the person's behaviour before the crisis.

   - The officer's questions should establish whether any warning signs are present, although warning sign will not always be present.

   - Other information, such as the person's age and religious beliefs, can help officers assess the risk of suicide.

3. Entry

   - The primary concern should be officer safety.

   - The next concern should be the legality of the entry.

   - If safe, knocking on the door and asking permission to enter is the preferred method of entry.

   - If unsafe, the officer should try to ensure that entry is legal.

   - Possible *Criminal Code* provisions that could allow entry are ss. 117.04(2) and 27.

   - The cases of *R v. Custer* and *R v. Godoy* discuss the legality of entry.

4. Intervention After Entry

- The primary concern should be officer safety.

- If the person is obviously injured or unconscious, assistance should be rendered if the situation is safe. The officer should take necessary precautions by using latex gloves and other safety equipment.

- If the person is conscious, the officer should be direct in questioning— "Do you intend to kill yourself?" "Why do you want to die?" Such questioning may have a psychological effect on the person by allowing him or her to realize the seriousness of the situation.

- Officers should try to ask questions and elicit answers that address the three Ps: plan, past, and partners.

- The three Ps also allow the officer to establish reasonable grounds allowing the use of s. 17 of the MHA if necessary.

- Negotiation is not an option. The person does not have anything to offer. (The person may believe that his or her life is worthless.)

- Officers should carefully consider requests made by a suicidal person before fulfilling them. Requests for alcohol or other drugs that interfere with the person's ability to reason should be refused.

- Requests to talk to a relative, friend, or clergy should be carefully considered by the officer in charge of the scene. The request may be a legitimate cry for help or the person may be planning to apologize for the hardship that he or she is about to impose—and then commit suicide.

SUICIDE INTERVENTIONS AND OFFICER STRESS

The stress of suicide interventions can be enormous. On the other hand, interventions that prevent a person from taking his or her life can be extremely rewarding. In such cases, the officers have fulfilled one of the greatest responsibilities that society has bestowed on them—the responsibility of saving people's lives.

It is not always possible to prevent a person from committing suicide. The stress of an intervention can be greatly amplified when the intervention fails to prevent a suicide. Police officers are taught that they are able to handle any situation. Their personalities usually reinforce this teaching. Most police officers have a "helping" personality—they want to assist anyone in trouble. Unsuccessful interventions can cause officers to question their abilities and how well they are fulfilling their obligation to society.

The duty of officers is to diligently provide assistance where circumstances permit. They must remember that although the person may have committed suicide, an intervention that ends in death does not necessarily mean that the officers were unsuccessful. If all reasonable attempts to prevent the person from harming himself or herself are made, the officers have carried out their duties diligently.

The final phase of any intervention is assessment. The officers must assess their response and decide whether their course of action was appropriate. If all that could have been done was done properly, but death occurred nevertheless, the proper conclusion is that the outcome was unavoidable. But an assessment can reveal a different strategy to follow the next time a similar situation arises. Because each situation is unique, the response must be unique. This uniqueness makes it impossible to determine one course of action that will be effective in all situations. The officers must remember that they are not infallible and that even if they do everything right, the outcome may be beyond their control. The officers must learn from the incident and then put it behind them. This does not necessarily mean that they must forget all about the victim to have closure. Although some officers believe that forgetting is the best way to cope with the stress, others believe that holding on to a compassionate memory of the victim facilitates coping. Police officers are individuals who must develop coping mechanisms tailored to their individual needs; it cannot be said that one method is superior to another.

Failure to successfully deal with the stress caused by suicide interventions may lead to post-traumatic stress disorder. Police officers should be aware of the early indicators of this disorder in order to prevent its development. Episodes where officers relive the incident in their thoughts or dreams or re-experience feelings of anxiety when thinking of or responding to similar occurrences may be early indicators of the disorder. (Chapter 1 expands upon these indicators.) If these early indicators are identified, the officer may, through proper treatment, be able to diminish their effect.

KEY TERMS

articulable cause

suicide by cop

inquest

three Ps (plan, past, and partners)

REFERENCES

Coroners Act. (1990). RSO 1990, c. C.37.

Criminal Code. (1985). RSC 1985, c. C-46, as amended.

Depressive and Manic Depressive Association of Ontario. (1994). Toronto: Author.

Gerberth, V. (July 1993). Inviting death from the hands of a police officer. *Law and Order*, 105–109.

Hafen, B., & Frandsen, K. (1985). *Psychological emergencies and crisis intervention.* Scarborough, ON: Prentice Hall.

McMains, M.J., & Mullins, W.C. (1996). *Crisis negotiations: Managing critical incidents and hostage situations in law enforcement and corrections.* Cincinnati, OH: Anderson Publishing.

Mental Health Act. (1990). RSO 1990, c. M.7.

Parent, R.B. (1996). Aspects of police use of deadly force in British Columbia: The phenomenon of victim-precipitated homicide. Master's thesis, Simon Fraser University.

Police Services Act. (1990). RSO 1990, c. P.15.

Provincial Offences Act. (1990). RSO 1990, c. P.33.

Royal Commission on Aboriginal Peoples. (1995). *Choosing life: Special report on suicide among aboriginal peoples.* Ottawa: Minister of Supply and Services Canada.

Schneidman, E. (1985). *A definition of suicide.* New York: Wiley.

Schneidman, E. (1996). The commonalities of suicide. In *The suicidal mind.* Oxford: Oxford University Press.

Van Zandt, C.R. (July 1993). Suicide by cop. *The Police Chief,* 24–30.

CLASS DISCUSSION: PERSONAL ATTITUDES ABOUT SUICIDE

The following questions may be used as a tool for assessing one's own personal attitude toward suicide. Answer the questions as truthfully as possible, and then in class discuss the answers and their implications for police work. Circle the code that corresponds most closely with your response to the question.

SA strongly agree   **A** agree   **D** disagree   **SD** strongly disagree

SA A D SD	1.	Suicide is wrong.
SA A D SD	2.	Suicide is all right for some people.
SA A D SD	3.	Anyone who commits suicide is mentally unstable.
SA A D SD	4.	A person who commits suicide is a coward.
SA A D SD	5.	I would attempt to stop anyone who tries to commit suicide.
SA A D SD	6.	Suicide is a sin.
SA A D SD	7.	I would feel shame if I ever considered suicide.
SA A D SD	8.	I would feel shame if anyone in my family attempted suicide.
SA A D SD	9.	Anyone who contemplates suicide is a "loser."
SA A D SD	10.	Police officers must remain emotionally detached from a suicidal person.

EXERCISES

True or False

_____ 1. Persons contemplating suicide always signal their intention by providing various warning signs.

_____ 2. The behaviour of persons with schizophrenia is usually quite predictable, which makes assessing the suicide risk of specific persons with schizophrenia an easy task.

_____ 3. Alcohol use is rarely a factor in suicidal behaviour.

_____   4. Gender has little bearing on suicide rates.

_____   5. Depressive illnesses are a contributing factor in a substantial number of suicides.

_____   6. As males enter old age, their risk of suicide drops dramatically.

Short Answer

1. Dorothy Williams calls 911 to report that her husband, Robbie, is attempting to hurt himself. On arriving at the Williams house, the responding officer learns from Dorothy that Robbie is schizophrenic, is acting irrationally, and told her that he was going to kill himself. The officer speaks to Robbie, who rationally tells the officer that his wife is not telling the truth, and that he does not wish to harm himself.

   Explain what the officer should do. Refer to the appropriate legislation in your answer.

2. Summarize the procedure for obtaining a physician's order for a psychiatric assessment under s. 15 of the *Mental Health Act*.

3. How does a justice of the peace's order for psychiatric examination under s. 16 of the *Mental Health Act* differ from a physician's order under s. 15?

4. What should be the primary concern of police officers on being called to a location where a person is threatening suicide?

5. How should officers cope with the stress of suicide interventions?

Case Analysis

Case 7.1

You are a police officer responding to a call for assistance. The information you have received is that Thelma Smith is worried that her former husband, Tom, will injure himself. Further details from dispatch are requested. Thelma called to report that Tom called her about five minutes ago. He seemed depressed over their divorce and loss of access to their children. Thelma lives in a community 500 kilometres away from Tom. Tom has never, to Thelma's knowledge, attempted suicide. He has never owned a firearm.

You, along with another officer, arrive at Tom's apartment. You knock on his door and identify yourself as a police officer. A person who identifies himself as Tom Smith answers the door and asks what you want. You tell him that you are concerned for his safety. He tells you that nothing is wrong and that you can leave. You ask to come inside so you can talk privately. He invites you in.

Once inside, you tell Tom about Thelma's concerns. He tells you that he did call her, adding that perhaps he is a little down because he hasn't seen his children in six months. He is unemployed and living on disability insurance he collects for a back problem. He doesn't have enough money to visit his children, nor does his wife have enough money to send the children to visit him. You continue to speak to Tom while observing the surroundings for any indication of a suicide plan. There are several empty beer bottles but nothing out of the ordinary is noted.

Tom begins to become upset, telling you that he doesn't believe that Thelma wants him to see the children. He tells you that he hasn't been able to send the children any gifts because he doesn't have any money. He has filed a claim with the workers' compensation board but has been denied benefits. He thinks he may have to go on social assistance. He can't make ends meet with the insurance money he receives.

You ask whether he intends to hurt himself. He tells you, "No, I just want an end to my problems." He also tells you that he doesn't own any firearms. You ask whether he would like to talk to someone about his problems. He tells you that he doesn't really have any friends in town and that he moved to town only a month ago. He is becoming agitated and says, "Please leave. I want to be alone." You tell him that you are only trying to help. He replies, "There's nothing wrong. I don't want help." He is becoming increasingly agitated and tells you to get out.

Using the CAPRA system discussed in chapter 2, describe what you will do in this situation.

Case 7.2

You are a police officer responding to an emergency call for assistance at 123 Main Street. On arrival you are met by Albert Rose, who lives next door at 125 Main Street. He believes that his neighbour, Hazel Malcolmson, is going to injure herself. Hazel called and asked him to wait an hour, then call the police. Her words were, "My life is over." He immediately called the police. Albert tells you that he knows Hazel quite well. She does not own any firearms, nor has she ever indicated a desire to die. Albert offers to stay around in case Hazel needs to talk to someone she knows. You thank him and ask him to remain in the area.

You cautiously approach the front door of Hazel's house. The door is unlocked. You open it and call out Hazel's name. There is no reply. You believe that you have reasonable grounds to enter the house. You enter and continue to call out her name while searching the house for her. In an upstairs bedroom, you find her sitting in a chair with a straight razor in her hand.

She looks at you and says, "You are not supposed to be here yet." She tells you not to come closer or she will cut herself and you. You ask her to tell you about her problems. She says that you would not understand, that the matter is very personal. When pressed for details, she becomes withdrawn and does not speak.

Albert suddenly enters the room, which enrages Hazel, who begins screaming, "This is your fault!" You tell Albert to leave the room. Hazel says that she wants him to stay so that he can "see what he has done." Her speech is becoming slurred. You ask whether she has taken any drugs, and she replies, "Two bottles of sleeping pills about twenty minutes ago."

You start to approach her, calmly speaking to her as you advance. She shouts, "Stop or I'll cut both of us. I want to die. My life is over anyway!" She holds the razor to her throat and makes a small cut. Blood begins to flow. She shouts, "Touch me and you are dead!" You retreat.

Using the CAPRA system discussed in chapter 2, describe what you will do in this situation.

Case 7.3

You are a police officer responding to a 911 call for assistance from an anonymous caller. On arrival at the address given by dispatch you are met at the door by Harold Bryant. He tells you that there is no problem and that he did not call. You ask Harold whether he wants to talk about anything and whether anything is wrong. He says that everything is fine but he wouldn't mind talking to someone for a while. He invites you inside and you cautiously accompany him to the living room. Harold asks, "Do you believe in God? Do you believe that you will go to hell if you commit a sin?" You tell him that you don't know.

After some prodding you learn that Harold is 33 years old and a high school teacher. He has been married five years and has daughters aged two and three.

Harold resumes his former line of conversation by asking, "Could you forgive your spouse for doing something really wrong?" You respond by telling him that you do not want to discuss your beliefs on that point. Harold says that he understands and does not speak for a couple of minutes. He then says, "Do you ever wonder what it would be like to die?" You ask him whether he intends to harm himself. He replies, "No. I don't think so. I just have some personal problems that I'm having difficulty dealing with. I did something that I'm not proud of and it has gotten me into serious trouble." You again ask whether he wants to talk about his problem. He replies, "No. It's between me and God." He thanks you for listening and tells you to leave.

Using the CAPRA system discussed in chapter 2, describe what you will do in this situation.

Case 7.4

You are a police officer responding to a call for assistance from Tim Jackson. He invites you into his house and tells you that his wife, Louisa, recently died of cancer. A lawyer has just sent him a letter that was written by Tim's wife shortly before her death and given to the lawyer on the understanding that it would be sent to Tim after she died. The letter states that she gave her permission to their family physician, Dr. Jane Wells, to administer a lethal dose of morphine if her suffering became unbearable and there was no possibility of recovery. Tim remarks that his wife had been suffering terribly but was able to talk rationally most of the time. He has asked Dr. Wells to come over. She should be arriving shortly. Tim feels betrayed by his wife's decision not to consult him before making her arrangement with Dr. Wells.

Dr. Wells arrives. Tim invites you and her into his living room. Dr. Wells states that the letter was written by Louisa about a week before she died. It was written with a lawyer present and was notarized to verify Louisa's signature. Louisa did not want to involve Tim in the decision because she knew that he would not want to let her go. Dr. Wells states that she had known Louisa for about 30 years and that Louisa "fought a good fight" but was suffering immensely and wanted to end her life on her own terms. Louisa, whose condition was terminal, had asked to be given something to allow her to "go gently." Dr. Wells states that she gave Louisa a large dose of morphine to allow her to end her life without further suffering. Dr. Wells begins to cry and says that she lost a true friend. Tim puts his arms around her and tells her that he forgives her.

Using the CAPRA system discussed in chapter 2, describe what you will do in this situation.

Case 7.5

You are a police officer responding to a call for assistance at 321 North Avenue, Smith Pharmaceuticals Company. Upon arrival you are met by the owner, Mr. Smith. Smith tells you that he is worried about the well-being of Dan Bayer, a sales representative whom he fired this morning. Bayer had been given two prior warnings about his alcohol consumption while making sales calls. Smith had received several further complaints from doctors and pharmacists about Bayer smelling of alcohol when he came to their offices.

Bayer told Smith that he has very large debts to pay and doesn't know how he will pay them. He begged Smith to reconsider. He said he would stop drinking if given another chance. Smith replied that he was not willing to jeopardize his business by keeping Bayer and told him he would not reconsider. Bayer became very upset and exclaimed, "Where else can I make a hundred thousand a year? I sold a lot of your drugs and this is what I get?"

Bayer then stormed out of Smith's office. About three hours later Smith received a call from Bayer, who was now at home. He sounded intoxicated. Bayer again asked Smith to reconsider and was told by Smith that he would not rehire him. Bayer began crying and said that he didn't know what he was going to do.

You attend Bayer's condominium, where the door is answered by Dan Bayer. He appears to be intoxicated and smells strongly of alcohol. You tell him that Smith is concerned about his well-being. He replies, "Then he should give me my job back!" You ask whether you can come in and talk. He tells you, "OK, come in."

Bayer offers you a drink, which you politely refuse. Bayer then pours himself a large glass of liquor and sits down. He begins to tell you about his financial problems: "I was making over a hundred thousand a year selling Smith's drugs. I bought this condo, new furniture, a new Porsche, and a few other toys. I drink a bit but that's not illegal. How am I going to pay all these bills? I'm not married and live alone. That's probably a blessing. At least I'm not hurting anyone else."

While he continues to tell you about how unfair it is that Smith fired him, he drinks another large glass of liquor. He tells you that he was good at his job and Smith will miss him. He is becoming more intoxicated and incoherent. He soon begins to fall asleep.

What will you do in this situation? Explain your answer. Be sure to quote authorities.

Case 7.6

Brian is a 14-year-old male in grade 9. He is having problems at school with other boys pushing him around and teasing him. He is very concerned about his small stature and has been using anabolic steroids for the past month in an effort to increase his weight. He has gained weight but has experienced many of the common side effects of steroid use. The worst, at least for Brian, is acne. He is now teased about his small stature and about his severe acne.

Brian tells his parents that he doesn't know if he can take the humiliation anymore. He tells his father, "I'm a loser. I'm never going to grow. You are small. Mom is small. I'll always be small!"

His father tells him about great achievers who were also of small stature such as Napoleon Bonaparte and Alexander the Great. Brian replies, "So what! I'll bet that no one pulled their pants down in the hallway at school! The bullying is driving me crazy! I can't take it anymore! I going to end it all! I'll, I'll, I'll … chop off my foot with an axe and bleed to death! That will show them!" Brian then runs out of the house and locks himself in the garage.

You are a police officer called to the scene. What will you do?

CHAPTER 8

Crime Victims

Chapter Objectives

After completing this chapter, you should be able to:

• Identify the rights given to crime victims under federal and Ontario legislation.

• Describe appropriate police responses to the needs of crime victims and others such as the families and friends of missing persons.

• Identify some of the community and other services available to crime victims.

INTRODUCTION

Police officers can become so involved in a criminal investigation that they forget the needs of the victim or victims. Politicians have tried to address the needs of victims through legislation such as Ontario's *Victims' Bill of Rights, 1995,* but legislation cannot teach an officer compassion. Compassionate officers are able to draw on experience and knowledge to relate to crime victims in a caring, professional manner.

Knowledge of the applicable legislation is an important part of addressing a victim's needs. Officers should know what a victim's rights are and be able to advise victims on restitution, compensation, and victim assistance programs. Officers are expected to meet the needs of victims in all respects, if not personally then through referrals to the appropriate community or social service agencies.

The following section discusses the rights of crime victims under federal and Ontario victims' rights legislation. Later sections focus in more detail on specific rights such as the rights to compensation and restitution.

VICTIMS' RIGHTS LEGISLATION

On October 1, 2003, Federal, Provincial, Territorial Ministers Responsible for Justice endorsed a new *Canadian Statement of Basic Principles of Justice for Victims of Crime, 2003.*

These principles are intended to promote fair treatment of victims and should be reflected in federal/provincial/territorial laws, policies, and procedures:

- Victims of crime should be treated with courtesy, compassion, and respect.

- The privacy of victims should be considered and respected to the greatest extent possible.

- All reasonable measures should be taken to minimize inconvenience to victims.

- The safety and security of victims should be considered at all stages of the criminal justice process and appropriate measures should be taken when necessary to protect victims from intimidation and retaliation.

- Information should be provided to victims about the criminal justice system and the victim's role and opportunities to participate in criminal justice processes.

- Victims should be given information, in accordance with prevailing law, policies, and procedures, about the status of the investigation; the scheduling, progress and final outcome of the proceedings; and the status of the offender in the correctional system.

- Information should be provided to victims about available victim assistance services, other programs and assistance available to them, and means of obtaining financial reparation.

- The views, concerns and representations of victims are an important consideration in criminal justice processes and should be considered in accordance with prevailing law, policies and procedures.

- The needs, concerns and diversity of victims should be considered in the development and delivery of programs and services, and in related education and training.

- Information should be provided to victims about available options to raise their concerns when they believe that these principles have not been followed.

The Victims' Bill of Rights, 1995 (Ontario)

The *Victims' Bill of Rights, 1995* (VBR) was proclaimed in force in June 1996. The VBR recognizes and supports the needs and rights of crime victims in both the criminal and civil justice systems. It establishes principles to support victims throughout the criminal justice process and makes it easier for victims to sue their assailants in civil actions. The VBR's statement of principles (in s. 2(1)) specifies how victims should be treated by judicial officials at different stages of the criminal justice process.

PRINCIPLES: VICTIMS' BILL OF RIGHTS, SECTION 2(1)

The following principles apply to the treatment of victims of crime:

1. Victims should be treated with courtesy, compassion and respect for their personal dignity and privacy by justice system officials.

2. Victims should have access to information about,

    i. the services and remedies available to victims of crime,

    ii. the provisions of this Act and of the *Compensation for Victims of Crime Act* that might assist them,

       iii. the protection available to victims to prevent unlawful intimidation,

       iv. the progress of investigations that relate to the crime,

       v. the charges laid with respect to the crime and, if no charges are laid, the reasons why no charges are laid,

       vi. the victim's role in the prosecution,

       vii. court procedures that relate to the prosecution,

       viii. the dates and places of all significant proceedings that relate to the prosecution,

       ix. the outcome of all significant proceedings, including any proceedings on appeal,

       x. any pretrial arrangements that are made that relate to a plea that may be entered by the accused at trial,

       xi. the interim release and, in the event of conviction, the sentencing of an accused,

       xii. any disposition made under section 672.54 or 672.58 of the *Criminal Code* (Canada) in respect of an accused who is found unfit to stand trial or who is found not criminally responsible on account of mental disorder, and

       xiii. their right under the *Criminal Code* (Canada) to make representations to the court by way of a victim impact statement.

3.   A victim of a prescribed crime should, if he or she so requests, be notified of,

       i. any application for release or any impending release of the convicted person, including release in accordance with a program of temporary absence, on parole or on an unescorted temporary absence pass, and

       ii. any escape of the convicted person from custody.

4.   If the person accused of a prescribed crime is found unfit to stand trial or is found not criminally responsible on account of mental disorder, the victim should, if he or she so requests, be notified of,

       i. any hearing held with respect to the accused by the Review Board established or designated for Ontario pursuant to subsection 672.38 (1) of the *Criminal Code* (Canada),

       ii. any order of the Review Board directing the absolute or conditional discharge of the accused, and

       iii. any escape of the accused from custody.

5.   Victims of sexual assault should, if the victim so requests, be interviewed during the investigation of the crime only by police officers and officials of the same gender as the victim.

6.   A victim's property that is in the custody of justice system officials should be returned promptly to the victim, where the property is no longer needed for the purposes of the justice system.

Section 3(1) of the VBR states that a person convicted of a crime prescribed by regulation by the lieutenant governor in council is liable for damages to the victim for emotional distress, and bodily harm resulting from the distress.

DAMAGES: VICTIM'S BILL OF RIGHTS, SECTION 3(1)

A person convicted of a prescribed crime is liable in damages to every victim of the crime for emotional distress, and bodily harm resulting from the distress, arising from the commission of the crime.

The prescribed crimes are identified in Ontario Regulation 456/96:

1. All crimes described in the *Criminal Code* (Canada) are prescribed for the purposes of paragraphs 3 and 4 of subsection 2(1) of the Act.

2. The crimes described in the following provisions of the *Criminal Code* (Canada) are prescribed for the purposes of subsection 3(1) of the Act:

1. Section 151. [Sexual Interference]

2. Section 152. [Invitation to Sexual Touching]

3. Section 153. [Sexual Exploitation]

4. Section 155. [Incest]

5. Section 159. [Anal Intercourse (Found To Violate s. 15 of the Charter)]

6. Section 170. [Parent or Guardian Procuring Sexual Activity]

7. Section 171. [Householder Permitting Sexual Activity]

8. Section 172. [Corrupting Children]

9. Section 220. [Causing Death by Criminal Negligence]

10. Section 221. [Causing Bodily Harm by Criminal Negligence]

11. Section 235. [Murder]

12. Section 236. [Manslaughter]

13. Section 239. [Attempt To Commit Murder]

14. Section 240. [Accessory After Fact to Murder]

15. Section 244. [Causing Bodily Harm with Intent—Firearm]

16. Section 264. [Criminal Harassment]

17. Section 264.1. [Uttering Threats]

18. Section 266. [Assault]

19. Section 267. [Assault with a Weapon or Causing Bodily Harm]

20. Section 268. [Aggravated Assault]

21. Section 269. [Unlawfully Causing Bodily Harm]

22. Section 271. [Sexual Assault]

23. Section 272. [Sexual Assault with a Weapon, Threats to a Third Party or Causing Bodily Harm]

24. Section 273. [Aggravated Sexual Assault]

25. Section 279. [Kidnapping]

26. Section 279.1. [Hostage Taking]

27. Section 280. [Abduction of Person Under Sixteen]

28. Section 281. [Abduction of Person Under Fourteen]

29. Section 283. [Abduction]

30. Section 344. [Robbery]

31. Section 372. [False messages, Indecent Phone Calls, Harassing Phone Calls]

Section 3(2) of the VBR makes it clear that a victim of domestic assault, sexual assault, or attempted sexual assault is presumed to have suffered emotional distress.

PRESUMPTION: VICTIMS' BILL OF RIGHTS, SECTION 3(2)

The following victims shall be presumed to have suffered emotional distress:

1. A victim of an assault if the victim is or was a spouse or same-sex partner, both within the meaning of section 29 of the *Family Law Act*, of the assailant.

2. A victim of a sexual assault.

3. A victim of an attempted sexual assault.

And subject to judicial discretion, the VBR applies the following provisions to civil actions brought by crime victims:

- An offender's sentence should not be considered when the court awards compensatory damages for the offender's crime.

- Victims who are successful in their lawsuits are presumed to be entitled to reimbursement for most of their legal costs by their assailant.

- Victims are entitled to receive interest on awards from the date of the crime to the date of trial.

- Victims who live outside Ontario and who are commencing a lawsuit usually should not have to post security at the outset of the proceeding.

The victim assistance fund account referred to in s. 60.1(4) of the *Provincial Offences Act* (POA) is continued as the victims' justice fund in the VBR so that money collected under the VBR will be dedicated solely to providing services for victims.

The money for the fund is collected through fine surcharges, which have been applied to all fines under the POA (except parking violations) since January 1, 1995. *Criminal Code* fine surcharge revenues are also added to this fund.

VICTIM FINE SURCHARGES

Victim fine surcharges are provided for in s. 60.1 of the *Provincial Offences Act* of Ontario and s. 737 of the *Criminal Code.*

Provincial Offences Act (Ontario)

SURCHARGE: PROVINCIAL OFFENCES ACT, SECTION 60.1(1)

If a person is convicted of an offence in a proceeding commenced under Part I or III and a fine is imposed in respect of that offence, a surcharge is payable by that person in the amount determined by regulations made under this Act.

COLLECTION: PROVINCIAL OFFENCES ACT, SECTION 60.1(2)

The surcharge shall be deemed to be a fine for the purpose of enforcing payment.

PRIORITIES: PROVINCIAL OFFENCES ACT, SECTION 60.1(3)

Any payments made by a defendant shall be credited towards payment of the fine until it is fully paid and then towards payment of the surcharge.

PART X AGREEMENTS: PROVINCIAL OFFENCES ACT, SECTION 60.1(3.1)

When an agreement made under Part X applies to a fine, payments made by the defendant shall first be credited towards payment of the surcharge, not as described in subsection (3).

SPECIAL PURPOSE ACCOUNT: PROVINCIAL OFFENCES ACT, SECTION 60.1(4)

Surcharges paid into the Consolidated Revenue Fund shall be credited to the victims' justice fund account and shall be deemed to be money received by the Crown for a special purpose.

Criminal Code

VICTIM SURCHARGE: CRIMINAL CODE, SECTION 737(1)

Subject to subsection (5), an offender who is convicted or discharged under section 730 of an offence under this Act or the *Controlled Drugs and Substances Act* shall pay a victim surcharge, in addition to any other punishment imposed on the offender.

AMOUNT OF SURCHARGE: CRIMINAL CODE, SECTION 737(2)

Subject to subsection (3), the amount of the victim surcharge in respect of an offence is

(a) 15 per cent of any fine that is imposed on the offender for the offence; or

(b) if no fine is imposed on the offender for the offence,

    (i) $50 in the case of an offence punishable by summary conviction, and

    (ii) $100 in the case of an offence punishable by indictment.

INCREASE IN SURCHARGE: CRIMINAL CODE, SECTION 737(3)

The court may order an offender to pay a victim surcharge in an amount exceeding that set out in subsection (2) if the court considers it appropriate in the circumstances and is satisfied that the offender is able to pay the higher amount.

AMOUNTS APPLIED TO AID VICTIMS: CRIMINAL CODE, SECTION 737(7)

A victim surcharge imposed under subsection (1) shall be applied for the purposes of providing such assistance to victims of offences as the lieutenant governor in council of the province in which the surcharge is imposed may direct from time to time.

THE INITIAL POLICE RESPONSE TO THE NEEDS OF CRIME VICTIMS

Victims expect thorough investigations. Victim dissatisfaction may arise whenever officers give the impression that the victim's complaint is not serious enough to justify the expenditure of police resources.

Crime victims have the right to courteous and compassionate treatment by the police. Their dignity and privacy must be respected. The qualities that allow an officer to behave in the appropriate way toward crime victims rest on the officer's integrity and life experience. Officers learn that more is required of them than simply responding to a victim's needs in a manner that is consistent with policy and addresses all of the legal aspects of an investigation.

Police want the cooperation of persons who report crimes. Without their help, the crime is probably not going to be solved. There may, however, be areas of conflict between police and victim expectations. Responding officers may seem remote, detached, uninterested, or unconcerned about the victim's plight. The victim may feel susceptible to further violation through the belief that the police will not provide any comfort. The victim may be reacting to the protective shield of emotional detachment often displayed by police officers who remain detached as a way of dealing with the daily encounters of policing.

Policing is a paramilitary profession that displays the characteristics of a military subculture—that is, an emphasis on toughness, camaraderie with fellow officers, suspicion of outsiders, and cynicism. Officers who subscribe to this subculture may approach the victim's personal tragedy in an impersonal, unemotional business-only manner. Victims can feel that they have been revictimized if an officer shows no understanding of their emotions following a crime. For an officer who has already investigated, say, 10 break-and-enters during the past week, it is possible to lose sight of the impact of the crime on the victim, who may be feeling horribly violated. If the officer fails to acknowledge the victim's emotional state, his or her actions may be construed as a lack of compassion. The officer can greatly enhance the victim's recovery by offering compassion, empathy, and timely advice at the outset.

The officer must try to preserve the victim's dignity by asking as few questions as possible, while still taking care to obtain the information needed to start an investigation. Asking too many personal questions may be interpreted by the victim as an indication that the victim is a suspect. If all the information needed to start an investigation is obtained during the initial contact with the victim, the officer can return later to seek further details, thus giving the victim the opportunity to at least partially recover from his or her turmoil.

The officer must be aware of the community and social service agencies that may be available to help the victim. Officers cannot help everyone with every problem, but are relied on by the public to at least provide information about where help can be obtained.

SPECIAL SITUATIONS

The following sections discuss certain situations that can be traumatic for victims and others: missing persons cases, the aftermath of a break-and-enter, and injury and death notifications. The information provided below is intended for general guidance only. Individual police services may have their own policies regarding the situations described below.

Missing Persons

CHILDREN

involuntarily missing
lost or abducted

A missing child should always be considered to be **involuntarily missing**. Information for a missing person report should be obtained (see appendix 8A at the end of this chapter) and that information relayed to other officers. The investigation should begin immediately. If the child is not located within a few hours, one may want to obtain permission from the child's parents or guardians to issue a news release. The safety of the child must be the primary concern. Although statistics show that the majority of missing children are runaways, police must presume that the child is involuntarily missing, at least until the evidence shows otherwise. The child may be lost, a victim of abuse, or abducted.

In 2004 there were 67,266 children reported missing in Canada, the vast majority of which were classified as runaways. The missing children were classified as follows (Royal Canadian Mounted Police, 2005):

- runaway: 52,280

- abduction by parent: 332

- abduction by stranger: 31

- accident: 27

- wandered off: 671

- other: 2,552

- unknown: 11,373.

The Canadian Police Information Centre provides definitions of the categories of missing children:

- *Runaway.* Includes children under 18 years of age who have run away from home or substitute home care (foster home, group home, or Children's Aid Society home or shelter). The causes may include a previous history of running away or a particular circumstance that leads to the subject's disappearance (for example, a family fight, or breakup with a boyfriend or girlfriend).

- *Abduction by parent.* Defined as when the subject is a child and he or she has been abducted by a parent. This category is divided into cases where a custody order has been granted, and cases where a custody order has not been granted.

- *Abduction by stranger.* Defined as an abduction by individuals other than the subject's parents or guardian. The abductor may be an uncle, sister, cousin, grandfather, neighbour, or close family friend. This definition also includes a child who has been briefly restrained from his or her intended destination. An example is a child who has been sexually assaulted and then released.

- *Accident.* This category is chosen when the probable cause for the child's disappearance is an accident of some kind and the body has not been recovered. This includes accidental drowning, fire/avalanche/hiking disappearance, and other types of accidents.

- *Wandered off/lost.* This category is used in the following cases: where the child is presumed to have wandered away in a confused state from a hospital, mental institution, or chronic care facility; where a child has become lost in the woods or has not returned when expected from hiking, camping, or hunting; where the child has wandered away or is lost from the family location; or where the child has not returned when expected from school, a friend's house, a meeting, etc.

- *Other.* This category is used when the child or youth has not returned to a detention home or institution housing young offenders.

- *Unknown.* This category is used when the police agency has no previous record on the missing child. The child has never run away, walked out, or wandered off before the incident was reported to police. The child has "no previous history."

(Note: The RCMP central database is Canada-wide and the statutory provisions that determine when a child may leave home without permission vary from province to province. This may account for any discrepancy in missing-child statistics. In Ontario, for example, the *Child and Family Services Act* [CFSA] allows a child to leave the parental home at age 16.)

The officer responding to a call of a missing child may not display empathy with the person who is reporting the missing child. The officer may know from the above statistics that the probability of the child being missing due to foul play or accident is very unlikely. This is of little comfort to the person reporting the missing child. The officer should therefore try to view the situation from the perspective of the person reporting the incident and act accordingly.

If the child is missing or has been missing for a lengthy period—which will be dictated by individual circumstances—there are organizations that may be helpful in locating the child. The following organizations use websites to post information about missing children:

- Our Missing Children: http://www.ourmissingchildren.ca/en.

- The National Center for Missing and Exploited Children: http://www.missingkids.org.

- Child Cybersearch: http://www.childcybersearch.org.

- Child Find Canada: http://www.childfind.ca.

- Missing Children's Network Canada: http://www.missingchildren.ca.

The information may be posted by the police or by the person who is reporting the missing child.

When a child who has run away from home is located, officers have the legal authority under s. 43(2) of the CFSA to apprehend and return the child to his or her parents or guardians if the child's safety in the home is not a concern.

ADULTS

voluntarily missing
missing from home as a result of a voluntary choice

The officer should first try to ascertain whether the person is **voluntarily missing** or involuntarily missing. The person may be running away from family problems, abuse, criminal conduct, or relationship problems, or may be attempting to start a new life. The police do not have the authority to apprehend an adult who is voluntarily missing.

Persons who are missing involuntarily may be victims of accidental death, murder, or abduction. Memory loss and Alzheimer's disease (see chapter 6) are other possibilities.

The officer must acquire as much information as possible about the missing person, including

- possible reasons for the disappearance;

- information on any past voluntary disappearances;

- a detailed physical description;

- a list of friends and relatives;

- employment information;

- information on habits and hobbies (for example, sports, clubs, support groups, and bars); and

- information on possible destinations.

Once the information has been gathered, the officer must use his or her judgment to determine whether the person is missing voluntarily or involuntarily. A missing person report should be filled out by the officer regardless of the determination.

The person reporting the disappearance may be very emotional. The investigating officer may believe, based on their analysis of the acquired information, that the missing person may be voluntarily missing. As with a missing child, the officer should view the situation from the perspective of the reporting person, regardless of whether the officer believes the disappearance to be voluntary, and display empathy with the reporting person. If the officer chooses to disclose what he or she thinks caused the disappearance, he or she should have regard for the possible emotional turmoil being experienced by the person reporting the disappearance. It may be advisable, depending on the circumstances and the officer's determination of the cause, to wait until the person's emotions are more under control before disclosing details.

If the person appears to be in turmoil, it may help to ask whether he or she would like assistance from a service such as the Victim Crisis Assistance and Referral Service program (discussed below).

Break-and-Enter

The crime of break-and-enter is common in many places. The frequency of its occurrence may lead an investigating officer to treat the crime as routine and forget how devastating it can be for the victim.

The property taken may, even if its monetary value is insignificant, have great sentimental value for the victim. And in addition to the property loss, the victim may feel violated because his or her personal space has been encroached upon. The victim may experience feelings of insecurity, shock, fear, and outrage.

The attending officer must, of course, perform his or her investigative duties, but should try to remain sensitive to the victim's needs. The officer should be empathetic and seek to view the event from the victim's perspective. And the officer should not create an unrealistic expectation that the property will be returned, because in many instances it cannot be recovered.

Information about preventing future break-and-enters may help alleviate some of the victim's fear and apprehension. The police can provide information on programs such as Neighbourhood Watch, on security devices such as alarm systems, and on security measures such as remembering to lock all doors and windows. This advice may seem insignificant, but imparting it may allow the victim to regain a sense of control over his or her domestic space.

A followup call by the police, and having an officer visibly present in the neighbourhood, will also help reinforce positive contact with the victim.

Restitution of Property

A person whose stolen property has been recovered may feel greatly inconvenienced and also revictimized if the property is withheld by the police for use as evidence. For this reason, the property should be returned as soon as possible once it is no longer needed for court proceedings or to preserve the continuity of evidence. The *Criminal Code* addresses restitution of property in ss. 489.1 and 491.2, below. The latter section concerns the use of photographs in court in lieu of the property itself.

RESTITUTION OF PROPERTY OR REPORT BY PEACE OFFICER: CRIMINAL CODE, SECTION 489.1(1)

Subject to this or any other Act of Parliament, where a peace officer has seized anything under a warrant issued under this Act or under section 487.11 or 489 or otherwise in the execution of duties under this or any other Act of Parliament, the peace officer shall, as soon as is practicable,

(a) where the peace officer is satisfied,

(i) that there is no dispute as to who is lawfully entitled to possession of the thing seized, and

(ii) that the continued detention of the thing seized is not required for the purposes of any investigation or a preliminary inquiry, trial or other proceeding,

return the thing seized, on being issued a receipt therefor, to the person lawfully entitled to its possession and report to the justice who issued the warrant or some other justice for the same territorial division or, if no warrant was issued, a justice having jurisdiction in respect of the matter, that he has done so; or

(b) where the peace officer is not satisfied as described in subparagraphs (a)(i) and (ii),

(i) bring the thing seized before the justice referred to in paragraph (a), or

(ii) report to the justice that he has seized the thing and is detaining it or causing it to be detained

to be dealt with by the justice in accordance with subsection 490(1).

"This section deals with the disposition of property that has been seized by a peace officer either under a warrant issued pursuant to ss. 258, 487, 487.01 or 487.1, or without warrant under ss. 487.11 or 489, or otherwise as a result of the execution of the peace officer's duties under any Act of Parliament.

"Subsection (1)(a) provides that where the peace officer is satisfied that lawful possession is not in issue and the continued detention of the thing seized is not required for the purposes of any investigation or court proceedings, the peace officer shall, as soon as practicable, return the item seized to the person lawfully entitled to it. The peace officer must obtain a receipt for the returned item and make a report to a justice having jurisdiction.

"Subsection (1)(b) states that where the peace officer is not satisfied as required in para. (a), he must bring the item seized to a justice having jurisdiction *or* report to the justice that the thing has been seized and is detained. The justice must then deal with the item in accordance with s. 490(1)." (*Martin's Annual Criminal Code, 2005*)

PHOTOGRAPHIC EVIDENCE: CRIMINAL CODE, SECTION 491.2(1)

Before any property that would otherwise be required to be produced for the purposes of a preliminary inquiry, trial or other proceeding in respect of an offence under section 334 [theft under $5,000], 344 [armed robbery], 348 [break-and-enter], 354 [possession of stolen property], 362 [false pretenses] or

380 [fraud] is returned or ordered to be returned, forfeited or otherwise dealt with under section 489.1 or 490 or is otherwise returned, a peace officer or any person under the direction of a peace officer may take and retain a photograph of the property.

CERTIFIED PHOTOGRAPH ADMISSIBLE IN EVIDENCE: CRIMINAL CODE, SECTION 491.2(2)

Every photograph of property taken under subsection (1), accompanied by a certificate of a person containing the statements referred to in subsection (3), shall be admissible in evidence and, in the absence of evidence to the contrary, shall have the same probative force as the property would have had if it had been proved in the ordinary way.

STATEMENTS MADE IN CERTIFICATE: CRIMINAL CODE, SECTION 491.2(3)

For the purposes of subsection (2), a certificate of a person stating that

(a) the person took the photograph under the authority of subsection (1),

(b) the person is a peace officer or took the photograph under the direction of a peace officer, and

(c) the photograph is a true photograph

shall be admissible in evidence and, in the absence of evidence to the contrary, is evidence of the statements contained in the certificate without proof of the signature of the person appearing to have signed the certificate.

SECONDARY EVIDENCE OF PEACE OFFICER: CRIMINAL CODE, SECTION 491.2(4)

An affidavit or solemn declaration of a peace officer or other person stating that the person has seized property and detained it or caused it to be detained from the time that person took possession of the property until a photograph of the property was taken under subsection (1) and that the property was not altered in any manner before the photograph was taken shall be admissible in evidence and, in the absence of evidence to the contrary, is evidence of the statements contained in the affidavit or solemn declaration without proof of the signature or official character of the person appearing to have signed the affidavit or solemn declaration.

At times it is not feasible to physically bring evidence to court (for example, if an object is large or perishable). In these cases a photograph that meets the requirements of s. 491.2 will be admissible.

Injury and Death Notifications

Injury and death notifications are a necessary but unpleasant aspect of policing. The reaction of the friend or relative who receives the news can range from calm acceptance to hysteria. Officers can prepare themselves to handle these situations and alleviate some of the turmoil experienced by those who receive the news by following the guidelines in this section.

The responding officer should ensure that he or she has all the pertinent information and that it is accurate. The following information is required:

- The name of the injured or deceased person. If the person has not been positively identified, a friend or family member may be required to identify him or her.

- The facts surrounding the injury or death.

- The exact location of the incident.

- The names of the attending officers (if the responding officer was not at the scene).

Once this information has been obtained, the officer attends the residence of the victim's partner or relative to notify him or her of the situation. Information should not be released to the media before notification. The following are some suggestions that may help alleviate the mental anguish experienced by friends and family:

- The officer must ensure that he or she is attending the proper address.

- If possible, another officer or resource person should attend at the residence along with the primary responding officer.

- The officer should introduce himself or herself and any others in attendance.

- The persons receiving the news should be asked to sit down (if they are outside the residence, they should be asked to go inside). In most instances, people are upset by the arrival of a police officer at their residence. An officer should not worsen matters by walking into a residence without first asking to be invited in.

- The officer must be polite, patient, respectful, and professional. The information relayed by the officer will be regarded as truthful, accurate, and sincere.

- Information about the incident should be relayed truthfully, but need not be graphic. If the case is a homicide and it is possible that details of a graphic nature will be discussed in court, the officer should, sometime before the trial date, disclose the details to the affected persons before they hear them in court.

- The officer should not speculate about what happened, but simply relay the facts.

- The officer should listen and respond to questions as truthfully as possible, and remain empathetic and compassionate. The officer should not rush matters.

- Within the limits of police service policies, all possible assistance should be provided to the persons being notified.

- The persons being notified should not be left alone. With their permission, a relative, friend, or representative of a service such as the Victim Crisis Assistance and Referral Service can be asked to stay.

- A followup call will help confirm that the police are compassionate and concerned.

VICTIM AND WITNESS ASSISTANCE PROGRAMS

Victim Crisis Assistance and Referral Service Program

Ontario has various programs for offering assistance to crime victims. One such program is the Victim Crisis Assistance and Referral Service program (VCARS).

VCARS offices, funded through the Victims' Justice Fund and administered by the Ontario Victim Services Secretariat, operate 24 hours a day, 7 days a week. They provide immediate, onsite comfort and support to crime and disaster victims. Police officers at a crime or accident scene can call on VCARS to send out a team of volunteers. The volunteers provide short-term assistance as well as followup services and referrals to community organizations.

During the first half of fiscal year 1996–97, VCARS volunteers responded to 2600 calls concerning homicides, abductions, car accidents, spousal assaults, and other incidents. Most calls involved domestic violence, and most of the assisted persons were women.

VCARS offices are managed by community-based organizations reporting to a locally selected board of directors and are staffed primarily by volunteers. VCARS volunteers work in conjunction with local police services, thus enabling the police to focus on other frontline duties.

The original 4 VCARS offices in Brantford, Toronto, Kingston, and Sault Ste. Marie have expanded to 40 in 2004.

Victim/Witness Assistance Program

The goal of the Victim/Witness Assistance Program (V/WAP) is to enhance victims' and witnesses' understanding of and participation in the criminal justice process. V/WAP offers courtroom orientation sessions, information about the criminal justice process generally, case-specific information (for example, the offender's bail and probation terms), and courtroom accompaniment services. It also acts as a liaison between victims and witnesses on the one hand and police officers and Crown attorneys on the other, provides referrals to community agencies for counselling and other support services, provides a public education and coordination function for government agencies and other government bodies within the community, and seeks community participation through the operation of an active volunteer program.

The program gives priority to acutely traumatized victims and witnesses. The groups most frequently helped comprise victims and witnesses involved in assaults against female spouses, sexual assault, and child abuse.

V/WAP provides training for Crown attorneys on the issues of spousal assault, sexual assault, and child abuse. It has developed an information and activity book for child witnesses that is available in both French and English. The V/WAP brochure itself is available in 13 languages.

The program has 45 offices in Ontario.

- *North:* For offices in North Region, contact 705-564-7269.
- *West:* For offices in West Region, contact 519-453-8973.
- *East:* For offices in East Region, contact 613-239-0392.

- *Central:* For offices in Central Region, contact 905-853-4852.

- *Central West:* For offices in Central West Region, contact 905-521-7590.

- *Toronto:* For offices in Toronto Region, contact 416-212-1310.

Victim Support Line

The Victim Support Line (VSL) is a program for crime victims. It is sponsored by the Ministry of the Attorney General and the Ministry of the Solicitor General and Correctional Services. The VSL operates in both English and French. By calling 1-888-579-2888 (or 416-314-2447 in Toronto), crime victims can obtain the following information 24 hours a day, 7 days a week:

- By registering with an automated callback system, the release status of any adult offender in the provincial corrections or parole system.

- Advice from a counsellor on appropriate services available in the victim's community (such as women's shelters and sexual assault counselling services).

- Tape-recorded information on arrest and release procedures, the court system, probation and parole, and other subjects of interest to crime victims.

- Information on how victims can ensure that their concerns are heard when a decision about releasing an offender is to be made.

THE VICTIM'S ACCESS TO INFORMATION ON OFFENDERS IN THE FEDERAL SYSTEM AFTER SENTENCING

(The following information does not apply to an accused who is a young offender.)

Section 26 of the *Corrections and Conditional Release Act* gives victims access to certain information about the offender after sentencing. If the National Parole Board decides that the victim's interests clearly outweigh the invasion of the offender's privacy, the victim or his or her agent may request information about the offender. The information that may be released includes:

- whether the offender is in custody, and if not, why;

- where the offender will be released;

- when the offender will be released;

- what type of release the offender has been released on—for example, parole, day pass, or work release; and

- any conditions attached to the offender's release.

victim impact statement
a written description of any harm to a victim or loss suffered by a victim due to an offence; it is considered by the courts in sentencing and by parole boards at parole hearings

The victim will not automatically be given this information. Application for the release of the information must be made by the victim or his or her agent. The victim or agent may also request ongoing information such as any movement of the offender from one correctional facility to another.

At any time, but preferably as soon as possible after the offender is sentenced, victims may also provide a **victim impact statement** to the National Parole Board. The statement should contain a written description of any harm done to the victim, any loss that he or she has suffered due to the offence, and any additional information that the victim feels may be important for the board to consider.

The board will use the information in its assessment of the likelihood of the offender reoffending or whether additional release conditions should be placed on the offender to enhance the protection of the victim.

The victim should be made aware that all the information provided will be disclosed to the offender with the exception of information about the victim's identification or other personal information.

Victims can attend parole board hearings as observers. Victims are not allowed to speak or participate in any way except through a victim impact statement.

For more information on parole, or to submit a victim impact statement, the victim can contact the Correctional Service of Canada (CSC). The CSC has five regional offices:

1. Pacific: 1-888-999-8828

2. Prairies: 1-800-616-5277

3. Ontario: 1-800-518-8817

4. Quebec: 514-283-9924

5. Atlantic: 1-800-265-8744

CRIMINAL INJURIES COMPENSATION

A victim injured as a result of a criminal act should be informed that he or she may be entitled to monetary compensation. This compensation does not prohibit the victim from seeking damages in civil court.

The Criminal Injuries Compensation Board is a quasi-judicial tribunal that provides compensation to victims of violent crime in Ontario (or their survivors). Applications may be made by victims who have been injured by a criminal act as defined under the *Criminal Code*, or by the survivors of persons killed as a result of such an act.

For the board to properly adjudicate a claim, credible evidence must be provided. A criminal conviction with respect to an act or negligent omission where a duty of care is required on which a claim is based is conclusive evidence that the offence has been committed.

Compensation may be awarded for

- expenses actually and reasonably incurred as a result of the victim's injury or death;

- emergency expenses such as medical expenses, funeral expenses up to $6,000, and interim counselling expenses up to $5,000;

- lost wages up to $250 a week, when the monetary loss is a consequence of a total or partial disability affecting the victim's capacity to work;

- financial losses suffered by the dependants of a deceased victim;

- pain and suffering; and

- maintenance of a child born as a result of a sexual assault.

More information can be obtained from the board's office:

Criminal Injuries Compensation Board
439 University Avenue, 4th Floor
Toronto, ON M5G 1Y8
Telephone: 1-800-372-7463

THE COURT PROCESS

The victim has the right to know the name of the accused unless the accused is a young offender. Also, information about the offence with which the accused is charged, and when and where court proceedings will commence, must be provided if requested.

Court procedures should be explained to victims in plain language. Victims, obviously, benefit from an understanding of the judicial process, and having this information can help them decide whether they wish to attend the proceedings. The possibility that a victim may see the accused in a public place while the accused is at large under the conditions of a judicial interim release or other release order should be explained to the victim. Conditions requiring the accused to abstain from contact with the victim should also be disclosed and explained.

If a victim is to be called as a witness, the procedures for testifying should be explained, including the possibility of cross-examination. The fact that the accused will be present in court should also be mentioned. Assuring a victim that he or she will be safe and that the accused will not be allowed to harm or harass him or her in court may alleviate a possible fear of testifying.

Victims should also be advised about their rights under s. 722 of the *Criminal Code*, which allows a victim to submit a victim impact statement before a convicted person is sentenced.

VICTIM IMPACT STATEMENT: CRIMINAL CODE, SECTION 722(1)

For the purpose of determining the sentence to be imposed on an offender or whether the offender should be discharged pursuant to section 730 in respect of any offence, the court shall consider any statement that may have been prepared in accordance with subsection (2) of a victim of the offence describing the harm done to, or loss suffered by, the victim arising from the commission of the offence.

"This section sets out the circumstances under which a victim impact statement is admissible. Where a statement is properly before the court then the court 'shall' consider the statement in determining the sentence. The court may, however, take into account any other evidence concerning the victim, for example, evidence given by the victim during the trial proper, in accordance with s. 724. The statement is to be prepared in writing and in the form and in accordance with the procedures established by a programme designated by the lieutenant governor in council." (*Martin's Annual Criminal Code, 2005*)

RESTITUTION

Victims should also be informed of the availability of a **restitution order** as described in s. 738 of the *Criminal Code*.

RESTITUTION TO VICTIMS OF OFFENCES: CRIMINAL CODE, SECTION 738(1)

Where an offender is convicted or discharged under section 730 of an offence, the court imposing sentence on or discharging the offender may, on application of the Attorney General or on its own motion, in addition to any other measure imposed on the offender, order that the offender make restitution to another person as follows:

(a) in the case of damage to, or the loss or destruction of, the property of any person as a result of the commission of the offence or the arrest or attempted arrest of the offender, by paying to the person an amount not exceeding the replacement value of the property as of the date the order is imposed, less the value of any part of the property that is returned to that person as of the date it is returned, where the amount is readily ascertainable;

(b) in the case of bodily harm to any person as a result of the commission of the offence or the arrest or attempted arrest of the offender, by paying to the person an amount not exceeding all pecuniary damages, including loss of income or support, incurred as a result of the bodily harm, where the amount is readily ascertainable; and

(c) in the case of bodily harm or threat of bodily harm to the offender's spouse or child, or any other person, as a result of the commission of the offence or the arrest or attempted arrest of the offender, where the spouse, child or other person was a member of the offender's household at the relevant time, by paying to the person in question, independently of any amount ordered to be paid under paragraphs (a) and (b), an amount not exceeding actual and reasonable expenses incurred by that person, as a result of moving out of the offender's household, for temporary housing, food, child care and transportation, where the amount is readily ascertainable.

"Restitution may be ordered in three circumstances. Under para. (1)(a), the offender can be required to pay to persons whose property was lost or destroyed the replacement value of the property, provided that the damage or loss or destruction of the property was the result of the commission of the offence or the arrest or attempted arrest of the offender. The amount to be paid cannot exceed the replacement value of the property at the time the order is made less the value of any of the property that has been returned to the person. Under para. (1)(b) the offender may be required to pay an amount not exceeding all pecuniary damages, including loss of income and support, to any person who suffered bodily harm as a result of the commission of the offence or the arrest or attempted arrest of the offender. Paragraph (1)(c) allows the court to order the offender to pay an amount not exceeding the actual and reasonable expenses incurred by a spouse, child or other person who was a member of the offender's household, as a result of moving out of the offender's household, for temporary housing, food, child care and transportation. Paragraph (1)(c) only applies in the case of bodily harm or threat of bodily harm to the offender's spouse, child or any other person as a result of the commission of the offence or the arrest or attempted arrest of the offender. In all cases the amount must be 'readily ascertainable.' " (*Martin's Annual Criminal Code, 2005*)

KEY TERMS

involuntarily missing   victim impact statement

restitution order   voluntarily missing

REFERENCES

Corrections and Conditional Release Act. (1992). SC 1992, c. 20.

Criminal Code. (1985). RSC 1985, c. C-46, as amended.

Martin's Annual Criminal Code, 2005. (2005). Aurora, ON: Canada Law Book.

Provincial Offences Act. (1990). RSO 1990, c. P.33.

Victims' Bill of Rights, 1995. (1995). SO 1995, c. 6.

EXERCISES

Short Answer

1. How are victim services programs funded in the province of Ontario?

2. Explain when photographs of seized property may be introduced into court as evidence.

3. Explain the purpose of the Victim Crisis Assistance and Referral Service program.

4. What is the purpose of the Victim/Witness Assistance Program?

5. How can a victim of crime ascertain the release status of an incarcerated adult offender?

6. What is the maximum monetary compensation available through the Criminal Injuries Compensation Board?

7. What is a restitution order?

APPENDIX 8A   MISSING PERSON REPORT

<u>**MISSING PERSON REPORT**</u>   OFFICER NO: _____
                                               OFFICER NAME: _____
                                               INCIDENT NO: _____

INCIDENT DATE: _____   TIME: _____   TO DATE: _____   TIME: _____
REPORT DATE: _____   TIME: _____

MISSING PERSON TYPE: 1__MISSING   2__ELOPEE   3__YOUNG OFFENDER

<u>PROBABLE CAUSE</u>

1__ABDUCT BY STRANGER   4__PARENT ABDUCT C/O   7__UNKNOWN
2__POSSIBLE ACCIDENT   5__PARENT ABDUCT NO C/O   8__OTHER
3__WANDER OFF   6__RUNAWAY

<u>MISSING FROM</u>

1__FAMILY RES.   4__VACATION TRAVEL   7__DISASTER   10__DETENTION CTR
2__SCHOOL   5__SHOP/PLAZA/MALL   8__CHILD CARE SERV   11__YOUTH CENTRE
3__OTHER INSTIT. 6__WORK RELATED   9__FOSTER HOME   12__OTHER

<u>DISABILITIES</u>

1__PHYSICAL   3__MEDICAL   5__ALCOHOL/DRUGS   7__NONE KNOWN
2__MENTAL   4__POSSIBLE SUICIDE   6__COMBINATION OF ALL

<u>AGE GROUP</u>

1__ 0-1 YR   4__ 6-8 YRS   7__ 14-15 YRS   10__ 22-29 YRS   13__ OVER 65
2__ 2-3 YRS   5__ 9-11 YRS   8__ 16-17 YRS   11__ 30-49 YRS
3__ 4-5 YRS   6__ 12-13 YRS   9__ 18-21 YRS   12__ 50-65 YRS

<u>HISTORY</u>

1__NO PREVIOUS HISTORY   2__REPEAT   3__HABITUAL OR CHRONIC

<u>DENTAL CHART</u>

1__AVAIL/ENTERED   2__AVAIL/NOT ENTERED   3__NOT REQ/NOT ENTERED   4__UNAVAIL

PHOTOGRAPH AVAILABLE (Y/N): _____   X-RAYS AVAILABLE (Y/N): _____
INSTITUTION NAME (ELOPEE): _____
ORDER EXPIRY DATE: _____   EMANCIPATION DATE: _____

LAST SEEN AT: _____   BY: _____
DATE LAST SEEN: _____ TIME: _____   TO DATE: _____ TIME: _____
PROBABLE DESTINATION: _____

LOCATED AT: _____ DATE: _____ TIME: _____ BY: _____
CIRCUMSTANCES: _____
PERSON ADVISED: _____ DATE: _____ TIME: _____ BY: _____

<u>REPORT NARRATIVE</u>

_____
_____
_____
_____
_____

PERSONS PHYSICAL DESCRIPTORS

SURNAME: _____ GIVEN 1: _____

HEIGHT (cm): _____   WEIGHT (kg): _____

OFFICER NO: _____
OFFICER NAME: _____
INCIDENT NO: _____

COMPLEXION

____

1__SALLOW   3__RUDDY   5__DARK/SWARTHY   7__DARK NEGRO   9__POCK MARKED
2__LIGHT/FAIR   4__FRECKLED   6__LIGHT NEGRO   8__NEGRO   10__OTHER

BUILD

1__SLENDER   2__MEDIUM   3__HEAVY   4__OTHER

HAIR COLOUR

1__BROWN   2__BLACK   3__BLOND   4__RED   5__GREY   6__WHITE   7__BALD

HAIR TYPE

1__BALD   4__LONG   7__UNKEMPT   10__DYED   13__TOUPEE/WIG
2__PART BALD   5__STRAIGHT   8__BUSHY   11__PONYTAIL   14__OTHER
3__SHORT   6__CURLY   9__WAVY   12__BRUSHCUT

FACIAL HAIR COLOUR

1__BROWN   2__BLACK   3__BLOND   4__RED   5__GREY   6__WHITE

FACIAL HAIR TYPE

1__MOUSTACHE   2__BEARD   3__OTHER

EYE COLOUR

1__BLACK   2__BLUE   3__BROWN   4__GREY   5__GREEN   6__HAZEL   7__MAROON

EYE LENS TYPE

1__GLASSES   2__CONTACTS   3__OTHER

TEETH

1__GOOD   4__VISIBLE GOLD   7__PROTRUD LOWER   10__OTHER
2__IRREGULAR   5__STAINED   8__VISIBLE DECAY
3__FALSE   6__PROTRUD UPPER   9__VISIBLE MISSING

SCARS/MARKS OR TATTOOS: _____

_____

ALIAS

SURNAME: _____ GIVEN 1: _____ GIVEN 2: _____

NICKNAME: _____

Glossary

abuse in the *Child and Family Services Act*, a state or condition of being physically harmed, sexually molested, or sexually exploited

active listening devoting complete attention to a message to ensure full and accurate understanding

acute stress a reaction to one or more specific critical incidents that are beyond the individual's ability to cope

ageism discriminatory belief that the elderly are generally frail, dependent, sick, and unproductive

Alzheimer's disease a progressive, degenerative disease that destroys brain cells and causes dementia

antisocial personality disorder condition characterized by a disregard for the moral and legal rules of society and for other people's rights

articulable cause suspicion based on some discernible fact

bipolar disorder illness characterized by alternating periods of mania and depression

CAPRA a problem-solving system with five components: clients (and communication skills), acquiring and analyzing information, partnerships, response, and assessment

child generally, a person under the age of 18; under some legislation, a person under the age of 16 or 14

child sexual abuse any activity or behaviour that is sexual in nature and directed toward a child

client anyone directly or indirectly involved in an occurrence, or in any way affected by it

clinical depression an illness that is characterized by a continually low, sad, and depressed mood and that interferes with the individual's ability to work, sleep, eat, and enjoy once-pleasurable activities

cognitive behavioural therapy pyschological treatment to change maladaptive thoughts, feelings, beliefs, and habits

conflict a disagreement that may not require police intervention

criminal harassment conduct that makes a person fear for his or her safety or for the safety of someone he or she knows; also called stalking

cumulative stress stress that is caused by long-term, frequent, low-level stress

dating violence any intentional physical, sexual, or psychological attack on one partner by the other in a dating relationship

delusion defect in belief or thought processes that is not reasonable

delusions of persecution false and irrational beliefs that a person is being harassed, cheated, poisoned, or conspired against

dementia mental deterioration characterized by confusion, memory loss, and disorientation

dependent personality   person who is overreliant on others for his or her physical and emotional needs

depression   an illness involving one's body, mood, and thoughts; characterized by persistent feelings of sadness and loss of interest

elder abuse   any violence or mistreatment directed toward an elderly person by someone on whom the elderly person depends for food, shelter, or other aid

elderly person   a person over the age of 60

emotional/psychological abuse   behaviour intended to control or instill fear in a person, cause a person to fear for his or her safety, or diminish a person's sense of self-worth

excited delirium   state of acute agitation and hyperactivity, usually accompanied by violent behaviour

financial abuse   actions that result in financial loss or financial harm to a person

hallucination   sensory perception that is real only to the person experiencing it

indictable offence   a crime that is more serious than a summary conviction offence, that carries heavier penalties, and that may be tried by a judge or a judge and jury

inquest   investigation by a coroner into the cause of a unexpected or sudden death

interpersonal stress   stress that emanates from the police service itself, including policies and procedures that govern and direct the officer's actions

intervention   any verbal or physical extraneous interference by police to change an event's negative outcome

intrapersonal stress   stress that can occur when a person believes that his or her abilities do not coincide with his or her position in life

involuntarily missing   lost or abducted

mediation   assisted negotiation in which a third party helps the disputants resolve their disagreement themselves

mental illness   for the purpose of police intervention, a departure from "normal" thinking that affects a person's ability to interact with his or her environment

neglect   caregiver omissions in providing adequate care that result in actual or potential harm to a child; failing to care for or meet the needs of elderly persons who are dependent and cannot meet their own needs

PARE   a problem-solving system with four components: problem identification, analysis, response, and evaluation

pedophile   a person who is sexually attracted to children

person in crisis   a person pushed beyond his or her ability to cope with stress from any source

physical abuse   the use of force in a way that injures a person or poses a risk of injury to a person

postpartum depression   symptoms of depression that can range from a brief attack of the "baby blues" to clinical depression

post-traumatic stress disorder (PTSD)   disorder in which a person is unable to recover from physical, emotional, and psychological stress caused by exposure to an extremely traumatic event

power of attorney   legal instrument that authorizes a person to carry out specific acts on behalf of another person

restitution order   a court order that instructs an offender to make a payment to a victim to compensate him or her for property damage and/or bodily harm

SARA   a problem-solving process with four components: scan, analysis, response, and assessment

schizophrenia   a family of psychological disorders characterized by psychotic thoughts, feelings, perceptions, and actions

sexual abuse   engagement in any form of sexual activity with a person without the full consent of that person; includes all forms of sexual assault, sexual harassment, or sexual exploitation

spousal abuse   the physical, sexual, emotional/psychological, or financial abuse of one spouse by another

spouse   any person involved in a relationship of cohabitation

stress   a response to a perceived threat or challenge or change; a physical or psychological response to a demand

stressor   something that causes a stress reaction or response

sudden infant death syndrome (SIDS)   the sudden, unexpected, and unexplained death of an infant during sleep

suicide by cop   the use of police to commit suicide, achieved by challenging police with a lethal or apparently lethal weapon, giving them no choice but to use lethal force to stop the threat

summary conviction offence   a crime that is less serious than an indictable offence and that is tried without a jury or preliminary hearing

three P's (plan, past, and partners)   a risk assessment tool that determines whether there is a plan for suicide, a past history of suicide attempts, and partners who can reduce the risk of suicide by helping the person solve his or her problems

unusual realities   perceptions of reality and views of the world that are sharply different from those of people who are not mentally ill and that may cause anxiety and confusion

victim impact statement   a written description of any harm to a victim or loss suffered by a victim due to an offence; it is considered by the courts in sentencing and by parole boards at parole hearings

violence   any unwanted act of aggression resulting in physical contact

voluntarily missing   missing from home as a result of a voluntary choice

Index